Risk
budgeting

Risk budgeting

*Portfolio Problem Solving
with Value-at-Risk*

NEIL D. PEARSON

John Wiley & Sons, Inc.

New York   Chichester   Weinheim   Brisbane   Singapore   Toronto

Published by John Wiley & Sons, Inc.

Published simultaneously in Canada.

This publication is designed to provide accurate and authoritative information in regard to the subject matter covered. It is sold with the understanding that the publisher is not engaged in rendering professional services. If professional advice or other expert assistance is required, the services of a competent professional person should be sought.

Library of Congress Cataloging-in-Publication Data:

Pearson, Neil D.
   Risk budgeting : portfolio problem solving with value-at-risk / Neil D. Pearson
     p. cm.—(Wiley finance series)
   Includes bibliographical references and index.
   ISBN 0-471-40556-6 (cloth : alk. paper)
   1. Portfolio management. 2. Risk management. 3. Financial futures.
  4. Investment analysis. I. Title. II. Series.

HG4529.5 .P4 2002
332.6--dc21   2001045641

10 9 8 7 6 5 4 3 2 1

To my wife, whose patience I have tried

preface

This book describes the tools and techniques of value-at-risk and risk decomposition, which underlie risk budgeting. Most readers will never actually compute a value-at-risk (VaR) estimate. That is the role of risk measurement and portfolio management systems. Nonetheless, it is crucial that consumers of value-at-risk estimates and other risk measures understand what is inside the black box. This book attempts to teach enough so the reader can be a sophisticated consumer and user of risk information. It is hoped that some readers of the book will actually use risk information to do risk budgeting.

While it is not intended primarily for a student audience, the level of the book is that of good MBA students. That is, it presumes numeracy (including a bit of calculus), some knowledge of statistics, and some familiarity with the financial markets and institutions, including financial derivatives. This is about the right level for much of the practicing portfolio management community. The book presents sophisticated ideas but avoids the use of high-brow mathematics. The important ideas are presented in examples. That said, the book does contain some challenging material.

Every effort has been made to make the book self-contained. It starts with the basics of value-at-risk before moving on to risk decomposition, refinements of the basic techniques, and issues that arise with VaR and risk budgeting. The book is organized into five parts. Part I (Chapters 1–2) presents the concept of value-at-risk in the context of a simple equity portfolio and introduces some of the ways it can be used in risk decomposition and budgeting. Then, Part II (Chapters 3–9) describes the basic approaches to computing value-at-risk and creating scenarios for stress testing. Following this description of value-at-risk methodologies, Part III (Chapters 11–13) turns to using value-at-risk in risk budgeting and shows how risk decomposition can be used to understand and control the risks in portfolios. A few refinements of the basic approaches to computing value-at-risk are described in Part IV (Chapters 14–16). Recognizing that value-at-risk is not perfect, Part V (Chapters 17–19) describes some of its limitations, and Part VI (Chapter 20) concludes with a brief discussion of some issues that arise in risk budgeting. Clearly some readers will want to skip the first few chapters on the basic value-at-risk techniques. The notes to the chapters guide diligent readers toward much of the original (and sometimes mathematically challenging) work on value-at-risk.

It should also be said that the book does not address credit, operational, or other risks. It is about measuring market risk. Also, it stays away from software packages, partly because it is hoped that the shelf life of the book will be longer than the life cycle of computer software. I will be sorely disappointed if this turns out to be incorrect.

contents

PART ONE

Introduction

CHAPTER 1
What Are Value-at-Risk and Risk Budgeting?   3

CHAPTER 2
Value-at-Risk of a Simple Equity Portfolio   13

PART TWO

Techniques of Value-at-Risk and Stress Testing

CHAPTER 3
The Delta-Normal Method   33

CHAPTER 4
Historical Simulation   55

CHAPTER 5
The Delta-Normal Method for a Fixed-Income Portfolio   75

CHAPTER 6
Monte Carlo Simulation   91

CHAPTER 7
Using Factor Models to Compute the VaR of Equity Portfolios   105

CHAPTER 8
Using Principal Components to Compute the VaR
of Fixed-Income Portfolios   115

CHAPTER 9
Stress Testing   135

PART THREE

Risk Decomposition and Risk Budgeting

CHAPTER 10
Decomposing Risk   153

CHAPTER 11
    A Long-Short Hedge Fund Manager   163

CHAPTER 12
    Aggregating and Decomposing the Risks of Large Portfolios   183

CHAPTER 13
    Risk Budgeting and the Choice of Active Managers   205

PART FOUR
    Refinements of the Basic Methods

CHAPTER 14
    Delta-Gamma Approaches   223

CHAPTER 15
    Variants of the Monte Carlo Approach   233

CHAPTER 16
    Extreme Value Theory and VaR   245

PART FIVE
    Limitations of Value-at-Risk

CHAPTER 17
    VaR Is Only an Estimate   263

CHAPTER 18
    Gaming the VaR   275

CHAPTER 19
    Coherent Risk Measures   287

PART SIX
    Conclusion

CHAPTER 20
    A Few Issues in Risk Budgeting   297

    References   303

    Index   315

one

Introduction

CHAPTER 1

What Are Value-at-Risk and Risk Budgeting?

It is a truism that portfolio management is about risk and return. Although good returns are difficult to achieve and good risk-adjusted returns can be difficult to identify, the concept and importance of return requires no explanation. Larger returns are preferred to smaller ones. This is true at the level of the pension plan, at the level of each asset manager or portfolio used by or within the plan, and at the level of the individual assets. It follows from the fact that the contribution of an asset to the portfolio return is simply the asset's weight in the portfolio.

Risk is more problematic. Risk is inherently a probabilistic or statistical concept, and there are various (and sometimes conflicting) notions and measures of risk. As a result, it can be difficult to measure the risk of a portfolio and determine how various investments and asset allocations affect that risk. Equally importantly, it can be difficult to express the risk in a way that permits it to be understood and controlled by audiences such as senior managers, boards of directors, pension plan trustees, investors, regulators, and others. It can even be difficult for sophisticated people such as traders and portfolio managers to measure and understand the risks of various instruments and portfolios and to communicate effectively about risk.

For years fund managers and plan sponsors have used a panoply of risk measures: betas and factor loadings for equity portfolios, various duration concepts for fixed income portfolios, historical standard deviations for all portfolios, and percentiles of solvency ratio distributions for long-term asset/liability analysis. Recently the fund management and plan sponsor communities have become interested in value-at-risk (VaR), a new approach that aggregates risks to compute a portfolio- or plan-level measure of risk. A key feature of VaR is that it is "forward-looking," that is, it provides an estimate of the aggregate risk of the current portfolio over the next measurement period. The existence of a forward-looking aggregate measure of risk allows plan sponsors to decompose the aggregate risk into its various sources: how much of the risk is due to each asset class, each portfolio manager, or even each security? Alternatively, how much of the risk is due to each underlying risk factor? Once the contribution to aggregate risk of the asset classes, managers, and risk factors has been computed, one can then go on to the next step and use these risk measures in the asset allocation process and in monitoring the asset allocations and portfolio managers.

The process of decomposing the aggregate risk of a portfolio into its constituents, using these risk measures to allocate assets, setting limits in terms of these measures, and then using the limits to monitor the asset allocations and portfolio managers is known as *risk allocation* or *risk budgeting*. This book is about value-at-risk, its use in measuring and identifying the risks of investment portfolios, and its use in risk budgeting. But to write that the book is about value-at-risk and risk budgeting is not helpful without some knowledge of these tools. This leads to the obvious question: What are value-at-risk and risk budgeting?

VALUE-AT-RISK

Value-at-risk is a simple, summary, statistical measure of possible portfolio losses due to market risk. Once one crosses the hurdle of using a statistical measure, the concept of value-at-risk is straightforward. The notion is that losses greater than the value-at-risk are suffered only with a specified small probability. In particular, associated with each VaR measure are a probability α, or a confidence level $1 - \alpha$, and a holding period, or time horizon, h. The $1 - \alpha$ confidence value-at-risk is simply the loss that will be exceeded with a probability of only α percent over a holding period of length h; equivalently, the loss will be less than the VaR with probability $1 - \alpha$. For example, if h is one day, the confidence level is 95% so that $\alpha = 0.05$ or 5%, and the value-at-risk is one million dollars, then over a one-day holding period the loss on the portfolio will exceed one million dollars with a probability of only 5%. Thus, value-at-risk is a particular way of summarizing and describing the magnitude of the likely losses on a portfolio.

Crucially, value-at-risk is a simple, summary measure. This makes it useful for measuring and comparing the market risks of different portfolios, for comparing the risk of the same portfolio at different times, and for communicating these risks to colleagues, senior managers, directors, trustees, and others. Value-at-risk is a measure of possible portfolio losses, rather than the possible losses on individual instruments, because usually it is portfolio losses that we care most about. Subject to the simplifying assumptions used in its calculation, value-at-risk aggregates the risks in a portfolio into a single number suitable for communicating with plan sponsors, directors and trustees, regulators, and investors. Finally, value-at-risk is a statistical measure due to the nature of risk. Any meaningful aggregate risk measure is inherently statistical.

VaR's simple, summary nature is also its most important limitation—clearly information is lost when an entire portfolio is boiled down to a single number, its value-at-risk. This limitation has led to the development of methodologies for decomposing value-at-risk to determine the contributions of the various asset classes, portfolios, and securities to the value-at-risk. The ability to decompose value-at-risk into its determinants makes it useful for managing portfolios, rather than simply monitoring them.

The concept of value-at-risk and the methodologies for computing it were developed by the large derivatives dealers (mostly commercial and investment banks) during the late 1980s, and VaR is currently used by virtually all commercial and investment banks. The phrase *value-at-risk* first came into wide usage following its appearance in the Group of Thirty report released in July 1993 (Group of Thirty 1993) and the release of the first version of RiskMetrics in October 1994 (Morgan Guaranty Trust Company 1994). Since 1993, the numbers of users of and uses for value-at-risk have increased dramatically, and the technique has gone through significant refinement.

The derivatives dealers who developed value-at-risk faced the problem that their derivatives portfolios and other trading "books" had grown to the point that the market risks inherent in them were of significant concern. How could these risks be measured, described, and reported to senior management and the board of directors? The positions were so numerous that they could not easily be listed and described. Even if this could be done, it would be helpful only if senior management and the board understood all of the positions and instruments, and the risks of each. This is not a realistic expectation, as some derivative instruments are complex. Of course, the risks could be measured by the portfolio's sensitivities, that is, how much the value of the portfolio changes when various underlying market rates or prices change, and the option deltas and gammas, but a detailed discussion of these would likely only bore the senior managers and directors. Even if these concepts could be explained in English, exposures to different types of market risk (for example, equity, interest rate, and exchange rate risk) cannot meaningfully be aggregated without a statistical framework. Value-at-risk offered a way to do this, and therefore helped to overcome the problems in measuring and communicating risk information.

WHY USE VALUE-AT-RISK IN PORTFOLIO MANAGEMENT?

Similar issues of measuring and describing risk pervade the investment management industry. It is common for portfolios to include large numbers of securities and other financial instruments. This alone creates demand for tools to summarize and aggregate their risks. In addition, while most investment managers avoid complex derivative instruments with risks that are difficult to measure, some investment managers do use them, and some use complicated trading strategies. As a result, for many portfolios the risks may not be transparent even to the portfolio manager, let alone to the people to whom the manager reports.

Moreover, pension plans and other financial institutions often use multiple outside portfolio managers. To understand the risks of the total portfolio, the management, trustees, or board of directors ultimately responsible for an investment portfolio must first aggregate the risks across managers. Thus, although developed by derivatives dealers in a different context, value-at-risk is valuable in portfolio management applications because it aggregates risks across assets, risk factors, portfolios, and asset classes. In fact, a 1998 survey of pensions, endowments, and foundations reported that 23% of large institutional investors used value-at-risk.

Derivatives dealers typically express the value-at-risk as a dollar amount, while in investment management value-at-risk may be expressed as a percentage of the value of the portfolio. Given this, it is clear that value-at-risk is closely related to portfolio standard deviation, a concept that has been used by quantitative portfolio managers since they first existed. In fact, if we assume that portfolio returns are normally distributed (an assumption made in some VaR methodologies), value-at-risk is proportional to the difference between the expected change in the value of a portfolio and the portfolio's standard deviation. In investment management contexts, value-at-risk is often expressed relative to the return on a benchmark, making it similar to the standard deviation of the tracking error. What then is new or different about value-at-risk?

Crucially, value-at-risk is a *forward-looking* measure of risk, based on current portfolio holdings. In contrast, standard deviations of returns and tracking errors are typically computed using historical fund returns and contain useful risk information only if one assumes both consistency on the part of the portfolio managers and stability in the market environment. Because value-at-risk is a forward-looking measure, it can be used to identify violations of risk limits, unwanted risks, and managers who deviate from their historical styles before any negative outcomes occur.

Second, value-at-risk is equally applicable to equities, bonds, commodities, and derivatives and can be used to aggregate the risk across different asset classes and to compare the market risks of different asset classes and portfolios. Since a plan's liabilities often can be viewed as negative or short positions in fixed-income instruments, value-at-risk can be used to measure the risk of a plan's net asset/liability position. Because it aggregates risk across risk factors, portfolios, and asset classes, it enables a portfolio manager or plan sponsor to determine the extent to which different risk factors, portfolios, and asset classes contribute to the total risk.

Third, the focus of value-at-risk is on the tails of the distribution. In particular, value-at-risk typically is computed for a confidence level of 95%, 99%, or even greater. Thus, it is a measure of "downside" risk and can be used with skewed and asymmetric distributions of returns.

Fourth, the popularity of value-at-risk among derivatives dealers has led to a development and refinement of methods for estimating the probability distribution of changes in portfolio value or returns. These methodologies are a major contribution to the development of value-at-risk, and much of this book is devoted to describing them.

Finally, and perhaps most importantly, the development of the concept of value-at-risk, and even the name itself, has eased the communication of information about risk. Phrases such as "portfolio standard deviation" and other statistical concepts are perceived as the language of nerds and geeks and are decidedly not the language of a typical pension plan trustee or company director. In contrast, *value* and *risk* are undeniably business words, and *at* is simply a preposition. This difference in terminology overcomes barriers to discussing risk and greatly facilitates the communication of information about it.

RISK BUDGETING

The concept of risk budgeting is not nearly as well defined as value-at-risk. In fact, it has been accused of being only a buzzword. Not surprisingly, it is also controversial. That it is a controversial buzzword is one thing upon which almost everyone can agree. But risk budgeting is more than a buzzword.

Narrowly defined, *risk budgeting* is a process of measuring and decomposing risk, using the measures in asset-allocation decisions, assigning portfolio managers *risk budgets* defined in terms of these measures, and using these risk budgets in monitoring the asset allocations and portfolio managers. A prerequisite for risk budgeting is risk decomposition, which involves

▪ identifying the various sources of risk, or risk factors, such as equity returns, interest rates, and exchange rates;
▪ measuring each factor's, manager's, and asset class's contribution to the total risk;
▪ comparing the *ex post* realized outcomes to the *ex ante* risk; and
▪ identifying the risks that were taken intentionally, and those taken inadvertently.

This risk decomposition allows a plan sponsor to have a better understanding of the risks being assumed and how they have changed, and to have more informed conversations with the portfolio managers. In the event that there are problems, it allows the sponsor to identify unwanted risks and managers who deviate from their historical styles before any negative outcomes occur.

If this risk decomposition is combined with an explicit set of risk allocations to factors, managers, or asset classes, it is called *risk allocation* or *risk budgeting*. The risk budgeting process itself consists of

▪ setting limits, or risk budgets, on the quantity of risk due to each asset class, manager, or factor;
▪ establishing asset allocations based on the risk budgets;
▪ comparing the risk budgets to the measures of the risk due to each factor on an ongoing basis; and
▪ adjusting the asset allocations to keep the risks within the budgeted limits.

Risk decomposition is crucial to risk budgeting, because the aggregate value-at-risk of the pension plan or other organization is far removed from the portfolio managers. At the risk of stating the obvious, the portfolio managers have control only over their own portfolios. For them, meaningful risk budgets are expressed in terms of their contributions to portfolio risk.

However, risk budgeting is more than a list of steps or procedures. Defined more broadly, risk budgeting is a way of thinking about investment and portfolio management. For this reason, to find a definition that attracts broad agreement is difficult, and perhaps impossible. The world view that underlies risk budgeting takes for granted reliance upon probabilistic or statistical measures of risk and the use of modern risk- and portfolio-management tools to manage risk. Thinking about the asset-allocation problem in terms of *risk* allocations rather than traditional *asset* allocations is a natural outgrowth of this world view.

From a logical perspective, there is no special relation between value-at-risk and risk budgeting. Risk budgeting requires a measure of portfolio risk, and value-at-risk is one candidate. It is a natural candidate, in that: (i) it is a measure of downside risk, and thus useful when the distribution of portfolio returns is asymmetric; and (ii) when returns are normally distributed, it is equivalent to a forward-looking estimate of portfolio standard deviation. However, the risk budgeting process could be implemented using any of a number of risk measures. For example, it could be implemented using either a forward-looking estimate of portfolio standard deviation or a scenario-based measure of the type advocated by Artzner, et al. (1997, 1999) and described in chapter 19. In fact, it is widely recommended that value-at-risk measures be used in combination with *stress testing* (procedures to estimate the losses that might be incurred in extreme or "stress" scenarios).

In practice, however, value-at-risk and risk budgeting are intimately related. Because risk budgeting involves the quantification, aggregation, and decomposition of risk, the availability of a well-recognized aggregate measure of portfolio risk is a prerequisite for its use and acceptance. In this sense, risk budgeting is an outgrowth of value-at-risk. But for the popularity and widespread acceptance of value-at-risk, you would likely not be hearing and reading about risk budgeting today. Nonetheless, value-at-risk has some well known limitations, and it may be that some other risk measure eventually supplants value-at-risk in the risk budgeting process.

DOES RISK BUDGETING USING VaR MAKE SENSE?

To those who share its underlying world view, the process of risk budgeting outlined above is perfectly natural — how else would one think about asset allocation? Of course, one can think about asset allocation in the traditional way, in terms of the fractions of the portfolio invested in each asset class. But seen through the lens of risk budgeting, the traditional approach is just an approximation to the process described above, where portfolio weights proxy for risk measures. An advantage of risk budgeting over this traditional view of asset allocation is that it makes explicit the risks being taken and recognizes that they change over time. In addition, risk budgeting provides a natural way to think about nontraditional asset classes, such as hedge funds and the highly levered strategies often pursued by them. In contrast to traditional asset classes, the dollar investment in a highly leveraged strategy often says little about the quantity of risk being taken, and the label "hedge fund" does not reveal the nature of the risks.

A significant part of the controversy stems from the broader definition of risk budgeting as the natural outgrowth of a way of thinking about investment and portfolio management. This is not about the precise definition of risk budgeting (i.e., whether the preceding list of the steps that define the risk budgeting process is better or worse than another) or whether risk budgeting is cost effective. Much of the controversy seems to stem from the fact that not all plan sponsors and portfolio managers share the same underlying paradigm. This is not just the source of the controversy; the difference in world views *is* much of the controversy. It is difficult to imagine that it will ever be resolved.

However, some of the disagreement about risk budgeting is eminently practical and can be addressed by a book. The computation of value-at-risk, and the processes of risk decomposition and risk budgeting, involve considerable trouble and expense. Given the imperfections of and errors in quantitative measures such as value-at-risk, reasonable people who share the view of portfolio management underlying risk budgeting may nonetheless conclude that it is not cost effective, that is, that the additional information about and understanding of portfolio risk provided by the risk budgeting process are not worth the cost that must be incurred. It is likely that the practical argument against risk budgeting will become less compelling over time, as increases in the extent of risk-management education and knowledge and the evolution of risk-measurement systems both increase the benefits and reduce the costs of the risk budgeting process. Regardless, to make an informed judgment about the benefits, limitations, and cost-effectiveness of value-at-risk and risk budgeting requires an understanding of them. One of the goals of this book is to provide enough information about value-at-risk methodologies and risk budgeting to enable readers to understand them and make informed choices about them.

NOTES

The development of value-at-risk is generally attributed to J.P. Morgan (e.g., see Guldimann 2000). To my knowledge, the first publication in which the phrase appeared was the widely circulated Group of Thirty report (Group of Thirty 1993). It was subsequently popularized by the RiskMetrics system originally developed by J.P. Morgan (Morgan Guaranty Trust Company 1994).

The use of the phrase "$1 - \alpha$ percent confidence VaR" to mean the loss that is exceeded with a probability of α percent over a holding period of length h is a misuse of the terminology "confidence" or "confidence level."

A better terminology would be to refer to the α or $1 - \alpha$ quantile VaR, because value-at-risk is the α quantile of the distribution of portfolio profits (or returns), or, equivalently, the $1 - \alpha$ quantile of the loss distribution. However, the misuse of the terminology *confidence* in the context of value-at-risk is well established, and this book will not try to fight it.

Since 1995, the Basel Committee on Banking Supervision and the International Organization of Securities Commissions have been examining the risk-management procedures and disclosures of leading banks and securities firms in the industrialized world. The latest surveys (Basel Committee on Banking Supervision and the International Organization of Securities Commissions 1999 and Basel Committee on Banking Supervision 2001) indicated that virtually all banks and securities firms covered by the survey used value-at-risk techniques to measure market risk. The finding that 23% of institutional investors use value-at-risk is from the 1998 Survey of Derivative and Risk Management Practices by U.S. Institutional Investors conducted by New York University, CIBC World Markets, and KPMG (Levich, Hayt, and Ripston 1999; Hayt and Levich 1999).

The nature of the controversy about risk budgeting is described by Cass (2000), who describes the debate at the Risk 2000 Congress in June 2000. Cass quotes Harris Lirtzman of the New York City Retirement Systems as saying: "There is almost a theological divide in this discussion among public plan sponsors—VaR versus non-VaR, risk budgeting versus asset allocation."

CHAPTER 2

Value-at-Risk of a Simple Equity Portfolio

To introduce the concept of *value-at-risk*, consider a simple example of a portfolio exposed to changes in the U.S. and U.K. stock market indexes. The portfolio consists of $110 million invested in a well-diversified portfolio of large-capitalization U.S. equities, together with positions in U.S. (S&P 500) and U.K. (FT-SE 100) index futures contracts. The portfolio of U.S. equities is well diversified, and its returns are highly correlated with the returns on the S&P 500 index. For simplicity, it is assumed that the returns on the portfolio are perfectly correlated with changes in the S&P 500 index. To gain exposure to the U.K. market, the portfolio manager has established a long position of 500 FT-SE 100 index futures contracts traded on the London International Financial Futures Exchange (LIFFE). Through the standard cost-of-carry formula for the futures price (see the notes to this chapter) and using the multiplier of £10, a one-point change in the FT-SE 100 index results in a £10.131 change in the position value. The current value of the FT-SE 100 is 5862.3, so the index futures position is equivalent to an investment of £29.696 million in the portfolio that underlies the index. At the current exchange rate of 1.6271 $/£, this is equivalent to an investment of $48.319 million in the portfolio underlying the index.

To reduce his exposure to the U.S. market, the portfolio manager has shorted 200 of the S&P 500 index futures contract traded on the Chicago Mercantile Exchange (CME). The current level of the S&P index is 1097.6, and the contract has a multiplier of 250, so, through the cost-of-carry formula, a one-point change in the index results in a $253.48 change in the position value, implying that this position is equivalent to a short position of $55.643 million in the portfolio that underlies the S&P 500 index. Combined with the $110 million invested in the "cash" market, the combined stock and futures position is equivalent to an investment of $54.357 million in the index portfolio.

It has been estimated that the standard deviation of monthly rates of return on the portfolio underlying the S&P 500 index is $\sigma_1 = 0.061$ (6.1%), the standard deviation of monthly rates of return on the portfolio underlying the FT-SE 100 index is $\sigma_2 = 0.065$ (6.5%), and the correlation between the monthly rates of return is estimated to be $\rho = 0.55$. The expected rates of change in the S&P 500 and FT-SE 100 indexes are estimated to be $\mu_1 = 0.01$ (1%) and $\mu_2 = 0.0125$ (1.25%) per month, respectively. In addition, the portfolio of U.S. stocks pays dividends at the rate of 1.4% per year, or $1.4/12 = 0.1167\%$ per month.

STANDARD VALUE-AT-RISK

To compute the value-at-risk, we need to pick a holding period and a confidence level $1 - \alpha$. We choose the holding period to be one month and somewhat arbitrarily pick a confidence level of $1 - \alpha = 95\%$, or $\alpha = 5\%$. Given these choices and the information above, it is easy to compute the value-at-risk if one assumes that the returns on the S&P 500 and FT-SE 100 are normally distributed. If they are, then the portfolio return is also normally distributed and the expected change and variance of the value of the portfolio can be calculated using standard mathematical results about the distributions of sums of normal random variables. Then, because the normal distribution is completely determined by the expected value and variance, we know the distribution of profit or loss over the month.

For example, suppose that the distribution of possible profits and losses on a portfolio can be adequately approximated by the probability density function shown in Figure 2.1. The distribution described by this density function has a mean of $1.2759 million and a standard deviation of $5.6845 million. A property of the normal distribution is that a critical value, or cutoff, equal to 1.645 standard deviations below the mean, leaves 5% of the probability in the left-hand tail. Calling this cutoff the 5% quantile of the distribution of profit and loss, we have

$$5\% \text{ quantile} = \begin{pmatrix} \text{mean change in} \\ \text{portfolio value} \end{pmatrix} - \left[1.645 \times \begin{pmatrix} \text{standard deviation of} \\ \text{change in portfolio value} \end{pmatrix} \right]$$
$$= 1.2759 - (1.645 \times 5.6845)$$
$$= -8.0752$$

million. That is, the daily mark-to-market profit will be less than −$8.0752 million with a probability of 5%. Then, since the 5% value-at-risk is defined as the *loss* that will be exceeded with a probability of 5%, the value-at-risk

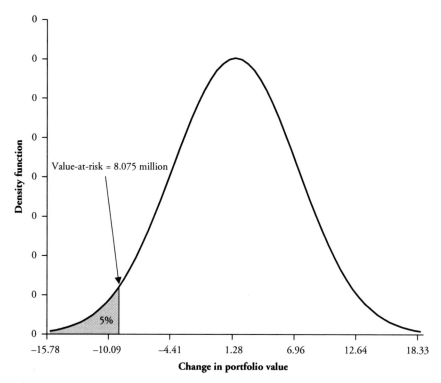

FIGURE 2.1 Density function of changes in portfolio value and value-at-risk for the portfolio consisting of positions in the U.S. and U.K. stock markets

is the negative of this quantile, or \$8.0752 million. This value-at-risk is also shown on Figure 2.1.

When there are two positions, the expected change in the value of the portfolio (including the dividends) is

$$E[\Delta V] \ = \ X_1\mu_1 + X_2\mu_2 + D,$$

where ΔV is the change in the value of the portfolio, X_1 and X_2 are the dollar amounts invested in the two positions, and $D = \$110(0.014/12)$ million are the dividends to be received during the next month. Using the fact that the portfolio is equivalent to a position of \$54.357 million invested in a portfolio that tracks the S&P 500 index and \$48.319 million in a portfolio that tracks the FT-SE 100 index, we have $X_1 = 54.357$ million and

X_2 = 48.319 million. The variance of monthly changes in the portfolio value depends on the standard deviations of changes in the value of the standardized positions, the correlation, and the sizes of the positions, and is given by the formula

$$\text{var}[\Delta V] = X_1^2\sigma_1^2 + X_2^2\sigma_2^2 + 2X_1X_2\rho_{12}\sigma_1\sigma_2.$$

Using these formulas, the expected value and variance of the change in value of the portfolio are

$$E[\Delta V] = 54.357(0.01) + 48.319(0.0125) + 110(0.14/12)$$
$$= 1.2759$$

and

$$\text{var}[\Delta V] = (54.357)^2(0.061)^2 + (48.319)^2(0.065)^2$$
$$+ 2(54.357)(48.319)(0.061)(0.065)(0.55)$$
$$= 32.3138.$$

Alternatively, letting V = U.S. \$110 million denote the value of the portfolio and $r = \Delta V/V$ the portfolio return, the expected value and variance of the portfolio return are

$$E[r] = \frac{54.357}{110}(0.01) + \frac{48.319}{110}(0.0125) + \frac{0.014}{12}$$
$$= 0.01160$$

and

$$\text{var}[r] = \left(\frac{54.357}{110}\right)^2(0.061)^2 + \left(\frac{48.319}{110}\right)^2(0.065)^2$$
$$+ 2\left(\frac{54.357}{110}\right)\left(\frac{48.319}{110}\right)(0.061)(0.065)(0.55)$$
$$= 0.0026706.$$

The standard deviation is, of course, simply the square root of the variance and is \$5.6845 million or 0.0517 (5.17%), respectively.

Using the fact that outcomes less than or equal to 1.645 standard deviations below the mean occur only 5% of the time, we can calculate the value-at-risk:

$$\begin{aligned}
\text{VaR} &= -(E[\Delta V] - 1.654 \times \text{s.d.}[\Delta V]) \\
&= -(1.2759 - 1.645 \times 5.6845) \\
&= 8.0752.
\end{aligned}$$

As a fraction of the initial value of the portfolio,

$$\begin{aligned}
\text{VaR} &= -(E[r] - 1.654 \times \text{s.d.}[r]) \\
&= -(0.01160 - 1.645 \times 0.05168) \\
&= 0.0734,
\end{aligned}$$

or 7.34% of the initial value of the portfolio.

In computing the value-at-risk estimate, it is sometimes assumed that the expected change in the value of the portfolio is zero. If this assumption is made, the value-at-risk is then $1.645(\$5.6845) = \$9.351$ million, or $1.645(0.05168) = 0.0850$, or 8.50%. The assumption of a zero-expected-change in the portfolio value is common when the time horizon of the value-at-risk estimate is one day.

In interpreting these value-at-risk estimates, it is crucial to keep in mind the holding period and confidence level, $1 - \alpha$, for different estimates will be obtained if different choices of these parameters are made. For example, to compute the value-at-risk using a confidence level of 99%, one would use the fact that, for the normal distribution, outcomes less than or equal to 2.326 standard deviations below the mean occur only 1% of the time. Thus, with a monthly holding period, the 99%–confidence value-at-risk estimate is

$$\begin{aligned}
\text{VaR} &= -\left(E\left[\frac{\Delta V}{V}\right] - 2.326 \times \text{s.d.}\left[\frac{\Delta V}{V}\right]\right) \\
&= -(0.01160 - 2.326 \times 0.05168) \\
&= 0.1086,
\end{aligned}$$

or 10.86% of the initial value. The choice of holding period can have an even larger impact, for the value-at-risk computed using this approach is approximately proportional to the square root of the length of the holding period, because return variances are approximately proportional to the length of the holding period. Absent appropriate adjustments, value-at-risk estimates for different holding periods and probabilities are not comparable.

BENCHMARK-RELATIVE VALUE-AT-RISK

In portfolio management it is common to think about risk in terms of a portfolio's return relative to the return on a benchmark portfolio. In particular, if the S&P 500 index is the benchmark, one might be concerned about the difference $r - r_{S\&P}$ instead of the return r, where $r_{S\&P}$ denotes the return on the portfolio underlying the S&P 500 index. Based on this idea (and using the normal distribution), the relative value-at-risk is determined by the expected value and variance of the relative return, $\text{var}(r - r_{S\&P})$. Using the example portfolio discussed above, the variance is

$$\text{var}(r - r_{S\&P}) = \text{var}(w_1 r_{S\&P} + w_2 r_{FT} - r_{S\&P})$$
$$= \text{var}((w_1 - 1) r_{S\&P} + w_2 r_{FT}),$$

where $w_1 = X_1/V$ and $w_2 = X_2/V$ are the portfolio weights. This expression is just the variance of a portfolio return, except that the position in the S&P 500 index has been adjusted to include a short position in that index. That is, the portfolio weight w_1 is replaced by $w_1 - 1$. Using the previous values of the parameters, the variance and standard deviation are 0.000798 and 0.02825, respectively. The expected relative return is

$$E[r - r_{S\&P}] = \left(\frac{54.357}{110}(0.01) + \frac{48.319}{110}(0.0125) + \frac{0.014}{12}\right) - \left(0.01 + \frac{0.014}{12}\right)$$
$$= 0.00043.$$

Finally, if we also use a probability of 5%, the benchmark-relative value-at-risk is

$$\text{relative VaR} = -(E[r - r_{S\&P}] - 1.645 \times \text{s.d.}[r - r_{S\&P}])$$
$$= -(0.00043 - 1.645 \times 0.02825)$$
$$= 0.0463.$$

The only difference between computing benchmark-relative and standard value-at-risk is that, in benchmark-relative VaR, the portfolio is adjusted to include a short position in the benchmark. Because the approach of adjusting the portfolio to include a short position in the benchmark also works with the other methods for computing value-at-risk, the computation of relative value-at-risk is no more difficult than the computation of standard VaR and can be accomplished using the same techniques. For this reason, the chapters on VaR methodologies focus on standard VaR.

RISK DECOMPOSITION

Having computed the value-at-risk, it is natural to ask to what extent the different positions contribute to it. For example, how much of the risk is due to the S&P 500 position, and how much to the FT-SE 100 position? How does the S&P 500 futures hedge affect the risk? The process of answering such questions is termed *risk decomposition.*

At the beginning of this chapter, the portfolio was described as a cash position in the S&P 500, hedged with a position in the S&P 500 index futures contract and then overlaid with a FT-SE 100 futures contract to provide exposure to the U.K. market. This description suggests decomposing the risk by computing the VaRs of three portfolios: (i) the cash S&P 500 position; (ii) a portfolio consisting of the cash S&P 500 position, combined with the S&P futures hedge; and (iii) the aggregate portfolio of all three positions. The risk contribution of the cash S&P 500 position would be computed as the VaR of portfolio (i); the contribution of the S&P futures position would be the incremental VaR resulting from adding on the futures hedge, that is, the difference between the VaRs of portfolios (ii) and (i); and the risk contribution of the FT-SE 100 index futures position would be the difference between the VaRs of portfolios (iii) and (ii).

However, equally natural descriptions of the portfolio list the positions in different orders. For example, one might think of the portfolio as a cash position in the S&P 500 (portfolio i), overlaid with a FT-SE 100 futures contract to provide exposure to the U.K. market (portfolio iv), and then hedged with a position in the S&P 500 index futures contract (portfolio iii). In this case, one might measure the risk contribution of the FT-SE 100 index futures position as the difference between the VaRs of portfolios (iv) and (i), and the contribution of the S&P futures position is the difference between the VaRs of portfolios (iii) and (iv). Unfortunately, different orderings of positions will produce different measures of their risk contributions, a limitation of the incremental risk decomposition. For example, risk decomposition based on the second ordering of the positions would indicate a greater risk-reducing effect for the short S&P 500 futures position, because it is considered after the FT-SE 100 overlay, as a result of which there is more risk to reduce. In fact, different starting points can yield extreme differences in the risk contributions. If one thinks of the portfolio as a short S&P 500 futures position, hedged with the cash S&P 500 position, and then overlaid with the FT-SE 100 futures position, the risk contributions of the S&P cash and futures positions will change sign.

This dependence of the risk contributions on the ordering of the positions is problematic, because for most portfolios there is no natural ordering. Even for this simple example, it is unclear whether the S&P futures position should be interpreted as hedging the cash position or vice versa and whether one should measure the risk contribution of the FT-SE 100 futures overlay before or after measuring the risk contribution of the S&P hedge. (Or one could think of the S&P positions as overlays on a core FT-SE 100 position, in which case one would obtain yet another risk decomposition.) A further feature is that each position's risk contribution measures the incremental effect of the entire position, not the marginal effect of changing it. Thus, the incremental risk contributions do not indicate the effects of marginal changes in the position sizes; for example, a negative risk contribution for the cash S&P 500 does not mean that increasing the position will reduce the VaR. These problems limit the utility of this incremental decomposition.

Marginal risk decomposition overcomes these problems. The starting point in marginal risk decomposition is the expression for the value-at-risk,

$$\text{VaR} = -(E[\Delta V] - 1.645 \times \text{s.d.}[\Delta V])$$

$$= -\left(E[X_1\mu_1 + X_2\mu_2 + D] - 1.645\sqrt{X_1^2\sigma_1^2 + 2X_1X_2\rho\sigma_1\sigma_2 + X_2^2\sigma_2^2} \right),$$

where the second equality uses the expressions for the expected value and standard deviation of ΔV. To carry out the marginal risk decomposition, it is necessary to disaggregate the S&P 500 position of $X_1 = 54.357$ million into its two components, cash and futures; here $X_1^c = 110$ million dollars and $X_1^f = -55.643$ million dollars are used to denote these two components, so that $X_1 = X_1^c + X_1^f$. Also, it is necessary to recognize that the dividend D depends on the magnitude of the cash position, $D = X_1^c (0.014/12)$. Using this expression and letting $X = (X_1^c, X_1^f, X_2)'$ represent the portfolio, one obtains

$$\text{VaR}(X) = -\left(E[X_1^c(\mu_1 + 0.014/12) + X_1^f\mu_1 + X_2\mu_2] \right.$$

$$\left. - 1.645\sqrt{X_1^2\sigma_1^2 + X_1X_2\rho\sigma_1\sigma_2 + X_2^2\sigma_2^2} \right).$$

From this formula one can see that VaR has the property that, if one multiplies each position by a constant k, that is, if one considers the portfolio

$kX = (kX_1^c, kX_1^f, kX_2)'$, the value-at-risk is multiplied by k. Carrying out this computation, the value-at-risk is

$$
\begin{aligned}
\mathrm{VaR}(kX) &= -\Big([kX_1^c(\mu_1 + 0.014/12) + kX_1^f\mu_1 + kX_2\mu_2] \\
&\quad -1.645\sqrt{k^2X_1^2\sigma_1^2 + k^2X_1X_2\rho\sigma_1\sigma_2 + k^2X_2^2\sigma_2^2}\,\Big) \\
&= -k\Big([X_1^c(\mu_1 + 0.014/12)] + X_1^f\mu_1 + X_2\mu_2] \\
&\quad -1.645\sqrt{X_1^2\sigma_1^2 + X_1X_2\rho\sigma_1\sigma_2 + X_2^2\sigma_2^2}\,\Big) \\
&= k\,\mathrm{VaR}(X).
\end{aligned}
$$

As we will see in chapter 10, this property of value-at-risk implies that it can be decomposed as

$$
\mathrm{VaR}(X) = \frac{\partial\mathrm{VaR}}{\partial X_1^c}X_1^c + \frac{\partial\mathrm{VaR}}{\partial X_1^f}X_1^f + \frac{\partial\mathrm{VaR}}{\partial X_2}X_2. \tag{2.1}
$$

This is known as the *marginal risk decomposition*. Each of the three terms on the right-hand side is called the *risk contribution* of one of the positions, for example, the term $(\partial\mathrm{VaR}/\partial X_1^c)X_1^c$ is the risk contribution of the cash S&P 500 position. The partial derivative $(\partial\mathrm{VaR}/\partial X_1^c)$ gives the effect on risk of increasing X_1^c by one unit; changing X_1^c by a small amount from X_1^c to X_1^{c*}, changes the risk by approximately $(\partial\mathrm{VaR}/\partial X_1^c)(X_1^{c*} - X_1^c)$. The risk contribution $(\partial\mathrm{VaR}/\partial X_1^c)X_1^c$ can then be interpreted as measuring the effect of percentage changes in the position size X_1^c. The change from X_1^c to X_1^{c*} is a percentage change of $(X_1^{c*} - X_1^c)/X_1^c$, and the change in value-at-risk resulting from this change in the position size is approximated by

$$
\frac{\partial\mathrm{VaR}}{\partial X_1^c}(X_1^{c*} - X_1^c) = \frac{\partial\mathrm{VaR}}{\partial X_1^c}X_1^c \times \frac{(X_1^{c*} - X_1^c)}{X_1^c},
$$

the product of the risk contribution and the percentage change in the position. The second and third terms, $(\partial\mathrm{VaR}/\partial X_1^f)X_1^f$ and $(\partial\mathrm{VaR}/\partial X_2)X_2$, of course, have similar interpretations.

A key feature of the risk contributions is that they sum to the portfolio risk, permitting the portfolio risk to be decomposed into the risk contributions of the three positions X_1^c, X_1^f, and X_2. Alternatively, if one divides both sides of (2.1) by the value-at-risk $\mathrm{VaR}(X)$, then the percentage risk contributions of the form $[(\partial\mathrm{VaR}/\partial X_1^c)X_1^c]/\mathrm{VaR}(X)$ sum to one, or 100%.

Computing each of the risk contributions, one obtains

$$\frac{\partial \text{VaR}}{\partial X_1^c} X_1^c = -(\mu_1 + 0.014/12) X_1^c$$

$$+ 1.645 \frac{(X_1 \sigma_1^2 + X_2 \rho \sigma_1 \sigma_2) X_1^c}{\sqrt{X_1^2 \sigma_1^2 + 2 X_1 X_2 \rho \sigma_1 \sigma_2 + X_2^2 \sigma_2^2}},$$

$$\frac{\partial \text{VaR}}{\partial X_1^f} X_1^f = -\mu_1 X_1^f + 1.645 \frac{(X_1 \sigma_1^2 + X_2 \rho \sigma_1 \sigma_2) X_1^f}{\sqrt{X_1^2 \sigma_1^2 + 2 X_1 X_2 \rho \sigma_1 \sigma_2 + X_2^2 \sigma_2^2}}, \qquad (2.2)$$

$$\frac{\partial \text{VaR}}{\partial X_2} X_2 = -\mu_2 X_2 + 1.645 \frac{(X_1 \rho \sigma_1 \sigma_2 + X_2 \sigma_2^2) X_2}{\sqrt{X_1^2 \sigma_1^2 + 2 X_1 X_2 \rho \sigma_1 \sigma_2 + X_2^2 \sigma_2^2}}.$$

The first term on the right-hand side of each equation reflects the effect of changes in the position size on the mean change in value and carries a negative sign, because increases in the mean reduce the value-at-risk. The second term on the right-hand side of each equation reflects the effect of changes in the position on the standard deviation. The numerator of each of these terms is the covariance of the change in value of a position with the change in value of the portfolio; for example, the term $(X_1 \sigma_1^2 + X_2 \rho \sigma_1 \sigma_2) X_1^c = (X_1 X_1^c \sigma_1^2 + X_2 X_1^c \rho \sigma_1 \sigma_2)$ is the covariance of changes in the value of the cash S&P 500 position with changes in the portfolio value. This captures a standard intuition in portfolio theory, namely, that the contribution of a security or other instrument to the risk of a portfolio depends on that security's covariance with changes in the value of the portfolio.

Table 2.1 shows the marginal risk contributions of the form $(\partial \text{VaR}/\partial X_1^c) X_1^c$ and the percentage risk contributions of the form $(\partial \text{VaR}/\partial X_1^c) X_1^c / \text{VaR}(X)$, computed using equations (2.2) and the parameters used earlier in this chapter. The S&P 500 cash position makes the largest risk contribution of 8.564 million, or 106% of the portfolio risk, for two reasons. First, the

TABLE 2.1 Marginal risk contributions of cash S&P 500 position, S&P 500 futures, and FT-SE 100 futures

Portfolio	Marginal Value-at-Risk ($ million)	Marginal Value-at-Risk (Percent)
Cash Position in S&P 500	8.564	106
S&P 500 Futures	−4.397	−54
FT-SE 100 Futures	3.908	48
Total	8.075	100

position is large and volatile; second, it is highly correlated with the total portfolio, because the net position in the S&P 500 index is positive, and because this position is positively correlated with the FT-SE 100 index futures position. The risk contribution of the short S&P futures position is negative because it is negatively correlated with the total portfolio, both because the net position in the S&P 500 index is positive and because the short S&P futures position is negatively correlated with the FT-SE 100 index futures position. Finally, the FT-SE 100 index futures position is positively correlated with the portfolio return, leading to a positive risk contribution.

In interpreting the risk decomposition, it is crucial to keep in mind that it is a marginal analysis. For example, a small change in the FT-SE 100 futures position, from $X_2 = 48.319$ to $X_2{}^* = 49.319$, changes the risk by approximately

$$
\begin{aligned}
\frac{\partial \text{VaR}}{\partial X_2}(X_2{}^* - X_2) &= \frac{\partial \text{VaR}}{\partial X_2} X_2 \times \frac{X_2{}^* - X_2}{X_2} \\
&= 3.908 \times \frac{(49.319 - 48.319)}{48.319} \\
&= 0.081
\end{aligned}
$$

million dollars, or from \$8.075 million to approximately \$8.156 million. This matches the exact calculation of the change in the value-at-risk to four significant figures. However, the marginal effects cannot be extrapolated to large changes, because the partial derivatives change as the position sizes change. This occurs because a large change in a position changes the correlation between the portfolio and that position; as the magnitude of a position increases, that position constitutes a larger part of the portfolio, and the correlation between the position and the portfolio increases. This affects the value-at-risk through the numerators of the second term on the right-hand side of each of the equations (2.2). Thus, the risk contribution of a position increases as the size of the position is increased. For this reason, the marginal risk contributions do not indicate the effect of completely eliminating a position.

USING THE RISK CONTRIBUTIONS

Although it may not be immediately obvious from this simple example, the marginal risk decomposition has a range of uses. The most basic is to identify unwanted or unintended concentrations of risk. For example, how much of the portfolio risk is due to technology stocks or other industry or sector concentrations? How much is due to CMOs, and how much is due to positions in foreign markets? How much is due to a particular portfolio or portfolio manager, for example, a hedge fund? As will be seen in

Chapter 12, it is also possible to compute the risk contributions of various market factors, for example, changes in the level or slope of the yield curve or changes to any of the factors in a model of equity returns. This allows one to identify unintended or unwanted factor bets.

The marginal risks of the various positions, asset classes, factor exposures, and allocations to portfolio managers are also key inputs in thinking about the risk-return tradeoff. A portfolio optimizing the risk-return tradeoff has the property that the marginal risk contributions of assets (or asset classes, managers, or factor exposures) are proportional to their expected return contributions. If this is not the case, for example, if two positions with the same risk contribution have different expected return contributions, then it is possible to increase the expected return without increasing the risk. While many plan sponsors and other investment management organizations reject formal portfolio optimization, this insight from it is still useful in thinking about asset allocation. In the example above, knowledge of the risk contributions allows one to assess whether the expected return from the FT-SE 100 futures contracts is large enough to justify the position. More generally, the marginal risk contributions (together with beliefs about expected returns) allow one to do the same assessment for various assets, asset classes, managers, and factor exposures in the portfolio.

Finally, the risk decomposition can be combined with an explicit set of risk allocations to factors, managers, or asset classes to create a risk allocation, or risk budgeting, system. In this approach, one sets limits, or *risk budgets,* in terms of the risk contributions and then monitors whether the risk contributions are within the budgeted limits. Part III (Chapters 10–13) includes examples of this.

OTHER APPROACHES TO COMPUTING VaR

The calculations above use a specific (normal) distribution to compute the value-at-risk estimates. An alternative approach called *historical simulation* does not specify the distribution of returns, but rather assumes that the distribution of returns over the next month is equal to the observed distribution of returns over some particular past period, for instance, the preceding N months. In essence, the approach involves using the historical returns to construct a distribution of potential future portfolio profits and losses and then reading off the value-at-risk as the loss that is exceeded only 5% of the time.

The distribution of profits and losses is constructed by taking the *current* portfolio and subjecting it to the *actual* returns experienced during each of the last N periods, here months. Suppose, for example, that the current date is 1 May, 1998, and we somewhat arbitrarily decide to use the last six years of monthly returns, so that N = 72. (This choice is not completely arbitrary, in that it represents an attempt to strike a balance between using a large time-series of returns, while avoiding the use of data from too far in the past.) In May 1992 (72 months earlier), the dollar-denominated percentage changes in the value of the S&P 500 and FT-SE 100 were 0.0964% and 4.9490%, respectively. Applying those returns to the current portfolio, the change in the value is $54.357(0.000964) + $48.319(0.049490) = $2.444 million. Adding the dividends of 110(0.014 / 12) million dollars, the profit is $2.572 million. Similar calculations were performed using the returns from each of the other past months in Table 2.2.

Table 2.3 sorts the changes in portfolio value from largest-to-smallest, whereas Figure 2.2 shows a histogram of the changes in value. If we use a probability of 5%, the value-at-risk is the loss that is exceeded 5% of the time. Since 3 / 72 = 0.0417 and 4 / 72 = 0.0556, the value-at-risk estimate should be somewhere between the third and fourth worst losses in Table 2.3, which

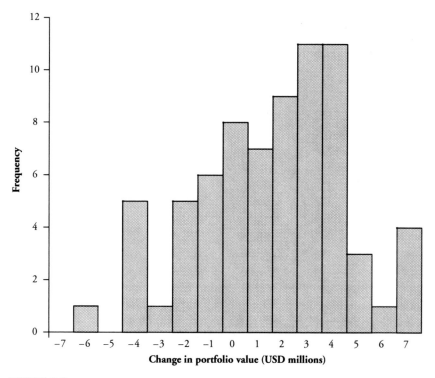

FIGURE 2.2 Histogram of changes in portfolio value for the portfolio consisting of positions in the U.S. and U.K. stock markets

TABLE 2.2 Hypothetical changes in portfolio value computed using the returns from the 72 months before May 1998. Amounts are in millions of U.S. dollars

Month	S&P 500 Percentage Change	FT-SE 100 Percentage Change	Change in Value of U.S. Equity Position (w/o Dividends)	Change in Value of U.K. Equity Position	Change in Portfolio Value (with Dividends of 0.1283)
May 92	0.096	4.949	0.0524	2.3913	2.5720
Jun. 92	−1.736	−2.988	−0.9436	−1.4438	−2.2591
Jul. 92	3.942	−3.694	2.1430	−1.7848	0.4865
Aug. 92	−2.402	−0.920	−1.3057	−0.4448	−1.6221
Sep. 92	0.913	−0.302	0.4963	−0.1458	0.4788
Oct. 92	0.211	−9.433	0.1145	−4.5578	−4.3150
Nov. 92	3.021	1.779	1.6423	0.8598	2.6304
Dec. 92	1.015	2.065	0.5520	0.9976	1.6779
Jan. 93	0.702	−2.909	0.3817	−1.4056	−0.8955
Feb. 93	1.048	−1.964	0.5699	−0.9492	−0.2510
.	.	.	.	.	.
.	.	.	.	.	.
.	.	.	.	.	.
Jul. 97	7.812	4.915	4.2465	2.3748	6.7497
Aug. 97	−5.745	−2.971	−3.1226	−1.4357	−4.4299
Sep. 97	5.315	8.723	2.8893	4.2148	7.2324
Oct. 97	−3.448	−4.555	−1.8741	−2.2011	−3.9469
Nov. 97	4.459	0.725	2.4236	0.3504	2.9024
Dec. 97	1.573	3.876	0.8551	1.8727	2.8562
Jan. 98	1.015	5.259	0.5517	2.5413	3.2214
Feb. 98	7.045	6.174	3.8294	2.9833	6.9410
Mar. 98	4.995	4.706	2.7149	2.2739	5.1171
Apr. 98	0.909	−0.096	0.4944	−0.0462	0.5765

are in the rows numbered 69 and 70. That is, the value-at-risk estimate is somewhere between \$4.367 million and \$4.389 million. A reasonable approach is to compute the value-at-risk by interpolating between these two losses in order to compute a loss that corresponds to a 5% probability. Specifically,

$$\text{value-at-risk} = \left(\frac{0.05 - 3/72}{4/72 - 3/72}\right)4.367 + \left(\frac{4/72 - 0.05}{4/72 - 3/72}\right)4.389 = 4.376.$$

Expressed as a fraction of the value of the portfolio, it is 4.367/110 = 0.03978, or 3.978%.

The historical simulation method can also easily be adapted to compute benchmark-relative VaR. To do this, one must subtract the change in the value of the benchmark portfolio from each of the entries in Table 2.3 before

TABLE 2.3 Hypothetical changes in portfolio value computed using the returns from the 72 months before May 1998 and sorted from largest profit to largest loss

Number	S&P 500 Percentage Change	FT-SE 100 Percentage Change	Change in Value of U.S. Equity Position (w/o Dividends)	Change in Value of U.K. Equity Position	Change in Portfolio Value (with Dividends of 0.1283)
1	5.315	8.723	2.8893	4.2148	7.2324
2	7.045	6.174	3.8294	2.9833	6.9410
3	7.338	5.494	3.9885	2.6547	6.7715
4	7.812	4.915	4.2465	2.3748	6.7497
5	5.858	5.235	3.1841	2.5296	5.8420
6	3.443	6.522	1.8716	3.1513	5.1512
7	4.995	4.706	2.7149	2.2739	5.1171
8	2.733	6.565	1.4855	3.1723	4.7862
9	3.762	4.749	2.0449	2.2945	4.4678
10	3.149	5.393	1.7117	2.6057	4.4457
.	.	.	.	.	.
.	.	.	.	.	.
.	.	.	.	.	.
63	−4.261	0.771	−2.3164	0.3723	−1.8157
64	−1.736	−2.988	−0.9436	−1.4438	−2.2591
65	−4.575	0.092	−2.4867	0.0444	−2.3140
66	−2.688	−4.165	−1.4610	−2.0124	−3.3450
67	−3.448	−4.555	−1.8741	−2.2011	−3.9469
68	0.211	−9.433	0.1145	−4.5578	−4.3150
69	−3.950	−4.859	−2.1474	−2.3479	−4.3669
70	−3.007	−5.967	−1.6343	−2.8830	−4.3889
71	−5.745	−2.971	−3.1226	−1.4357	−4.4299
72	−4.577	−7.406	−2.4878	−3.5785	−5.9379

sorting them and finding the loss that corresponds to a probability of 5%. The change in the value of the benchmark portfolio is simply the return on the benchmark, multiplied by the value of the portfolio, $110 million. Carrying out this calculation for May 1992, the difference between the change in the value of the portfolio and the benchmark is $[54.357 (0.000964) + 48.319(0.049490) + (0.014/12)110] − [110(0.000964) + (0.014/12)110] = \$2.338$ million. Carrying out the computation for each of the past 72 months, the benchmark-relative value-at-risk is $3.571 million.

An advantage of the historical simulation method is that it does not require that one make any specific assumption about the distribution of changes in the two indexes. (However, it does require that one assume that the distribution of returns is identical to the distributions from which the returns used to construct the value-at-risk estimate were drawn.) This, however, comes at the cost of being very data-intensive. Estimating the value-at-risk comes down to estimating the lower tail of the distribution, and large numbers of observations (many more than 72) are required to do this with any accuracy. For this reason, the historical simulation approach is best suited to computing value-at-risk for short holding periods such as one or two days, because reasonably large samples of one- or two-day returns are usually available. Even with a short holding period and large numbers of observations, the estimate of value-at-risk is still determined by a relatively small number of observations in the tail of the distribution. As a result, the estimate can be inaccurate.

Yet another method of computing the value-at-risk is to use a *Monte Carlo simulation* approach. In this approach, one simulates the hypothetical future values of the portfolio by drawing pseudo-random return vectors from an assumed joint distribution of the percentage changes in the two stock market indexes and then computing hypothetical new values of the stock market indexes and hypothetical new values of the portfolio. These provide an estimate of the distribution of possible future values of the portfolio from which the value-at-risk may be determined. This approach is most interesting for portfolios that include options, and we defer discussion of it until a later chapter. There are also variants of the different methods, designed to deal with the complexities of actual portfolios. Despite the differences in details and implementation, all methods share the goal of estimating the distribution of possible future values of the portfolio from which the value-at-risk estimate is obtained.

NOTES

Some authors use different terminology in referring to the various methods for computing values-at-risk. For example, Simons (1995) identifies three methods for computing values-at-risk: the parametric method, the historical method, and simulation. She then identifies two variants of simulation, historical simulation and Monte Carlo simulation, resulting in a total of four methods. This book identifies three basic methods, the delta-normal, historical simulation, and Monte Carlo simulation, as well as variants of the basic methods (e.g., the delta-gamma-theta-normal method and variants of Monte Carlo simulation). The delta-normal and parametric methods are the same and have yet a third name, the *variance-covariance method*. The approach Simons calls the *historical method* is that labeled the *"naïve" historical simulation* in chapter 4.

The cost-of-carry formula is $F = S \exp [(r - d)(T - t)]$, where F is the futures price, S is the current level of the index, r is the continuously compounded interest rate, d is the (continuous) dividend yield, and $T - t$ is the time remaining until the final settlement date of the futures contract. The example uses the parameters $r = 0.05$, $d = 0.016$, and $T - t = 0.3836$ for the FT-SE 100 contract, so this becomes $F = 1.0131S$. Since the multiplier of the FT-SE 100 index futures contract is 10, this implies that a holder of a futures contract gains or loses £10.131 when the index value changes by one unit. For the S&P 500 index futures contract, the example uses $r = 0.05$, $d = 0.014$, $T - t = 0.3836$, and a multiplier of 250, implying that a one-point change in the index results in a $253.48 change in the value of the S&P 500 contract.

In the interest of simplicity, the example "cheats" by interpreting the S&P 500 index futures contract as equivalent to a position in the stock portfolio underlying the index and thereby ignores the leverage or short-bond position implicit in a long futures position. Including this bond position would slightly affect the estimate of the expected change in the value of the portfolio, thus slightly affecting the value-at-risk. The situation with the FT-SE 100 futures contract is more complicated. The example first (incorrectly) ignores the embedded bond position and thereby treats the futures position as equivalent to a cash position in the portfolio underlying the FT-SE 100. However, this position is exposed to the risk of changes in the dollar/pound exchange rate. The example sidesteps this issue by neglecting to specify whether the parameters μ_2, σ_2, and ρ_{12} apply to the pound- or dollar-denominated returns in the FT-SE 100 index. The next chapter interprets these parameters as applying to the pound-denominated returns. This actually gives the correct result here, because (except that stemming from any margin balance) the FT-SE 100 index futures position has no exchange-rate risk due to the zero net investment in the position. This issue is addressed explicitly in the next chapter.

The key properties of the multivariate normal distribution used repeatedly in this book are as follows. Let $x_1, x_2, \ldots, x_N$ be normal random variables, and use μ_i and σ_i to denote the mean and standard deviation of the ith random variable x_i and ρ_{ij} to denote the correlation between x_i and x_j, where $\rho_{ii} = 1$. Then the random variable y, given by the linear combination

$$y = a_0 + \sum_{i=1}^{N} a_i x_i$$

$$= a_0 + a'x,$$

has a normal distribution with mean and variance

$$E[y] = a_0 + \sum_{i=1}^{N} a_i \mu_i$$

$$= a_0 + a'\mu$$

and

$$\text{var}[y] = \sum_{i=1}^{N} \sum_{j=1}^{N} a_i a_j \rho_{ij} \sigma_i \sigma_j$$

$$= a'\Sigma a,$$

respectively, where $a = (a_1, \ldots, a_N)'$, $x = (x_1, \ldots, x_N)'$, $\mu = (\mu_1, \ldots, \mu_N)'$, and Σ is an $N \times N$ matrix with elements of the form $\rho_{ij}\sigma_i\sigma_j$.

The approach to risk decomposition in this book is that of Litterman (1996), which has become standard. Chapter 10 includes a more detailed discussion of risk decomposition.

Techniques
of Value-at-Risk
and Stress Testing

The Delta-Normal Method

In the previous chapter, the first calculation of value-at-risk using the normal distribution was very easy. We simply needed the expected values and covariance matrix (i.e., the standard deviations and correlations) of the returns on the two indexes and the dollar values of the positions in the two markets. We then computed the mean and variance of changes in the value of the portfolio using formulas for the mean and variance of linear combinations of normally distributed random variables. Finally, we computed the standard deviation of changes in the value of the portfolio and the value-at-risk.

Even if we restrict our attention to equity portfolios, the computation of value-at-risk is not quite so easy for most actual portfolios. The approach in the previous chapter involved determining the investment in each asset (e.g., market index) and the means and covariances of returns on the assets. Once these were determined the VaR computation was simply an application of standard formulas. However, actual portfolios can include hundreds or even thousands of different common and preferred stocks, convertible bonds, options, index futures contracts, and other derivative instruments. To estimate directly the covariance matrix of the returns or changes in value of hundreds or thousands of different instruments is simply not feasible, especially because the risks of some of the instruments (e.g., options and convertible bonds) can change dramatically as the levels of stock prices change. Thus, it is essential to simplify the problem.

The procedure to do this is known as *risk mapping*. It involves taking the actual instruments and mapping them to a set of simpler, standard positions or instruments. The standard positions are chosen so that each of them is associated with a single market factor (e.g., the return on a market index such as the S&P 500) and the covariance matrix of their returns or changes in value may be readily estimated. Once the standard positions and the covariance matrix of their changes in value have been determined, the standard deviation of any portfolio of the standardized positions can be computed using known formulas. In essence, for any actual portfolio one finds a portfolio of the standard positions that is (approximately) equivalent to the original portfolio in the sense that it has the same sensitivities to changes in the values of the market factors. One then computes the value-at-risk of that equivalent portfolio. If the set of standard positions is reasonably rich, and the actual portfolio does not include many options or option-like instruments, then little is lost in the approximation.

There are two dimensions in which this simplification, or risk mapping, must be done. First, options and other instruments with values that are nonlinear functions of the prices of their underlying assets must be replaced by (approximately) equivalent positions in the underlying assets. Second, there must be some procedure for mapping thousands of individual stocks onto a limited number of stock market indexes. This chapter illustrates the mapping of options using the example of a portfolio in U.S. and U.K. stock market indexes that we consider in Chapter 2, except that now we add some index options to the portfolio. Chapter 7 describes a procedure for mapping individual stocks onto a limited number of market indexes.

THE PORTFOLIO

As before, the portfolio consists of $110 million invested in a well-diversified portfolio of large-capitalization U.S. equities, the returns of which are perfectly correlated with changes in the S&P 500 index. The portfolio manager has reduced his exposure to the U.S. market by shorting 200 of the S&P 500 index futures contracts and gained exposure to the U.K. market by establishing a long position of 500 FT-SE 100 index futures contracts. As in Chapter 2, at the current S&P level of 1097.6 the combined stock and futures position is equivalent to an investment of $54.357 million in the portfolio underlying the index. At the current FT-SE 100 level of 5862.3 and exchange rate of 1.6271 $/£, this position is equivalent to an investment of £29.696 million or $48.319 million in the portfolio that underlies the FT-SE 100 index.

In addition, the portfolio manager has written 600 of the September FT-SE 100 index call options with a strike level of 5875 traded on the LIFFE and has written 800 of the September S&P 500 index call options with a strike level of 1100 traded on the Chicago Board Options Exchange. Combining the (written) options positions with the $110 million invested in U.S. equities, the net value of the portfolio is $101,485,220. The delta of the entire portfolio with respect to the S&P 500 index is 4863.7, and the portfolio delta with respect to the FT-SE 100 index is 2821.5. The gammas of the two positions with respect to the S&P 500 index and FT-SE 100 index are −218.5 and −4.68, respectively.

Figure 3.1 shows the value of the portfolio as a function of the levels of the S&P 500 and FT-SE 100 indexes. The current levels of the S&P 500 and FT-SE 100 indexes are 1097.6 and 5862.3, respectively, so that the current portfolio value is in the middle of the graph. Figure 3.2 shows the value of the portfolio as a function of the level of the S&P 500 index, holding the FT-SE 100 index fixed at its current level of 5862.3, while Figure 3.3 shows the value of the portfolio as a function of the level of the FT-SE 100 index, holding the S&P 500 index fixed at its current level of 1097.6.

As before, the standard deviation of monthly percentage changes in the S&P 500 index is $\sigma_1 = 0.061$ (6.1%), the standard deviation of monthly percentage changes in the FT-SE 100 index is $\sigma_2 = 0.065$ (6.5%), and the correlation between the monthly percentage changes is 0.55. The expected percentage changes in the S&P 500 and FT-SE 100 indexes are $\mu_1 = 0.01$ (1%) and $\mu_2 = 0.0125$ (1.25%) per month, respectively. Again, we choose the holding period to be one month and the probability to be 5%.

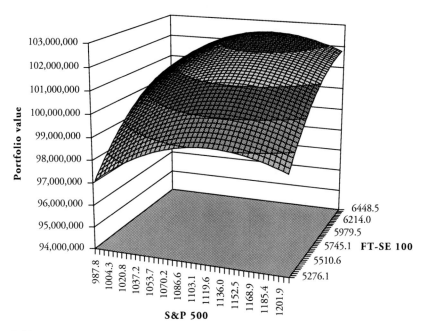

FIGURE 3.1 Current value of the portfolio as a function of the levels of the S&P 500 and FT-SE 100 indexes

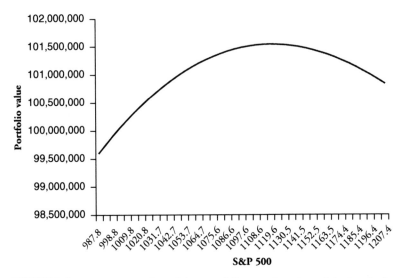

FIGURE 3.2 The current value of the portfolio as a function of the level of the S&P 500 index, holding fixed the value of the FT-SE index

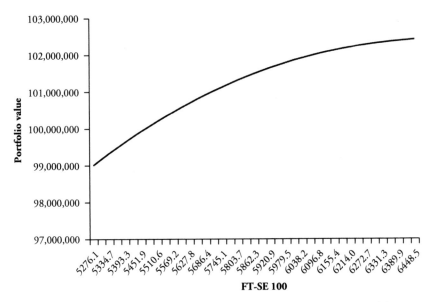

FIGURE 3.3 The current value of the portfolio as a function of the level of the FT-SE 100 index, holding fixed the value of the S&P 500 index

MAPPING OPTIONS

Equity and index options typically are mapped into *delta equivalent* positions in the underlying stock or equity index. An *option delta* is the partial derivative of the option price with respect to the price of the underlying asset or index level, or the rate at which the option value changes as the value of the underlying asset or index changes. Letting V denote the value of the option and S denote the value of the underlying asset or index, the delta is $\Delta = \partial V / \partial S$. The change in the option price resulting from a change in the spot price can be calculated from the delta and the change in price of the underlying asset or index level,

$$\text{Change in } V \approx \Delta \times \text{change in } S.$$

For example, if the option is on the S&P 500 index with $\Delta = 60$ (recall that the multiplier of the S&P 500 index option is 100, so that this corresponds to $\Delta = 0.6$ on a "per index" basis), the predicted change in the option price is 60 times the change in the index value. One interpretation of this is that for small changes in the index an option is equivalent to the investment of an amount, $\Delta \times S$, in a portfolio that is perfectly correlated with the index, because the change in the portfolio value is also given by the product of Δ and the change in the index level. Loosely, the option acts like Δ indexes.

To appreciate the power of this procedure, one need simply recognize that there exist an immense variety of options. Even if one considers just ordinary options, wide ranges of both strike prices and expiration dates are possible, and of course there are both calls and puts. In addition, there are exotic options that can have virtually any terms. This procedure allows the ith option to be mapped to an investment of $\Delta_i S$ in a portfolio that is perfectly correlated with the index, where the terms of the option matter only to the extent that they determine the option delta, Δ_i. Since the procedure can be applied to each option, it allows a portfolio of N different positions to be mapped to an investment of $\sum_{i=1}^{N} \Delta_i S$ in a portfolio that tracks the index.

For the example portfolio, the investment of $54.357 million in the portfolio perfectly correlated with the S&P 500 index has a delta of $49{,}524 = 54.357$ million$/1097.6$. Each of the S&P 500 index call options has a delta of 55.825, so the delta of the position of 800 written options is $-800 \times 55.825 = -44{,}660$, and the portfolio delta with respect to the S&P 500 index is $49{,}524 - 44{,}660 = 4863.7$ dollars. Thus, the positions based on the S&P 500 are mapped to a position consisting of an investment of

$4863.7 \times 1097.6 = \$5.338$ million in a portfolio that tracks the S&P 500 index.

There are 500 FT-SE 100 index futures contracts, each with a multiplier of 10 pounds, and the delta of the FT-SE 100 index futures position is 5065.6. Each of the FT-SE 100 index options has a delta of 5.553, implying that the delta of the position of 600 written options is $-600 \times 5.553 = -3331.6$, and the portfolio delta with respect to the FT-SE 100 index is $5065.6 - 3331.6 = 1734$. Thus, the FT-SE 100 index futures and options positions are mapped to a position consisting of an investment of £1734 $\times$ 5862.3 = £10.166 million in a portfolio that tracks the FT-SE 100 index, or 1734 units of the index. At the current exchange rate of 1.6271 dollar/pound, this is equivalent to an investment of \$16.541 million in a portfolio that tracks the index.

Having mapped the portfolio, we can now proceed as we did in Chapter 2. The expected change in and variance of the value of the portfolio are

$$
\begin{aligned}
E[\Delta V] &= X_1 \mu_1 + X_2 \mu_2 + D \\
&= 5.338(0.01) + 16.541(0.0125) + 110(0.014/12) \\
&= 0.3885
\end{aligned}
$$

and

$$
\begin{aligned}
\mathrm{var}[\Delta V] &= X_1^2 \sigma_1^2 + X_2^2 \sigma_2^2 + 2X_1 X_2 \rho_{12} \sigma_1 \sigma_2 \\
&= (5.338^2)(0.061^2) + (16.541^2)(0.065^2) \\
&\quad + 2(5.338)(16.541)(0.061)(0.065)(0.55) \\
&= 1.647
\end{aligned}
$$

The standard deviation of changes in the value of the portfolio is $1.283 = \sqrt{1.647}$, and the value-at-risk is

$$
\begin{aligned}
\mathrm{VaR} &= -(E[\Delta V] + 0.1283 - 1.645 \times \mathrm{s.d.}[\Delta V]) \\
&= -(0.3885 - 1.645 \times 1.283) \\
&= 1.723
\end{aligned}
$$

million. As a percentage of the value of the portfolio, the value-at-risk is $1.723/101.485 = 0.01698$ or 1.698%. Just as in Chapter 2, benchmark relative value-at-risk can be computed by adjusting the position in the S&P 500 to include a short position in the benchmark portfolio. Doing this, the relative VaR turns out to be 9.405% of the value of the portfolio. This is larger than the value-at-risk of 1.698% because in that calculation the portfolio weight on the S&P 500 is only 5.338/101.485 = 0.0526 or 5.26% due to the short positions in the S&P index futures and options. Since the benchmark portfolio has a weight of 100% in the S&P 500, the weight on the S&P 500 used in the calculation of relative value-at-risk is 5.26% – 100% = –94.74%.

EXPLICIT CONSIDERATION OF FX RISK

The value-at-risk calculation carried out above sidesteps the issue of exchange rate risk. Do the parameters μ_2, σ_2, ρ_{12} and apply to the local currency (i.e., pound-denominated) percentage changes in the FT-SE 100 index, or the dollar-denominated changes? Given that the FT-SE 100 futures contract was mapped to a cash position in the portfolio underlying the index, the correct approach seems to be to interpret them as applying to the dollar-denominated returns. If the parameters apply to the pound-denominated returns, the VaR calculation above would not capture the exchange rate risk of the position in the U.K. market.

While the preceding calculation is simple, a drawback of organizing the calculations in terms of the dollar-denominated returns is that the expected returns and covariance matrix depend upon the perspective or base currency of the person or organization performing the calculations. For example, a U.S. investor or organization would use the expected dollar-denominated returns and the covariance matrix of dollar-denominated returns, while a U.K. investor would use a set of parameters describing the distribution of pound-denominated returns. Unfortunately the expected returns and covariance matrices are generally different, depending on the base currency. This is inconvenient for companies or other organizations in which different subsidiaries or other units use different base currencies, as well as for software vendors whose customers do not all use the same base currency.

More importantly, while the calculation carried out above illustrates the main idea of mapping, it is incorrect. Even though the FT-SE 100 futures and options have the U.K. equity market risk of £10.166 million invested in a portfolio that tracks the FT-SE 100 index, there has not been a cash investment of £10.166 million. Rather, the FT-SE 100 index futures contract has a value of zero at the end of each day, so only the value of the written position in the FT-SE 100 index options is exposed to exchange rate risk. The procedure of mapping the futures and options positions to an investment of £10.166 million in a portfolio that tracks the FT-SE 100 index incorrectly treats this entire amount as if it were exposed to exchange rate risk.

These two difficulties can be overcome by considering the exchange rate to be a separate market factor or source of risk and interpreting the portfolio as having three risk factors, S_1, S_2, and e, where the new risk factor e is the exchange rate expressed in terms of dollars per pound. To do this, we must be careful about how the exchange rate affects the value of the portfolio.

First, the exchange rate does not affect the value of the positions in the S&P 500 index, so the portfolio delta with respect to the S&P 500 index remains 4863.7 dollars and the positions based on the S&P 500 are mapped to a position consisting of an investment of $\$4863.7 \times 1097.6 =$ $5.338 million in a portfolio that tracks the S&P 500 index.

The positions based on the FT-SE 100 index are affected by the exchange rate, though in different ways, and we consider them separately. These positions will be mapped using their deltas, or partial derivatives.

The FT-SE 100 index futures contracts affect the profit or loss on the portfolio through their daily resettlement payments. Even though the values of the futures contracts are zero at the end of each day, the daily resettlement payments must be included in the profit or loss because they are paid or received by the owner of the portfolio. To determine how the daily resettlement payment is affected by changes in S_2 and e, we use the cost-of-carry formula $F(S_2, t) = S_2 \exp[(r_2 - d_2)(T_2 - t)]$, where T_2 is the final settlement date of the FT-SE 100 index futures contract, t is the current date, r_2 is the £ interest rate, and d_2 is the dividend yield on the portfolio underlying the FT-SE 100 index. Because the futures contract has value zero following each resettlement payment, one need only consider the effects of changes in the market factors on the value of the first daily resettlement payment. This is given by

$$£500(10)\{S_2 \exp[(r_2 - d_2)(T_2 - t)] - 5862.3\exp[(r_2 - d_2)(T_2 - t_0)]\},$$

where t_0 is the initial time (i.e., the end of the previous day) and 10 is the multiplier for the FT-SE contract. In dollar terms, it is

$$\begin{pmatrix} \text{dollar value of daily} \\ \text{resettlement payment} \end{pmatrix} = 500(10)e\{S_2 \exp[(r_2 - d_2)(T_2 - t)]$$
$$-5862.3 \exp[(r_2 - d_2)(T_2 - t_0)]\}$$

Computing the deltas, or partial derivatives

$$\partial \begin{pmatrix} \text{dollar value of daily} \\ \text{resettlement payments} \end{pmatrix} \Big/ \partial S_2$$

and

$$\partial\left(\begin{array}{c}\text{dollar value of daily}\\\text{resettlement payments}\end{array}\right)\Big/\partial e$$

and then evaluating them at the initial values $S_1 = 1097.6$, $S_2 = 5862.3$, $e = 1.6271$, and t_0, we obtain

$$\partial\left(\begin{array}{c}\text{dollar value of daily}\\\text{resettlement payment}\end{array}\right)\Big/\partial S_2 = 5065.6e = 8242.3,$$

$$\partial\left(\begin{array}{c}\text{dollar value of daily}\\\text{resettlement payment}\end{array}\right)\Big/\partial e = 0. \tag{3.1}$$

The exchange rate delta of the futures contract is zero because when $S_2 = 5862.3$ and $t = t_0$ the value of the daily resettlement payment is zero, regardless of the exchange rate.

The written position of 600 FT-SE 100 index call options has a pound value of $-600C_2(S_2, t)$ and a dollar value of $-600eC_2(S_2, t)$, where the function C_2 gives the value (including the effect of the multiplier) of the FT-SE 100 index call option as a function of the index level and time. The partial derivatives are

$$\frac{\partial(-600eC_2(S_2,t))}{\partial S_2} = -600e\frac{\partial C_2(S_2,t)}{\partial S_2} = -3331.6e = -5420.8$$

$$\frac{\partial(-600eC_2(S_2,t))}{\partial e} = -600C(S_2,t) = -2{,}127{,}725 \tag{3.2}$$

where again the derivatives are evaluated at the initial values $S_1 = 1097.6$, $S_2 = 5862.3$, $e = 16271$, and $t = t_0$.

Combining the deltas of the FT-SE 100 futures and options positions, we have

$$\frac{\partial V}{\partial S_1} = 4863.7,$$

$$\frac{\partial V}{\partial S_2} = 8242.3 - 5420.8 = 2821.5, \tag{3.3}$$

$$\frac{\partial V}{\partial e} = 0 - 2{,}127{,}725 = -2{,}127{,}725,$$

where for $\partial V/\partial S_2$ and $\partial V/\partial e$ the right-hand sides consist of the sums of the futures and options deltas. The interpretation of these deltas is that one-unit changes in S_1, S_2, and e result in changes of 4863.7, 2,821.5, and $-2,127,725$ in the dollar value of the portfolio, respectively. Thus, the change in the dollar value of the portfolio can be approximated as

$$\text{change in } V \approx 4863.7(\text{change in } S_1) + 2821.5(\text{change in } S_2)$$
$$- 2,127,725(\text{change in } e).$$

Writing the changes in the risk factors in percentage terms,

$$\text{change in } V \approx 4863.7 S_1 \left(\frac{\text{change in } S_1}{S_1}\right) + 2821.5 S_2 \left(\frac{\text{change in } S_2}{S_2}\right)$$
$$-2,127,725 e\left(\frac{\text{change in } e}{e}\right) \tag{3.4}$$

or

$$\text{change in } V \approx 5,338,445\left(\frac{\text{change in } S_1}{1097.6}\right) + 16,540,531\left(\frac{\text{change in } S_2}{5862.3}\right)$$
$$-3,462,022\left(\frac{\text{change in } e}{1.6271}\right). \tag{3.5}$$

The upshot of this analysis is that the portfolio is mapped to $X_1 = 4863.7 \times 1097.6 = 5.338$ million dollars exposed to the risk of percentage changes in the S&P 500, $X_2 = 2821.5 \times 5862.3 = 16.541$ million dollars exposed to the risk of percentage changes in the FT-SE 100, and $X_3 = -21,27,725 \times 1.6271 = -3.462$ million dollars exposed to the risk of percentage changes in the exchange rate.

Examining the partial derivatives in (3.1) and (3.2) and following the role they play in equations (3.3) through (3.5), one can see that the written position in the FT-SE 100 index call option with value $-\$600 e C2(S_2,t)$ is exposed to the risk of changes in both S_2 and e. As a result, it contributes to both of the last two terms on the right-hand sides of (3.4) and (3.5). In contrast, the futures contract is not exposed to the risk of changes in e and does not contribute to the last term on the right-hand side of (3.4) and (3.5). Thus, this mapping captures the fact that the position in the FT-SE 100 index futures contract is not exposed to the risk of changes in the \$/£ exchange rate.

The mapping amounts to replacing the portfolio with a linear approximation

$$V = 5{,}338{,}445\left(\frac{S_1}{1097.6}\right) + 16{,}540{,}531\left(\frac{S_2}{5862.3}\right)$$
$$- 3{,}462{,}022\left(\frac{e}{1.6271}\right) + 83{,}068{,}266 \tag{3.6}$$
$$= 4863.7S_1 + 2821.5S_2 - 2{,}127{,}725e + 83{,}068{,}266.$$

The constant on the right-hand side is chosen so that, when $S_1 = 1097.6$, $S_2 = 5862.3$, and $e = 1.6271$, the right-hand side equals the actual initial value of the actual portfolio, \$101,485,220. This linear approximation is shown in Figures 3.4 and 3.5. Figure 3.4 shows the value of the portfolio as a function of the level of the S&P 500 index, holding the FT-SE 100 index and exchange rate fixed at their current levels of 5862.3 and 1.6271, along with the linear approximation of the value of the portfolio. Figure 3.5 shows the value of the portfolio and the linear approximation as a function of the level of the FT-SE 100 index, holding fixed the S&P 500 index and the exchange rate.

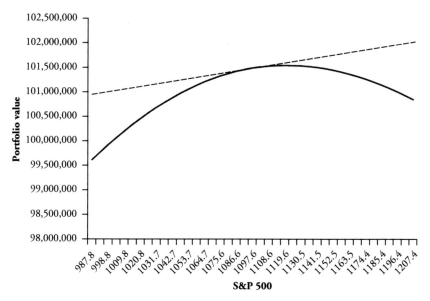

FIGURE 3.4 The current value of the portfolio as a function of the level of the S&P 500 index and the linear approximation used in computing delta-normal value-at-risk

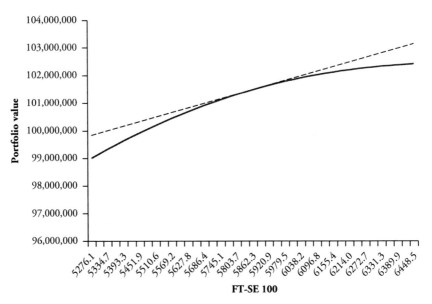

FIGURE 3.5 The current value of the portfolio as a function of the level of the FT-SE 100 index and the linear approximation used in computing delta-normal value-at-risk

Using equation (3.3), the expected change in the value of the portfolio is

$$E[\Delta V] = X_1\mu_1 + X_2\mu_2 + X_3\mu_3 + D,$$

where $\mu_1 = 0.01$, $\mu_2 = 0.0125$, and $\mu_3 = 0$ are the expected percentage changes in the three risk factors. The variance of monthly changes in portfolio value is given by the formula

$$\mathrm{var}[\Delta V] = X_1^2\sigma_1^2 + X_2^2\sigma_2^2 + X_3^2\sigma_3^2 + 2X_1X_2\rho_{12}\sigma_1\sigma_2$$
$$+ 2X_1X_3\rho_{13}\sigma_1\sigma_3 + 2X_2X_3\rho_{23}\sigma_2\sigma_3,$$

where $\sigma_1 = 0.061$ is the standard deviation of monthly percentage changes in the S&P 500 index, $\sigma_2 = 0.065$ is the standard deviation of monthly percentage changes in the FT-SE 100 index, $\sigma_3 = 0.029$ is the standard deviation of monthly percentage changes in the exchange rate, and $\rho_{12} = 0.55$, $\rho_{13} = 0.05$, and $\rho_{23} = -0.30$ are the correlation coefficients. Using these parameters and the mapping $X_1 = 5.338$ million, $X_2 = 16.541$ million, and $X_3 = -3.462$ million, the expected value and standard deviation of the change in value of the portfolio are

$$E[\Delta V] = 5.338(0.01) + 16.541(0.0125) - 3.462(0.0) + 110(0.014/12)$$
$$= 0.3885,$$

$$\begin{aligned}
\text{var}[\Delta V] = {} & (5.338^2)(0.061^2) + (16.541^2)(0.065^2) + (-3.462^2)(0.029^2) \\
& + 2(5.338)(16.541)(0.061)(0.065)(0.55) \\
& + 2(5.338)(-3.462)(0.061)(0.029)(0.05) \\
& + 2(16.541)(-3.462)(0.065)(0.029)(-0.30) \\
= {} & 1.719.
\end{aligned}$$

The standard deviation is, of course, simply the square root of the variance, or \$1.311 million, and the value-at-risk is

$$\begin{aligned}
\text{VaR} &= -(E[\Delta V] - 1.645 \times \text{s.d.}[\Delta V]) \\
&= -(0.3885 - 1.645 \times 1.311) \\
&= 1.768.
\end{aligned}$$

As a fraction of the initial value of the portfolio,

$$\begin{aligned}
\text{VaR} &= -\left(E\left[\frac{\Delta V}{V}\right] - 1.645 \times \text{s.d.}\left[\frac{\Delta V}{V}\right]\right) \\
&= -(0.00383 - 1.645 \times 0.0129) \\
&= 0.0174,
\end{aligned}$$

or 1.74% of the initial value of the portfolio.

Alternatively, when the time horizon of the value-at-risk estimate is one day, it is common to assume that the expected change in the portfolio value is zero. If this assumption is made, the value-at-risk is then \$1.645 million(1.311) = \$2.157 million, or 1.645(0.0129) = 0.0213 or 2.13% of the value of the portfolio.

COVARIANCE MATRIX ESTIMATES AND EXPONENTIAL WEIGHTING

The delta-normal method and others based on the normal distribution, such as the delta-gamma-theta-normal method and the implementations of the Monte Carlo simulation method, all require an estimate of the covariance matrix of changes in the market factors. Almost always, the estimate is obtained from historical data. For the diagonal terms of the covariance matrix (i.e., the variances), a natural choice is the classical variance estimator

$$\sigma_i^2 = \frac{1}{N-1}\sum_{n=1}^{N}(x_{i,t-n} - \bar{x}_i)^2,$$

where σ_i^2 is the estimate of the variance of changes in the ith market factor, $x_{i,t-n}$ is the change in the ith market factor n periods in the past, N is the number of past observations to be used, and

$$\bar{x}_i = \frac{1}{N}\sum_{n=1}^{N}x_{i,t-n}$$

is an estimate of the mean change in the ith market factor. The off-diagonal terms of the covariance matrix (i.e., the covariances) can be estimated using the formula

$$\sigma_i\sigma_j\rho_{ij} = \frac{1}{N-1}\sum_{n=1}^{N}(x_{i,t-n} - \bar{x}_i)(x_{j,t-n} - \bar{x}_j),$$

where $\sigma_i\sigma_j\rho_{ij}$ is the estimate of the covariance between changes in the ith and jth market factors. When the changes in the market factors are measured over short horizons such as one day, often it is assumed that $\bar{x}_i = 0$ and the formulas above are replaced by

$$\sigma_i^2 = \frac{1}{N}\sum_{n=1}^{N}x_{i,t-n}^2 , \tag{3.7}$$

and

$$\sigma_i\sigma_j\rho_{ij} = \frac{1}{N}\sum_{n=1}^{N}x_{i,t-n}x_{j,t-n} , \tag{3.8}$$

which seem to perform better.

An alternative is to use exponentially weighted estimators of the form

$$\sigma_i^2 = \frac{1-\lambda}{1-\lambda^N}\sum_{n=1}^{N}\lambda^{n-1}x_{i,t-n}^2 , \qquad (3.9)$$

and

$$\sigma_i\sigma_j\rho_{ij} = \frac{1-\lambda}{1-\lambda^N}\sum_{n=1}^{N}\lambda^{n-1}x_{i,t-n}x_{j,t-n} , \qquad (3.10)$$

where $\lambda < 1$ and N is chosen to be large enough that the terms for $n > N$ are negligible. The coefficient $(1-\lambda)/(1-\lambda^N)$ appears because the sum of the weights is $\sum_{n=1}^{N}\lambda^{n-1} = (1-\lambda^N)/(1-\lambda)$, or approximately $1/(1-\lambda)$ when N is large. Thus, this coefficient makes the sum of the weights approximately equal to one. The effect of this weighting scheme is that the more recent returns receive more weight in the estimation of the variance. For example, in the RiskMetrics methodology $\lambda = 0.94$ with daily data, so that the most recent observation receives a weight of 0.06, the next most recent observation receives a weight 0.06(0.94), and so on. Having more recent returns receive larger weight seems desirable because volatility both changes and is persistent; that is, large (in absolute value) returns are typically followed by additional large returns. Thus, when a large (in absolute value) return is observed, the volatility estimate should be increased, and when a small return is observed, it should be decreased. This is accomplished by placing a heavy weight on the recent returns.

A key issue in both the classical and exponentially weighted estimators is how much past data should be used, that is, the choice of N and λ. Were volatility constant, it would be optimal to use the equally weighted estimator with N chosen to be as large as possible, that is, equal to the number of available observations. However, if volatility changes over time, only recent data will be relevant and either N should be small or an exponentially weighted estimator with a relatively small value of λ should be used so that the weights decay rapidly. Morgan Guaranty Trust Company (1994; 1996) claims that $\lambda = 0.94$, which makes the weights decay relatively rapidly, is a good choice. With this choice of λ the weight is less than 0.01 for the observation 30 days in the past and is less than 0.001 for the observation 66 days in the past. Hendricks's (1996) comparison of value-at-risk estimators using equally weighted covariance matrix estimators also suggests that good choices of N are relatively small, and his results using exponentially weighted estimators are consistent with the claim that $\lambda = 0.94$ is a good choice.

LIMITATIONS OF THE DELTA-NORMAL APPROACH

First, an assumption in virtually all VaR methods is that the portfolio does not change during the holding period. Either explicitly or implicitly, VaR is an estimate of the risk of the *current* portfolio over the stated holding period or time horizon. To the extent that the portfolio changes, the distribution of profit and loss will be different from that used in the computation of the VaR estimate.

It is clear from equations (3.1) through (3.6) and Figures 3.4 and 3.5 that the delta-normal method is based on a linear or delta approximation of the value of the portfolio. Thus, the method will work well when a linear approximation adequately describes the changes in the value of the portfolio. From Figures 3.4 and 3.5, one can see that the adequacy of a linear approximation will depend on the curvature of the function expressing the value of the portfolio in terms of the underlying market factors. This curvature is measured by the portfolio gammas (second derivatives) with respect to each of the underlying market factors. Gamma, or curvature in the value function, is a characteristic of options and option-like instruments, implying that the adequacy of the linear approximation is determined by the number of options in the portfolio and their characteristics. As a result, the delta-normal method may not provide accurate VaR estimates for portfolios that contain large numbers of options.

In particular, it is clear from examining the figures that for portfolios with downward curvature, or gamma less than zero, the linear approximation is always greater than the actual portfolio value, so that an estimate of the loss based on the linear approximation will be less than the actual loss. Thus, the delta-normal method underestimates the value-at-risk for such portfolios. Conversely, for portfolios with positive gamma the linear approximation lies below the true portfolio value, so that an estimate of the loss based on the linear approximation will exceed the actual loss. For such portfolios the delta-normal method overestimates the value-at-risk. Portfolios in which the options are exclusively or predominantly purchased have positive gamma, while portfolios in which the options are exclusively or predominantly written have negative gamma. Thus, the delta-normal method will tend to underestimate the value-at-risk for portfolios of written options and overestimate it for portfolios of bought options.

The delta-normal method also uses the assumption that changes in the market factors are normally distributed. Unfortunately, the actual distributions of changes in financial rates and prices typically have fat tails relative to the normal distribution. That is, in the actual distributions both extreme changes and small changes are more frequent than predicted by a normal distribution with the same variance. (If small changes were not also more frequent the distributions would not have the same variance; thus, it is changes of intermediate size that are less frequent.) Many different models generate such distributions of changes in the values of the market factors. Two popular classes of models that generate fat tails are: (i) *stochastic volatility* models, including the popular ARCH and GARCH models; and (ii) models in which the change in the value of the market factor is a mixture of a normal market movement drawn from a normal distribution and one or more other random variables, either drawn from normal distributions with different parameters or from distributions of other types. There is a voluminous literature on such models, a small part of which is cited in the notes to this chapter.

The delta-normal method is perfectly compatible with non-normality in returns or changes in market factors due to stochastic volatility, because in many stochastic volatility models the returns or changes in market factors have conditional normal distributions, and conditional normality is all that is needed for the delta-normal method. (The unconditional distribution of returns in such models has fat tails relative to the normal distribution because it is a mixture of normal random variables with different parameters.) In fact, the exponentially weighted covariance matrix estimator described above is a special case of the popular GARCH(1,1) model described briefly in the notes. Thus, such implementations of the delta-normal method capture stochastic volatility of this form. However, the exponentially weighted scheme does not fully capture other forms of stochastic volatility, and implementations of the delta-normal method using equally weighted covariance matrix estimators will not capture even this special case of stochastic volatility.

However, the conditional distribution of the changes in market factors may be non-normal. In principle, this can be handled through the use of other distributions, for example the t distribution or mixtures of normal distributions. This would result in a delta-t or delta-mixture-of-normals method of computing value-at-risk. This approach is typically not taken, both because it sacrifices much of the tractability of the delta-normal approach and because selecting an appropriate fat-tailed distribution and estimating its parameters are extremely difficult problems. By definition, there are relatively few extreme realizations of changes in market factors. As a result, the data contain only limited information about the fatness of the tails.

The non-normality of the distribution of changes in market factors is not a problem when computing 95% confidence value-at-risk. In fact, because of the lower frequency of market factor changes of intermediate size, the correct 95% confidence VaR can often be less than the VaR computed using the delta-normal approach. The delta-normal approach typically understates 99% confidence VaR, but the bias is often not too severe. However, the problem can be significant when value-at-risk is computed using higher confidence levels. The risks of such extreme outcomes are typically assessed using stress-testing, described in Chapter 9.

NOTES

The calculations of the futures prices of the S&P 500 and FT-SE 100 index futures contracts use the cost-of-carry formula $F = S \exp[(r - d)(T - t)]$, where S is the current index value, r is the interest rate, d is the dividend yield on the portfolio underlying the index, and $T - t$ is the time until the final settlement of the futures contract. For the S&P contract the parameter values are $r = 0.05$, $d = 0.014$, and $T - t = 0.3836$, while for the FT-SE 100 contract they are $r = 0.05$, $d = 0.016$, and $T - t = 0.3836$.

The calculation of the expected change in the value of the portfolio in the example ignores the return on the implicit synthetic bond position embedded in the call options and futures contracts. Equivalently, the calculation ignores the time derivative of the position value, the position theta. This is standard in the delta-normal approach; including the time derivative would result in a delta-theta-normal approach. Over the short horizons for which the delta-normal approach is usually used, the resulting error is small, except for portfolios with significant options content or bond positions that are very large relative to the VaR. As indicated in the body of the chapter, when the time horizon of the value-at-risk estimate is one day, it is common also to ignore the expected changes in the values of the market factors and simply assume that the expected change in the portfolio value is zero.

J.P. Morgan's release of the RiskMetrics data and methodology in 1994 gave considerable prominence to the delta-normal method (see Morgan Guaranty Trust 1994); the most recent version of the RiskMetrics system is described by Morgan Guaranty Trust Company (1996) and Mina and Xiao (2001). Morgan Guaranty Trust Company (1994; 1996) provides an extensive discussion of mapping and covariance matrix estimation using the exponentially weighted approach, though the focus is on fixed-income instruments.

Figlewski (1997) presents evidence that the variance estimator (3.7) that treats the expected change as equal to zero performs better than the classical variance estimator. An intuitive explanation for this is that the two estimators differ materially only when the sample mean return is much different from zero. But for financial data one knows the expected daily return is close to zero. Thus, if the average return in the sample is much different from zero, then one knows that the sample mean is a poor estimate of the expected return and should be disregarded. The same reasoning applies to the covariance estimator (3.8).

At first glance, using historical estimates of the covariance matrix might seem like a poor choice, because value-at-risk is intended as a measure of the possible *future* changes in market value. In light of this, it might seem valuable to exploit the information available in option-implied volatilities, which can be interpreted as *the market's* forward-looking volatility forecasts. However, this is typically not done, for two reasons.

First, the dimension of the covariance matrix used in VaR calculations is often quite large. For example, if the government bond or LIBOR yield curve in each currency is mapped to between 15 and 20 standard positions, then the value-at-risk system of a bank or pension fund with positions in fixed-income instruments denominated in most or all of the actively traded currencies along with equity positions in most of the major stock markets could involve 400 or more basic market factors. While implied volatilities for some market factors could be readily computed, there are not enough actively traded options to allow for all of the relevant implied volatilities to be computed. In addition, a $K \times K$ covariance matrix involves $(K^2 - K)/2$ different correlation coefficients. The computation of implied correlation coefficients requires the prices of options that depend on both underlying market factors (e.g., spread options). For many pairs of market factors, such options either do not exist or their prices are not readily available.

Second, value-at-risk is often used to monitor or control traders or portfolio managers. Monitoring takes place through the reporting of VaR estimates to senior managers, company directors, or pension plan trustees, and value-at-risk is sometimes used to control traders through position limits based on VaR estimates. Basing VaR estimates on implied volatilities can be problematic because the computation of implied volatilities often requires input from the trading desk or portfolio manager. To the extent that value-at-risk is used in monitoring and controlling traders and portfolio managers, they may have incentives to shade or bias the computation of implied volatilities. For this reason, it is often thought desirable that the covariance matrix be estimated objectively based on historical data.

Autoregressive Conditional Heteroscedasticity (ARCH) and Generalized Autoregressive Conditional Heteroscedasticity (GARCH) models are a popular approach for estimating time-varying conditional volatilities. GARCH models describe the conditional variance in terms of weighted averages of past conditional variances and squared past returns. In a GARCH(p,q) model, the conditional variance of the return or change in market factor x_t, σ_t^2 is modeled as

$$\sigma_t^2 = \alpha_0 + \sum_{n=1}^{q} \alpha_i x_{t-n}^2 + \sum_{n=1}^{p} \beta_i \sigma_{t-n}^2 , \tag{3.11}$$

where p and q determine the order of the GARCH process, x_{t-n} is the return or change in the market factor n periods in the past, and the αs and βs are parameters to be estimated. Typically this is done using the method of maximum likelihood. A common choice is to let $p = q = 1$, resulting in a GARCH(1,1) model, which can be written in the form

$$\sigma_t^2 = \frac{\alpha_0}{1 - \beta_1} + \sum_{n=1}^{\infty} \alpha_1 \beta_1^{n-1} x_{t-n}^2 . \tag{3.12}$$

That is, the conditional variance σ_t^2 is equal to a constant $\alpha_0 / 1 - \beta_1$, plus a geometrically declining weighted sum of past returns. Comparing this to equation (3.9) reveals that the exponentially weighted covariance matrix estimator is a special case of the GARCH(1,1) model with $\alpha_0 = 0$.

A univariate GARCH model like (3.11) or (3.12) would be applied separately to each market factor. When the covariance matrix is of low dimension ($K \leq 3$ or 4), multi-dimensional GARCH models may be used. Unfortunately, the available procedures for estimating multivariate GARCH models become impractical when K is larger than this. Thus, such sophisticated procedures for estimating the covariance matrix are often only useful when the object is to estimate the value-at-risk of a portfolio exposed to only a few market factors, for example, the trading book of a single trading desk.

The literature on GARCH and other stochastic volatility models is too large to survey here. Boudoukh, Richardson, and Whitelaw (1997) discuss GARCH and other methods for estimating volatility in the context of value-at-risk models. Duffie and Pan (1997) discuss a range of approaches for estimating volatilities in the context of VaR estimation, including GARCH and multivariate GARCH models, other stochastic volatility models, and jump-diffusion models.

Koedjik, Huisman, and Pownall (1998) propose the use of the t-distribution to capture the fat tails typically found in financial returns data. Zangari (1996b) proposes a simple version of a mixture of normals approach, while Venkataraman (1997) is a recent example of the use of mixtures of normals to compute value-at-risk. Gibson (2001) proposes modeling extreme returns by grafting a model of large price jumps onto a (perhaps normal) model for ordinary market movements.

Evidence that non-normality does not have much impact on 95% confidence VaR estimates is described by Morgan Guaranty Trust Company (1994; 1996) and Duffie and Pan (1997), which present evidence about the distributions of a number of different market factors. Evidence for emerging market exchange rates and equity indexes is presented in Finger (1996) and Zangari (1996d).

CHAPTER 4

Historical Simulation

Historical simulation represents a markedly different approach to the problem of estimating value-at-risk. It does not impose *a priori* a specific assumption about the distribution of changes in the market factors and does not rely on the delta or linear approximation central to the delta-normal method. Instead, it relies on the assumption that the distribution of possible changes in the market factors over the next period is identical to the distribution observed over a sample of N past periods. This chapter illustrates the use of this approach to measure the risk of a simple fixed-income portfolio.

In Chapter 2, the historical simulation method of computing the value-at-risk of a simple-equity portfolio could be interpreted as pretending that one held the current portfolio during each of the last N periods and seeing what would have happened to the value of the portfolio during each of the periods. While this is also the spirit of a historical simulation calculation of the value-at-risk of a fixed-income portfolio, one needs to take a bit more care with the interpretation. First, it is crucial to be careful about what is meant by the *current portfolio*. For concreteness, consider a very simple portfolio consisting of a zero-coupon bond maturing on date T, one year from today, and having a face, or par, value of F and a current market value of V. In this case, *current portfolio* means V invested in a zero-coupon bond with one year remaining until maturity. It does not mean a zero-coupon bond with face value F maturing on date T, because during each of the last N periods a bond maturing on date T had more than one year remaining until maturity and likely was riskier than the current portfolio. Also, on each of the past N days the market value of a bond maturing on date T was almost certainly not identical to today's market value V.

Second, one does not use the interest rates that prevailed during the last N periods, because they may be very different from current market interest rates. Rather, starting from the current levels of interest rates, one subjects the portfolio to the interest rate *changes* that were observed during the last

N periods. Thus, the historical simulation method of estimating the value-at-risk of a fixed-income portfolio consists of taking the current portfolio and subjecting it to the interest rate changes that were observed during the last N periods.

This is in the spirit of pretending that one held the portfolio for each of the last N periods, but for the two reasons above is not quite the same thing. Despite these subtle differences, the historical simulation calculation of the value-at-risk of a simple equity portfolio performed in Chapter 2 was correct. Because common stocks do not have a fixed maturity, the issue of the varying time to maturity does not arise with simple equity portfolios. For such portfolios the naïve historical simulation approach of pretending that one held the portfolio for each of the last N periods used in Chapter 2 is identical to taking the current portfolio and subjecting it to the equity returns that were observed during the last N periods, provided one interprets "held the portfolio" to mean maintained a constant dollar investment in the portfolios underlying each of the two indexes. However, the two approaches are not equivalent for equity portfolios that include options or convertible securities, because such instruments do expire or mature. For equity portfolios that include options or option-like instruments, one should use a historical simulation approach analogous to that described in this chapter.

To describe it a bit more precisely, the historical simulation approach involves using historical changes in market rates and prices to estimate the distribution of potential future portfolio profits and losses. The estimate of the distribution is constructed by taking the current portfolio and subjecting it to the actual changes in the basic market factors experienced during each of the last N periods, typically days. Specifically, the current values of the market factors and the changes observed during the last N periods are used to construct N sets of hypothetical future values of the market factors. Once these hypothetical future values of the market factors have been constructed, N hypothetical mark-to-market portfolio values are computed using the appropriate formulas or models for computing the market values of the instruments that make up the portfolio. Subtracting the actual current mark-to-market portfolio value from each of the hypothetical future values, N hypothetical mark-to-market profits and losses on the portfolio are computed. These N hypothetical mark-to-market profits or losses provide the estimate of the distribution of profits and losses, from which the value-at-risk estimate is obtained.

The use of the actual historical changes in rates and prices to compute the hypothetical profits and losses is the distinguishing feature of historical simulation and the source of the name. Though the actual changes in rates and prices are used, the mark-to-market profits and losses are hypothetical because the current portfolio was not held on each of the last N periods. The historical simulation approach is typically used with a short holding period, such as one day, because reasonably accurate estimation of value-at-risk using this methodology requires that one have access to the changes in market rates and prices over a large number of (nonoverlapping) past periods. For many markets, data spanning large numbers of long (e.g., one month or one quarter) past holding periods simply are not available, rendering simple versions of the historical simulation method unsuitable for the calculation of value-at-risk over long holding periods.

A SIMPLE FIXED-INCOME PORTFOLIO

We illustrate the approach by applying it to a simple fixed-income portfolio consisting of positions in the U.S. dollar and Thai baht. We use a holding period of one day and a confidence level of 95% and assume that the current date is Friday, 30 January. The value-at-risk will be computed for the one (business) day holding period from Friday, 30 January to Monday, 2 February. Somewhat arbitrarily, the most recent 250 periods ($N = 250$) are used to compute the changes in the values of the market factors and the hypothetical profits and losses on the portfolio. Again, the analysis is performed from the perspective of a dollar-based investor. This simply means that the portfolio values and profits and losses are denominated in U.S. dollars.

The portfolio consists of the following two positions: (i) A one-year Thai baht (THB) denominated note with a face value of 5 billion Thai baht, paying semiannual interest at the rate of 22.5% per year. The note will make an interest payment of THB $0.5 \times 0.25 \times 5$ billion = THB 562.5 billion in one-half year. After one year, it will make another interest payment of THB 562.5 million and also return the principal of THB 5 billion; (ii) This position is partially financed by a U.S. dollar-denominated loan with a principal amount of $50 million paying semiannual interest at the rate of 6% per year. The loan requires the borrower to make an interest payment of U.S. $0.5 \times 0.06 \times 50$ million = U.S. $1.5 million in one-half year and to make another interest payment of U.S. $1.5 million and repay the principal of U.S. $50 million in one year.

The current value of the Thai baht note is THB $5,047,516,023 \times 0.01860465$ $/baht = $93,907,275$, and the present value of the liability on the dollar-denominated loan is $50,201,942. Thus, the current value of the portfolio is $93,907,275 - $50,201,942 = $43,705,333.

ANALYSIS OF THE PORTFOLIO

The key steps in the historical simulation method are to construct N sets of hypothetical future values of the market factors and then to use these to compute N hypothetical mark-to-market portfolio values using the appropriate formulas or models. Thus, it is necessary to identify the basic market factors that determine the value of the portfolio and to determine a formula or model that allows the value of the portfolio to be computed as a function of these factors. Achieving both of these goals is facilitated by decomposing the instruments in the portfolio into simpler instruments directly related to the underlying market risk factors and then interpreting the actual instruments as portfolios of the simpler instruments. For the example portfolio, the Thai baht-denominated bond is equivalent to a six-month zero-coupon bond with a face value of THB 562.5 million and a one-year zero-coupon bond with a face value of THB 5.5625 billion, while the dollar-denominated loan is equivalent to a six-month zero-coupon bond with a face value of $1.5 million and a one-year zero-coupon bond with a face value of $51.5 million. This decomposition of the portfolio is shown in Table 4.1 and yields the following formula for the current mark-to-market value (in dollars) of the position:

U.S. dollar mark-to-market value =

$$S_{\text{THB}} \times \left[\frac{\text{THB 562.5 million}}{1 + 0.5 r_{\text{THB},6}} + \frac{\text{THB 5.5625 billion}}{1 + r_{\text{THB},12}} \right] \\ - \left[\frac{\text{USD 1.5 million}}{1 + 0.5 r_{\text{USD},6}} + \frac{\text{USD 51.5 million}}{1 + r_{\text{USD},12}} \right] \quad (4.1)$$

Examining Table 4.1 and equation (4.1), one can see that the current U.S. dollar market value of the Thai baht bond depends on three basic market factors: S_{THB}, the spot exchange rate expressed in dollars per baht; $r_{\text{THB},6}$, the six-month baht interest rate; and $r_{\text{THB},12}$, the 12-month baht interest rate. The current market value of the U.S. dollar bond depends on two basic market factors: $r_{\text{USD},6}$, the six-month dollar interest rate; and $r_{\text{USD},12}$, the 12-month dollar interest rate. Thus, we have succeeded in expressing the value of the portfolio as a function of five variables: S_{THB}, $r_{\text{THB},6}$, $r_{\text{THB},12}$, $r_{\text{USD},6}$, and $r_{\text{USD},12}$. It is natural to take these to be the basic market factors, because spot exchange rates are widely quoted, and six and 12 months are standard maturities for which interest rate quotes are readily available.

TABLE 4.1 Decomposition of the fixed income portfolio into simple instruments directly related to the basic market factors

Position	Current USD Value of Position	Cash Flow in 6 Months	Cash Flow in 12 Months
Long position in 6-month THB zero-coupon bond with face value of THB 562.5 million	$S_{THB} \times \dfrac{\text{THB } 562.5 \text{ million}}{1 + 0.5 r_{THB,6}}$	Receive THB 562.5 million	
Long position in 12-month THB zero-coupon bond with face value of THB 5.5625 billion	$S_{THB} \times \dfrac{\text{THB } 5.5625 \text{ billion}}{1 + r_{THB,12}}$		Receive THB 5.5625 billion
Short position in 6-month USD zero-coupon bond with face value of USD 1.5 million	$-\dfrac{\text{USD } 1.5 \text{ million}}{1 + 0.5 r_{USD,6}}$	Pay USD 1.5 million	
Long position in 12-month USD zero-coupon bond with face value of USD 51.5 million	$-\dfrac{\text{USD } 51.5 \text{ million}}{1 + r_{USD,12}}$		Pay USD 51.5 million

One issue that is not apparent in this simple example is that one would continue to use interest rates for standard maturities as the market factors even if the payment dates of the instruments in the portfolio did not coincide with the standard maturities. For example, if the interest payment of U.S. $1.5 million was to be made in eight months instead of six, one would continue to use the six- and 12-month U.S. interest rates as the market factors.

To do this, the market value of the interest payment to be made in eight months might be computed as

$$\text{market value} = -\frac{\text{USD 1.5 million}}{1 + [(2/3)r_{\text{USD},6} + (1/3)r_{\text{USD},12}]},$$

where $(2/3)r_{\text{USD},6} + (1/3)r_{\text{USD},12} = \left(\frac{12-8}{6}\right)r_{\text{USD},6} + \left(\frac{8-6}{6}\right)r_{\text{USD},12}$ is an estimate of the eight-month interest rate obtained by interpolating from the six- and 12-month interest rates. (Of course, one might use interpolation schemes more sophisticated than linear interpolation.) It is necessary to do this first, because for most currencies interest rate quotes are readily available for only a limited number of standard maturities. In addition, it is necessary to identify a limited number of basic market factors simply because otherwise the complexity and data requirements of the method become overwhelming. Even if we restrict our attention to bonds, virtually any maturities and interest payment dates are possible. If the market factors are chosen to be the interest rates for each possible payment date, a portfolio of bonds denominated in just one currency would require thousands of market factors, because there are potentially thousands of different days on which payments could be made. Thus, an essential first step is to express the instruments' values in terms of a limited number of basic market factors.

Most actual portfolios will include bonds with many different payment dates, perhaps spread over a number of years, and many will involve bonds denominated in more than one currency. As a result, most will have values that depend upon more than five market factors. A typical set of market factors might include the interest rates on zero-coupon bonds with a range of maturities for each currency in which the company has positions, along with the spot exchange rates. For example, the maturities used in the fourth version of the RiskMetrics system are one, three, six, and 12 months, and two, three, four, five, seven, nine, 10, 15, 20, and 30 years (Morgan Guaranty Trust 1996). As a result, the portfolio of a bank or investment management organization with fixed-income positions in many or most of the actively traded currencies could easily be exposed to several hundred different market factors. Regardless of the number of different market factors, the key is still to obtain a formula expressing the value of the portfolio as a function of the various market factors.

The second step is to obtain historical values of the market factors for the last $N + 1$ days, and from them construct the previous N changes in the market factors. For our portfolio, this means collecting the six- and 12-month baht and dollar interest rates and the spot dollar/baht exchange rate for the last 251 business days, that is, from 6 February of the prior year to 30

January of the current year. Thus, the first of the previous 250 periods is from 6 to 7 February of the prior year, while the last is from 29 to 30 January of the current year. The actual daily changes in the market factors over these 250 periods will be used to construct hypothetical values of the market factors used in the calculation of hypothetical profits and losses.

The key step is to subject the current portfolio to the actual changes in the market factors that occurred over these 250 periods and to calculate the daily profits and losses that would occur if comparable daily changes in the market factors occurred over the next day (from 30 January to 2 February) and the current portfolio is marked-to-market. We first apply the 250 historical percentage changes in the market factors to the current (30 January) market factors to compute 250 sets of hypothetical market factors for 2 February. These hypothetical market factors are then used to calculate the 250 hypothetical mark-to-market portfolio values, again for 2 February. For each of the hypothetical portfolio values, we subtract the actual mark-to-market portfolio value on 30 January to obtain 250 hypothetical daily profits and losses. With this procedure, the hypothetical 2 February market factors are based upon, but *not* equal to, the historical values of the market factors over the previous 250 days.

Table 4.2 shows the calculation of the first of the 250 hypothetical changes in value using the changes in the market factors from 6 to 7 February of the prior year. We start by using the 30 January values of the market factors and equation (4.1) to compute the mark-to-market value of the portfolio on 30 January, which is \$43,705,333 and is shown on line 1. Next, we determine a 2 February hypothetical value by applying the percentage changes in the market factors from 6 to 7 February of the prior year to the actual values on 30 January. Lines 2 through 4 show the values of the market factors on 6 and 7 February of the prior year and the percentage changes. Line 5 shows the actual values of the market factors on 30 January, while line 6 applies the percentage changes in line 4 to the 30 January values shown in line 5 to compute hypothetical values of the market factors for 2 February. These hypothetical values of the market factors for 2 February are then used to compute a hypothetical mark-to-market value of the portfolio using the formula

U.S. dollar mark-to-market value =

$$
\hat{S}_{\text{THB}} \times \left[\frac{\text{THB } 562.5 \text{ million}}{(1 + 0.5\hat{r}_{\text{THB},6})^{179.5/182.5}} + \frac{\text{THB } 5.5625 \text{ billion}}{(1 + \hat{r}_{\text{THB},12})^{362/365}} \right] \\
- \left[\frac{\text{USD } 1.5 \text{ million}}{(1 + 0.5\hat{r}_{\text{USD},6})^{179.5/182.5}} + \frac{\text{USD } 51.5 \text{ million}}{(1 + \hat{r}_{\text{USD},12})^{362/365}} \right], \quad (4.2)
$$

TABLE 4.2 Calculation of hypothetical 2 February 1998 mark-to-market profit/loss on the fixed income portfolio using market factors from 30 January 1998 and changes in market factors from 6 to 7 February 1997

	Market Factors					
Start with actual values of market factors and portfolio at close of business on 30 Jan. 1998:	6-Month USD Interest Rate (% per year)	1-Year USD Interest Rate (% per year)	6-Month THB Interest Rate (% per year)	1-Year THB Interest Rate (% per year)	Exchange Rate (USD/THB)	Mark-to-Market Value of Portfolio (USD)
(1) Actual values on 30 Jan. 1998	5.62500	5.65625	22.02500	22.50000	0.01860465	43,705,333
Compute actual past changes in market factors:						
(2) Actual values on 6 Feb. 1997	5.62500	5.84766	11.39500	10.65000	0.03848374	
(3) Actual values on 7 Feb. 1997	5.63281	5.85156	11.16500	10.42000	0.03846154	
(4) Percentage change from 6 Feb. 1997 to 7 Feb. 1997	0.13884%	0.06669%	−2.01843%	−2.15962%	−0.057687%	
Use these to compute the hypothetical future values of the market factors and the mark-to-market value of the portfolio:						
(5) Actual values on 30 Jan. 1998	5.62500	5.65625	22.02500	22.50000	0.01860465	
(6) Hypothetical future values calculated using rates from 30 Jan. 1998 and percentage changes from 6 to 7 Feb. 1997	5.63281	5.66002	21.58044	22.01408	0.01859392	44,140,027
(7) Hypothetical mark-to-market profit/loss on portfolio						434,694

where $\hat{S}_{THB}$, $\hat{r}_{THB,6}$, $\hat{r}_{THB,12}$, $\hat{r}_{USD,6}$, and $\hat{r}_{USD,12}$ are the simulated values of the market factors and $179.5/182.5$ and $362/365$ are, respectively, the fractions of a half-year and year remaining after the three days from 30 January to 2 February have passed. The value of $44,140,027 computed using this formula is shown in the right-hand column of line 6. The profit or loss on the portfolio is just the difference between this hypothetical mark-to-market value and the actual value of $43,705,333 from line 1 and is shown in line 7.

This calculation is repeated 249 more times, using the values of the market factors on 30 January and the percentage changes in the market factors from the second through 250th past periods. This results in 250 hypothetical mark-to-market portfolio values for 2 February, and the 250 hypothetical mark-to-market profits or losses shown in Table 4.3.

The final step is to select the loss that is equaled or exceeded 5% of the time, that is, the value-at-risk. This is facilitated by sorting the mark-to-market profits and losses from the largest profit to the largest loss. The sorted profits/losses are shown in Table 4.4, and range from a profit of $7,418,019 to a loss of $13,572,640. Since we have used 250 past periods and 5% of 250 is 12.5, the 95% confidence value-at-risk is between the twelfth and thirteenth worst losses, or between the losses of $2,738,866 and $2,777,376, which appear in the rows numbered 238 and 239. Interpolating between these two values, the 95% confidence value-at-risk is $0.5(2,738,866) + 0.5(2,777,376) = 2,758,121$. An alternative approach would be to smooth the histogram to obtain a nonparametric estimate of the probability density of changes in value and then obtain the value-at-risk from the estimated density.

Figure 4.1 shows the distribution of hypothetical profits and losses. The loss that is exceeded with a probability of only 5%, that is, the value-at-risk, is the loss that leaves 5% of the probability in the left-hand tail. This is indicated by the arrow located toward the left-hand side of the graph.

INCLUDING OPTIONS AND OTHER MORE COMPLICATED INSTRUMENTS

Options and option-like instruments are somewhat more complicated but can be handled using the same basic approach. Again, the key is to express the option values in terms of the basic market factors. The trick is that option pricing formulas and models typically give the option value as a function of the price of the underlying asset (and other parameters), and typically the underlying asset will not coincide with one of the basic market

TABLE 4.3   Historical simulation of 250 hypothetical daily mark-to-market profits and losses on a fixed income portfolio

			Market Factors				
Number	6-Month USD Interest Rate (% per year)	1-Year USD Interest Rate (% per year)	6-Month THB Interest Rate (% per year)	1-Year THB Interest Rate (% per year)	Exchange Rate (USD/THB)	Hypothetical Portfolio Value (USD)	Change in Hypothetical Port. Value
1	5.6328	5.6600	21.5804	22.0141	0.01859	44,140,027	434,694
2	5.6055	5.6185	22.3209	22.8239	0.01864	43,780,410	75,078
3	5.6133	5.6563	21.3242	22.0956	0.01862	44,209,050	503,718
4	5.6250	5.6563	22.7287	22.7818	0.01856	43,401,250	−304,083
5	5.6250	5.6563	21.5185	22.2431	0.01859	43,964,983	259,650
6	5.5936	5.6258	23.8396	24.0592	0.01853	42,321,906	−1,383,427
7	5.6092	5.6257	22.3566	22.4392	0.01865	44,070,216	364,883
8	5.6171	5.6563	21.7709	21.7486	0.01863	44,477,397	772,065
9	5.6290	5.6563	21.8047	22.6891	0.01862	43,810,108	104,776
10	5.6369	5.6870	20.9678	21.7083	0.01863	44,553,678	848,346
11	5.6250	5.6563	21.7133	22.3273	0.01863	44,080,360	375,027
12	5.6250	5.6715	20.9974	21.9342	0.01863	44,407,123	701,790
13	5.6250	5.6524	22.3774	22.7679	0.01863	43,749,104	43,771
14	5.6566	5.6753	21.9760	22.6103	0.01862	43,848,062	142,729
15	5.6878	5.7779	21.4197	22.1488	0.01858	44,035,091	329,759
.	.						.
.	.						.
.	.						.
236	5.5318	5.5630	20.9700	21.5000	0.01768	39834277	−3871056

TABLE 4.3 Historical simulation of 250 hypothetical daily mark-to-market profits and losses on a fixed income portfolio (Continued)

	Market Factors						
Number	6-Month USD Interest Rate (% per year)	1-Year USD Interest Rate (% per year)	6-Month THB Interest Rate (% per year)	1-Year THB Interest Rate (% per year)	Exchange Rate (USD/THB)	Hypothetical Portfolio Value (USD)	Change in Hypothetical Port. Value
237	5.6566	5.6878	19.3521	19.6221	0.01912	48658747	4953414.3
238	5.6564	5.7034	20.3712	22.6800	0.01991	50423457	6718123.8
239	5.6016	5.6095	23.5619	22.5000	0.01814	41393052	−2312281
240	5.6485	5.6877	20.2865	21.8750	0.01862	44449532	744198.91
241	5.6563	5.6875	21.7701	22.7449	0.01834	42354782	−1350551
242	5.5939	5.6368	23.3881	23.0148	0.01866	43691449	−13883.72
243	5.6250	5.6446	22.1638	23.6842	0.01831	41533743	−2171590
244	5.6250	5.6563	22.0250	22.5000	0.01848	43224483	−480850.2
245	5.6250	5.6563	24.9498	23.0625	0.01835	42042003	−1663330
246	5.6328	5.6875	22.3446	24.6951	0.01866	42620007	−1085326
247	5.6172	5.6563	22.0250	22.5000	0.01883	44983704	1278370.7
248	5.6563	5.6873	22.0250	22.5000	0.01843	42982520	−722813.2
249	5.6250	5.6563	22.0250	22.5000	0.01867	44189864	484530.8
250	5.5939	5.5944	22.0250	22.5000	0.01860	43811324	105991.32

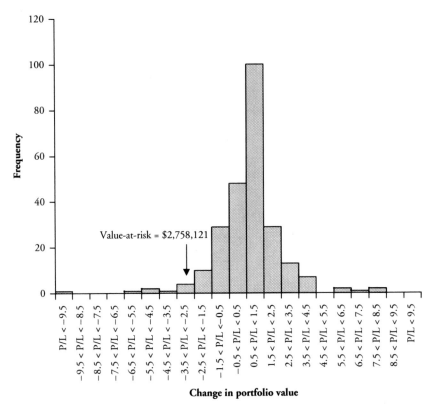

FIGURE 4.1 Histogram of hypothetical daily mark-to-market profits and losses on the fixed-income portfolio

factors. This is handled by expressing the value of the underlying asset as a function of the market factors, which will make the option price a compound function of the values of the market factors. For example, the value of a bond option depends on the price of the underlying bond, which in turn depends on the market factors (interest rates), perhaps using the interpolation approach described above. Option volatilities may be handled either by treating them as additional market factors that must be estimated and collected for each of the past periods or else by treating the volatilities as constants and disregarding the fact that they change randomly over time.

To handle realistic portfolios with many instruments does not require any change in the approach described above, though it does involve a bit more computation. Instruments with payment dates that do not correspond to the standard maturities of the market factors can be handled using the interpolation approach described above, while longer maturity bonds or bonds denominated in additional currencies can be handled by introducing additional market factors. Of course, there may be a great many market factors. These factors must be identified, data on their historical values must be collected, and pricing formulas expressing the instruments' values in terms of the market factors must be obtained. Finally, the change in the value of the portfolio must be computed using the appropriate formulas and taking into account all of the instruments in the portfolio. All of this may be a great deal of work, but the nature of the work is no different from that described above.

ADVANTAGES AND LIMITATIONS OF HISTORICAL SIMULATION

Historical simulation is easy to understand and explain. The key calculations in Table 4.4 can be explained to and understood by audiences without any statistical training. Through the reliance on revaluation of the portfolio rather than a delta approximation, the procedure also captures the fact that the prices of options and some other instruments are nonlinear functions of the underlying market factors.

A key limitation of the approach is that it requires large samples of past data. Even though the procedure involves revaluing the portfolio N times, the value-at-risk estimate is determined by the realizations in the tail of the distribution. Almost by definition, there are relatively few observations in the tail, so that the effective sample size is much smaller than N. For this reason, reasonably accurate estimation of value-at-risk, using the historical simulation method, requires large sample sizes, for example, 1000 or 2000 past observations (that is, approximately four or eight years of daily data). The drawback is that the use of such a large sample requires the assumption that the distribution of changes in the market factors is constant over long periods, and in particular that data from four or eight years ago are relevant for estimating the current risk of a portfolio.

Unfortunately, it is easy to think of examples where such an assumption would have been badly wrong. For example, in late June 1997, immediately prior to the collapse of the Thai baht, there was widespread speculation that the Thai authorities would be unable to maintain the basket regime. Thus, it was clear that Thai baht positions were very risky. However, a historical simulation analysis of the value-at-risk of a Thai baht position would not have revealed this risk, because during the preceding few years only small changes in the dollar/baht exchange rate had been

TABLE 4.4 Historical simulation of 250 hypothetical daily mark-to-market profits and losses on a fixed income portfolio, sorted from largest profit to largest loss

Number	Market Factors					Hypothetical Portfolio Value (USD)	Change in Hypothetical Port. Value
	6-Month USD Interest Rate (% per year)	1-Year USD Interest Rate (% per year)	6-Month THB Interest Rate (% per year)	1-Year THB Interest Rate (% per year)	Exchange Rate (USD/THB)		
1	5.6250	5.6563	13.1214	17.9392	0.019300	51,123,351	7,418,019
2	5.6564	5.7034	20.3712	22.6800	0.019914	50,423,457	6,718,124
3	5.6250	5.6563	20.7286	20.6221	0.019453	49,549,737	5,844,404
4	5.6176	5.6563	22.9457	22.5000	0.019663	49,149,919	5,444,586
5	5.6566	5.6878	19.3521	19.6221	0.019121	48,658,747	4,953,414
6	5.6250	5.6563	18.4215	18.7500	0.018728	47,283,712	3,578,379
7	5.6250	5.6563	21.9734	20.8696	0.019029	47,146,895	3,441,562
8	5.6250	5.6563	19.0078	22.6406	0.019236	47,063,621	3,358,289
9	5.6250	5.6563	21.1543	22.5000	0.019166	46,716,501	3,011,168
10	5.6324	5.6857	19.2140	20.6107	0.018865	46,623,405	2,918,073
11	5.6250	5.6563	20.6064	22.5000	0.019124	46,528,409	2,823,076
12	5.6552	5.7158	21.7049	22.9563	0.019181	46,471,839	2,766,507
13	5.6250	5.6563	22.0250	22.5000	0.019079	46,238,105	2,532,772
14	5.6250	5.6563	24.0053	22.5000	0.019057	46,040,706	2,335,373
15	5.6250	5.6563	19.4520	21.8132	0.018891	45,880,487	2,175,154
.	.	.	.	.	.	.	.
.	.	.	.	.	.	.	.
.	.	.	.	.	.	.	.

TABLE 4.4 Historical simulation of 250 hypothetical daily mark-to-market profits and losses on a fixed income portfolio, sorted from largest profit to largest loss (Continued)

Number	Market Factors					Hypothetical Portfolio Value (USD)	Change in Hypothetical Port. Value
	6-Month USD Interest Rate (% per year)	1-Year USD Interest Rate (% per year)	6-Month THB Interest Rate (% per year)	1-Year THB Interest Rate (% per year)	Exchange Rate (USD/THB)		
236	5.6250	5.6563	23.6499	24.2308	0.018297	41,067,304	−2,638,029
237	5.6438	5.6818	24.6006	22.5000	0.018073	41,060,627	−2,644,706
238	5.6250	5.6563	24.2022	24.4565	0.018311	40,966,466	−2,738,866
239	5.6250	5.6266	21.1437	23.2500	0.018123	40,927,957	−2,777,376
240	5.5692	5.5697	22.1109	22.5000	0.018027	40,877,074	−2,828,259
241	5.6250	5.6633	30.2855	28.8529	0.018890	40,746,746	−2,958,587
242	5.6401	5.6857	26.6243	25.8333	0.018331	40,094,856	−3,610,477
243	5.5318	5.5630	20.9700	21.5000	0.017683	39,834,277	−3,871,056
244	5.5949	5.5967	22.8471	23.3710	0.017900	39,645,581	−4,059,752
245	5.5954	5.6089	24.4857	23.5420	0.017879	39,369,526	−4,335,807
246	5.6250	5.6416	27.1248	28.7395	0.018420	38,664,935	−5,040,398
247	5.6250	5.6195	23.3857	24.1598	0.017697	38,113,393	−5,591,940
248	5.5645	5.5961	24.0063	23.4084	0.017555	37,842,065	−5,863,268
249	5.6250	5.6563	28.8501	24.4737	0.017579	37,137,405	−6,567,927
250	5.5954	5.6275	20.2191	19.8214	0.015573	30,132,693	−13,572,640

observed. This problem can be overcome by adjusting the historical changes in the market factors to be consistent with a current estimate of the covariance matrix, as described below and in sources cited in the notes. However, doing this sacrifices one of the principal advantages of the historical simulation method, its simplicity.

A second key limitation is that historical simulation responds slowly to changes in volatility. Because large returns are typically associated with increases in volatility, large returns should lead to increases in the value-at-risk estimate. This happens, for example, when the delta-normal method is used with an exponentially weighted volatility estimator. With the historical simulation method, a large negative return, such as a market crash, will shift the ranking of the returns; what was the eleventh worst return will become the twelfth worst, and what was the twelfth worst will become the thirteenth, and so on. If, as in the example in this chapter, one is computing a 95% confidence VaR estimate using 250 past returns, then the VaR is computed from the twelfth and thirteenth worst returns. If the eleventh, twelfth, and thirteenth worst returns are all relatively close in value, then the market crash and shifting described above will have little impact on the VaR estimate. Perhaps even worse, large positive returns will have no impact on the VaR estimate, even though positive returns are also associated with volatility increases.

REFINEMENTS TO THE HISTORICAL SIMULATION APPROACH

Historical simulation can be adapted to reflect recent market volatility by exponentially weighting the hypothetical changes in portfolio value. One first computes the hypothetical changes in the portfolio value using the changes in the market factors from N past periods, just as in standard historical simulation. Letting ΔV_n denote the change in portfolio value computed using the changes in market factors from n periods in the past, one then applies weight $\alpha \lambda^{n-1}$ to the change in value ΔV_n, where $\lambda < 1$, the coefficient $\alpha = (1 - \lambda)/(1 - \lambda^N)$ is chosen to make the sum of the weights equal 1, and N is the total number of past observations used. The weights α, $\alpha\lambda$, $\alpha\lambda^2$, ..., $\alpha\lambda^{n-1}$, ..., $\alpha\lambda^{N-1}$ are then used to construct the empirical distribution (histogram) of the changes in portfolio value by acting as if a proportion $\alpha\lambda^{n-1}$ of the observations had change in value ΔV_n, and the VaR estimate is read off the empirical distribution.

Because $\lambda < 1$, this scheme gives relatively more weight to the recent past (n is small) and less to the more distant past (n close to N). In particular, the weights on the simulated changes in value based on recent changes in the market factors are greater than $1/N$, the weights implicitly used in standard historical simulation, while the weights applied to the more distant past are less than $1/N$. This is the mechanism through which the scheme allows the VaR estimate to reflect recent volatility. However, a limitation of this approach is that it does not update the VaR estimate to reflect recent large increases in the value of the portfolio, which also will be associated with subsequent higher volatility. A further disadvantage is that the exponentially weighted approach can exacerbate the estimation error in the historical simulation VaR because deweighting the past observations is similar to using a smaller sample.

It is possible to overcome this drawback while still reflecting recent volatility by scaling the past changes in market factors using volatility estimates. This is done by computing daily volatility estimates for every market factor for both the current date and every day during the period covered by the historical data, scaling the historical changes in market factors by the ratios of current to past volatilities, and then using these scaled changes in place of the original ones. Specifically, let t denote the current date, $x_{i,t-n}$ the change in the ith market factor n days in the past, $\sigma_{i,t-n}$ the estimate of the volatility of the change $x_{i,t-n}$, and $\sigma_{i,t}$ the estimate of the current volatility of the ith factor. These volatilities may be estimated using either exponentially weighted moving averages of squared returns or GARCH models. The approach is to compute the hypothetical changes in the portfolio value using the scaled changes in market factors $(\sigma_{i,t}/\sigma_{i,t-n})x_{i,t-n}$ (or $(\sigma_{i,t}/\sigma_{i,t-n})[x_{i,t-n} - E(x_{i,t-n})]$) in place of the (unscaled) changes $x_{i,t-n}$ or $[x_{i,t-n} - E(x_{i,t-n})]$, form the empirical distribution (histogram) from the profits and losses, computed using the scaled changes in market factors, and then obtain the VaR estimate from this distribution. The advantage of this approach is that it reflects current estimates of market volatility through the scaled changes in the market factors, while still using a long historical sample to provide information about the fatness of the tails. Sources cited in the notes describe a slightly more general approach that can also incorporate changes in correlations among the market factors.

The historical simulation approach can be adapted to estimate value-at-risk over multiple-day horizons by repeatedly sampling from the empirical distribution of daily changes in the market factors and then cumulating the daily changes to obtain the simulated changes over multiple-day horizons. For example, suppose one wanted to estimate the value-at-risk of the portfolio analyzed above over a horizon of one month (21 days). One would begin by randomly selecting (with replacement) 21 vectors of changes in the market factors from the available sample of observed past changes. Let x_{1t} denote the tth of the 21 percentage changes in the first market factor (the spot exchange rate), x_{2t} denote the tth of the 21 percentage changes in the second market factor (the six-month THB interest rate), and so on. The simulated values of the market factors at the end of the 21-day horizon can then be obtained by cumulating these percentage changes; for example, the simulated value of the spot exchange rate is

$$\hat{S}_{\text{THB}} = S_{THB}\prod_{t=1}^{21}(1 + x_{1t}),$$

where S_{THB} is the current value of the spot exchange rate and $\hat{S}_{\text{THB}}$ is the simulated end-of-month value, and similarly for the other market factors. Then, the simulated values $\hat{S}_{\text{THB}}$, $\hat{r}_{\text{THB},6}$, $\hat{r}_{\text{THB},12}$, $\hat{r}_{\text{USD},6}$, and $\hat{r}_{\text{USD},12}$ can be combined with a formula similar to that in equation (4.2) (the time remaining to maturity will differ) to compute a simulated mark-to-market value of the portfolio, yielding one simulated realization of the mark-to-market value and, by subtracting the current value, one simulated realization of the change in value. Repeating the process a large number of times generates an estimate of the distribution of changes in value, and thus the value-at-risk.

NOTES

Historical simulation is used in portfolio management settings, though its use in this context does not appear to be widespread. Roth and Layng (1998) describe the development and implementation of a VaR model for measuring the risks of portfolios consisting of emerging market equities and convertible bonds. In this implementation, the market factors are the prices of the individual equities. The choice to use individual equity returns as the market factors instead of the common choice to use the returns on market indexes permits the system to capture the risk of arbitrage and relative value trading strategies. De Bever, Kozun, and Zvan (2000) describes the use of historical simulation at the Ontario Teachers Pension Plan, including the use of historical simulation over a multiple-day horizon.

The calculation in equation (4.1) computes the price for immediate settlement, reflects the simplifying assumption that the payments are to be made or received in exactly one-half year (182.5 days) and one year (365 days), and assumes that the six-month rates are compounded twice per year and the 12-month rates are compounded once per year. Typically, the interest rates would be either derived from the prices of government securities or else LIBOR term structures would be constructed from the rates on interbank deposits, forward rate agreements, futures contracts on interbank deposit rates, and interest rate swaps (or from some subset of these instruments). The calculation in equation (4.2) reflects the simplifying assumption that the payments are to be made or received in exactly one-half year (182.5 days) and one year (365 days) after the current date of 30 January and also that the rates for 179.5 and 362 days observed on 2 February are identical to the rates for one-half year and one year, respectively.

Butler and Schachter (1996; 1998) propose implementing the historical simulation approach by using a kernel estimator to produce a nonparametric estimate of the probability density function of changes in portfolio value. The nonparametric estimate of the probability density can be interpreted as a smoothed histogram, so this approach is in the spirit of standard historical simulation. Butler and Schachter also go on to develop a confidence interval around the historical simulation estimate of value-at-risk.

Zangari (1997b) describes a procedure termed *portfolio aggregation*, which is closely related to the historical simulation approach. This involves constructing the portfolio returns as in historical simulation, but then fitting a parametric distribution to them instead of simply constructing their histogram. Alternatives to fitting a parametric distribution are the regression quantile approach of Engle and Manganelli (1999) and extreme value theory described in Chapter 16. Advantages of portfolio aggregation are that it allows for more flexible time-series volatility models (e.g., ARCH, GARCH, and related models), and that one can then use the fitted volatility model to develop a VaR estimate over a multi-day horizon using a Monte Carlo approach. A disadvantage is that risk decomposition becomes difficult, perhaps impossible.

The exponentially weighted historical simulation approach is due to Boudoukh, Richardson, and Whitelaw (1998). Shimko, Humphreys, and Pant (1998) suggest weighting the simulated changes in value using other criteria. For example, for portfolios that depend on prices that display seasonal differences in volatility, one might place more weight on past data from the same season or month. The volatility scaling approach is due to Duffie and Pan (1997), Hull and White (1998), and Barone-Adesi, Giannopoulos, and Vosper (1999; 2000a; 2000b), who term it *filtered historical simulation*. Duffie and Pan (1997) and Pritsker (2001) also explain how to rescale the factor changes to incorporate changing correlations. This is accomplished by using scaled changes of the form $\Sigma_t^{1/2} \Sigma_{t-n}^{-1/2} x_{t-n}$ or

$\Sigma_t^{1/2} \Sigma_{t-n}^{-1/2} x_{t-n} [x_{t-n} - E(x_{t-n})]$, where $x_{t-n} = (x_{1,t-n}, x_{2,t-n}, ..., x_{K,t-n})'$ is a vector of changes in the K market factors, $\Sigma_{t-n}^{1/2}$ is a matrix square root of the estimate of the covariance matrix of x_{t-n}, and $\Sigma_t^{1/2}$ is a matrix square root of the estimate of the covariance matrix of x_t. A limitation of this procedure is that correlation estimates tend to be unstable, suggesting that any corrections for changing correlation estimates should be used with caution. Pritsker (2001) analyzes some limitations of historical simulation and these variants of it, including their response to changes in volatility.

The Delta-Normal Method for a Fixed-Income Portfolio

The value-at-risk of fixed-income portfolios can also be computed using the delta-normal method presented in Chapters 2 and 3. Though the analysis of fixed-income portfolios is more complicated, the basic approach is identical to the earlier analysis of the simple-equity portfolios.

As in Chapters 2 and 3, the delta-normal approach is based on the assumptions that: (i) the probability distribution of changes in the underlying market factors can be adequately approximated by a multivariate normal distribution; and (ii) the probability distribution of possible portfolio profits and losses or returns is adequately approximated by a (univariate) normal distribution. These two assumptions are mutually consistent if the returns of the instruments in the portfolio are linearly related to the changes in the market factors. While this will rarely be exactly true, it is often approximately so, and a linear approximation lies at the heart of the delta-normal method. Given this approximation, assumptions (i) and (ii) are consistent. Once the distribution of changes in portfolio value has been determined, the quantiles of the normal distribution are used to determine the loss that will be equaled or exceeded with probability α, that is, the $1 - \alpha$ confidence value-at-risk.

Given the reliance on the normal distribution, the computation of the mean and standard deviation of changes in portfolio value or returns is the focus of the delta-normal method. The mean and standard deviation are computed through a procedure of mapping the actual instruments in the portfolio into positions in a relatively small set of market factors or standard instruments. In effect, this involves approximating the changes in the value of the actual portfolio, which may include large numbers of complicated instruments (e.g., ordinary and exotic options, callable and puttable bonds, mortgage-backed securities, etc.), in terms of changes in the values of the market factors. Once this has been done, the mean and variance of its return are computed using formulas for the mean and variance of linear combinations of normal random variables. These computations are based on the fact that the statistical properties of the returns on a portfolio are just the statistical properties of linear combinations of the returns on the instruments that make up the portfolio.

Chapter 3 presented a simple example of a mapping in which index options were mapped to their delta-equivalent positions in the standard instruments using their partial derivatives, or deltas. This same approach is used to map bond and interest-rate options in a fixed-income portfolio, that is, they are mapped to their delta-equivalent positions. However, mapping a fixed-income portfolio is usually more complicated than the mapping of the options in Chapter 3. The complexity is not primarily due to the possible presence of options in the portfolio but rather to the fact that most fixed-income portfolios have cash flows on many different days and therefore have values that depend on many different interest rates. As in Chapter 4, it would be unmanageable to take the interest rate for each payment date to be a separate risk factor, and some simplification is necessary. This is achieved by choosing a relatively small number of market risk factors (bond prices or interest rates) that capture the risk of the portfolio and then expressing the portfolio value in terms of these market factors. The complexity of mapping a fixed-income portfolio stems from this need to express the values of cash flows paid or received on hundreds or thousands of different dates in terms of a limited number of market factors.

Even this brief description makes the method seem complicated. This is unavoidable; the method *is* complicated. In order to make the steps clear, the calculation is illustrated using the simple fixed-income portfolio from the previous chapter. As above, this portfolio consists of a long position in a one-year Thai baht-denominated note with a face value of 5 billion THB, paying semiannual interest at the rate of 22.5% per year, and a short position (a loan) in U.S. dollar-denominated bond with a principal amount of $50 million paying semiannual interest at the rate of 6% per year. As in the last chapter, we perform the analysis from the perspective of a dollar-based investor, use a holding period of one day and a probability of 5% ($\alpha = 0.05$) or confidence level of 95% and use the most recent 250 business days ($N = 250$) to estimate the covariance matrix of changes in the values of the market factors.

The preceding description of the approach started with the goal of computing the mean and standard deviation of the changes in portfolio value and then briefly described the steps to achieve this goal. In actually carrying out the computations, one starts with the details of the choice of risk factors and the mapping and then builds up to the computation of the mean and variance of the possible change in the portfolio value. This requires the four steps below.

IDENTIFY THE BASIC MARKET FACTORS AND STANDARD POSITIONS

The value-at-risk estimate measures the risk of changes in the market factors. Thus, the choice of market factors is a key step in the design of the risk-measurement system, for the choice of the market factors amounts to a choice of what risks to measure. For example, a system that uses the prices of or yields on government bonds as the basic market factors will capture the risk of changes in the level and shape of the yield curve but will be unable to capture the risk of changes in the yield spreads between government and corporate bonds. In contrast, a system that includes both government and corporate prices or yields as market factors is able to capture this risk. The choice of the number of different maturities to include among the market factors reflects a choice of how finely to measure the shape of the yield curve. For example, a system that uses the yields on three-month, two-year, and 10-year bonds or the first three principal components (see Chapter 8) as the market factors measures the shape of the yield curve less finely than a system that uses 15 or 20 different yields (e.g., the yields on, or prices of, bonds with maturities of one month, three months, six months, one year, two years, etc.).

The designer of the risk measurement system has considerable flexibility in the choice of market factors and therefore has considerable flexibility in the mapping. Here we make a simple choice in order to illustrate the procedure. Based on the previous decomposition of the portfolio into long positions in six- and 12-month Thai baht and U.S. dollar zero-coupon bonds, it is natural to choose five market factors: the prices of, or equivalently yields on, six- and 12-month dollar-denominated zero-coupon bonds; the prices of or yields on six- and 12-month Thai baht-denominated zero-coupon bonds; and the spot dollar/baht exchange rate. There are five market factors even though there are only four cash flows because the dollar value of the Thai baht note depends on three market factors: the six- and 12-month baht bond prices/interest rates and the dollar/baht exchange rate. Thus, each of the Thai baht cash flows must be mapped to positions in two market factors: (i) bond position exposed only to changes in the baht interest rate of that maturity; and (ii) a spot position in baht exposed only to changes in the exchange rate.

MAPPING THE PORTFOLIO INTO POSITIONS
IN THE STANDARD INSTRUMENTS

Mapping the portfolio consists of expressing the values of the positions in terms of the market factors. We use bond prices rather than interest rates as the market factors, because this choice makes the delta-normal method a bit simpler. With this choice, expressing the values of the positions in terms of the market factors amounts to computing the dollar values of positions in the zero-coupon bonds and spot Thai baht.

The positions in six- and 12-month dollar-denominated zero-coupon bonds are computed by discounting the cash flows using the six- and 12-month dollar interest rates. Letting X_1 and X_2 denote the dollar values of the positions in the first and second standard instruments and using negative signs to represent short positions,

$$X_1 = -\frac{\$1.5 \text{ million}}{1 + 0.5 r_{USD, 6}} = -\frac{\$1.5 \text{ million}}{1 + 0.5(.05625)} = -\text{U.S. } \$1,458,967,$$

$$X_2 = -\frac{\$51.5 \text{ million}}{1 + r_{USD, 12}} = -\frac{\$51.5 \text{ million}}{1 + (.0565625)} = -\text{U.S. } \$48,742,975.$$

As discussed above, the Thai baht note must be mapped into three positions because its value depends on three market factors: the six- and 12-month baht bond prices and the spot dollar/baht exchange rate. The magnitudes of the positions are determined by separately considering how changes in each of the market factors affect the value of the baht cash flows, holding the other factors constant. The dollar values of the two baht cash flows are given by

$$X_3 = (S \text{ dollar/baht}) \times \left(\frac{\text{THB } 562.5 \text{ million}}{1 + 0.5 r_{THB, 6}}\right)$$

$$= (0.001860465 \text{ dollar/baht}) \times \left(\frac{\text{THB } 562.5 \text{ million}}{1 + 0.5 r_{THB, 6}}\right)$$

$$= \$9,426,971$$

and

$$X_4 = (S \text{ dollar/baht}) \times \left(\frac{\text{THB } 5562.5 \text{ million}}{1 + r_{THB, 12}}\right)$$

$$= (0.001860465 \text{ dollar/baht}) \times \left(\frac{\text{THB } 5562.5 \text{ million}}{1 + r_{THB, 12}}\right)$$

$$= \$84,480,304.$$

The first term, X_3, represents the dollar value of the six-month Thai baht cash flow and does not depend on the 12-month baht interest rate, while the second term, X_4, represents the dollar value of the 12-month cash flow and does not depend on the six-month interest rate. Holding constant the exchange rate S, the baht note has the risk of $X_3 = \$9,426,971$ invested in six-month baht-denominated bonds and $X_4 = \$84,480,304$ invested in 12-month baht bonds. In addition, both components are exposed to the risk of changes in the dollar/baht exchange rate. The Thai baht note has a value of $X_3 + X_4 = \$9,426,971 + 84,480,304 = \$93,907,275$ and has the exchange rate risk of a baht spot position with this dollar value. Thus, the position in the fifth market factor consists of $X_5 = \$93,907,275$ invested in a spot baht position. We have the relation $X_5 = X_3 + X_4$ because both X_5 and the sum $X_3 + X_4$ represent the dollar value of the Thai baht note. As discussed above, the dollar value of the Thai baht note appears twice in the mapped position because, from the perspective of a U.S. investor, a position in a baht-denominated bond is exposed to changes in both bond price/interest rate and exchange rate risk.

Having completed this mapping, the portfolio is now described by the magnitudes of the positions X_1 through X_5, and the delta-normal method proceeds by computing the risk of the portfolio consisting of X_1 through X_5. Alternatively, the delta-normal method can be interpreted in terms of a Taylor series approximation of the value of the portfolio about the current values of the market factors, and this alternative interpretation can be used to justify the mapping carried out above. This alternative interpretation is a special case of the delta-gamma-theta method described in chapter 14 and is useful when interest rates, rather than bond prices, are used as market factors.

DETERMINE THE DISTRIBUTION OF CHANGES IN THE VALUES OF THE MARKET FACTORS

The third step is to assume that percentage changes in the basic market factors have a multivariate normal distribution and to estimate or otherwise select the parameters of that distribution. This is the point at which the delta-normal procedure captures any expected change or trend in the market factors, and their variability and comovement. The variability is captured by the standard deviations (or variances) of the normal distribution, and the comovement by the correlation coefficients. Typically the parameters are estimated from historical data on the (percentage or log) changes in the market factors. This use of the historical data differs from their use in the historical simulation method, because here the data are not used directly but affect the value-at-risk through the estimates of the parameters of the distribution.

The means, standard deviations, and correlation coefficients of daily percentage changes in the market factors estimated from the previous 250 daily changes are shown in Table 5.1. The mean percentage change in the exchange rate change is strongly negative, equal to approximately –0.27% per day. This reflects the depreciation of the Thai baht that occurred during the summer of 1997. Similarly, the large estimated standard deviations for the Thai bond prices and the dollar/baht exchange rate reflect the extremely high THB interest and exchange rate volatility that was observed during 1997. Combined with the large long position in the Thai baht-denominated note, these estimates will lead to a negative estimate of the expected change in the value of the portfolio and a relatively high estimate of the standard deviation of changes in the value of the portfolio.

One might wonder why an investor would be interested in holding this portfolio, given that the estimate of the expected change in value is negative. The explanation is that the historical average percentage change in the dollar/baht exchange rate of –0.27% that drives the estimate of the expected change in the portfolio value is obtained from an unusual historical period in which the Thai baht collapsed and is clearly not a reasonable estimate of future expected exchange-rate changes. In fact, it is notoriously difficult to estimate the expected changes in financial rates and prices with any precision. Partly because of this, when value-at-risk is computed using a holding period of one day, it is common to assume that the expected changes in the values of the market factors are zero. In our example, an assumption of a zero expected change in the dollar/baht exchange rate in place of the historical estimate of –0.27% per day would probably result in a more accurate estimate of the value-at-risk. Nonetheless, the nonzero expected change is used in order to illustrate the delta-normal approach in its most general form. One might want to replace this simple estimate based on historical data with one derived from a model of interest and exchange rate changes.

The estimated standard deviations of the dollar/baht exchange rate and the baht bond prices are also derived from the same unusual historical period and reflect more volatility than one might reasonably expect to occur in the future. These estimates highlight the need to be careful in relying on historical data.

TABLE 5.1   Means and standard deviations of, and correlations between, percentage changes in market factors

Market Factor	Means of % Changes	Standard Deviations of % Changes	Market Factor	Correlations Between % Changes in Market Factors				
				6-month USD bond price	1-year USD bond price	6-month THB bond price	1-year THB bond price	USD/THB bond price
6-month USD bond price	0.000%	0.0107%	6-month USD bond price	1.0000	0.8762	-0.0226	0.0167	-0.2250
1-year USD bond price	0.0006%	0.0300%	1-year USD bond price	0.8762	1.0000	-0.0442	0.0004	-0.2305
6-month THB bond price	-0.0582%	0.8003%	6-month THB bond price	-0.0226	-0.0442	1.0000	0.7657	0.0425
1-year THB bond price	-0.0861%	1.0810%	1-year THB bond price	0.0167	0.0004	0.7657	1.0000	-0.0862
USD/THB exchange rate	-0.2727%	1.8474%	USD/THB exchange rate	-0.2250	-0.2305	0.0425	-0.0862	1.0000

COMPUTE THE PORTFOLIO VARIANCE, STANDARD DEVIATION, AND THE VALUE-AT-RISK

Given the standard deviations of, and correlations between, changes in the values of the market factors, the variance and standard deviation of changes in the value of the portfolio can be computed using standard mathematical results about the distributions of linear combinations of normal random variables. The expected change in the mark-to-market portfolio value depends on the sizes of the positions in the market factors and the expected percentage changes in them and is given by the formula

$$E(\Delta V) = \sum_{i=1}^{5} X_i E\left(\frac{\text{change in } x_i}{x_i}\right), \tag{5.1}$$

where x_i denotes the value of the ith market factor and X_i is the position in the ith market factor. The variance of changes in mark-to-market portfolio value depends upon the standard deviations of changes in the values of the standard instruments, the correlations, and the sizes of the positions, and is given by the formula

$$\text{var}[\Delta V] = \sum_{i=1}^{5} \sum_{j=1}^{5} X_i X_j \rho_{ij} \sigma_i \sigma_j, \tag{5.2}$$

where σ_i is the standard deviation of percentage changes in the value of the ith market factor and ρ_{ij} is the correlation between percentage changes in the values of the ith and jth market factor. The portfolio standard deviation is, of course, simply the square root of the variance. Using the values of the X_i computed above and the means, standard deviations, and correlation coefficients in Table 5.1, the expected change in portfolio value is –334,608, the portfolio variance is $\text{var}[\Delta V] = 3.7052 \times 10^{12}$, and the standard deviation is $\sigma_{\text{portfolio}} = 1,924,881$. The value-at-risk is then

$$\begin{aligned}
\text{VaR} &= -(E[\Delta V] - 1.645 \times \text{s.d.}[\Delta V]) \\
&= -(-334,608 - 1.645 \times 1,924,881) \\
&= 3,501,037.
\end{aligned}$$

Figure 5.1 shows the probability density function for a normal distribution with a mean of –334,608 and a standard deviation of 1,924,881, along with this value-at-risk estimate.

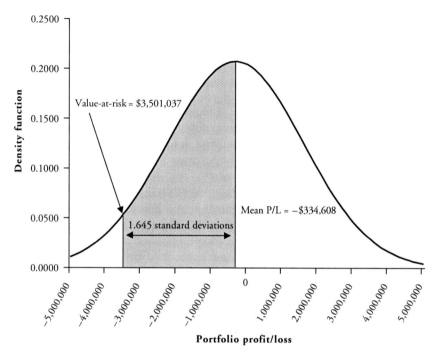

FIGURE 5.1 Estimated density function of daily mark-to-market profits and losses on the fixed-income portfolio and the value-at-risk

The computation of value-at-risk is more complicated for most realistic portfolios. First, most actual portfolios are exposed to the risk of changes in more than five market factors. In general, the means, standard deviations, and correlations must be estimated for all of the market factors, and then the mean and variance must be calculated using formulas similar to equations (5.1) and (5.2), except that, of course, the sums are over the number of market factors. More significantly, in actual portfolios the dates on which payments are received or made do not necessarily coincide with the maturities of the market factors. Further, many portfolios will include options and bonds with option-like features.

DIFFERING PAYMENT DATES

The choice of an example portfolio in which the payment dates coincide with the maturities of the bonds used as the market factors was particularly convenient. It implied that each dollar cash flow maps directly into a position in one market factor, and each Thai baht cash flow maps into positions in two market factors, a spot Thai baht position and a bond position. As discussed in the previous chapter, cash flows received or paid at intermediate dates between the maturities of these bonds do not result in additional market factors. However, it does complicate the risk mapping. Consider, for example, an eight-month cash flow, when the market factors are bonds with maturities of six and 12 months. The approach is to split the eight-month cash flow between the six- and 12-month bonds, so that the eight-month cash flow is replaced by a portfolio of six- and 12-month positions, where the portfolio of six- and 12-month positions is chosen to have the same risk as the eight-month position. The details of how to do this depend on the definition of risk used in the preceding sentence. The simplest scheme replaces the eight-month cash flow with a portfolio of the six- and 12-month bonds that has the same duration.

To do this, one uses the fact that the duration of a portfolio is the weighted average of the durations of its components, where the weights are the fractions of the portfolio invested in each of the components. For a portfolio of six- and 12-month zero-coupon bonds, we have

$$\text{portfolio duration} = a/2 + (1 - a),$$

where a is the fraction of the portfolio invested in the six-month bond, $1 - a$ is the fraction of the portfolio in the 12-month bond, and we have used the fact that the durations of the six- and 12-month bonds are 1/2 and 1, respectively. We then chose a so that the portfolio duration is equal to the duration of the eight-month bond, that is, we chose a so that

$$2/3 = (1/2)a + (1 - a),$$

implying that $a = 2/3$. Thus, an eight-month cash flow with a present value of X is mapped to an investment of $(2/3)X$ in the six-month bond and $(1/3)X$ in the 12-month bond.

An instrument with multiple cash flows at different dates, for example a 10-year bond, is handled by mapping each of the 20 semiannual cash flows into positions in the two nearby standard instruments. For example, suppose the standard instruments consist of one-, three-, and six-month, and one-, two-, three-, four-, five-, seven-, 10-, 15-, 20-, and 30-year zero-coupon bonds, and that $4\frac{1}{2}$ months have passed since the bond was issued, so that the next interest payment will be received in $1\frac{1}{2}$ months. This payment would be split between the one- and three-month bonds. Then, the interest payment to be received in $7\frac{1}{2}$ months would be split between the six-month and one-year bonds, the interest payment to be received in $13\frac{1}{2}$ months would be split between the one- and two-year bonds, and so on. Finally, the last six cash flows would all be split between the seven- and 10-year standard instruments, though in different proportions.

MAPPING INTEREST-RATE SWAPS

At first glance, mapping an interest-rate swap appears difficult. How does one handle the random cash flows, based on unknown future values of LIBOR? Fortunately, the problem can be solved by the use of two simple, but powerful, ideas.

The first idea is that a generic or "plain-vanilla" interest-rate swap can be interpreted as a portfolio of: (i) a floating-rate note based on LIBOR with principal equal to the swap notional principal; and (ii) some "left over" fixed cash flows. The second idea is that on each reset date, the floating-rate note trades at par, that is, the face value is equal to the present value of the remaining cash flows. One implication of this is that the floating-rate note into which the swap is decomposed has present value zero, so that the value of the swap is equal to the present value of the "left over" fixed cash flows. These fixed cash flows are handled in the same fashion as the cash flows of any other fixed-rate note or bond, using the approach for mapping multiple cash flows at different dates described above. Thus, for purposes of valuation and mapping we can substitute the "left over" fixed cash flows for those of the swap. This decomposition and mapping of the swap is explained in detail in the Appendix to this chapter.

Many other swaps can be handled similarly. For example, currency swaps can be interpreted as portfolios of bonds or notes denominated in the two different currencies. However, a limitation of the approach is that it relies on the fact that the floating leg of a generic swap with payments every τ years has reset dates τ years prior to the corresponding payments. Thus, it will not work for floating legs that do not follow this convention regarding the timing of reset dates relative to payment dates. Swaps with such non-standard timing, embedded options, or other complicated features must be mapped using the approach for options described next.

MAPPING OPTIONS

At first glance, it seems that an option on one of the bonds used as the market factors could be mapped to a position in its underlying asset using the approach in Chapter 3. For example, if the market factors included six-month and one-year maturities, a six-month European option on a one-year bond could be mapped to a "delta-equivalent" position in the underlying asset, the one-year bond. As in Chapter 3, this would be done using the option delta; for example, if the option had a delta of 1/2 with respect to the price of the one-year bond, it would be mapped to 1/2 of a bond. However, this does not finish the job, because exercising the option involves paying the exercise price on the expiration date. As a result, the option price has an exposure to, or its value depends upon, the six-month interest rate or the price of a six-month zero-coupon bond. This can be handled by computing the option price sensitivity (i.e., delta) with respect to the price of the six-month bond and mapping the option to an equivalent position in the six-month bond. Thus, the six-month option on a one-year bond would be mapped to two zero-coupon bonds, with maturities of six months and one year.

The mapping becomes more complicated if the underlying asset and expiration of the option do not coincide with the maturities of the standard instruments. Consider, for example, an eight-month option on an 18-month bond, when the market factors consist of zero-coupon bonds with maturities of six, 12, and 24 months. One approach would be to map the option to delta-equivalent positions in eight- and 18-month bonds and then map these eight- and 18-month bonds to positions in the market factors. A more natural approach is to express the option price as a function of the values of the basic market factors. To do this, note that typically the option price would be a function of the eight- and 18-month bond prices or interest rates. The eight- and 18-month bond prices or interest rates would then be expressed either as functions of the market factors, the six-, 12-, and 24-month bond prices or interest rates. This can be done using the interpolation approach in Chapter 4; for example, the eight-month interest rate can be expressed as a linear combination of the six- and 12-month rates. Once the option price has been expressed as a function of the market, the option price sensitivities with respect to the standard instruments can be computed, and these can be used to map the option to its delta-equivalent position in the standard instruments. This approach will work for any instrument for which there is a pricing model expressing its value in terms of the basic market factors.

NOTES

Duration was used to split the cash flows of the eight-month bond between the six- and 12-month bonds primarily because it is the simplest mapping approach. Henrard (2000) compares this mapping scheme to five others and reports that it works well, though a mapping scheme based on interpolation of interest rates described by Mina (1999) appears to work slightly better.

Comparison of the mapping of the fixed-income portfolio to the mapping of the simple equity portfolio in Chapter 3 might suggest that fixed-income portfolios are more difficult to handle, due to the need to map the cash flows occurring on many different dates to a small number of standard maturities. However, an issue of roughly similar complexity arises in actual equity portfolios consisting of hundreds or thousands of different common stocks and other instruments. For such portfolios, the dependence of the portfolio value on the many different stock prices must be approximated in terms of a limited number of common equity market factors. Methods for doing this are discussed in Chapter 7.

Finally, all of the limitations of the delta-normal approach discussed in Chapter 4 also apply to its use in measuring the risk of fixed-income portfolios.

APPENDIX. MAPPING AN INTEREST-RATE SWAP

We show how a generic or "plain-vanilla" interest-rate swap can be mapped by decomposing it into a portfolio of a fixed-rate note and a floating-rate note based on LIBOR, using an example of a hypothetical pay-fixed, receive-floating interest-rate swap with a notional principal of $100 million and payments every six months based on six-month LIBOR. The swap fixed rate is 8% per year, and six payments remain, with payment dates occurring $t = 0.25, 0.75, \ldots,$ and 2.75 years in the future. This situation might arise if the swap originally had a tenor of three years and was entered into three months in the past. The timing of reset dates and payments follows the usual convention; for example, the payment at $t = 0.75$ is based on LIBOR quoted six months previously, at $t = 0.25$. In general, the payment at time t is based on six-month LIBOR quoted at time $t - 0.5$, denoted $r_{t-0.5}$.

With these assumptions, the cash flows of the fixed and floating legs of the swap at time t are $-\$100[0.5(0.08)]$ million and $\$100[0.5r_{t-0.5}]$ million, respectively, where $r_{t-0.5}$ is six-month LIBOR quoted at time $t - 0.5$ for a loan from $t - 0.5$ to t and 0.08 or 8% is the fixed rate. The coefficient 0.5 is the length of the payment period and reflects a decision to ignore the details of day-count conventions. Similarly, we ignore certain other details of the timing, for example, the fact that LIBOR quoted at time t typically covers a deposit period beginning two banking days after time t. Table 5.2 shows these swap cash flows for the six payment dates as functions of the floating rates observed on the reset dates.

TABLE 5.2   Cash flows of a hypothetical three-year interest rate swap entered into three months prior to the current date

Time	Swap Cash Flows ($million)
0.25	$100[0.5(0.075) - 0.5(0.08)]$
0.75	$100[0.5r_{0.25} - 0.5(0.08)]$
1.25	$100[0.5r_{0.75} - 0.5(0.8)]$
1.75	$100[0.5r_{1.25} - 0.5(0.8)]$
2.25	$100[0.5r_{1.75} - 0.5(0.8)]$
2.75	$100[0.5r_{2.25} - 0.5(0.8)]$

Table 5.3 decomposes the swap cash flows shown in the second column into a set of fixed cash flows (third column) and the cash flows that would ensue from buying a floating-rate note at time 0.25 (fourth column). In particular, in the fourth column the cash flow of -$100 at time 0.25 is the amount paid to purchase the floating-rate note, the cash flows of the form $100[0.5r_{0.25}]$, $100[0.5r_{0.75}]$, etc., are the interest payments, and the cash flow of $100[0.5r_{2.25}] + 100$ at time 2.75 represents the final interest payment and the return of the principal. Because time 0.25 is a reset date, an investor who purchases the note on this date will receive the prevailing market six-month rate over each six-month period during the remaining life of the note, implying that the note should trade at par on this date. As a result, the payment of $100 to purchase the note is exactly equal to the present value of the remaining cash flows, and the set of cash flows in the fourth column has present value zero as of time 0.25. This then implies that the set of cash flows in the fourth column has present value zero as of time 0.

But if the swap is equivalent to the sum of the cash flows in the third and fourth columns and the present value of the cash flows in the fourth column is zero, then the present value of the swap cash flows must equal the present value of the cash flows in the third column. Thus, for purposes of valuation, we can substitute the fixed cash flows in the third column for those of the swap. If the market factors consist of zero-coupon bonds, these fixed cash flows can then be mapped onto the zero-coupon bonds using the approach discussed in this chapter.

TABLE 5.3 Decomposition of the swap into fixed cash flows and the purchase of a floating rate note

Time	Swap Cash Flows	Fixed Cash Flows	Cash Flows of Floating Rate Note Bought at Time 0.25
0.25	$100[0.5(0.075) - 0.5(0.08)]$	$100 + 100[0.5(0.8) - 0.5(0.075)]$	-100
0.75	$100[0.5r_{0.25} - 0.5(0.8)]$	$-100[0.5(0.8)]$	$100[0.5r_{0.25}]$
1.25	$100[0.5r_{0.75} - 0.5(0.8)]$	$-100[0.5(0.8)]$	$100[0.5r_{0.75}]$
1.75	$100[0.5r_{1.25} - 0.5(0.8)]$	$-100[0.5(0.8)]$	$100[0.5r_{1.25}]$
2.25	$100[0.5r_{1.75} - 0.5(0.8)]$	$-100[0.5(0.8)]$	$100[0.5r_{1.75}]$
2.75	$100[0.5r_{2.25} - 0.5(0.8)]$	$-100[0.5(0.08)] - 100$	$100[0.5r_{2.25}] + 100$

CHAPTER 6

Monte Carlo Simulation

The Monte Carlo simulation approach has a number of similarities to historical simulation. Most importantly, the method is able to capture the risk of portfolios that include options and other instruments whose values are nonlinear functions of the underlying market factors. Like historical simulation, Monte Carlo simulation accomplishes this by repeatedly revaluing the portfolio, using hypothetical new values of the underlying market factors that determine the portfolio value. Because the exact portfolio value is computed for every realization of the market factors considered, the method captures any nonlinearities in the value of the portfolio.

The main difference between the two approaches is that the Monte Carlo method does not conduct the simulation using the observed changes in the market factors over the last N periods to generate N hypothetical portfolio profits or losses. Instead, one chooses a statistical distribution that is believed to adequately capture or approximate the possible changes in the market factors. Then, a pseudo-random number generator is used to generate thousands, or perhaps tens of thousands, of hypothetical changes in the market factors. These are then used to construct the distribution of possible portfolio profit or loss. Finally, the value-at-risk is determined from this distribution.

The approach is illustrated using the example portfolio analyzed using the delta-normal method in Chapter 3. It consists of $110 million invested in a well-diversified portfolio of large capitalization U.S. equities, where it is assumed that the returns on this portfolio are perfectly correlated with changes in the S&P 500 index. The portfolio manager has reduced his exposure to the U.S. market by shorting 200 of the S&P 500 index futures contracts and obtained exposure to the U.K. market by establishing a long position of 500 FT-SE 100 index futures contracts. In addition, the portfolio manager has written 800 of the September S&P 500 index call options with a strike of 1100 and has written 600 of the September FT-SE 100 index call options with a strike price of 5875. Combining the written options positions with the portfolio of U.S. equities, the net value of the portfolio is approximately $101,485,220.

To analyze this portfolio, we perform the same steps we carried out in the historical simulation method, except that collecting data on the past realizations of changes in the basic market factors will be replaced by selecting a statistical distribution from which to draw pseudo-random changes. The steps consist of: (i) identifying the market factors; (ii) selecting a statistical distribution from which to draw pseudo-random hypothetical changes in the value of the market factors; (iii) applying these hypothetical pseudo-random changes in the market factors to the current portfolio; and (iv) identifying the value-at-risk. Once again, we use a probability of 5% and a holding period of one month.

IDENTIFY THE MARKET FACTORS

The first step is to identify the basic market factors and obtain a formula expressing the mark-to-market value of the portfolio in terms of the market factors. The basic market factors have already been identified in Chapter 3. In this chapter, we select the second of the two possible choices of the basic market factors, so that for this chapter the market factors are taken to be the levels of the S&P 500 and FT-SE 100 stock market indexes S_1 and S_2, and the dollar/pound exchange rate e.

To obtain a formula giving the value of the portfolio as a function of the levels of the two indexes and the exchange rate, note that an investment of $110 million in a portfolio that underlies the S&P 500 is equivalent to 110,000,000/ 1097.6 = 100,219 units of the index, with a value of $100,219S_1$. The written position of 800 S&P 500 index call options has a value of $-800C_1(S_1, t)$, where the function C_1 gives the value of an index call option as a function of the index level and time. The written position of 600 FT-SE 100 index call options has a pound value of $-600C_2(S_2, t)$ and a dollar value of $-600eC_2(S_2, t)$, where the function C_2 gives the value of the FT-SE 100 index call option as a function of the index level and time. Both the functions C_1 and C_2 include the effects of the option multipliers of 100 and 10, respectively.

As discussed in Chapter 3, the futures contracts affect the profit or loss on the portfolio through their daily resettlement payments. The daily settlement payments on the S&P 500 futures contract are determined by the changes in futures prices, and their sum is given by

$$
\begin{aligned}
\binom{\text{S\&P settlement}}{\text{payments}} &= -200(250)\sum_{k=1}^{K}\{S_1(t_k)\exp[(r_1-d)(T_1-t_k)] \\
&\quad - S_1(t_{k-1})\exp[(r_1-d_1)(T_1-t_{k-1})]\} \\
&= -200(250)\{S_1(t_k)\exp[(r_1-d)(T_1-t)] \\
&\quad - 1097.6\exp[(r_1-d_1)(T_1-t_0)]\},
\end{aligned}
\tag{6.1}
$$

where t_k is the kth day during the month, $S(t_k)$ is the index value on t_k, t_0 is the initial date, K is the number of days in the month, 250 is the multiplier of the futures contract, and we have used the fact that $S_1(t_0) = 1097.6$. For the position in the FT-SE 100, the pound value of the settlement payments is given by

$$
\begin{pmatrix} \text{FT-SE 100 settlement} \\ \text{payments} \end{pmatrix} = -500(10) \sum_{k=1}^{K} \{S_2(t_k)\exp[(r_2 - d)(T_2 - t_k)]
$$
$$
- S_2(t_{k-1})\exp[(r_2 - d_2)(T_2 - t_{k-1})]\}
$$
$$
= -500(10)\{S_2(t_K)\exp[(r_2 - d)(T_2 - t_K)]
$$
$$
- 5862.3\exp[(r_2 - d_2)(T_2 - t_0)]\},
$$

where 10 is the multiplier for the FT-SE 100 index contract, and we have used the fact that $S_2(t_0) = 5862.3$. The dollar value of the daily resettlement payments during the month is

$$
\begin{pmatrix} \text{Dollar value of} \\ \text{FT-SE settlement} \\ \text{payments} \end{pmatrix} = -500(10) \sum_{k=1}^{K} e(t_k)\{S_2(t_k)\exp[(r_2 - d)(T_2 - t_k)]
$$
$$
- S_2(t_{k-1})\exp[(r_2 - d_2)(T_2 - t_{k-1})]\}, \tag{6.2}
$$

where each day's settlement payment is converted at the exchange rate $e(t_k)$ prevailing on that day. Primarily for convenience, we approximate this by

$$
\begin{pmatrix} \text{Dollar value of} \\ \text{FT-SE 100 settlement} \\ \text{payments} \end{pmatrix} = -500(10)e(t_K)\{S_2(t_K)\exp[(r_2 - d)(T_2 - t_K)]
$$
$$
- 5862.3\exp[(r_2 - d_2)(T_2 - t_0)]\}, \tag{6.3}
$$

which involves the assumption that the cash flows are converted using $e(t_K)$, the exchange rate at the end of the month.

Putting this all together, the formula expressing the portfolio value as a function of the market factors and time is

$$
\begin{aligned}
V(S_1, S_2, e, t) = {} & 100{,}219 S_1 - 800 C_1(S_1, t) - 600 e C_2(S_2, t) \\
& - 50{,}000\{S_1 \exp[(r_1 - d_1)(T_1 - t)] \\
& - 1097.6\exp[(r_1 - d_1)(T_1 - t_0)]\} \\
& + 5000 e\{S_2 \exp[(r_2 - d_2)(T_2 - t)] \\
& - 5862.3\exp[(r_2 - d_2)(T_2 - t_0)]\} \\
& + 110(0.014/12)(t - t_0),
\end{aligned} \tag{6.4}
$$

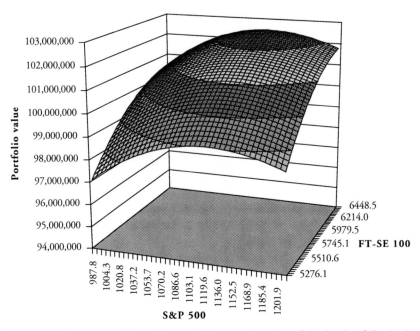

FIGURE 6.1 Current value of the portfolio as a function of the levels of the S&P 500 and FT-SE 100 indexes, holding the exchange rate fixed at $e = 1.6721$

where the final term is the value of the dividends on the portfolio of U.S. equities. Using the Black-Scholes formula with the appropriate choices for the strike price and volatility to compute the option prices, Figure 6.1 shows the portfolio value as a function of S_1 and S_2, with $t = t_0 = 0$ and e fixed at its initial value of 1.6271. At the initial values of $S_1 = 1097.6$ and $S_2 = 5862.3$, the option prices are $C_1(1097.6, 0) = 63.16$ and $C_2(5862.3, 0) = 354.62$, and the initial value of the portfolio is $V(1097.6, 5862.3, 1.6271, 0) = 101,485,220$. This point is in the middle of the surface shown in Figure 6.1.

SELECT A STATISTICAL DISTRIBUTION FROM WHICH TO DRAW PSEUDO-RANDOM CHANGES IN THE VALUE OF THE MARKET FACTORS

The second step is to determine or assume a specific distribution for the changes in the market factors and to estimate or otherwise select the parameters of that distribution. As in Chapter 3, we continue to assume that percentage changes in the basic market factors have a multivariate normal distribution and that the expected monthly percentage changes in the three market factors are $\mu_1 = 0.01$, $\mu_2 = 0.0125$, and $\mu_3 = 0$, the standard deviations of monthly percentage changes are $\sigma_1 = 0.061$, $\sigma_2 = 0.065$, and $\sigma_3 = 0.029$, and the correlation coefficients are $\rho_{12} = 0.55$, $\rho_{13} = 0.05$, and $\rho_{23} = -0.30$.

A natural alternative would be to assume that the changes in the market factors are described by a multivariate lognormal distribution rather than the multivariate normal distribution. The assumption of lognormality is appealing because it is consistent with the assumptions underlying the Black-Scholes formula. Nonetheless, we stick with the assumption of multivariate normality because of its slightly greater convenience and in order that the computations in this chapter be comparable to those in Chapter 3.

The natural interpretations of the parameters and the ease with which they can be estimated weigh in favor of the normal and lognormal distributions, though the distribution need not be one of these two. For example, if one wanted to capture the fat tails in financial data, one might chose the multivariate student's *t* distribution or another distribution that has fat tails relative to the normal. The ability to pick the distribution is a feature that distinguishes Monte Carlo simulation from the historical simulation and delta-normal methods. In these other methods, the distribution of changes in the market factors must be either the empirical distribution observed over the past N days or the normal distribution, respectively. In contrast, with the Monte Carlo approach the designers of the risk-management system are free to choose any distribution that they think reasonably describes possible future changes in the market factors. However, in practice most implementations of the Monte Carlo approach do not exploit this freedom, but rely on the normal and lognormal distributions.

APPLY THE HYPOTHETICAL PSEUDO-RANDOM CHANGES IN THE MARKET FACTORS TO THE CURRENT PORTFOLIO

Once the distribution has been selected, the next step is to use a pseudo-random generator to generate N hypothetical values of changes in the market factors, where the number of trials N is almost certainly greater than 1000 and perhaps greater than 10,000. Combining the changes with the initial values of the market factors results in N hypothetical sets of market factors, each consisting of a triple (S_1, S_2, e). These hypothetical market factors are then used in conjunction with equation (6.4) to calculate N hypothetical mark-to-market portfolio values. Subtracting each of these hypothetical portfolio values from the initial mark-to-market portfolio value, one obtains N hypothetical daily profits and losses. The appendix to this chapter briefly describes methods for simulating multivariate normal random vectors.

IDENTIFY THE VALUE-AT-RISK

Figure 6.2 shows the distribution of the hypothetical mark-to-market profits and losses, using a sample of $N = 10,000$ pseudo-random trials. Using a probability of 5%, the estimate of the value-at-risk is the loss that is equaled or exceeded on 5% of the trials. For this portfolio and sample, the value-at-risk estimate turns out to be 2,582,663 and is shown on the figure.

Strikingly, the distribution of possible profits and losses is asymmetric: the right tail of the distribution is truncated, and there is a long left tail. This asymmetry is due to the presence of written options in the portfolio. Because of them, the portfolio benefits only slightly from increases in the FT-SE 100 index and, except for a small range, does not benefit from increases in the S&P 500 index. However, the portfolio remains exposed to the risk of decreases in these indexes. Graphically, the presence of the options in the

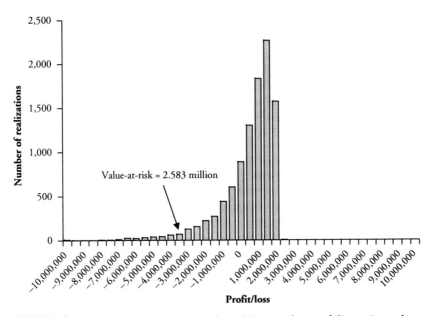

FIGURE 6.2 Distribution of possible profit and loss on the portfolio, estimated using the full Monte Carlo method

portfolio is manifested in the downward curvature shown in Figure 6.1. Using the jargon of the Greek letter risks, this reflects the fact that the gammas $\partial^2 V / \partial S_1^2$ and $\partial^2 V / \partial S_2^2$ are negative.

The ability of the Monte Carlo simulation method to capture the nonlinear effect of options on the value of the portfolio is its principal advantage over the delta-normal approach. That is, the Monte Carlo method captures the curvature of the portfolio value function shown in Figure 6.1, and the resulting asymmetry in the distribution of possible profits and losses. In contrast, the delta-normal approximation is based on the linear approximation in equation (3.6), and the estimate of the distribution obtained using the delta-normal approach is symmetric. This can be seen in Figure 6.3, which shows the estimate of the distribution obtained using the delta-normal method for the same portfolio and parameter values. The distributions are strikingly different, and the value-at-risk estimate of 1,768,081 obtained using the delta-normal method is much smaller than the estimate of 2,582,663 obtained using the Monte Carlo method.

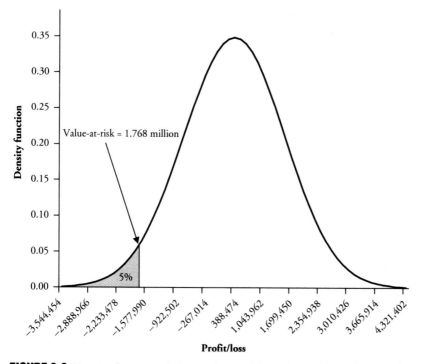

FIGURE 6.3 Density function of changes in portfolio value and the value-at-risk, computed using the delta-normal method

As discussed in Chapter 3 and shown in Figures 3.4 and 3.5, for portfolios with written options the linear approximation is always above the actual portfolio value and thus understates the loss. As a result, for such portfolios the delta-normal method understates the value-at-risk, which is what is seen in this example. For portfolios that include only purchased options, the delta-normal method overstates the value-at-risk.

While this example is of an equity portfolio, there is no difficulty in adapting the method to handle fixed-income portfolios. For fixed-income portfolios, the market factors will typically consist of bond prices, interest rates, or linear combinations of changes in interest rates (the principal components), and it will be necessary to have formulas expressing the values of options and other instruments in terms of these market factors. This adds nothing new, as the issues that arise in doing this have been discussed in Chapters 4 and 5. Realistic portfolios containing many different instruments of different types are likely to be exposed to the risk of changes in many more market factors, including interest rates, equity returns, exchange rates, and perhaps commodity prices. These factors must be identified, and pricing formulas expressing the instruments' values in terms of the market factors must be obtained.

LIQUIDITY-ADJUSTED VALUE-AT-RISK AND OTHER DYNAMIC TRADING STRATEGIES

Standard VaR measures the risk of a portfolio over a fixed, usually short, holding period. Inherent in it is the implicit assumption that the risk can be eliminated by the end of the holding period, by either liquidating or hedging the portfolio. In periods of market illiquidity, this implicit assumption may not be valid. Even in normal periods it is unlikely to be valid for all assets. In the Monte Carlo framework, this issue can be addressed through the computation of *liquidity-adjusted VaR* (LaVaR).

LaVaR recognizes that there are limits to the rate at which a portfolio can be liquidated. To illustrate its computation, consider a portfolio of only a single asset and assume that only b units of the asset can be sold each day; for example, a 100-unit portfolio requires $n = 100/b$ days to liquidate. If liquidation of the portfolio becomes necessary, a possible strategy would be to liquidate b units each day and invest the proceeds at the risk-free rate r. The proceeds from selling the b units are thus no longer exposed to market risk, while the positions that have not yet been liquidated remain so exposed. Under this liquidation strategy, b units are exposed to market risk for one day and then invested at the risk-free rate r for the remaining $n - 1$

days; another b units would be exposed to market risk for two days and then invested at r for $n - 2$ days; another b units would be exposed to market risk for three days and then invested at r for $n - 3$ day, ands so on. If the initial price per unit is S_0 and the return on the ith day is r_i, at the end of n days this strategy results in a liquidated value of

$$\text{liquidated value} = bS_0\left[(1 + r_1)(1 + r)^{n-1} + (1 + r_1)(1 + r_2)(1 + r)^{n-2}\right.$$
$$\left. + (1 + r_1)(1 + r_2)(1 + r_3)(1 + r)^{n-3} + \cdots + \prod_{i=1}^{n}(1 + r_i)\right].$$

LaVaR is then obtained by estimating the distribution of this liquidated value, similar to the way standard VaR is obtained by estimating the distribution of the mark-to-market portfolio value. Since LaVaR measures portfolio risk over an n-day horizon, it follows that LaVaR will exceed a standard VaR over a one-day horizon whenever $n > 1$ but will be less than standard VaR over an n-day horizon.

Realistic implementations of LaVaR will allow for different liquidation rates for different securities and can incorporate the fact that illiquidity is correlated with extreme market movements by making the liquidation rates depend on the outcomes for the market factors. A few seconds of thought lead to the insight that liquidating a portfolio is only one possible dynamic trading strategy. An approach that allows for gradual portfolio liquidation can also handle other dynamic trading strategies, for example, reinvesting coupons or dividends or rebalancing hedges. Thus, it becomes possible to overcome the limitation that value-at-risk measures the risk of the *current* portfolio and does not reflect any changes to the portfolio that might be made during the holding period. An issue is that doing this requires that the dynamic trading strategy be specified, which may be difficult or impossible. A further drawback is that LaVaR and similar calculations require simulation of the entire sample path of each of the market factors, increasing the computational burden of the calculation.

ADVANTAGES AND LIMITATIONS
OF THE MONTE CARLO METHOD

As indicated above, the main advantage of the Monte Carlo method is its ability to capture the nonlinearities in the portfolio value created by the presence of options in the portfolio. This can be important for portfolios with significant options positions, and especially for portfolios that include exotic options. Additional advantages are that it can be used with a range of different distributions for the market factors and can be used to measure the risk of dynamic trading strategies, such as LaVaR.

For short holding periods such as one day, an offsetting factor is that the nonlinearities are much less important. This is true because: (i) for short holding periods, the typical changes in the values of the market factors are much smaller; and (ii) linear (and quadratic) approximations work better for small changes in the variables. Thus, the delta-normal method and the delta-gamma-theta-normal method described in Chapter 14 often work well over short holding periods.

An advantage of the Monte Carlo method over the historical simulation method is that it is not constrained to rely on relatively small samples (small N). Thus, the problem of relying on small samples to estimate the tail probabilities that are inherent to historical simulation is not shared by Monte Carlo simulation. However, the number of Monte Carlo trials required for estimating the α quantile accurately can be surprisingly large, especially when α is small.

If the Monte Carlo simulation method has such advantages, then why is its use not universal? The answer is that it does suffer from one significant drawback. Earlier, it was carefully stated that there is no *conceptual* difficulty in extending the Monte Carlo method to handle realistic portfolios with many different instruments. However, the computational burden of the procedure can present a practical problem. Letting N denote the number of hypothetical future scenarios used (i.e., the number of samples or "draws" in the simulation), K the number of market factors, and M the number of instruments in the portfolio, a naïve application of the Monte Carlo simulation method will involve generating $N \times K$ pseudo-random variables and performing $N \times M$ valuations of financial instruments. Such straightforward application of the Monte Carlo method is termed *full* Monte Carlo. In actual applications, N might exceed 10,000, K can range from 2 or 3 to 400 or more in systems that employ detailed modeling of yield curves in different currencies, and M can range from only a few to thousands or even tens of thousands. Using reasonable values of $N = 10,000$, $K = 100$, and $M = 1000$, a straightforward application of the Monte Carlo simulation method would involve generating one million pseudo-random variables and performing 10 million valuations of financial instruments. For the interest-rate swap "book" of a large derivatives dealer, M could be 30,000 or more, so a naïve use of the Monte Carlo method would involve hundreds of millions of swap valuations.

Options portfolios typically do not involve so many positions, and for them K is often small. However, the value of options with American-style exercise features typically requires computations on "trees" or lattices, and the prices of some exotic options may be computed using various numerical methods. For this reason, using full Monte Carlo with even a moderately sized options portfolio can be time consuming. In contrast, the delta-normal method requires only that the instrument's deltas be evaluated once, for the current values of the market factors. The difference between doing this and performing NM instrument valuations can be the difference between seconds and days of computation.

NOTES

As in Chapter 3, the calculations of the futures prices of the S&P 500 and FT-SE 100 index futures contracts use the cost-of-carry formula $F = S\exp[(r - d)(T - t)]$, where S is the current index value, r is the interest rate, d is the dividend yield on the portfolio underlying the index, and $T - t$ is the time until the final settlement of the futures contract. For the S&P contract, the parameter values are $r = 0.05$, $d = 0.014$, and $T - t = 0.3836$, while for the FT-SE 100 contract they are $r = 0.05$, $d = 0.016$, and $T - t = 0.3836$.

This calculation of the futures contract settlement payments in equation (6.1) and the similar calculation for the FT-SE 100 index futures contract ignore the fact that positive cash flows would likely be deposited at interest and negative cash flows would either incur financing costs or require a reduction in the investment in the portfolio. We translate the FT-SE 100 futures contract settlement payments to U.S. dollars using (6.3) instead of (6.2) primarily for convenience, because if we used (6.2) we would be forced to simulate the entire path of index values and exchange rates during the month. However, (6.3) is not necessarily a worse assumption than (6.2) and may be better. Equation (6.2) ignores any pound balance in the margin account and assumes that the pound flows in and out of the account are converted to, or from, dollars each day. Equation (6.3) assumes that the pound flows in and out of the account are allowed to accumulate until the end of the month and then converted to, or from, dollars at the month-end exchange rate. It is almost certain that neither assumption is exactly correct. As a practical matter, the exchange-rate risk of the futures contract is sufficiently small that the difference between these two assumptions does not have a significant impact on the calculated value-at-risk, and we use (6.3) because it is more convenient.

The need for large numbers of Monte Carlo trials can be reduced through use of variance reduction techniques. While these are beyond the scope of this book, Glasserman, Heidelberger, and Shahabuddin (2000) provide an introduction to them in the context of value-at-risk estimation.

Most Monte Carlo approaches are based on the multivariate normal and lognormal distributions, though there has been some limited work outside this framework. Recently, Hull and White (1998) and Hosking, Bonti, and Siegel (2000) have suggested approaches that involve simulating multivariate normal random vectors and then transforming them to have marginal distributions that better fit the known properties of changes in financial market factors. The heavy reliance on the normal and lognormal distributions seems to be driven by two considerations. First, these distributions are convenient and tractable. Second, while distributions with fat tails relative to the normal are available, the data provide little guidance about which fat-tailed distribution should be selected. The whole issue is how much probability should be in the tails, but almost by definition there have been very few realizations in the tails. Thus, it is difficult to resolve this issue by looking at the data, and the designer has little basis to select and/or parameterize a particular fat-tailed distribution.

The use of Monte Carlo simulation to evaluate the risk of time- and path-dependent portfolio strategies, such as that underlying LaVaR is pushed by Dembo, Aziz, Rosen, and Zerbs (2000) under the rubric *Mark-to-Future*. An alternative approach to adjusting for liquidity is described by Berkowitz (2000).

APPENDIX: SIMULATING MULTIVARIATE NORMAL RANDOM VARIABLES

In the Monte Carlo method, it is necessary to simulate vectors of pseudo-random multivariate normal random variables with a specified covariance matrix. That is, if there are K market factors and the changes in them have a covariance matrix Σ, then it is necessary to simulate vectors

$$
x = \begin{bmatrix} x_1 \\ \vdots \\ x_i \\ \vdots \\ x_K \end{bmatrix}
$$

such that $\text{cov}[x_i, x_j] = \sigma_i \sigma_j \rho_{ij}$. To do this, we use the fact that if

$$e = \begin{bmatrix} e_1 \\ \vdots \\ e_i \\ \vdots \\ e_K \end{bmatrix}$$

is a vector of independent standard normal random variables (that is, $\text{var}[e_i] = 1$ and $\text{cov}[e_i, e_j] = 0$ for $i \neq j$) and A is a $K \times K$ matrix, then the vector of random variables x given by the product $x = Ae$ has a covariance matrix given by the matrix product AA', where A' is the transpose of A. Given this fact, we need to pick A such that $AA' = \Sigma$, that is, such that $A = \Sigma^{1/2}$ is the square root of the matrix Σ. There is always at least one square root (and generally more than one) whenever Σ is a legitimate covariance matrix, so that there always exists an appropriate square root A.

Thus, to generate a vector of random variables x with covariance matrix Σ, we first generate a vector of independent standard normal random variables e and then construct x as $x = \Sigma^{1/2}e$. The elements of the vector x have covariance matrix Σ, but they do not yet correspond to the changes in the market factors because they have expected values of zero. However, the changes in the market factors can be constructed simply by adding to each component of x the expected change in the corresponding market factor.

The remaining issues are how to generate the e_i, and how to construct the square root $A = \Sigma^{1/2}$. A realization of a standard normal pseudo-random variable can be constructed by applying the inverse of the cumulative standard normal distribution function to a pseudo-random variable uniformly distributed on the interval [0,1]. That is, if F^{-1} denotes the inverse of the cumulative standard normal distribution function and u is a uniform pseudo-random variable, then $e_i = F^{-1}(u)$ is a standard normal pseudo-random variable. However, this approach is not the most efficient; other approaches are discussed in Chapter 13 of Johnson, Kotz, and Balakrishnan (1994). Many software packages include both functions to generate uniform pseudo-random variables and the inverse of the cumulative standard normal distribution function. Alternatively, computer codes to perform these computations are available in many software libraries and in standard references (e.g., Press, Teukolsky, Vetterling, and Flannery 1992). The square root $\Sigma^{1/2}$ is typically computed as the Cholesky decomposition of the covariance matrix, which is described in standard references (e.g., Press, Teukolsky, Vetterling, and Flannery 1992) and is available in many statistical packages and software libraries.

CHAPTER 7

Using Factor Models to Compute the VaR of Equity Portfolios

The example equity portfolio discussed in Chapters 2, 3, and 5 was carefully constructed, so that the portfolio returns depended only on the changes in the S&P 500 and FT-SE 100 stock market indexes. In particular, it was assumed that the portfolio of U.S. equities was so well-diversified that its returns could be assumed perfectly correlated with percentage changes in the S&P 500 index, and the other positions in the portfolio consisted of index futures and options. Actual portfolios include instruments that are neither perfectly nor even highly correlated with one of the popular market indexes. This raises the question of what should be used as the underlying market factor or factors that affect the value of the portfolio. It is impractical to treat all of the securities prices as market factors, because actual equity portfolios may include hundreds, or even thousands, of stocks. Rather, one needs to find a limited number of market factors that explain most of the variability in the value of the portfolio.

Factor models of equity (and other) returns provide a solution to this problem. Such models express the return on a security or portfolio of securities in terms of the changes in a set of common factors and a residual or idiosyncratic component. For example, the return on the ith security, denoted r_i, might be expressed as

$$r_i = \alpha_i + \beta_{i1}f_1 + \beta_{i2}f_2 + \ldots + \beta_{iK}f_K + \varepsilon_i, \qquad (7.1)$$

where $f_1, f_2, \ldots, f_K$ denote the changes in K common factors, $\beta_{i1}, \beta_{i2}, \ldots, \beta_{iK}$ denote the factor loadings of the ith security on the K factors, α_i is a constant component of the return of the ith security, and ε_i is a residual or idiosyncratic component of the return. The number of factors K is usually relatively small, ranging from as few as one in simple single-index models to as many as 50. A common, and even standard, assumption is that the residuals are independent across securities, that is, ε_i is independent of ε_j for $i \neq j$. Factor models are used for a variety of different purposes and differ in

105

their choice of factors and methodologies for estimating the factor loadings. In some models, the factors consist of the returns on stock market indexes or portfolios (e.g., broad-based market indexes, industry indexes, or the returns on portfolios of small- or large-capitalization stocks), in others they consist of macroeconomic factors, such as unexpected changes in industrial production or inflation, and in others they consist of purely statistical factors (the principal components) extracted from the covariance matrix of returns.

Factor models provide a very intuitive way of thinking about the risk of a portfolio. If the changes in the factors (the f_ks) in equation (7.1) are the returns on portfolios, then (7.1) can be loosely interpreted as saying that one dollar invested in the ith security behaves like a portfolio of β_{i1} dollars invested in the first portfolio, β_{i2} dollars in the second portfolio, . . . , and β_{iK} dollars in the Kth portfolio. If the f_ks are not the returns on portfolios, then equation (7.1) can be interpreted as saying that one dollar invested in the ith security behaves like a portfolio of β_{ik} dollars invested in a portfolio with returns that are perfectly correlated with changes in the kth factor. In addition, there is a constant component of the return α_i and an idiosyncratic component ε_i, which is small if the factors explain most of the variation in the portfolio return. If one ignores the residual ε_i, then equation (7.1) corresponds to the mapping performed in earlier chapters. That is, the factor model maps the ith security onto the common factors.

DELTA-NORMAL VALUE-AT-RISK

The properties of factor models are especially convenient for computing value-at-risk using the delta-normal approach. The factor loadings of a portfolio consist of the weighted (by proportion of market value) averages of the factor loadings of the securities that make up the portfolio. If the residuals ε_i are independent across securities, the variance of the portfolio residual can also be easily computed from the portfolio weights and the residual variances of the individual securities. The factor model for a portfolio return r is

$$r = \alpha + \beta_1 f_1 + \beta_2 f_2 + \ldots + \beta_K f_K + \varepsilon,$$

where the kth portfolio factor loading $\beta_k = \sum_{i=1}^{N} w_i \beta_{ik}$, $\alpha = \sum_{i=1}^{N} w_i \alpha_i$, $\varepsilon = \sum_{i=1}^{N} w_i \varepsilon_i$, w_i is the proportion of the value of the portfolio invested in the ith security, and the variance of ε is

$$\text{var}(\varepsilon) = \text{var}\left(\sum_{i=1}^{N} w_i \varepsilon_i \right) = \sum_{i=1}^{N} w_i^2 \, \text{var}(\varepsilon_i). \qquad (7.2)$$

If the portfolio is well-diversified (i.e., if all of the w_is are small) then the variance of ε will be small, and it is sometimes treated as zero. The variance of the portfolio return is

$$\text{var}(r) = \sum_{j=1}^{K} \sum_{k=1}^{K} \beta_j \beta_k \sigma_j \sigma_k \rho_{jk} + \text{var}(\varepsilon) \equiv \sigma^2, \tag{7.3}$$

where σ_j is the standard deviation of changes in the jth factor and ρ_{jk} is the correlation between changes in the jth and kth factors. Letting V denote the value of the portfolio, the variance of the dollar value of the portfolio is $\sigma^2 V^2$, the standard deviation is σV, and the value-at-risk will be proportional to σV. For example, if the desired probability is 1%, the value-at-risk is $2.326\sigma V$. Expressed as a fraction of the value of the portfolio, it is simply 2.326σ.

To illustrate these computations, consider an example with four common stocks and two factors, interpreted as growth and value indexes. The portfolio value is $V = \$100$ million, and the portfolio weights of the four stocks are $w_1 = 0.4$, $w_2 = 0.1$, $w_3 = 0.3$, and $w_4 = 0.2$ The factor loadings of the four stocks on the two factors are

$$\begin{bmatrix} \beta_{11} & \beta_{12} \\ \beta_{21} & \beta_{22} \\ \beta_{31} & \beta_{32} \\ \beta_{41} & \beta_{42} \end{bmatrix} = \begin{bmatrix} 2.5 & -1.1 \\ 2.1 & -0.8 \\ -0.1 & 1.2 \\ 0.2 & 0.8 \end{bmatrix}, \tag{7.4}$$

suggesting that we label the first two stocks *growth* and the second two *value*. The different stocks' residuals are independent of each other, and the residual variances are $\text{var}(\varepsilon_1) = 0.08^2 = 0.0064$, $\text{var}(\varepsilon_{21}) = 0.07^2 = 0.0049$, $\text{var}(\varepsilon_3) = 0.06^2 = 0.0036$, and $\text{var}(\varepsilon_4) = 0.055^2 = 0.003025$. The standard deviations of the (monthly) changes in the factors are $\sigma_1 = 0.043$, or 4.3%, and $\sigma_2 = 0.041$, or 4.1%, and the correlation between changes in the factors is $\rho = 0.8$.

Using these parameters, the portfolio factor loadings are

$$\beta_1 = \sum_{i=1}^{4} w_i \beta_{i1} = 1.22,$$

$$\beta_2 = \sum_{i=1}^{4} w_i \beta_{i2} = 0.00,$$

and the portfolio residual variance is

$$\text{var}(\varepsilon) = \sum_{i=1}^{4} w_i^2 \, \text{var}(\varepsilon_i) = 0.0025 \sum_{i=1}^{4} w_i^2 = 0.001518.$$

The variance of the portfolio return is then

$$\sigma^2 = \beta_1^2 \sigma_1^2 + \beta_2^2 \sigma_2^2 + 2\beta_1 \beta_2 \sigma_1 \sigma_2 \rho + \text{var}(\varepsilon) = 0.002752,$$

and the variance and standard deviation of the dollar value of the portfolio are $\sigma^2 V^2 = 2.752 \times 10^{13}$ and $\sigma V = 5{,}246{,}000$. The value-at-risk can then be computed by using this estimate of the standard deviation and an estimate of the expected return.

If we want to compute the value-at-risk relative to the return r_B on a benchmark portfolio such as the portfolio underlying the S&P 500 index, then we are interested in the standard deviation of the return $r - r_B$. The factor loadings for this return are obtained by subtracting the factor loadings of the benchmark portfolio from the factor loading of the portfolio with return r. That is, if the benchmark return is described by a factor model

$$r_B = \alpha_B + \beta_{B1} f_1 + \beta_{B2} f_2 + \cdots + \beta_{BK} f_K + \varepsilon_B,$$

the factor model for the difference $r - r_B$ is

$$\begin{aligned} r - r_B = {}& (\alpha - \alpha_B) + (\beta_1 - \beta_{B1}) f_1 + (\beta_2 - \beta_{B2}) f_2 + \cdots \\ & + (\beta_K - \beta_{BK}) f_K + (\varepsilon - \varepsilon_B). \end{aligned}$$

Thus, the computation of the variance is identical to that in equation (7.3), except that each β_j is replaced by a term of the form $\beta_j - \beta_{Bj}$ and the term $\text{var}(\varepsilon)$ is replaced by

$$\text{var}(\varepsilon - \varepsilon_B) = \text{var}\left(\sum_{i=1}^{N} w_i (\varepsilon_i - \varepsilon_B) \right) = \sum_{i=1}^{N} w_i^2 \, \text{var}(\varepsilon_i) + \text{var}(\varepsilon_B),$$

where in the last equality it has been assumed that ε_B is uncorrelated with each of the ε_i. Often the return on the benchmark will consist of the return on a factor portfolio or a linear combination of such returns, in which case $\text{var}(\varepsilon_B) = 0$. Given the variance or $r - r_B$, it is then straightforward to compute the standard deviation and the relative value-at-risk.

In the example above, suppose that the factor loadings of the benchmark portfolio are $\beta_{B1} = 0.5$ and $\beta_{B2} = 0.5$. Then the factor loadings for $r - r_B$ are

$$
\begin{bmatrix}
\beta_{11} - \beta_{1B} & \beta_{11} - \beta_{2B} \\
\beta_{21} - \beta_{1B} & \beta_{22} - \beta_{2B} \\
\beta_{31} - \beta_{1B} & \beta_{32} - \beta_{2B} \\
\beta_{41} - \beta_{1B} & \beta_{42} - \beta_{2B}
\end{bmatrix}
=
\begin{bmatrix}
2.0 & -1.6 \\
1.6 & -1.3 \\
-0.6 & 0.7 \\
-0.3 & 0.3
\end{bmatrix},
$$

and these would be used in place of those in (7.3). To complete the computation, one would also need to specify the residual variance $\text{var}(\varepsilon_B)$, which will often be zero.

INCLUDING OPTIONS IN COMPUTING DELTA-NORMAL VALUE-AT-RISK

Options can be handled in a straightforward fashion similar to the way they were handled in Chapter 3. Letting V^{option} denote the value (on a per-share basis) of an option on security i, the option is mapped to a position of $\Delta \equiv \partial V^{\text{option}}/\partial S_i$ shares. For an option on the ith stock, the factor loading for the kth factor is related to that of the underlying stock through the formula

$$
\beta_{ik}^{\text{option}} = \Omega_i \beta_{ik}^{\text{stock}}, \tag{7.5}
$$

where S_i is the stock price and $\Omega_i \equiv (\partial V^{\text{option}}/\partial S_i)(S_i/V^{\text{option}}) = \Delta(S_i/V^{\text{option}})$ is the *option elasticity*, which can be interpreted as the percentage change in the option price resulting from a 1% change in the stock price. The option factor loadings depend on the prices through the option elasticity because the factor loadings apply to returns or percentage changes rather than dollar changes. Similarly, the option residual is given by $\varepsilon_{ik}^{\text{option}} = \Omega_i \varepsilon_{ik}^{\text{stock}}$, so its variance is

$$
\text{var}(\varepsilon_i^{\text{option}}) = \Omega_i^2(\varepsilon_i^{\text{stock}}).
$$

If one ignores the portfolio residual variance by assuming that $\text{var}(\varepsilon) = 0$, then the option can be interpreted as another security with factor loadings given by (7.5). However, this approach does not make sense if one incorporates the residual variance using (7.2), because if the N securities in the portfolio include both the underlying stock and options on the stock it is impossible for the residuals to be uncorrelated. Instead, one can include options by adjusting the factor loadings of their underlying common stocks and the residual variances. (Alternatively, one can give up the assumption that the residuals are uncorrelated.)

To do this, think of the stock and options together as making up the total position in that stock, and let γ denote the proportion of the value of the total position contributed by the value of the options. The factor loading for the total position is then a weighted average of the factor loadings of the stock and option positions. Specifically, for the kth factor loading

$$\beta_{ik} = \gamma \beta_{ik}^{\text{option}} + (1 - \gamma)\beta_{ik}^{\text{stock}}. \tag{7.6}$$

Using the fact that the option residual is $\varepsilon_{ik}^{\text{option}} = \Omega_i \varepsilon_{ik}^{\text{stock}}$, the residual of the total position is $\varepsilon_{ik} = \gamma \varepsilon_{ik}^{\text{option}} + (1 - \gamma)\varepsilon_{ik}^{\text{stock}} = (\gamma \Omega_i + (1 - \gamma))\varepsilon_{ik}^{\text{stock}}$. Thus, its variance is

$$\text{var}(\varepsilon_{ik}^{\text{option}}) = (\gamma \Omega_i + (1 - \gamma))^2 \, \text{var}(\varepsilon_{ik}^{\text{stock}}). \tag{7.7}$$

If the portfolio includes different series of options, the γ in these formulas is interpreted as the value of all of the options together, and similarly for the option elasticity that appeared earlier. Alternatively, (7.6) and (7.7) can be modified to include additional terms corresponding to additional options series. Once the factor loadings and variance have been adjusted to incorporate the options using (7.6) and (7.7), the value-at-risk is computed just as it was above.

Returning again to the earlier example, suppose that the portfolio manager liquidates one-half of the position in the fourth stock and uses the proceeds to buy call options on the first stock. Assuming that the delta of this call is 0.55 (per share) and that $S_1 / V^{\text{option}} = 20$, the option elasticity is $0.55 \times 20 = 11$ and the options' factor loadings are

$$\beta_{11}^{\text{option}} = 11(2.5) = 27.5,$$

$$\beta_{12}^{\text{option}} = 11(-1.1) = -12.1.$$

Since 10% of the value of the portfolio is invested in the option and 40% is invested in the first stock, the weight $\gamma = 0.10/0.4 = 0.25$. The factor loadings for the total position (option and stock) in the first stock are then

$$\beta_{11} = 0.25(27.5) + 0.75(-1.1) = 8.75,$$
$$\beta_{12} = 0.25(-12.1) + 0.75(-1.1) = -3.85.$$

These are used instead of the values 2.5 and –1.1 that appear in (7.4). After the residual variance is adjusted using (7.7), the portfolio variance can be computed using the new portfolio weights $w_1 = 0.50$, $w_2 = 0.1$, $w_3 = 0.3$, and $w_4 = 0.1$. Then, the value-at-risk can be computed in the usual fashion.

In the context of factor models, this approach of mapping the option to a position of Δ shares has exactly the same limitations discussed in Chapter 3. That is, it fails to capture the nonlinearity of the option price as a function of the value of the underlying asset. Here, because the option was purchased, the linear approximation will exceed the value of the portfolio and the delta-normal method will tend to overstate the risk of the portfolio.

FULL MONTE CARLO VALUE-AT-RISK

The appendix to the previous chapter describes how multivariate normal random variables may be simulated using the equation

$$x = \Sigma^{1/2} e, \tag{7.8}$$

where e is a vector of independent standard normal random variables, Σ is the covariance matrix or an estimate of it, and $\Sigma^{1/2}$ is a square root of Σ. If it is assumed that the changes to the factors are normally distributed, then we can use this equation with x interpreted as a vector of changes to the market factors. The calculation in (7.8) is inconvenient if each of the N stock prices is treated as a market factor, because then Σ is $N \times N$, and x and e are $N \times 1$. Actual portfolios can contain thousands of different stocks, so N can be as large as several thousand.

Factor models such as (7.1) simplify the computations involved in computing value-at-risk using the full Monte Carlo method because the number of common market factors in (7.1) is sometimes very small (e.g., one to three) and rarely much greater than 50. If a factor model is used, the calculation (7.8) is replaced by the two equations

$$f = \Sigma_f^{1/2} e, \tag{7.9}$$

$$r_i = \alpha_i + \beta_{1i} f_1 + \beta_{2i} f_2 + \ldots + \beta_{Ki} f_K + \varepsilon_i, \text{ for } i = 1, \ldots, N, \tag{7.10}$$

where f is the $K \times 1$ vector of changes to the market factors, Σ_f is the $K \times K$ covariance matrix of changes to the market factors, and e is $K \times 1$ vector of independent standard normal random variables. First, (7.9) is used to simulate changes in the market factors, and then, given f, (7.10) is used for each stock to simulate the stock returns. These returns then allow the computation of the stock prices, the prices of options on the stocks and any other derivatives, the hypothetical new value of the portfolio, and the hypothetical change in value. The Monte Carlo simulation then consists of repeating this procedure many times.

This procedure can be illustrated using the two-factor example discussed earlier. The lower triangular square root of the covariance matrix is

$$\Sigma_f^{1/2} = \begin{bmatrix} \sigma_1 & 0 \\ \rho\sigma_2 & \sqrt{1 - \rho^2}\sigma_2 \end{bmatrix} = \begin{bmatrix} 0.043 & 0 \\ 0.8(0.041) & \sqrt{1 - 0.8^2}(0.041) \end{bmatrix},$$

where σ_1 and σ_2 are the volatilities of the two market factors and ρ is the correlation between them. Then, using (7.9),

$$\begin{bmatrix} f_1 \\ f_2 \end{bmatrix} = \begin{bmatrix} 0.043 & 0 \\ 0.8(0.041) & \sqrt{1 - 0.8^2}(0.041) \end{bmatrix} \begin{bmatrix} e_1 \\ e_2 \end{bmatrix}$$

$$= \begin{bmatrix} 0.043 e_1 \\ 0.8(0.041) e_1 + \sqrt{1 - 0.8^2}(0.041) e_2 \end{bmatrix}.$$

If, for concreteness, we suppose that $(e_1, e_2)' = (0.62, -0.37)$, then

$$\begin{bmatrix} f_1 \\ f_2 \end{bmatrix} = \begin{bmatrix} 0.043 & 0 \\ 0.8(0.041) & \sqrt{1 - 0.8^2}(0.041) \end{bmatrix} \begin{bmatrix} 0.62 \\ -0.37 \end{bmatrix} = \begin{bmatrix} 0.0267 \\ -0.0574 \end{bmatrix}.$$

The returns can then be constructed using a pseudo-random realization of $\varepsilon' = (\varepsilon_1, \varepsilon_2, \varepsilon_3, \varepsilon_4)'$, the factor model

$$r_i = \alpha_i + \beta_{1i}f_1 + \beta_{2i}f_2 + \varepsilon_i,$$

the factor loadings above, and estimates of the α_i. The simulated stock prices can then be computed from these returns. Then, given the stock prices, one can compute the prices of any options or other derivative instruments, the hypothetical new value of the portfolio, and the hypothetical change in value. Repeating this procedure many times completes the Monte Carlo simulation.

OTHER METHODS

If full Monte Carlo is too costly, factor models may be used with the delta-gamma-theta Monte Carlo approach described in Chapter 14. Instead of computing the option prices exactly as in full Monte Carlo, one simply uses delta-gamma-theta or delta-gamma approximations to their values.

Factor models also simplify the computation of value-at-risk using other methods, provided that one is willing to assume that the variance of e_i s (the residual in equation 7.1) is zero. If this assumption is made and the number of factors K is small (typically this means $K \le 3$), then *grid Monte Carlo* methods described in Chapter 15 may be used. In general, factor models do not simplify grid Monte Carlo methods, because the limiting factor in grid Monte Carlo method is the number of stock prices on which option prices depend. Factor models do not change this, but only simplify the process of simulating the stock prices.

The historical simulation method can also be simplified by the use of factor models, provided that one assumes $\text{var}(\varepsilon) = 0$. In this case, the simulation requires the use of only the observed past changes in the market factors. However, a drawback of using factor models with the historical simulation approach is that they eliminate one of the main claimed advantages of the historical simulation approach, namely, its lack of dependence on any model. However, it does eliminate the need to assume a specific distribution for the factors.

NOTES

In some models, α_i is equal to the rate of interest available on a riskless security r, in which case the model is often written as

$$r_i - r = \beta_{1i}f_1 + \beta_{2i}f_2 + \ldots + \beta_{Ki}f_K + \varepsilon_i.$$

Factor models are described in investments textbooks such as Bodie, Kane, and Marcus (1993, Chapter 9) and in many other places, such as in Grinold and Kahn (1994), Burmeister, Roll, and Ross (1994), and Elton and Gruber (1994).

CHAPTER 8

Using Principal Components to Compute the VaR of Fixed-Income Portfolios

The *principal components decomposition* can be viewed as a particular kind of factor model. As with other factor models, its role in risk measurement is to reduce the dimensionality of the problem, that is, to reduce the number of underlying sources of uncertainty or market factors that must be considered. In the principal components decomposition, the market factors are not specified in advance but rather consist of the principal components of the data, which are linear combinations of the variables being explained. For example, if the variables being explained consist of the changes in the yields of zero-coupon bonds, the first principal component consists of the linear combination of yield changes that best explains (in a sense made precise below) the variability of the yields. The second, third, and subsequent principal components then each consist of the linear combinations of yield changes that best explain the variability not explained by the previous components.

The number of principal components is equal to the number of linearly independent variables to be explained. At first glance, this suggests that there may be no advantage to the principal components decomposition because the principal components do not achieve any reduction in dimensionality. However, in many situations in finance, and especially in modeling the variability in interest rates, the data are so highly correlated that the first few principal components explain most of their variability, and the remaining components can be safely ignored. Thus, the principal components decomposition can provide a way of constructing a factor model with a small number of factors, often as few as two or three.

This chapter first explains the principal components decomposition in this statistical context as a particular way of constructing a factor model to explain the data, beginning with a simple two-variable example. It then illustrates the use of principal components in describing the variability of changes in the yields of zero-coupon bonds, and finally applies it to compute the value-at-risk of a simple bond portfolio. While it is not the focus of this chapter, mathematically inclined readers may already be familiar with the principal components decomposition. It is equivalent to the eigensystem decomposition of the covariance matrix, with the eigenvalues and associated eigenvectors ordered from the largest to smallest eigenvalue.

DECOMPOSING A RANDOM VECTOR

Consider a two-dimensional random vector $x = (x_1, x_2)'$ with covariance matrix

$$\Sigma = E[(x - E[x])(x - E[x])']$$

$$= \begin{bmatrix} \sigma_1^2 & \rho\sigma_1\sigma_2 \\ \rho\sigma_1\sigma_2 & \sigma_2^2 \end{bmatrix}. \tag{8.1}$$

For simplicity assume that $E[x] = 0$, allowing us to work with x instead $x - E[x]$; thus the covariance matrix becomes $\Sigma = E[xx']$. In this chapter, the vector x is interpreted as the changes in the yields of zero-coupon bonds, though in other contexts it could consist of changes in forward rates, the returns on common stocks or other assets, or the changes in commodity or currency prices.

The vector x can be written as a linear combination of orthogonal (uncorrelated) random variables, that is,

$$\begin{bmatrix} x_1 \\ x_2 \end{bmatrix} = \begin{bmatrix} a_{11} & a_{12} \\ a_{21} & a_{22} \end{bmatrix} \begin{bmatrix} \varepsilon_1 \\ \varepsilon_2 \end{bmatrix}, \tag{8.2}$$

or equivalently $x = A\varepsilon$, where $A = \{a_{ij}\}$ is the matrix on the right-hand side of equation (8.2), ε is the vector $\varepsilon = (\varepsilon_1, \varepsilon_2)'$, and ε_1 and ε_2 are uncorrelated random variables each with mean zero and variance one. In carrying out the value-at-risk calculation, we make the additional assumption that the ε_i s are normally distributed, so the lack of correlation implies they are independent. Combining (8.1) and (8.2) and letting I denote the two-dimensional identity matrix,

$$\Sigma = E[A\varepsilon\varepsilon'A'] = AE[\varepsilon\varepsilon']A' = AIA' = AA'.$$

This indicates that, if we are to write the vector x as a linear combination of uncorrelated random variables, we must chose the elements of A so that

$$
\begin{bmatrix} \sigma_1^2 & \rho\sigma_1\sigma_2 \\ \rho\sigma_1\sigma_2 & \sigma_2^2 \end{bmatrix} = \begin{bmatrix} a_{11} & a_{12} \\ a_{21} & a_{22} \end{bmatrix} \begin{bmatrix} a_{11} & a_{21} \\ a_{12} & a_{22} \end{bmatrix}
$$

$$
= \begin{bmatrix} a_{11}^2 + a_{12}^2 & a_{11}a_{21} + a_{12}a_{22} \\ a_{11}a_{21} + a_{12}a_{22} & a_{21}^2 + a_{22}^2 \end{bmatrix}.
$$

(8.3)

This set of equations always has a solution. In fact, as suggested by the presence of three parameters ρ, σ_1, and σ_2 on the left-hand side and four a_{ij}s on the right, in general there are infinitely many combinations of the a_{ij}s that satisfy the equations. The easiest choice involves setting $a_{12} = 0$, in which case $a_{11} = \sigma_1$, $a_{21} = \rho\sigma_2$, and $a_{22} = \sigma_2\sqrt{1-\rho^2}$. However, this is not the choice made in principal components.

Rather, the principal components decomposition involves writing the matrix A as

$$
A = \begin{bmatrix} a_{11} & a_{12} \\ a_{21} & a_{22} \end{bmatrix} = \begin{bmatrix} \nu_{11} & \nu_{12} \\ \nu_{21} & \nu_{22} \end{bmatrix} \begin{bmatrix} \sqrt{\lambda_1} & 0 \\ 0 & \sqrt{\lambda_2} \end{bmatrix},
$$

(8.4)

where λ_1 and λ_2 are positive scalars and $\nu_1 = (\nu_{11} \ \nu_{21})'$ and $\nu_2 = (\nu_{12} \ \nu_{22})'$ are orthonormal vectors, that is, $\nu_1'\nu_1 = \nu_{11}^2 + \nu_{21}^2 = 1$, $\nu_2'\nu_2 = \nu_{12}^2 + \nu_{22}^2 = 1$ (each vector has length 1), and $\nu_1'\nu_2 = \nu_{11}\nu_{12} + \nu_{21}\nu_{22} = 0$ (the two vectors are orthogonal). This choice implies

$$
\begin{bmatrix} \sigma_1^2 & \rho\sigma_1\sigma_2 \\ \rho\sigma_1\sigma_2 & \sigma_2^2 \end{bmatrix} = \begin{bmatrix} \nu_{11} & \nu_{12} \\ \nu_{21} & \nu_{22} \end{bmatrix} \begin{bmatrix} \lambda_1 & 0 \\ 0 & \lambda_2 \end{bmatrix} \begin{bmatrix} \nu_{11} & \nu_{21} \\ \nu_{12} & \nu_{22} \end{bmatrix}
$$

$$
= \begin{bmatrix} \nu_{11}^2\lambda_1 + \nu_{12}^2\lambda_2 & \nu_{11}\nu_{21}\lambda_1 + \nu_{12}\nu_{22}\lambda_2 \\ \nu_{11}\nu_{21}\lambda_1 + \nu_{12}\nu_{22}\lambda_2 & \nu_{21}^2\lambda_1 + \nu_{22}^2\lambda_2 \end{bmatrix}
$$

(8.5)

$$
= \begin{bmatrix} \nu_{11}^2 & \nu_{11}\nu_{21} \\ \nu_{11}\nu_{21} & \nu_{21}^2 \end{bmatrix}\lambda_1 + \begin{bmatrix} \nu_{12}^2 & \nu_{12}\nu_{22} \\ \nu_{12}\nu_{22} & \nu_{22}^2 \end{bmatrix}\lambda_2.
$$

By choosing A as in (8.4) we have decomposed the covariance matrix into two terms, one involving only λ_1 and elements of the first vector ν_1 and another involving λ_2 and elements of the second vector ν_2. To interpret this decomposition, return to equations (8.2), writing the vector x in terms of ε, and (8.4), writing the matrix A in terms of the ν_{ij}s and λ_js. Combining (8.2) and (8.4), we obtain

$$
\begin{bmatrix} x_1 \\ x_2 \end{bmatrix} = \begin{bmatrix} \nu_{11} & \nu_{12} \\ \nu_{21} & \nu_{22} \end{bmatrix} \begin{bmatrix} \sqrt{\lambda_1} & 0 \\ 0 & \sqrt{\lambda_2} \end{bmatrix} \begin{bmatrix} \varepsilon_1 \\ \varepsilon_2 \end{bmatrix}
$$
$$
= \begin{bmatrix} \nu_{11} \\ \nu_{21} \end{bmatrix} \sqrt{\lambda_1} \varepsilon_1 + \begin{bmatrix} \nu_{12} \\ \nu_{22} \end{bmatrix} \sqrt{\lambda_2} \varepsilon_2.
$$

(8.6)

The two terms on the right-hand side of the second line of (8.5) are the portions of the covariance matrix Σ due to the two terms on the right-hand side of equation (8.6), that is,

$$
\begin{bmatrix} \nu_{11}^2 & \nu_{11}\nu_{21} \\ \nu_{11}\nu_{21} & \nu_{21}^2 \end{bmatrix} \lambda_1 = E\left(\begin{bmatrix} \nu_{11} \\ \nu_{21} \end{bmatrix} \sqrt{\lambda_1} \varepsilon_1 \right) \left(\varepsilon_1 \sqrt{\lambda_1} \begin{bmatrix} \nu_{11} & \nu_{21} \end{bmatrix} \right)
$$

and

$$
\begin{bmatrix} \nu_{12}^2 & \nu_{12}\nu_{22} \\ \nu_{12}\nu_{22} & \nu_{22}^2 \end{bmatrix} \lambda_2 = E\left(\begin{bmatrix} \nu_{12} \\ \nu_{22} \end{bmatrix} \sqrt{\lambda_2} \varepsilon_2 \right) \left(\varepsilon_2 \sqrt{\lambda_2} \begin{bmatrix} \nu_{12} & \nu_{22} \end{bmatrix} \right).
$$

Since the vectors ν_1 and ν_2 have the same size (length equal to one), the importance of the two terms on the right-hand side of (8.6) is determined by the magnitudes of λ_1 and λ_2.

THE PRINCIPAL COMPONENTS

In equations (8.6) and (8.5) above we decomposed the random vector x and its covariance matrix Σ into the components due to uncorrelated random variables ε_1 and ε_2. Our ability to do this depends only on the existence of a solution to (8.2) of the form (8.3). Although we do not demonstrate this fact, equation (8.2) will always have a solution of the form of (8.3), implying that we can always decompose the random vector x into the components due to uncorrelated random variables ε_1 and ε_2 as in (8.6). But what are ε_1 and ε_2? Rewrite (8.6) slightly to yield

$$
\begin{bmatrix} x_1 \\ x_2 \end{bmatrix} = \begin{bmatrix} \nu_{11} & \nu_{12} \\ \nu_{21} & \nu_{22} \end{bmatrix} \begin{bmatrix} \sqrt{\lambda_1}\,\varepsilon_1 \\ \sqrt{\lambda_2}\,\varepsilon_2 \end{bmatrix}
$$
$$
= \begin{bmatrix} \nu_{11} & \nu_{12} \\ \nu_{21} & \nu_{22} \end{bmatrix} \begin{bmatrix} p_1 \\ p_2 \end{bmatrix},
\tag{8.7}
$$

where $p_1 \equiv \sqrt{\lambda_1}\,\varepsilon_1$ and $p_2 \equiv \sqrt{\lambda_2}\,\varepsilon_2$. The question "what are ε_1 and ε_2?" is equivalent to the question "what are p_1 and p_2?" The answer comes from rearranging (8.7). The matrix $V = \{\nu_{ij}\}$ is an orthogonal matrix (i.e., a matrix composed of orthonormal vectors); a key property of such a matrix is that its inverse is simply its tranpose. Using this property,

$$
\begin{bmatrix} p_1 \\ p_2 \end{bmatrix} = \begin{bmatrix} \nu_{11} & \nu_{12} \\ \nu_{21} & \nu_{22} \end{bmatrix}^{-1} \begin{bmatrix} x_1 \\ x_2 \end{bmatrix}
$$
$$
= \begin{bmatrix} \nu_{11} & \nu_{21} \\ \nu_{12} & \nu_{22} \end{bmatrix} \begin{bmatrix} x_1 \\ x_2 \end{bmatrix}
\tag{8.8}
$$

Thus, $p_1 = \nu_{11} x_1 + \nu_{21} x_2$ is a linear combination of the x_is, and similarly for p_2. Each p_i is associated with a vector, $\nu_i = (\nu_{1i} \ \nu_{2i})'$, and a scalar, λ_i. If we order the p_is, ν_is, and λ_is from the largest to smallest λ_i, then the p_is are called the principal components and the ν_is are the factor loadings of the principal components. This last terminology can be understood by slightly rearranging (8.7) to yield

$$
\begin{bmatrix} x_1 \\ x_2 \end{bmatrix} = \begin{bmatrix} \nu_{11} & \nu_{12} \\ \nu_{21} & \nu_{22} \end{bmatrix} \begin{bmatrix} p_1 \\ p_2 \end{bmatrix}
$$
$$
= \begin{bmatrix} \nu_{11} \\ \nu_{21} \end{bmatrix} p_1 + \begin{bmatrix} \nu_{12} \\ \nu_{22} \end{bmatrix} p_2.
\tag{8.9}
$$

This is a key equation for interpreting the principal components. It expresses each x_i in terms of random factors p_1 and p_2 and factor loadings ν_{i1} and ν_{i2}, which are analogous to factor model beta coefficients. From the relations $p_1 = \sqrt{\lambda_1}\,\varepsilon_1$ and $p_2 = \sqrt{\lambda_2}\,\varepsilon_2$ it is clear that the eigenvalue λ_1 is the variance of the first principal component p_1, while λ_2 is the variance of p_2; in the general case λ_i is the variance of p_i. The sum $\lambda_1 + \lambda_2 = \text{var}(p_1) + \text{var}(p_2)$ is the total variance of the principal components.

The eigenvalues λ_1 and λ_2 also have an interpretation in terms of the variance of the vector x. From (8.5), the sum $\text{var}(x_1) + \text{var}(x_2) = \sigma_1^2 + \sigma_2^2$ is given by

$$\sigma_1^2 + \sigma_2^2 = (\nu_{11}^2 + \nu_{21}^2)\lambda_1 + (\nu_{21}^2 + \nu_{22}^2)\lambda_2 = \lambda_1 + \lambda_2.$$

Thus, the sum of eigenvalues $\lambda_1 + \lambda_2$ is also the total variance of x, $\sigma_1^2 + \sigma_2^2$, and the eigenvalues λ_1 and λ_2 are interpreted as the contributions of the two principal components to the total variance of x.

The p_is are uncorrelated because they are defined by $p_i \equiv \sqrt{\lambda_i}\varepsilon_i$, implying that they can be interpreted as the separate or "independent" risk factors that explain the variation in x. Because they are ordered from largest to smallest value of λ_i, p_1 is the factor that explains the largest possible part of the variability of x, while p_2 is the factor uncorrelated with p_1 that explains the largest possible part of the remaining variability of x. Here, with only two elements of x, the component p_2 simply explains the remaining variability not explained by p_1; in the general case, with $K > 2$ factors, each principal component is the factor uncorrelated with the previous principal components that explains the largest possible part of the remaining variability of x. The ith eigenvalue λ_i is the contribution of the ith principal component to the total variance.

One further feature of this decomposition is that the signs of the vectors ν_1 and ν_2 are arbitrary, in that ν_1 could be replaced by $-\nu_1$ or ν_2 replaced by $-\nu_2$. An easy way to see this is to observe that equation (8.6) continues to hold if ε_1 is replace by $-\varepsilon_1$ and ν_1 by $-\nu_1$, or if ε_2 is replaced by $-\varepsilon_2$ and ν_2 by $-\nu_2$. But since $-\varepsilon_1$ and $-\varepsilon_2$ have the same statistical properties as ε_1 and ε_2, this choice must be irrelevant. Alternatively, the elements of ν_1 and ν_2 appear in equation (8.5) only when multiplied by other elements of the same vector, implying that the signs of these vectors can be switched without affecting (8.5).

COMPUTING THE PRINCIPAL COMPONENTS

To compute the principal components, note that equation (8.6) implies

$$\text{cov}\left(\begin{bmatrix} x_1 \\ x_2 \end{bmatrix}\right) = \text{cov}\left(\begin{bmatrix} \nu_{11} & \nu_{12} \\ \nu_{21} & \nu_{22} \end{bmatrix}\begin{bmatrix} \sqrt{\lambda_1} & 0 \\ 0 & \sqrt{\lambda_2} \end{bmatrix}\begin{bmatrix} \varepsilon_1 \\ \varepsilon_2 \end{bmatrix}\right)$$

or

$$\Sigma = \begin{bmatrix} \nu_{11} & \nu_{12} \\ \nu_{21} & \nu_{22} \end{bmatrix} \begin{bmatrix} \lambda_1 & 0 \\ 0 & \lambda_2 \end{bmatrix} \begin{bmatrix} \nu_{11} & \nu_{21} \\ \nu_{12} & \nu_{22} \end{bmatrix}.$$

Post-multiplying by the matrix

$$V = \begin{bmatrix} \nu_{11} & \nu_{12} \\ \nu_{21} & \nu_{22} \end{bmatrix},$$

using the fact that this is an orthogonal matrix, and doing some rearranging results in

$$\Sigma \begin{bmatrix} \nu_{11} & \nu_{12} \\ \nu_{21} & \nu_{22} \end{bmatrix} - \begin{bmatrix} \lambda_1 & 0 \\ 0 & \lambda_2 \end{bmatrix} \begin{bmatrix} \nu_{11} & \nu_{12} \\ \nu_{21} & \nu_{22} \end{bmatrix} = 0,$$

or equivalently,

$$(\Sigma - \lambda_i I) \begin{bmatrix} \nu_{1i} \\ \nu_{2i} \end{bmatrix} = 0 \text{ for } i = 1, 2. \tag{8.10}$$

The system (8.10) has a solution with $\nu_i \neq 0$ for the λ_i such that the matrix $(\Sigma - \lambda_i I)$ is singular, that is, for the λ_i such that

$$\det(\Sigma - \lambda_i I) = 0. \tag{8.11}$$

Thus, the λ_is are the solutions of (8.11), and the factor loadings $\nu_i = (\nu_{1i} \ \nu_{2i})'$ are the corresponding solutions of (8.10). The principal components p_1 and p_2 are then determined by (8.8).

Equations (8.10) and (8.11) are the equations for the eigenvectors and eigenvalues of Σ; thus, the ν_is is and λ_is are precisely the eigenvectors and eigenvalues. This observation provides an approach for computing the principal components, because most mathematical software packages and libraries have functions or subroutines to compute eigenvectors and eigenvalues and also provide an alternative interpretation of them mentioned briefly in the notes.

NUMERICAL EXAMPLE

To illustrate the principal components decomposition, let $\sigma_1 = 0.20$, $\sigma_2 = 0.30$, and $\rho = 0.50$, so the covariance matrix is

$$\Sigma = \begin{bmatrix} \sigma_1^2 & \rho\sigma_1\sigma_2 \\ \rho\sigma_1\sigma_2 & \sigma_2^2 \end{bmatrix} = \begin{bmatrix} 0.04 & 0.03 \\ 0.03 & 0.09 \end{bmatrix}.$$

The eigenvalues of this matrix are $\lambda_1 = 0.1041$ and $\lambda_2 = 0.0259$, and the eigenvectors are

$$\begin{bmatrix} \nu_{11} \\ \nu_{21} \end{bmatrix} = \begin{bmatrix} 0.4242 \\ 0.9056 \end{bmatrix} \text{ and } \begin{bmatrix} \nu_{12} \\ \nu_{22} \end{bmatrix} = \begin{bmatrix} 0.9056 \\ -0.4242 \end{bmatrix}.$$

Thus, the two principal components are $p_1 = 0.4242x_1 + 0.9056x_2$ and $p_2 = 0.9056x_1 - 0.4242x_2$ with variances of $\text{var}(p_1) = \lambda_1 = 0.1041$ and $\text{var}(p_2) = \lambda_2 = 0.0259$, respectively. For the first principal component the weight on x_2 is larger than that on x_1 because x_2 is more variable; if x_1 and x_2 had the same variance, the first principal component would have equal weights on the two variables. These two principal components explain the vector x in the sense of equations (8.7) and (8.9), that is,

$$\begin{bmatrix} x_1 \\ x_2 \end{bmatrix} = \begin{bmatrix} \nu_{11} \\ \nu_{21} \end{bmatrix} p_1 + \begin{bmatrix} \nu_{12} \\ \nu_{22} \end{bmatrix} p_2$$

$$= \begin{bmatrix} 0.4242 \\ 0.9056 \end{bmatrix} (0.4242x_1 + 0.9056x_2) + \begin{bmatrix} 0.9056 \\ -0.4242 \end{bmatrix} (0.9056x_1 - 0.4242x_2).$$

But note that this "explanation" of x in terms of the principal components follows mechanically from the construction of p_1 and p_2; finishing the computations on the right-hand side of the preceding equation,

$$\begin{bmatrix} 0.4242 \\ 0.9056 \end{bmatrix} (0.4242x_1 + 0.9056x_2) + \begin{bmatrix} 0.9056 \\ -0.4242 \end{bmatrix} (0.9056x_1 - 0.4242x_2)$$

$$= \begin{bmatrix} (0.4242)^2 + (0.9056)^2 \\ (0.4242)(0.9056) - (0.4242)(0.9056) \end{bmatrix} x_1$$

$$+ \begin{bmatrix} (0.4242)(0.9056) - (0.4242)(0.9056) \\ (0.4242)^2 + (0.9056)^2 \end{bmatrix} x_2$$

$$= \begin{bmatrix} 1 \\ 0 \end{bmatrix} x_1 + \begin{bmatrix} 0 \\ 1 \end{bmatrix} x_2 = \begin{bmatrix} x_1 \\ x_2 \end{bmatrix}.$$

Also, from equation (8.5) the principal components explain the covariance matrix, that is,

$$
\begin{bmatrix} 0.04 & 0.03 \\ 0.03 & 0.09 \end{bmatrix} = \begin{bmatrix} \sigma_1^2 & \rho\sigma_1\sigma_2 \\ \rho\sigma_1\sigma_2 & \sigma_2^2 \end{bmatrix} = \begin{bmatrix} v_{11}^2 & v_{11}v_{21} \\ v_{11}v_{21} & v_{21}^2 \end{bmatrix}\lambda_1 + \begin{bmatrix} v_{12}^2 & v_{12}v_{22} \\ v_{12}v_{22} & v_{22}^2 \end{bmatrix}\lambda_2
$$

$$
= \begin{bmatrix} 0.0187 & 0.0400 \\ 0.0400 & 0.0853 \end{bmatrix} + \begin{bmatrix} 0.0213 & -0.0100 \\ -0.0100 & 0.0047 \end{bmatrix}.
$$

THE GENERAL CASE

In the general case when x is a K-dimensional vector, the covariance matrix Σ is $K \times K$, there will be K principal components, and the vectors v_i of the principal components' factor loadings (i.e., the eigenvectors) will be K-dimensional; but otherwise the situation is essentially unchanged. Equations (8.6) and (8.9) become

$$
\begin{aligned}
x &= v_1\sqrt{\lambda_1}\varepsilon_1 + v_2\sqrt{\lambda_2}\varepsilon_2 + \cdots + v_K\sqrt{\lambda_K}\varepsilon_K \\
&= v_1 p_1 + v_2 p_2 + \cdots + v_K p_K,
\end{aligned} \tag{8.12}
$$

where the ε_is are uncorrelated random variables each with mean zero and variance one, $p_i = \sqrt{\lambda_i}\varepsilon_i$ is the ith principal component, λ_i is the variance of the ith principal component (and also the ith eigenvalue of Σ, if the eigenvalues are ordered from largest to smallest), and $v_i = (v_{1i} \ v_{2i} \ \cdots \ v_{Ki})'$ is the vector of factor loadings for the ith principal component (and also the ith eigenvector). The decomposition of the covariance matrix in equation (8.5) becomes

$$
\Sigma = E[xx'] = (v_1 v_1')\lambda_1 + (v_2 v_2')\lambda_2 + \cdots + (v_K v_K')\lambda_K, \tag{8.13}
$$

where we have used the fact that the principal components are uncorrelated. Also similar to the two-dimensional case, the total variance is $\sum_{i=1}^{K} \sigma_i^2 = \sum_{i=1}^{K} \lambda_i$, and the ith eigenvalue λ_i is still interpreted as the contribution of the ith principal component to the total variance.

Not surprisingly, the approach for computation of the principal components is also unchanged. The eigenvalues λ_i are the solutions of a K-dimensional version of (8.11), and the eigenvectors satisfy a K-dimensional version of (8.10),

$$(\Sigma - \lambda_i I)\nu_i = 0 \text{ for } i = 1, 2, \ldots, K, \qquad (8.14)$$

where here I is the K-dimensional identity matrix. The principal components themselves can then be computed from a K-dimensional version of (8.8),

$$p = V'x, \qquad (8.15)$$

where $p = (p_1 \ p_2 \ \ldots \ p_K)'$ is the K-dimensional vector of principal components and $V = (\nu_1 \ \nu_2 \ \ldots \ \nu_K)$ is a $K \times K$ matrix formed from the K eigenvectors of Σ.

A TERM STRUCTURE EXAMPLE

We now turn to illustrating the use of principal components in describing changes in the term structure of interest rates. Table 8.1 shows a hypothetical correlation matrix of the changes in the yields of zero-coupon bonds of 10 different maturities ranging from three months to 30 years, along with their annual volatilities (in basis points). These yields are naturally thought of as either the yields on zero-coupon government bonds, or as zero-coupon yields constructed from benchmark interest-rate swap quotes. They are the underlying basic risk factors, which will be further summarized through the use of principal components. Often, when the underlying risk factors are the yields of zero-coupon bonds, they are called *key rates* (Ho 1992), and we use this terminology below.

Through this choice of risk factors, the value-at-risk will fail to include the risks of changes in credit or liquidity spreads. If spread and liquidity risks are important for the portfolio, one would need to expand the correlation matrix to include the correlations and volatilities of these spreads and also to measure the exposures of the various instruments to these spreads.

Table 8.2 shows the covariance matrix corresponding to the correlations and volatilities in Table 8.1. One feature of the choice of maturities in Tables 8.1 and 8.2 is that the "short end" of the term structure is not captured in great detail, the three-month maturity being the only maturity of less than one year. This choice is reasonable for many portfolio management applications involving measuring the risk of portfolios that include medium- and long-term bonds, but would be less useful for bank portfolios in which short-term instruments play a more important role.

TABLE 8.1 Hypothetical volatilities and correlations of changes in yields of zero-coupon bonds

Maturities	3 mos.	1 year	2 years	3 years	5 years	7 years	10 years	15 years	20 years	30 years
Volatilities (basis points)	72	98	116	115	115	112	107	102	100	85

Correlations:

	3 mos.	1 year	2 years	3 years	5 years	7 years	10 years	15 years	20 years	30 years
3 mos.	1.00	0.75	0.65	0.64	0.55	0.52	0.50	0.46	0.43	0.41
1 year	0.75	1.00	0.85	0.84	0.77	0.74	0.71	0.68	0.65	0.61
2 years	0.65	0.85	1.00	0.99	0.97	0.95	0.92	0.88	0.86	0.83
3 years	0.64	0.84	0.99	1.00	0.98	0.97	0.94	0.91	0.89	0.86
5 years	0.55	0.77	0.97	0.98	1.00	0.99	0.97	0.95	0.93	0.91
7 years	0.52	0.74	0.95	0.97	0.99	1.00	0.98	0.97	0.96	0.95
10 years	0.50	0.71	0.92	0.94	0.97	0.98	1.00	0.99	0.98	0.97
15 years	0.46	0.68	0.88	0.91	0.95	0.97	0.99	1.00	0.99	0.98
20 years	0.43	0.65	0.86	0.89	0.93	0.96	0.98	0.99	1.00	0.99
30 years	0.41	0.61	0.83	0.86	0.91	0.95	0.97	0.98	0.99	1.00

TABLE 8.2 Hypothetical covariances of changes in yields of zero-coupon bonds

Maturity	3 mos.	1 year	2 years	3 years	5 years	7 years	10 years	15 years	20 years	30 years
3 mos.	5184	5292	5429	5299	4554	4194	3852	3378	3096	2509
1 year	5292	9604	9663	9466	8678	8123	7445	6797	6370	5081
2 years	5429	9663	13,456	13,207	12,940	12,342	11,419	10,412	9976	8184
3 years	5299	9466	13,207	13,228	12,962	12,489	11,564	10,675	10,234	8410
5 years	4554	8678	12,940	12,962	13,226	12,748	11,934	11,144	10,694	8898
7 years	4194	8123	12,342	12,489	12,748	12,552	11,749	11,079	10,754	9037
10 years	3852	7445	11,419	11,564	11,934	11,749	11,451	10,804	10,487	8818
15 years	3378	6797	10,412	10,675	11,144	11,079	10,804	10,405	10,098	8498
20 years	3096	6370	9976	10,234	10,694	10,754	10,487	10,098	10,000	8413
30 years	2509	5081	8184	8410	8898	9037	8818	8498	8413	7231

Table 8.3 shows the factor loadings of the principal components, that is, the eigenvectors. These explain the changes in yields through equation (8.12); for example, the entries in the column headed "1" indicate the effect of the first principal component on the 10 different yields. As pointed out above, the sign of each vector ν_i is arbitrary, implying that switching the signs of the entries in any column of Table 8.3 (or any set of columns) would yield an equivalent decomposition.

Table 8.4 shows variances of the principal components (the eigenvalues), the fraction of the total variance explained by each of the principal components, the percentage of the total variance explained by each, and the cumulative percentages. The first principal component explains 89.24% of the variance, the first two together explain 96.42%, and the first three together explain a total of 98.15%. This finding that the first three principal components together explain more than 95% of the total variance of yields is a common one, and as a result users of principal components often restrict attention to the first three components. A second consideration reinforcing this is that the first three principal components have intuitive interpretations as corresponding to changes in level, slope, and curvature, discussed next.

Figure 8.1 shows the term structure shifts due to 100 basis point changes in each of the first three principal components. The plain solid line shows the assumed initial yield curve, rising from a yield of 6% for the shortest maturity to a 7% yield at the longest. The dashed line above it

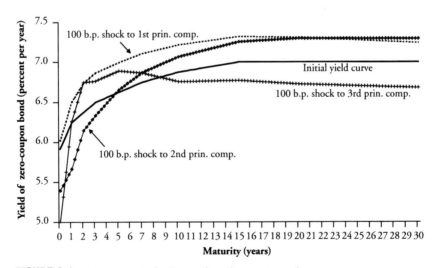

FIGURE 8.1 Yield curve shifts due to first three principal components

TABLE 8.3 Factor loadings of principal components (eigenvectors) of covariance matrix

Maturity	Factors Loadings v_i of Principal Components (Eigenvectors)									
	1	2	3	4	5	6	7	8	9	10
3 mos.	0.1390	−0.5369	−0.6864	0.4602	0.0148	−0.0679	0.0264	−0.0479	0.0077	−0.0402
1 year	0.2563	−0.5832	0.0122	−0.7586	0.0393	−0.0808	0.0769	0.0298	0.0444	−0.0418
2 years	0.3650	−0.2296	0.3706	0.2343	−0.1498	0.5834	0.2813	−0.2099	−0.3686	0.0055
3 years	0.3669	−0.1649	0.2637	0.1901	0.1232	0.0415	−0.6854	0.2933	0.1830	0.3556
5 years	0.3694	0.0282	0.2656	0.1957	−0.0893	−0.5707	0.3722	−0.3261	0.3459	0.2363
7 years	0.3603	0.1201	0.1141	0.1157	0.5593	−0.2255	0.0213	0.1740	−0.2062	−0.6265
10 years	0.3412	0.1925	−0.1193	−0.0102	−0.5893	0.1258	0.1113	0.4816	0.3358	−0.3348
15 years	0.3200	0.2542	−0.2289	−0.1503	−0.3460	−0.3236	−0.2429	−0.1017	−0.6639	0.1529
20 years	0.3093	0.2973	−0.2755	−0.1806	0.1238	0.3246	−0.2699	−0.6164	0.3356	−0.1459
30 years	0.2577	0.2940	−0.3094	−0.1216	0.3969	0.2106	0.4017	0.3285	−0.0172	0.5149

TABLE 8.4 Variance explained by principal components

	Principal Component									
	1	2	3	4	5	6	7	8	9	10
Variance (eigenvalues λ_i)	94900	7636	1834	1338	203.1	186.9	122.1	70.8	36.7	11.0
Annual volatility (basis points)	308.06	87.38	42.82	36.57	14.25	13.67	11.05	8.41	6.05	3.32
Monthly volatility (basis points)	88.93	25.22	12.36	10.56	4.11	3.95	3.19	2.43	1.75	0.96
Percentage of variance explained	89.24	7.18	1.72	1.26	0.19	0.18	0.11	0.07	0.03	0.01
Cumulative percentage	89.24	96.42	98.15	99.41	99.60	99.77	99.89	99.96	99.99	100

shows the effect of a 100 basis point realization of the first principal component, with the other principal components fixed at zero. The changes in the 10 key rates are computed using (8.12) with $p_1 = 100$ basis points, the elements of v_1 set equal to the values in the column headed "1" in Table 8.3, and $p_2 = p_3 = \ldots = p_K = 0$. Doing this results in a relatively small change of $x_1 = 0.1390 \times 100$ basis points = 13.90 basis points for the three-month maturity and larger changes in the range of 25.63 to 36.94 basis points for the other key rates. The changes for the maturities in between those of the key rates are then computed by linear interpolation; for example, the change for the six-month maturity was interpolated from the changes for the three-month and one-year maturities. These shifts were then added to the initial yield curve to create the dashed curve labeled "100 b.p. shock to 1st prin. comp." This curve illustrates that the first principal component can be interpreted as corresponding with a shift in the overall level of interest rates. Because the signs of the factor loadings are arbitrary, this shift can be either an increase or decrease in rates.

The two curves labeled "100 b.p. shock to 2nd prin. comp." and "100 b.p. shock to 3rd prin. comp." were computed similarly, except that p_2 and p_3 were set equal to 100 basis points and v_2 and v_3 were used with elements set equal to the values in the columns headed "2" and "3" in Table 8.3. Due to the pattern of negative and positive factor loadings on the second principal component, the curve corresponding to the second principal component is below the initial yield curve for the short maturities and above it for the long maturities, illustrating that the second principal component can be interpreted as corresponding to a change in the slope of the yield curve. Due to the pattern of negative and positive factor loadings on the third principal component, the curve corresponding to the third principal component is below the initial yield curve for the very shortest maturities, above it for intermediate maturities, and then again below it for the long maturities. This pattern is often called a change in the curvature of the yield curve.

One caveat worth mentioning is that Figure 8.1 overstates the relative importance of the second and third components, because the shocks to the principal components p_1, p_2, and p_3 were each set equal to the same value of 100 basis points. Table 8.4 shows that, on a monthly basis, the volatility (standard deviation) of the first principal component p_1 is 88.93 basis points, so a change of 100 basis points is only $100/88.93 = 1.12$ standard deviations and is not unusual. However, the monthly volatilities of the second and third principal components are 25.22 and 12.36 basis points, respectively, so changes of 100 basis points correspond to $100/25.22 = 3.97$ and $100/12.36 = 8.09$ standard deviations, respectively. Thus, the relative importances of the second and third factors are slightly more than one-fourth and one-eighth as large as the differences between the curves in Figure 8.1 suggest.

USING THE PRINCIPAL COMPONENTS TO COMPUTE VALUE-AT-RISK

After all of this work we are finally ready to compute the value-at-risk of a hypothetical bond portfolio, which we do using the delta-normal approach. The portfolio consists of three bonds: 20% of the portfolio's value is invested in a five-year bond paying semiannual interest at the rate of 6.5% per year; 40% of it is invested in a 10-year, 6.75% bond; and 40% is invested in a 30-year, 7% bond. Since we have already selected the market factors (the 10 zero-coupon yields or key rates), estimated their covariance matrix, and decomposed the covariance matrix into its principal components, the most important remaining task is to estimate the exposures of each of the bonds to the principal components.

The value of each bond depends upon the zero-coupon interest rates for all maturities, which will be interpolated from the key rates. These in turn depend on the principal components and factor loadings through equation (8.12). We compute the changes in value due to each of the first three principal components by shifting the term structures in a fashion similar to the construction of Figure 8.1, except that now the shifts are small enough (one basis point) that the resulting changes in the bond prices can be interpreted as (approximations to) the partial derivatives with respect to the principal components. Letting ΔP_{ki} denote the change in the price of the kth bond due to a one basis point change in the ith principal component, the exposure of the kth bond to the ith principal component is

$$\beta_{ki} = \frac{(\Delta P_{ki}/0.0001)}{P_{ki}}.$$

For example, if $\beta_{ki} = -1.59$, then a 10 basis point change in the ith principal component results in a change in the bond price of -1.59×10 basis points $= -1.59 \times 10 \times 10^{-4} = -0.00159$, or -0.159% of its value.

Table 8.5 shows the exposures of the three bonds to the first three principal components. The exposure to the first principal component is negative for all three bonds, consistent with the interpretation of the first principal component as corresponding to a shift in the level of interest rates (and the choice of the sign of the factor loadings). The exposure of the five-year bond to the second principal component is approximately zero because a large part of the value of this bond is due to the return of the principal at the end of the years, and the factor loading five-year zero-coupon rate on the second principal component is only 0.0282 (see Table 8.3). The effect of this factor loading on the bond price is then offset by the negative factor loadings for the shorter maturities. The 10- and 30-year bonds have negative exposures to the second principal component because the long-term zero-coupon rates have positive factor loadings on the second principal component. Similarly, the bonds' exposures to the third principal component depend upon the zero-coupon rates that determine the bond prices and the factor loadings of these rates on the third principal component. For example, the 30-year bond has a positive exposure because the long-term interest rates have negative factor loadings on the third principal component.

TABLE 8.5 Exposures of the bonds to the first three principal components

			Principal Components		
Bond	Value	Weight	1	2	3
1 (5-year)	100	0.2	−1.59	0.00	−0.11
2 (10-year)	200	0.4	−2.55	−1.08	0.35
3 (30-year)	200	0.4	−3.72	−2.91	2.47
Portfolio:	500		−2.83	−1.60	1.10
Volatility: (basis points)			88.93	25.22	12.36

Given these exposures, the first-order approximation to the portfolio variance used in the delta-normal approach is

$$\text{portfolio variance} = \beta_{p1}^2 \lambda_1 + \beta_{p2}^2 \lambda_2 + \beta_{p3}^2 \lambda_3$$
$$= [(-2.83^2)(94,900) + (-1.60^2)(7636)$$
$$+ (1.10^2)(1834)] \times 10^{-8}$$
$$= 0.007797,$$

where, as above, λ_i is the variance of the ith principal component, we have used the exposures from Table 8.5 and the variances (eigenvalues) from Table 8.4, and the factor 10^{-8} adjusts for the fact that the volatilities in Table 8.1 are expressed in basis points (1 basis point = 10^{-4}). This formula for the portfolio variance does not include any covariance terms because the principal components are uncorrelated. Also, because the covariance matrix in Table 8.2 is expressed in annual terms, the λ_is and this portfolio variance also are in annual terms. The monthly portfolio variance and volatility are then $0.007797/12 = 6.4973 \times 10^{-4}$ and $\sqrt{0.007797/12} = 0.02549$, or 2.549% of the value of the portfolio.

The formula for the delta-normal value-at-risk is

$$\text{VaR} = -k(E[\text{return}] - \text{portfolio volatility}),$$

where as usual the constant k is determined by the confidence level of the value-at-risk. One remaining detail is that we need the expected changes in the bond prices, which in turn depend on the expected changes in the principal components. The expected changes in the principal components can be computed using equation (8.15) along with a model giving the expected changes in interest rates x, and the expected rate of return on the portfolio is given by $E[\text{return}] = \beta_{p1}E[p_1] + \beta_{p2}E[p_2] + \beta_{p3}E[p_3]$. Rather than go through these steps, for simplicity we assume that the expected rate of return on the portfolio is 1/2% per month. Using this assumption, the monthly volatility computed above, and a horizon of one month, the 95% confidence delta-normal value-at-risk is

$$\text{VaR} = -k(E[\text{return}] - \text{portfolio volatility})$$
$$= -1.645(0.005 - 0.0255)$$
$$= 0.0371,$$

or 3.71% of the value of the portfolio.

The benchmark-relative VaR can be computed by adjusting the portfolio to reflect a short position in the benchmark. Using the 10-year bond as a benchmark, the adjusted portfolio exposures are $\beta_{p1}^{\text{relative}} = -2.83 - (-2.55) = (-2.26)$

$\beta_{p2}^{\text{relative}} = -1.60 - (-1.08) = -0.52$, and $\beta_{p3}^{\text{relative}} = 1.10 - (-0.35) = 0.75$, and the monthly volatility is 0.0029, or 0.29% per month. Assuming that the expected relative return is zero, the benchmark-relative VaR is

$$
\begin{aligned}
\text{Relative VaR} &= -k(E[\text{relative return}] - \text{portfolio volatility}) \\
&= -1.645(0.000 - 0.0029) \\
&= 0.0048,
\end{aligned}
$$

or 0.48% per year.

USING THE PRINCIPAL COMPONENTS WITH MONTE CARLO SIMULATION

While the use of principal components in computing value-at-risk was illustrated using the delta-normal approach, the reduction in dimensionality associated with the use of principal components comes into its own with the Monte Carlo simulation approach, and especially in modifications—such as grid Monte Carlo (see Chapter 15)—intended to reduce the computational burden of the Monte Carlo simulation.

To use principal components in a Monte Carlo simulation, one would start by decomposing the covariance matrix into its eigenvalues and eigenvectors, as illustrated above. The simulation is then carried out by drawing pseudo-random realizations of the underlying random variables ε_i and then using equation (8.12) to compute the random changes in the key rates x. Then, the changes in the key rates are given by $x + m$, where m is a vector of the expected changes in interest rates, as estimated by an appropriate model. (Recall that most of this chapter, including equation (8.12), uses the simplifying assumption that the expected changes in interest rates are zero. This assumption is likely adequate for computing value-at-risk over short holding periods but may not be adequate for longer holding periods. When it is not adequate, it is necessary to adjust x to reflect the expected changes in interest rates.) Given the simulated changes in key rates $x + m$, the rates for all maturities can be interpolated from the key rates. Once the rates for all maturities have been computed, the various instruments in the portfolio can be valued. Repeating the process the requisite number of times yields the distribution of profit and loss and the value-at-risk.

LIMITATIONS OF THE USE OF PRINCIPAL COMPONENTS

The key advantage of principal components, the reduction in dimensionality, is also its most important limitation. The reduction in dimensionality inherently means that some risks are not measured. For example, restricting attention to the first three principal components implies that the value-at-risk captures only the risks of changes in the level, slope, and curvature of the yield curve. More complicated yield curve reshapings are assumed to be impossible. While in many situations this is reasonable because such complicated yield curve reshapings account for only a small fraction of the portfolio risk, restricting attention to the first few principal components treats these events as impossible, when in fact they can happen.

The error in measuring risk resulting from the reduction of dimensionality is likely not a problem for most investment portfolios, because the bulk of the risk of such portfolios typically stems from their exposures to the first three principal components: changes in the level, slope, and curvature of the yield curve (in addition to spread risks). However, the error resulting from the reduction in dimensionality can be a problem for well-hedged portfolios. Once changes in the level and slope of the term structure have been hedged, the remaining risk in the portfolio will be due to more complicated yield curve reshapings. These are precisely the risks that are not captured by the first few principal components. In other forms, this problem pervades risk measurement systems. All risk measurement systems involve some simplification and reduction in dimensionality and thus omit some risks; if these omitted risks are important for the portfolio, the value-at-risk will be understated.

The interaction of the reduction in dimensionality and hedging is particularly a problem for grid Monte Carlo approaches based on principal components. In such approaches, one strategy for reducing the computational burden of portfolio revaluations is to use a cruder grid for the second and third principal components. The justification is that these components explain a much smaller proportion of the variability in interest rates; thus, there is little cost to using a crude approximation to measure their impact on the portfolio value. But if the effect of the first one or two principal components is hedged, then the risk of the portfolio is due primarily to the second principal component, or the combination of the second and third. In this case, measuring the impact of the second and third principal components on the value of the portfolio using a crude approximation can have a significant impact on the value-at-risk.

NOTES

Numerous books on multivariate statistics discuss the principal components decomposition, for example Anderson (1984), Joliffe (1986), and Mardia, Kent, and Bibby (1979), and it is implemented in most statistical software packages.

This chapter approached the principal components decomposition as a particular kind of factor model, and equation (8.9) was interpreted as saying that the principal components p_1 and p_2 explain the random vector x through the factor loadings v_{if}. However, the principal components decomposition is equivalent to a decomposition of the covariance matrix into its eigenvectors and eigenvalues, and these need not be given a statistical interpretation. In mathematical terms, the vectors $v_1 = (v_{11}\ v_{21})'$ and $v_2 = (v_{21}\ v_{22})'$ make up an orthonormal basis for $\Re^2$ (or more generally, $\Re^K$), which can be seen from equation (8.9) expressing the vector $x = (x_1\ x_2)'$ in terms of the two orthogonal vectors $v_1 = (v_{11}\ v_{21})'$ and $v_2 = (v_{21}\ v_{22})'$ and the coefficients p_1 and p_2. Eigenvectors and eigenvalues are developed in this way in many books on linear algebra, which are too numerous to mention here.

Litterman and Scheinkman (1991) was one of the first papers carrying out the principal components decomposition of changes in the term structure of interest rates. Since then, the use of principal components in modeling changes in interest rates has become standard, appearing for example in Golub and Tilman (2000), Hull (2000), James and Webber (2000), Jarrow (1996), Rebanoto (1998), Wilson (1994), and many others. Frye (1997), Golub, and Tilman (1997) and Singh (1997) were among the first to describe the use of principal components in computing value-at-risk. Principal components grid Monte Carlo is described by Frye (1998).

Multiple term structures in different currencies can be handled either by finding a set of principal components that explains the common variation across multiple term structures, as in Niffikeer, Hewins, and Flavell (2000), or by carrying out a principal components decomposition of each term structure. As above, the K principal components that describe each term structure will be uncorrelated with each other; however, the principal components of the term structures for different currencies will be correlated. In general, all of the principal components will be correlated with changes in exchange rates. Reflecting these nonzero correlations, the covariance matrix used in the value-at-risk calculation will not be diagonal. While this does add some complexity, the advantage of the separate decompositions of each market vis-à-vis a single "simultaneous" principal components decomposition of all world fixed-income markets is that the market factors (the principal components) resulting from the separate decompositions will produce the market factors most useful for the separate risk analyses of each market. In particular, the separate decompositions will yield for each market principal components that have natural interpretations as level, slope, and curvature.

CHAPTER 9

Stress Testing

After considering all of the issues, your organization has chosen a method and computed the value-at-risk. Using a critical probability of α or confidence level of $1-\alpha$, the value-at-risk over the chosen holding period is consistent with your organization's risk appetite. You have also decomposed the risk and confirmed that you are within budgeted limits. You are almost ready to relax. But before you manage to sneak out the door, your boss finds you with a series of questions: "What happens in extreme market conditions?" "When the value-at-risk is exceeded, just how large can the losses be?" And finally, "What risks have been left out of the VaR?"

Stress testing provides partial answers to these questions. The phrase *stress testing* is a general rubric for performing a set of analyses to investigate the effects of extreme market conditions. Stress testing involves three basic steps. (i) The process usually begins with a set of extreme, or *stressed*, market scenarios. These might be created from actual past events, such as the Russian government default during August 1998; possible future market crises, such as a collapse of a major financial institution that leads to a "flight to quality"; or stylized scenarios, such as assumed five or 10 standard deviation moves in market rates or prices. (ii) For each scenario, one then determines the changes in the prices of the financial instruments in the portfolio and sums them to determine the change in portfolio value. (iii) Finally, one typically prepares a summary of the results showing the estimated level of mark-to-market gain or loss for each stress scenario and the portfolios or market sectors in which the loss would be concentrated.

It seems clear that such analyses can provide useful information beyond the value-at-risk estimate. Most obviously, value-at-risk does not provide information on the magnitude of the losses when the value-at-risk is exceeded. Due to possible nonlinearities in the portfolio value, one cannot reliably estimate such losses by extrapolating beyond the value-at-risk estimate. Further, to say that the $1 - \alpha$ confidence value-at-risk over a horizon of one month is only a small percentage z of the portfolio value does not reveal what will happen in the event of a stock market crash. It

135

could mean that the portfolio has no exposure to a stock market crash, or it could mean that it has a significant exposure but that the probability of a crash (and all other events that result in a loss greater than z) is less than α.

Second, the value-at-risk estimate provides no information about the direction of the risk exposure. For example, if the value-at-risk is z, the risk manager does not know whether a loss of this magnitude is realized in a stock market decline or in a sudden rise in prices.

Value-at-risk also says nothing about the risk due to factors that are omitted from the value-at-risk model, either for reasons of simplicity or due to lack of data. For example, the value-at-risk model might include only a single yield curve for a particular currency, thereby implicitly assuming that the changes in the prices of government and corporate bonds of the same maturity move together. Even if it includes multiple yield curves, it may not include sufficient detail on credit and maturity spreads to capture the risks in the portfolio.

Stress tests address these shortcomings by directly simulating portfolio performance conditional on particular changes in market rates and prices. Because the scenarios used in stress testing can involve changes in market rates and prices of any size, stress tests can capture the effect of large market moves whose frequency or likelihood cannot reliably be estimated. Combined with appropriate valuation models, they also capture the effect of options and other instruments whose values are nonlinear functions of the market factors. Because they examine specific selected scenarios, stress tests are easy for consumers of risk estimates to understand and enable meaningful participation in discussion of the risks in the portfolio. Provided that the results are presented with sufficiently fine granularity, stress tests allow portfolio and risk managers to identify and structure hedges of the unacceptable exposures. Finally, a consistent set of stress tests run on multiple portfolios can identify unacceptable concentrations of risk in extreme scenarios.

Despite recent advances in approaches to stress testing, there is no standard way to stress test a portfolio, no standard set of scenarios to consider, and even no standard approach for generating scenarios. This chapter illustrates a number of available approaches for constructing stress scenarios using the example equity portfolio discussed previously in Chapters 3, 5, and 6. As described there, this portfolio includes a cash position in large capitalization U.S. equities, a short position in S&P 500 index futures contracts, written S&P 500 index call options, a long position in FT-SE 100 index futures contracts, and written FT-SE 100 index options. As a result, it has exposures to the S&P 500 index, the FT-SE 100 index, and the dollar/pound exchange rate.

CONSTRUCTING STRESS SCENARIOS

The most challenging aspect of stress testing is generating credible extreme market scenarios that are relevant to current portfolio positions. Which market factors should be changed, and by how much? The scenarios need to consider both the magnitudes of the movements of the individual market factors and the interrelationships (correlations) among them. For example, suppose the stress scenario is a U.S. stock market crash accompanied by a flight to quality, defined as a decrease in the yields on U.S. government obligations. Should the assumed decline in the S&P 500 index be 10, 20, or 30%? By just how much do U.S. Treasury yields decline in the event of a flight to quality? If one settles on an assumed 20% decline in the S&P 500 and a 50 basis point decline in U.S. Treasury yields, what should one assume about the returns on other stock market indexes, either in the United States or overseas? What should one assume about changes in commodity prices, exchange rates, and other interest rates and bond market spreads?

The sheer number of market factors makes this exercise complicated, because a stress scenario needs to specify what happens to every market factor. To do this in an internally consistent and sensible way can be difficult. There exist a number of approaches, of varying degrees of sophistication, to generate scenarios.

USING ACTUAL PAST MARKET EVENTS

A defensible approach is to base stress scenarios on actual past extreme market events. In this approach, one generates the stress scenario by assuming that the changes in market factors are identical to those that were experienced during the past event. For the example portfolio, it is natural to use the October 1987 U.S. stock market crash and to use a horizon that matches what we have generally been using to estimate value-at-risk: one month. During October 1987, the S&P 500 index fell by 21.76%, the FT-SE 100 fell by 26.04%, and the U.S. dollar price of a U.K. pound rose from 1.6255 to 1.7220, or 5.94%. In this scenario, the cash S&P position and long FT-SE futures position lose heavily, with these losses being offset by the S&P futures and options and the FT-SE options. Overall, the value of the portfolio declines by approximately $18 million, or 17.5% of its initial value. This calculation is shown in the column of Table 9.1 headed "Actual."

Other examples of actual extreme market events include the 1992 exchange rate crisis, the changes in U.S. dollar interest rates during the spring

TABLE 9.1 Example Stress Tests

	Initial Value	Actual (Oct. 1987)	Zero-Out	Predictive	Stressed Covariances
Market Factors:					
S&P 500	1097.6	858.73	879.10	878.1	878.1
FT-SE 100	5862.3	4335.5	5862.30	5214.1	4886.1
USD/GBP	1.6271	1.7237	1.6271	1.6190	1.5946
Position Values:					
Cash S&P 500 Position	110,000,000	86,060,653	88,102,667	88,000,000	88,000,000
S&P 500 Futures	0	12,240,026	11,210,175	11,261,953	11,134,969
S&P 500 Options	−5,052,759	−66,920	−115,434	−112,435	−220,767
FT-SE 100 Futures	0	−13,438,302	−136,709	−5,437,106	−7,890,540
FT-SE 100 Options	−3,462,022	−18,381	−3,024,496	−677,671	−365,557
Total	101,485,220	84,777,075	96,036,203	93,034,742	90,658,105
$ Gain/Loss		−16,708,145	−5,449,017	−8,450,478	−10,827,115
% Gain/Loss		−16.5	−5.4	−8.3	−10.7

of 1994, the 1995 Mexican crisis, the East Asian crisis during the summer of 1997, the Russian devaluation of August 1998 and its aftermath, and the Brazilian devaluation of 1999. An advantage of using past events is that it is clear that such events can happen; it is difficult to dismiss them as impossible or unrealistic. Another advantage is that the past event provides all of the market factors, provided they were captured and stored. A perhaps obvious disadvantage is that the historical event may not be relevant to the current portfolio.

APPLYING ASSUMED SHOCKS TO MARKET FACTORS: ZERO-OUT STRESS SCENARIOS

A simple approach to generate stress scenarios is to apply assumed shocks to certain key or core market factors. This approach provides the flexibility of allowing one to consider shocks of any size and also to examine the effect of changing either individual market factors or small groups of factors. The other peripheral market factors are handled by assuming that they do not change, that is, they are *zeroed-out*. For our example portfolio, assuming that the S&P 500 declines by 20% and zeroing-out the changes in the FT-SE 100 and dollar/pound exchange rate results in a loss of approximately $5.7 million, or about 5.5% of the initial value of the portfolio. As shown in the column of Table 9.1 headed "Zero-Out," the S&P positions account for the bulk of the changes in value. (There are small gains and losses on the FT-SE positions despite the fact that the FT-SE 100 is zeroed-out due to the dependence of futures and options prices on time. This is the only dimension in which the horizon length affects the zero-out stress test.)

This approach has the advantages of simplicity and ease of implementation. However, its lack of realism is a clear disadvantage, which is made clear by comparing the zero-out scenario to the actual scenario: zeroing out the other factors means neglecting the losses on the FT-SE positions. In fixed-income and commodity markets, thoughtless application of this approach can even result in market rates and prices that imply the existence of arbitrage opportunities.

APPLYING ASSUMED SHOCKS TO MARKET FACTORS: ANTICIPATORY STRESS SCENARIOS

A less mechanical approach is to develop stress scenarios by specifying a possible market, economic, or political event and then thinking through the event's implications for all major markets. For example, a Middle East crisis that spreads to the Persian Gulf region and causes a sudden spike in oil prices would almost certainly have effects on the equity markets, interest rates, and exchange rates of the major industrial countries. One would think through all of these interrelated effects and specify the magnitudes of the changes in the various market factors. Because thinking carefully about hundreds of market factors is not a sensible use of time, at some point the peripheral market factors would be either zeroed-out or else computed mechanically using the covariance matrix, as in the predictive stress test described next.

A benefit of this approach is that it at least offers the possibility of designing realistic stress scenarios that are relevant for the current market environment. But this issue cuts both ways. Stress tests are useful only if they use extreme scenarios that the users consider plausible; stress tests involving extreme scenarios too remote to be worthy of attention are of little value. Sophisticated methodology offers little help here and cannot substitute for the judgment of the risk manager. Further, the credibility of the stress tests and the weight placed on them may depend on the rhetorical skills of risk managers in convincing their superiors of the plausibility of the market scenarios.

PREDICTIVE ANTICIPATORY STRESS SCENARIOS

Once the stress scenarios for the core risk factors have been specified, statistical tools can be used to determine the scenarios for other factors. The *predictive stress test* generates scenarios by combining assumed changes in the core risk factors with the covariance matrix of changes in the market factors to compute the changes in the peripheral market factors. For example, suppose the stress scenario is a U.S. stock market crash, defined as a 20% decline in the S&P 500. Rather than set the changes in the other market factors equal to zero or specify them in an ad hoc fashion, the predictive stress test would use the covariance matrix (and expected changes, if these are nonzero) of the market factors to compute the conditional expectations of the peripheral market factors and then set them equal to their conditional expectations.

This exercise requires a fact about conditional expectations. Suppose there are K market factors taking values $x = (x_1, x_2, \ldots, x_K)'$, with a $K \times K$ covariance matrix Σ and means given by a $K \times 1$ vector μ. The first $H < K$ market factors are the core factors that will be specified directly in the stress test, while the other $H - K$ are the peripheral factors that will be computed based on the assumed changes in the first H.

Partition the vector x into the core and peripheral market factors $x^{\text{core}} = (x_1, x_2, \ldots, x_H)'$ and $x^{\text{periph.}} = (x_{H+1}, x_{H+2}, \ldots, x_K)'$, with expected values μ^{core} and $\mu^{\text{periph.}}$, respectively. Similarly, partition the covariance matrix Σ as

$$ \Sigma = \begin{bmatrix} A & B \\ B' & D \end{bmatrix}, $$

where A is the $H \times H$ covariance matrix of the core market factors, D is the $(K - H) \times (K - H)$ covariance matrix of the peripheral market factors, and B is the $H \times (K - H)$ matrix formed from the covariances between the core and peripheral factors. Given the outcomes for the core market factors x^{core}, the conditional expected values of the peripheral market factors are given by

$$E[x^{\text{periph.}}|x^{\text{core}}] = \mu^{\text{periph.}} + B'A^{-1}(x^{\text{core}} - \mu^{\text{core}})$$
$$= \mu^{\text{periph.}} - B'A^{-1}\mu^{\text{core}} + B'A^{-1}\mu^{\text{core}}. \tag{9.1}$$

If the unconditional expected changes μ^{core} and $\mu^{\text{periph.}}$ are treated as zero, this simplifies to

$$E[x^{\text{periph.}}|x^{\text{core}}] = B'A^{-1}x^{\text{core}}. \tag{9.2}$$

Equation (9.1) has a nice intuitive interpretation. Consider

$$E[x_{H+j}|x^{\text{core}}],$$

the jth element of the vector of conditional expectations $E[x^{\text{periph.}}|x^{\text{core}}]$. Equation (9.1) says that

$$E[x_{H+j}|x^{\text{core}}] = E[x_{H+j}] - [\sigma_{1,H+j} \quad \sigma_{2,H+j} \quad \cdots \quad \sigma_{H,H+j}]A^{-1}E[x^{\text{core}}]$$
$$+ [\sigma_{1,H+j} \quad \sigma_{2,H+j} \quad \cdots \quad \sigma_{H,H+j}]A^{-1}x^{\text{core}}$$
$$= \beta_{H+j,0} + \sum_{i=1}^{H}\beta_{H+j,i}x_i,$$

where the intercept

$$\beta_{H+j,0} = E[x_{H+j}] - [\sigma_{1,H+j} \quad \sigma_{2,H+j} \quad \cdots \quad \sigma_{H,H+j}]A^{-1}E[x^{\text{core}}]$$

and each coefficient $\beta_{H+j,i}$ is the ith element of the vector

$$[\sigma_{1,H+j} \quad \sigma_{2,H+j} \quad \cdots \quad \sigma_{H,H+j}]A^{-1}.$$

Examination of virtually any econometrics or multivariate statistics book (and recognition that $b'A^{-1}x^{\text{core}} = (x^{\text{core}})'A^{-1}b$ for all vectors b) reveals that $\beta_{H+j,i}$ is the ith slope coefficient in the regression of the jth peripheral factor x_{H+j} on the core market factors, and $\beta_{H+j,0}$ is the intercept. Thus, the values of the peripheral factors in the predictive stress tests are the forecasts of these market factors that would be obtained by regressing each of the peripheral market factors on the core market factors.

In our example, we treat the S&P 500 as the core market factor and the FT-SE 100 and exchange rate as the peripheral factors. Thus, we have

$$A = \sigma_1^2, \quad B = [\sigma_1\sigma_2\rho_{12} \quad \sigma_1\sigma_3\rho_{13}],$$

and

$$
D = \begin{bmatrix} \sigma_2^2 & \sigma_2\sigma_3\rho_{23} \\ \sigma_2\sigma_3\rho_{23} & \sigma_3^2 \end{bmatrix}.
$$

Equation (9.1) reduces to

$$
E[x_2 \,|\, x_1] = \mu_2 - \frac{\sigma_1\sigma_2\rho_{12}}{\sigma_1^2}(\mu_1) + \frac{\sigma_1\sigma_2\rho_{12}}{\sigma_1^2}(x_1),
$$

$$
E[x_3 \,|\, x_1] = \mu_3 - \frac{\sigma_1\sigma_3\rho_{13}}{\sigma_1^2}(\mu_1) + \frac{\sigma_1\sigma_3\rho_{13}}{\sigma_1^2}(x_1),
$$

where $\sigma_1\sigma_2\rho_{12}/\sigma_1^2$ and $\sigma_1\sigma_3\rho_{13}/\sigma_1^2$ are the slope coefficients that would be obtained by regressing x_2 and x_3 on x_1, $\mu_2 - (\sigma_1\sigma_2\rho_{12}/\sigma_1^2)(\mu_1)$ and $\mu_3 - (\sigma_1\sigma_3\rho_{13}/\sigma_1^2)(\mu_1)$ are the intercepts from these two regressions, and $\mu_i = E[x_i]$. Using the parameter estimates $\sigma_1 = 0.061$, $\sigma_2 = 0.065$, $\sigma_3 = 0.029$, $\rho_{12} = 0.55$, $\rho_{13} = 0.05$, $\rho_{23} = -0.30$, $\mu_1 = 0.01$, $\mu_2 = 0.0125$, and $\mu_3 = 0$, the expected percentage changes in the peripheral market factors are

$$
\begin{aligned}
E[x_2 \,|\, x_1] &= 0.0125 - \frac{0.061(0.065)(0.55)}{(0.061)^2} \times 0.01 \\
&\quad + \frac{0.061(0.065)(0.55)}{(0.061)^2} \\
&\quad \times 0.20 \\
&= -0.1106,
\end{aligned}
$$

$$
\begin{aligned}
E[x_3 \,|\, x_1] &= 0 - \frac{0.061(0.029)(0.05)}{(0.061)^2} \times 0.01 \\
&\quad + \frac{0.061(0.029)(0.05)}{(0.061)^2} \\
&\quad \times 0.20 \\
&= -0.0050.
\end{aligned}
$$

The column of Table 9.1 labelled "Predictive" shows that the loss in this scenario is $9.5 million, or 9.3% of the initial value of the portfolio. It exceeds the loss in the zero-out scenario precisely because this scenario reflects the fact that declines in the S&P 500 are typically associated with declines in the FT-SE 100 about one-half as large and with small declines in the dollar/pound exchange rate.

This is the stress loss over a one-month horizon, which is reflected by the use of the monthly means, volatilities, and correlations, and by the recognition of the time decay of the options positions. If we desire the stress loss over a different horizon, we need to use the parameters appropriate for that horizon. For example, for a one-day horizon

$$E[x_2 | x_1] = \frac{1}{21}(0.0125) - \frac{(1/21)^2}{(1/21)^2} \times \frac{0.061(0.065)(0.55)}{(0.061)^2} \times \frac{1}{21}(0.01)$$

$$+ \frac{(1/21)^2}{(1/21)^2} \times \frac{0.061(0.065)(0.55)}{(0.061)^2} \times 0.20$$

$$= -0.1169,$$

$$E[x_3 | x_1] = \frac{1}{21}(0) - \frac{0.061(0.029)(0.05)}{(0.061)^2} \times \frac{1}{21}(0.01)$$

$$+ \frac{0.061(0.029)(0.05)}{(0.061)^2} \times 0.20$$

$$= -0.0048,$$

where it is assumed that the means and volatilities are proportional to the length of the horizon and the correlations do not depend on the horizon. Note that under these assumptions the length of the horizon has little effect on the market factors x_2 and x_3, and almost the same values would be obtained by treating the means as zero. The stress loss is approximately $10 million instead of $9.5 million, but only about half of the difference is due to the different market factors. The remainder is due to the difference in the time decay of the options positions with the shorter holding period.

The principal advantage of this approach is that it results in generally sensible stress scenarios that are consistent with the volatilities and correlations used in the value-at-risk calculation. The disadvantage, aside from the additional complexity relative to the zero-out approach, is that the covariance matrix may change during periods of market stress. If this is the case, then the changes in the peripheral market factors are computed using the wrong covariance matrix.

ANTICIPATORY STRESS SCENARIOS WITH "STRESS" CORRELATIONS

This last drawback can be addressed by combining the predictive stress test with a separate estimate of the covariance matrix that applies during periods of market stress. To illustrate it, we arbitrarily assume that the volatilities increase by one-half to $\sigma_1 = 1.5(0.061) = 0.0915$, $\sigma_2 = 1.5(0.065) = 0.0975$, and $\sigma_3 = 1.5(0.029) = 0.435$, and that the correlations between the S&P 500 index and the two peripheral factors increase to $\rho_{12} = 0.80$ and $\rho_{13} = 0.20$. The other correlation coefficient, $\rho_{23} = -0.30$, and the means are assumed to remain unchanged. The conditional expected percentage changes in the peripheral market factors are now

$$E[x_2 | x_1] = 0.0125 - \frac{(1.5)^2(0.061)(0.065)(0.80)}{(1.5)^2(0.061)^2} \times 0.01$$

$$+ \frac{(1.5)^2(0.061)(0.065)(0.80)}{(1.5)^2(0.061)^2} \times 0.20$$

$$= -0.1665,$$

$$E[x_3 | x_1] = 0.00 - \frac{(1.5)^2(0.061)(0.029)(0.20)}{(1.5)^2(0.061)^2} \times 0.01$$

$$+ \frac{(1.5)^2(0.061)(0.029)(0.20)}{(1.5)^2(0.061)^2} \times 0.20$$

$$= -0.0200.$$

These changes in the market factors are considerably larger, due to the higher correlations. (Note that, because only the ratios of volatilities enter the calculation, the increase in volatilities has no effect on $E[x_2 | x_1]$ and $E[x_3 | x_1]$.) The stress loss is now $12 million and is shown in the column of Table 9.1 headed "Stress Covariances."

This approach seems easy, but where does one obtain the estimates of correlations during stress scenarios? The example above simply relied on the conventional wisdom that correlations increase during periods of market stress and adjusted them in an ad hoc fashion to reflect this. A significant drawback is that this can result in nonsensical correlation and covariance matrices. This problem is further described in the next section, and methods of addressing it are described in sources cited in the notes.

An alternative, the *broken arrow stress test*, is to assume that the available data on factor changes represent a mixture of realizations from stressed and nonstressed market environments and to estimate a statistical model that allows for different covariance matrices in the different market environments. This approach results in generally sensible stress scenarios that are consistent with the data from past periods of market stress and are thus defensible. However, the complexity of the procedure is a drawback.

STRESSING VALUE-AT-RISK ESTIMATES

The rubric *stress testing* is also used to refer to analyses that examine the effects of changes in the volatilities and correlations used in value-at-risk calculations, resulting in a *stressed VaR*. Commonly, this is intended to capture the conventional wisdom that volatilities and correlations increase in periods of market stress. While volatilities can be increased or decreased like market rates or prices, a delicate issue is that seemingly natural changes in the correlation coefficients can result in correlation (and covariance) matrices that are not positive definite, resulting in predictive stress scenarios that make no sense.

Using the original volatilities and correlations, the delta-normal VaR is $1.768 million (Chapter 3) and the Monte Carlo VaR is $2.583 million (Chapter 6). With the stressed volatilities and correlations $\sigma_1 = 1.5(0.061) = 0.0915$, $\sigma_2 = 1.5(0.065) = 0.0975$, $\sigma_3 = 1.5(0.0290) = 0.435$, $\rho_{12} = 0.80$, $\rho_{13} = 0.20$, and $\rho_{23} = -0.30$ used above, the delta-normal VaR is $2.998 million and the Monte Carlo VaR is $6.722.

It is clear that such stressed value-at-risk estimates can be valuable. For example, prior to the spring and summer of 1997, the historical correlation of the Thai baht/U.S. dollar and Japanese yen/U.S. dollar exchange rates was about 0.8. All of the methods for computing value-at-risk rely on historical data and therefore assume that future volatilities and correlations will be like those observed in the past. Thus, prior to the collapse of the Thai baht in July 1997, all methods would have indicated that from the perspective of a U.S. dollar investor a long position in baht combined with a short position in yen had a relatively low value-at-risk. Yet by the end of June there was considerable speculation that the Thai currency regime would collapse and thus that, in the future, the correlation was likely to be much lower than 0.8. This circumstance cried out for stressed value-at-risk estimates computed using correlations much less than 0.8 and volatilities much greater than the historical volatility.

The problem is that seemingly reasonable changes in the correlations can result in nonsensical or even nonexistent value-at-risk estimates. The choice to set the above correlations to $\rho_{12} = 0.80$, $\rho_{13} = 0.20$, and $\rho_{23} = -0.30$ was a sensible one, that is, it resulted in a positive definite correlation matrix. All valid correlation (and covariance) matrices are positive semidefinite, and most correlation (and covariance) matrices that arise in finance are positive definite. However, the choice of $\rho_{12} = 0.90$, $\rho_{13} = 0.20$, and $\rho_{23} = -0.30$, which at first glance seems equally reasonable, results in a correlation matrix that is not positive semidefinite. Intuitively, if the first two factors are very highly correlated, then ρ_{13} must be close to ρ_{23}, and the correlations $\rho_{13} = 0.20$ and $\rho_{23} = -0.30$ are not close enough. In the extreme case, when the first two factors are perfectly correlated, we must have $\rho_{13} = \rho_{23}$. The financial implication of a correlation (covariance) matrix that is not positive definite is that it is possible to form negative-variance portfolios, which makes no sense. The financial implication of a correlation (covariance) matrix that is positive semidefinite but not positive definite is that it is possible to form zero-variance portfolios, or equivalently, that some combination of the assets is a perfect hedge for another combination of the assets.

With three factors, the requirement that the correlation (covariance) matrix be positive definite does not present a significant problem, because it is both easy to check whether a three-by-three covariance matrix is positive definite and easy to see and understand the nature of this constraint. However, the problem is more severe the larger the number of factors. Seemingly reasonable changes to the correlation matrix can easily result in correlation and covariance matrices that are not positive semidefinite and value-at-risk estimates that are nonsensical, or, if the Monte Carlo method is used, nonexistent. A source cited in the notes explains one approach to addressing this problem.

STRESSING FACTORS LEFT OUT OF THE MODEL

None of the value-at-risk calculations in this book treats option-implied volatilities as market factors, which is a common modeling choice. But changes in option-implied volatilities, and sometimes large changes, are observed. Stress tests can be used to assess the exposure to factors such as these that are not included in the value-at-risk model. The demands of simplicity, tractability, and data availability also typically require that the value-at-risk model make simplifying assumptions that certain interest rate and commodity price spreads are constant, while the mapping procedure assumes that cost-of-carry relationships between spot and futures markets hold. The exposure to the risk of changes in such relationships can be examined using stress tests.

PORTFOLIO-SPECIFIC STRESS TESTS

None of the procedures discussed so far guarantees that the stress tests are relevant for the current portfolio. For our example, it is clear that the loss is greatest with a simultaneous sharp fall in both S&P 500 and FT-SE 100, together with an increase in implied volatilities (because the portfolio involves written options). Another stress-testing approach searches for stress scenarios by analyzing the vulnerabilities of the portfolio in question. These may be identified by conducting a historical or Monte Carlo simulation on a portfolio and searching for all scenarios that cause a loss exceeding a high threshold. If this is used as the stress test scenario, this amounts to asking what scenarios cause the VaR. Alternatively, it can be used as the basis for constructing an extreme stress scenario. For example, if the Monte Carlo simulation indicates that the portfolio is exposed to a yield curve twist, one can use stress tests that involve severe yield curve twists.

OTHER ISSUES IN DESIGNING GOOD STRESS TESTS

The discussion above focused on designing sensible stress scenarios that are relevant to both the current portfolio and the current market environment. This point is worth emphasizing: the success of stress testing depends crucially upon the selection of sensible scenarios. The only meaningful stress scenarios are those that could occur in the current market environment.

Useful stress tests also reveal the details of the exposures, for example, which positions are responsible for the profits and losses. Absent this information, it is difficult to identify which positions to eliminate or hedge in order to reduce any undesirable exposures. In fact, a great part of the value of stress testing stems precisely from the process of systematically thinking through the effects of shocks on different positions and markets and what can be done to ameliorate them.

In addition, organizations whose risk-management strategies depend on the ability to frequently adjust or rebalance their portfolios need to consider the impact of crises on market liquidity, because it may be difficult or impossible to execute transactions at reasonable bid/ask spreads during crises. Finally, organizations that use futures contracts to hedge relatively illiquid securities or other financial instruments should consider the cash flow requirements of the futures contracts. Gains or losses on futures contracts are received or paid immediately, while gains or losses on other instruments are often not received or paid until the positions are closed out. Thus, using futures contracts to hedge the changes in the values of other instruments can lead to timing mismatches between when funds are required and when they are received.

A common criticism of stress tests is that stress tests as usually conducted are not probabilistic and thus lie outside the value-at-risk framework. The typically subjective choice of stress scenarios complicates external review of a stress-testing program, and the failure to assign probabilities renders back testing impossible. In response to these concerns, various methods of attaching probabilities to stress scenarios have been proposed. While these approaches provide either objectivity or its appearance, they are a step away from stress testing, back toward the computation of value-at-risk using a low probability or high confidence level. While extreme tail value-at-risk estimates are useful, stress testing is a distinct activity.

NOTES

The zero-out and historical stress test approaches have been standard (see e.g., Kupiec 1998) for some time. Kupiec (1998) proposes the use of predictive stress scenarios and also discusses the possibility of combining them with stressed volatilities and correlations. All of these approaches are implemented in at least some risk measurement software. The more recent *broken arrow stress test* is due to Kim and Finger (2000).

Finger (1997) proposes an approach for modifying parts of a correlation matrix while ensuring that the matrix remains positive definite. The drawback, pointed out by Brooks, Scott-Quinn, and Whalmsey (1998), is that the property of positive definiteness is maintained by changing the other parts of the correlation matrix in an unintuitive and uncontrolled fashion. Rebonato and Jäckel (1999/2000) present an efficient method for constructing a valid correlation matrix that is as close as possible to a desired target correlation matrix, where closeness can be defined in a number of different ways. They also explain how principal components analysis can be used to obtain easily approximately the same correlation matrix as their proposed approach.

The conventional wisdom is that correlations increase during periods of market stress. For example, Alan Greenspan's oft-quoted speech on measuring financial risk includes the phrase, ". . . joint distributions estimated over periods without panics will misestimate the degree of asset correlation between asset returns during panics," while Bookstaber (1997) writes, "During periods of market stress, correlations increase dramatically." Brooks and Persand (2000) document the existence of such changes in measured correlations. However, the correct interpretation of such statements and evidence is delicate. They are certainly correct if understood to mean that the measured correlations are higher when returns are large; however, it is not clear that the distributions generating the data actually change.

Boyer, Gibson, and Loretan (1997) show that apparent correlation breakdowns can be found in data for which the true underlying distribution has a constant correlation coefficient. Specifically, they derive an expression for the conditional correlation coefficient of data generated from a bivariate normal distribution and find that the conditional correlation is larger when one conditions on large rather than small returns. Thus, one expects measured correlations to be larger during periods of high returns or market volatility, even if the distribution generating the data has not changed. A similar result is cited by Ronn, Sayrak, and Tompaidis (2000), who credit Stambaugh (1995) for it. Boyer, Gibson, and Loretan (1999) find no evidence for nonconstant correlations in a limited empirical analysis of exchange rate changes, while Cizeau, Potters, and Bouchaud (2001) argue that a simple non-Gaussian one-factor model with time-independent correlations can capture the high measured correlations among equity returns observed during extreme market movements. In contrast, Kim and Finger (2000) estimate a specific (mixture of distributions) model that allows for correlation changes and find evidence of such changes for four of the 18 market factors they consider. Thus, there is evidence of correlation changes, though overall the evidence argues against their ubiquity.

Berkowitz (1999/2000) argues that the typically subjective choice of stress scenarios makes external review of a stress-testing program difficult, and the failure to assign probabilities renders back testing impossible. In response to these concerns, Berkowitz proposes that risk managers explicitly assign (perhaps subjective) probabilities to stress scenarios and then combine the resulting stress distribution with the factor distribution for normal market conditions to generate a single forecast distribution. He argues that this will impose needed discipline on the risk manager and enable back testing. This approach is also advocated by Aragonés, Blanco, and Dowd (2001). Similar approaches are suggested by Cherubini and Della Lunga (1999) and Zangari (2000), who use Bayesian tools to combine subjective stress scenarios with historical data.

A different approach is taken by Longin (2000), who proposes the use of *extreme value theory* (see chapter 16) to model the extreme tails of the distribution of returns. As discussed there, multivariate extreme value theory is not well developed, and current proposals for using EVT involve fitting the tails of the distribution of portfolio returns, without consideration of the detail that causes these returns. A limitation is that this amounts to an extreme tail VaR and thereby sacrifices some of the benefits of stress testing.

Risk Decomposition and Risk Budgeting

Decomposing Risk

Risk decomposition was introduced in Chapter 2 in the context of a simple equity portfolio exposed to two market factors. The next few chapters turn to more realistic examples of the use of risk decomposition, without which risk budgeting cannot exist. As a preliminary, this chapter summarizes the mathematics of risk decomposition. Risk decomposition is crucial to risk budgeting, because the aggregate value-at-risk of the pension plan, or other organization, is far removed from the portfolio managers. At the risk of stating the obvious, the portfolio managers have control over only their own portfolios. For them, meaningful risk budgets are expressed in terms of their contributions to portfolio risk.

In fact, meaningful use of value-at-risk in portfolio management almost requires risk decomposition. Value-at-risk, or any other risk measure, is useful only to the extent that one understands the sources of risk. For example, how much of the aggregate risk is due to each of the asset classes? If we change the allocations to asset classes, what will be the effect on risk? Alternatively, how much of the risk is due to each portfolio manager? How much is due to tracking error? Is it true that the hedge fund managers do not add to the overall risk of the portfolio? All of these questions can be answered by considering risk decomposition. This chapter first describes risk decomposition and then turns to another issue, the model for expected returns.

RISK DECOMPOSITION

Let $w = (w_1, w_2, \ldots, w_N)'$ denote the vector of portfolio weights on N assets, instruments, asset classes, or managers, and let $\sigma(w)$ and $\text{VaR}(w)$ denote the portfolio standard deviation and value-at-risk, which depend on the positions or weights w_i. Imagine multiplying all of the portfolio weights by the same constant, k, that is, consider the vector of portfolio weights $kw = (kw_1, kw_2, \ldots, kw_N)'$ and the associated portfolio standard deviation $\sigma(kw)$ and value-at-risk $\text{VaR}(kw)$. A key property of the portfolio standard deviation is that scaling all positions by the common factor k scales the standard deviation by the same factor, implying $\sigma(kw) = k\sigma(w)$. This is also true of the value-at-risk, because scaling every position by k clearly scales every profit or loss by k, and thus scales the value-at-risk by k.

In mathematical terminology, the result that $\text{VaR}(kw) = k\text{VaR}(w)$ for $k > 0$ means that function giving the value-at-risk is *homogenous of degree 1*, or *linear homogenous*. From a financial perspective, this property of value-at-risk is almost obvious: if one makes the same proportional change in all positions, the value-at-risk also changes proportionally.

Though very nearly obvious, this property has an important implication. If value-at-risk is linear homogenous, then Euler's law (see the notes to this chapter) implies that both the portfolio standard deviation and VaR can be decomposed as

$$\sigma(w) = \frac{\partial \sigma(w)}{\partial w_1} w_1 + \frac{\partial \sigma(w)}{\partial w_2} w_2 + \cdots + \frac{\partial \sigma(w)}{\partial w_N} w_N \qquad (10.1)$$

and

$$\text{VaR}(w) = \frac{\partial \text{VaR}(w)}{\partial w_1} w_1 + \frac{\partial \text{VaR}(w)}{\partial w_2} w_2 + \cdots + \frac{\partial \text{VaR}(w)}{\partial w_N} w_N, \qquad (10.2)$$

respectively. The ith partial derivative, $\partial\sigma(w)/\partial w_i$ or $\partial\text{VaR}(w)/\partial w_i$, is interpreted as the effect on risk of increasing w_i by one unit; in particular, changing the ith weight by a small amount, from w_i to w_i^*, changes the risk by approximately $(\partial\sigma(w)/\partial w_i)(w_i^* - w_i)$, or $(\partial\text{VaR}(w)/\partial w_i)(w_i^* - w_i)$. The ith term, $(\partial\sigma(w)/\partial w_i)w_i$ or $(\partial\text{VaR}(w)/\partial w_i)w_i$, is called the *risk contribution* of the ith position and can be interpreted as measuring the effect of percentage changes in the portfolio weight w_i. For example, the change from w_i to w_i^* is a percentage change of $(w_i^* - w_i)/w_i$, and the change in portfolio standard deviation resulting from this change in the portfolio weight is

$$\frac{\partial \sigma(w)}{\partial w_i}(w_i^* - w_i) = \frac{\partial \sigma(w)}{\partial w_i} w_i \times \frac{(w_i^* - w_i)}{w_i},$$

the product of the risk contribution and the percentage change in the weight.

A key feature of the risk contributions is that they sum to the portfolio risk, permitting the portfolio risk to be decomposed into the risk contributions of the N positions w_i. Similarly, we can define $((\partial\sigma(w)/\partial w_i)w_i)/\sigma(w)$ or $((\partial\text{VaR}(w)/\partial w_i)w_i)/\text{VaR}(w)$ to be the percentage contribution to portfolio risk of the ith position. It is straightforward to compute these risk contributions when risk is measured by standard deviation. Computing the derivative with respect to the ith portfolio weight,

$$\frac{\partial\sigma(w)}{\partial w_i} = \frac{\sum_{j=1}^{N} w_i \,\text{cov}(r_i,r_j)}{\sigma(w)}, \tag{10.3}$$

where the numerator $\sum_{j=1}^{N} w_i \,\text{cov}\,(r_i,r_j)$, is the covariance between the return r_i and the portfolio return $\sum_{i=1}^{N} w_j r_j$. Thus, the risk contribution of the ith position or asset

$$\frac{\partial\sigma(w)}{\partial w_i} w_i = \frac{\sum_{j=1}^{N} w_i \,\text{cov}(r_i,r_j)}{\sigma(w)} w_i$$

is proportional to the covariance between the return on the ith position and the portfolio, and is zero either when that position is uncorrelated with the portfolio or when the weight $w_i = 0$. The percentage contribution to portfolio risk is

$$\frac{\partial\sigma(w)}{\partial w_i} \frac{w_i}{\sigma(w)} = \frac{\sum_{j=1}^{N} w_i \,\text{cov}(r_i,r_j)}{\sigma^2(w)} w_i$$
$$= \beta_i \omega_i,$$

where β_i is the regression coefficient, or beta, of the ith market return on the return of the portfolio. By construction, the weighted sum of the betas is 100% or one, that is, $\sum_{i=1}^{12} \beta_i w_i = 1$. This is exactly analogous to the standard result in portfolio theory that the market beta of one is the weighted average of the betas of the stocks constituting the market.

Decomposing delta-normal value-at-risk is almost equally easy. Recognizing that delta-normal VaR is of the form

$$\text{VaR}(w) = -\left[\sum_{i=1}^{N} w_i E[r_i] - k\sigma(w)\right],$$

the ith partial derivative and risk contribution of the ith asset are

$$\frac{\partial \text{VaR}(w)}{\partial w_i} = -E[r_i] + k\frac{\partial \sigma(w)}{\partial w_i}$$

and

$$\frac{\partial \text{VaR}(w)}{\partial w_i} w_i = -E[r_i]w_i + k\frac{\partial \sigma(w)}{\partial w_i} w_i,$$

respectively. The only difference (besides the constant k) between this and equation (10.3) is the expected return component $-E[r_i]w_i$, which appears because larger expected returns shift the distribution upward and reduce the probability of loss.

The key insight from these results is that the risk contribution of a position crucially depends on the covariance of that position with the existing portfolio. This covariance is zero when the position is uncorrelated with the existing portfolio, in which case the risk contribution is zero. When the correlation is positive, the risk contribution is positive; when it is negative, the position serves as a hedge, and the risk contribution is negative.

In interpreting risk decomposition, it is crucial to keep in mind that it is a marginal analysis; a small change in the portfolio weight from w_i to w_i^* changes the risk by approximately $(\partial \sigma(w)/\partial w_i)(w_i^* - w_i)$, or $(\partial \text{VaR}(w)/\partial w_i)(w_i^* - w_i)$. Alternatively, if the risk decomposition indicates that the ith position accounts for one-half of the risk, increasing that position by a small percentage will increase risk as much as increasing all other positions by the same percentage. The marginal effects cannot be extrapolated to large changes, because the partial derivatives $\partial \sigma(w)/\partial w_i$ and $\partial \text{VaR}(w)/\partial w_i$ change as the position sizes change. In terms of correlations, a large change in market position changes the correlation between the portfolio and that market. For example, if the ith market is uncorrelated with the current portfolio, the risk contribution of a small change in the allocation to the ith market is zero. However, as the allocation to the ith market increases, that market constitutes a larger fraction of the portfolio and the portfolio is no longer uncorrelated with the ith market. Thus, the risk contribution of the ith market increases as the position in that market is increased.

RISK DECOMPOSITION FOR HISTORICAL AND MONTE CARLO SIMULATION

The expression $(\partial \text{VaR}(w)/\partial w_i)(w_i)$ for the risk contribution of the ith position suggests computing the risk contributions by perturbing the position weights w_i by small amounts and then recomputing the value-at-risk to obtain estimates of the partial derivatives $\partial \text{VaR}(w)/\partial w_i$ and then multiplying by the weights w_i. While it is a natural first thought, there are two severe disadvantages to this approach. First, if there are N positions, this requires $N + 1$ VaR calculations. Given that the computational burden is a significant drawback of the Monte Carlo approach, this is unappealing. Second, even if the computational burden does not rule out that approach, in practice the simulation error is too large to permit an accurate estimate of the partial derivatives and risk contributions. However, all is not lost, as a good approach is available.

Trivially, the value-at-risk estimate can be characterized as the (negative of the) expected loss, conditional on the set of scenarios such that the (negative of the) expected loss is equal to the VaR. For example, if we compute a 95%-confidence value-at-risk using 100 simulation trials, the value-at-risk estimate is the loss given by the 95th worst scenario. Changing a portfolio weight w_i, then, has two effects. First, it affects the loss in the set of scenarios such that the (negative of the) expected loss is equal to the VaR. Letting $r_i^{1-\alpha}$ denote the return on the ith asset in the scenario used to compute a $(1 - \alpha)$-confidence VaR, the loss in this scenario is $\sum_{i=1}^{N} w_i r_i^{1-\alpha}$ and the effect of changing w_i on the loss in this scenario is

$$\frac{\partial \left(\sum_{i=1}^{N} w_i r_i^{1-\alpha} \right)}{\partial w_i} = r_i^{1-\alpha}. \tag{10.4}$$

Second, the change in w_i might have an effect on the scenarios used to compute the value-at-risk. A bit of thought suggests that this latter effect will be small: the probability that a very small change in one of the weights w_i causes a different scenario to be the 95th (or 950th or 9500th) worst scenario will typically be zero and will almost certainly be small. In fact, this second effect disappears in the limit as the change in $w_i \to 0$, implying that the partial derivative can be computed from (10.4). The risk contribution of the ith position is then simply

$$\frac{\partial \text{VaR}(w)}{\partial w_i} w_i = r_i^{1-\alpha} w_i. \tag{10.5}$$

If more than one scenario is used to compute the value-at-risk, the term $r_i^{1-\alpha}$ on the right-hand side of (10.5) is replaced by the average return in the scenarios used to compute the value-at-risk.

EXPECTED RETURNS: WHOSE MODEL?

Investment managers are typically interested in holding periods longer than those used by the derivatives dealers who originally developed value-at-risk. The longer holding period makes the model of expected returns more important and gives a strong push in the direction of using Monte Carlo simulation to compute VaR measures. One role of the expected-returns model is obvious through the appearance of $E[r]$ in formulas such as

$$\text{VaR} = -(E[r] - k\sigma).$$

Less obviously, the expected returns model also impacts the estimate of σ.

To see this, consider a simple example with an equity portfolio, a portfolio manager, and a risk manager, perhaps employed by a plan sponsor. The portfolio manager is skilled at predicting expected returns and selecting stocks. Let η denote the component of the portfolio return that he or she is able to predict (i.e., he or she knows η), and let ε denote the unpredictable component. The portfolio return $r = \eta + \varepsilon$ is the sum of the predictable and unpredictable components. For concreteness, one can think of either η or ε as the return on an industry factor and the other term as the idiosyncratic component of return. Assume ε is normally distributed, and the conditional expectation of ε, given η, is $E[\varepsilon|\eta] = 0$.

From the perspective of the portfolio manager, the unpredictable component ε is the only source of uncertainty, because he or she knows η. Thus, from his or her perspective, the expected value and standard deviation of portfolio return are $E[r|\eta] = E[\eta + \varepsilon|\eta] = \eta$ and $\sigma_\varepsilon = \sqrt{\text{var}(\varepsilon)}$, and the 95%-confidence value-at-risk is $\text{VaR}_1 = -(\eta - 1.645\sigma_\varepsilon) = 1.645\sigma_\varepsilon - \eta$.

The risk manager does not have the information to predict expected returns and therefore does not know η. Further, the risk manager either does not believe or is unwilling to assume that the portfolio manager knows η, and therefore calculates value-at-risk as if η is unknown. Again for simplicity, assume that, from the portfolio manager's perspective, η is normally distributed with expected value $E[\eta] = \mu$, where μ is the expected return on a passive benchmark. Thus, to the risk manager the expected value and standard deviation of portfolio returns are $E[r] = E[\eta + \varepsilon] = \mu$ and $\sigma = \sqrt{\text{var}(\eta) + \text{var}(\varepsilon)} > \sigma_\varepsilon$, and the 95%-confidence value-at-risk is $\text{VaR}_2 = -(\mu - 1.645\sigma) = 1.645\sigma - \mu$.

In the portfolio manager's computation $\text{VaR}_1 = -(\eta - 1.645\sigma_\varepsilon) = 1.645\sigma_\varepsilon - \eta$, the term η will always be positive because, if the portfolio manager predicted returns less than μ on some stocks, he or she could either select different stocks, establish short positions in the stocks for which he or she predicted negative returns, or simply invest in the passive benchmark. Comparing this to the risk manager's computation $\text{VaR}_2 = -(\mu - 1.645\sigma) = 1.645\sigma - \mu$, one can see that the risk manager's value-at-risk estimate will always exceed that of the portfolio manager, because $\sigma > \sigma_\varepsilon$ and $\mu < \eta$. The result that the risk manager's value-at-risk estimate exceeds that of the portfolio manager will remain true if one uses the expected returns as the benchmarks for defining loss, because then the VaRs are proportional to the standard deviations $\text{VaR}_1 = 1.645\sigma_\varepsilon$ and $\text{VaR}_2 = 1.645\sigma$.

Though this is only a simple example, the point holds more generally. To the extent that a portfolio manager is able to predict expected returns, the predictive model will explain some of the variability of returns. Thus, the variability of the unexplained component of returns, namely, the residual, will be less than the variability of returns computed when assuming that the expected return is constant. As a result, VaR estimates computed with the use of forecast errors from the predictive model of returns will indicate less risk than VaR estimates computed when assuming that the expected return is constant.

Given this, how should VaR be computed? For a bank that is warehousing a portfolio of interest-rate and other derivatives, the answer is clear. In this setting, a key use of VaR is to monitor and control the individual risk-takers and risk-taking units, for example, traders, trading "desks," and larger business units. To the extent that the VaR estimates used for internal risk-management rely on the traders' models, forecasts, and beliefs, this monitoring and control function is defeated. More generally, "best practice" is for the internal risk-management unit to be independent of the risk-taking units. Thus, it is standard for a bank's internal VaR models to use naïve estimates of expected returns, typically setting them to zero. This argument in favor of the use of naïve estimates of expected price changes is reinforced by the fact that assumptions about expected returns have a limited impact on the VaR model when a one-day holding period is used, because volatilities are roughly proportional to the square root of time and expected price changes are proportional to time.

In portfolio-management uses of VaR, the answer is less clear. Investors or plan sponsors acting on their behalf entrust portfolio managers with their funds, expecting returns; the portfolio manager, acting on behalf of the investors or plan sponsors, must construct portfolios that balance the anticipated returns against the risks accepted to earn those returns. This portfolio construction is based, explicitly or implicitly, on the manager's beliefs about expected returns. In this situation, the risk is due to the fact that the realized asset-returns may deviate from the manager's forecasts, and VaR measures should measure the risk of such deviations. These are determined by the extent to which the realized values of the market factors deviate from the expected values, given the manager's information, unlike traditional VaR measures, which are based on the magnitudes of deviations from naïve expectations.

This approach to computing VaR numbers is used at two different levels, for two different purposes. First, the discussion above implies that it is the correct approach at the level of an individual fund, when VaR estimates are being computed for use in portfolio construction and managing the risk-taking process. In this case, the VaR would be computed based on deviations from the model used by the portfolio manager in forecasting returns. The next chapter provides several examples of this use of VaR. Second, this is also a reasonable approach at the level of the plan sponsor, both when it makes asset-allocation decisions among asset classes and when it allocates funds to portfolio managers within each asset class. When it does this, the plan sponsor is playing a role analogous to a portfolio manager, but selecting among asset classes and portfolio managers rather than among individual securities. In this case, the VaR would be computed based on deviations from the expected returns in the plan sponsor's strategic asset-allocation model. Chapter 13 provides an extended example of this use of VaR.

Plan sponsors also play a second role, that of monitoring their portfolio managers. This is akin to that of the internal risk-management function at a bank or other derivatives dealer. For this purpose, it is reasonable to use naïve estimates of expected returns. This provides a check on the managers in case the portfolio manager incorrectly thinks that he or she has the ability to predict expected returns when he or she does not, and so that the portfolio manager's model understates the risk of deviations from his or her forecasts.

NOTES

The approach to risk decomposition in this book is that of Litterman (1996), which has become standard. Adding confusion, some (e.g., Mina and Xiao 2001) defy standard usage of the word *marginal* and switch the definitions of marginal and incremental risk. That is, in RiskMetrics, marginal VaR is the change in risk resulting from selling the entire position and incremental VaR measures the effect of a small change in a position (Mina and Xiao 2001: Sections 6.2–6.3).

Euler's law is obvious in the one-variable case, because only functions of the form $f(w) = bw$ are homogenous of degree 1, implying that, for such functions, $f(kw) = kbw$ and $\partial f(kw)/\partial k = bw = f(w)$.

To obtain Euler's law in the general case, one starts with the statement that the value-at-risk of a portfolio kw is $\mathrm{VaR}(kw) = k\mathrm{VaR}(w)$ and differentiates both sides of this equation with respect to k. This differentiation amounts to asking what the effect is of a proportionate increase in all positions.

The right-hand side of the equation means that the portfolio value-at-risk is proportional to k and thus increases at the rate $\mathrm{VaR}(w)$ as k changes. Thus, the derivative of the right-hand side is

$$\frac{\partial(k\,\mathrm{VaR}(w))}{\partial k} = \mathrm{VaR}(w). \tag{10.6}$$

To compute the derivative of the left-hand side, write it as $\mathrm{VaR}(kw) = \mathrm{VaR}(y_1, y_2, \ldots, y_N) = \mathrm{VaR}(y)$, where $y_1 = kw_1$, $y_2 = kw_2, \ldots, y_N = kw_N$, and y is the vector $y = (y_1, y_2, \ldots, y_N)'$. Then,

$$\frac{\partial \mathrm{VaR}(y)}{\partial k} = \frac{\partial \mathrm{VaR}(y)}{\partial y_1} \times \frac{\partial y_1}{\partial k} + \frac{\partial \mathrm{VaR}(y)}{\partial y_2} \times \frac{\partial y_2}{\partial k} + \cdots + \frac{\partial \mathrm{VaR}(y)}{\partial y_N} \times \frac{\partial y_N}{\partial k}.$$

This says that the effect on the value-at-risk of increasing k is determined by the effects of y_i on VaR and the effects of k on y_i. Then, using the facts that $\partial y_1/\partial k = w_1$, $\partial \mathrm{VaR}(y)/\partial y_1 = \partial \mathrm{VaR}(w)/\partial w_1$, and similarly for the other y_is, one obtains

$$\frac{\partial \text{VaR}(y)}{\partial k} = \frac{\partial \text{VaR}(y)}{\partial y_1} w_1 + \frac{\partial \text{VaR}(y)}{\partial y_2} w_2 + \cdots + \frac{\partial \text{VaR}(y)}{\partial y_N} w_N$$

$$= \frac{\partial \text{VaR}(X)}{\partial w_1} w_1 + \frac{\partial \text{VaR}(w)}{\partial w_2} w_2 + \frac{\partial \text{VaR}(X)}{\partial w_N} w_N.$$

(10.7)

Combining (10.6) and (10.7) yields equation (10.2) in the body of the chapter. A similar analysis will yield the decomposition of the standard deviation in equation (10.1)

CHAPTER 11

A Long-Short Hedge Fund Manager

We start our series of examples illustrating the use of value-at-risk in risk decomposition and risk budgeting by looking at the simplest possible case, a quantitative portfolio manager who uses value-at-risk internally in order to measure, manage, and optimize the risks of its portfolios. This manager, MPT Asset Management (MPT), specializes in predicting the relative returns in the stock, bond, and currency markets of some of the developed countries over short horizons and uses these predictions in managing long-short hedge funds. Both MPT's predictions of expected returns and its estimates of market risks change frequently, requiring that it rapidly alter its portfolios to reflect the changes in its beliefs and optimize the risk-return tradeoff. Due to their high liquidity, low transaction costs, and (for the futures contracts) lack of credit risk, futures and currency forward contracts are MPT's preferred investment vehicles. In particular, for each country it follows it uses the leading stock index futures contract, a futures contract on a benchmark government bond, and currency forward contracts.

The futures and forward contracts involve no cash outlay (other than the required margin or collateral), so in addition to the futures contracts each of MPT's funds includes a portfolio of securities. These asset portfolios are not actively managed but rather are chosen to match the returns on the benchmarks used by the various funds. For example, some of MPT's funds are *absolute return funds,* benchmarked to the riskless return; for these the asset portfolio consists of high-grade money market instruments. Other funds are benchmarked to large-capitalization U.S. equity indexes, and for these the asset portfolios consist of passively managed portfolios of U.S. equities. Thus, each of MPT's portfolios consists of an active portfolio of liquid futures (and sometimes forward) contracts, along with a passively managed benchmark asset portfolio. Such simple portfolios provide a good setting in which to begin illustrating the use of value-at-risk in portfolio management because they allow us to illustrate some of the main ideas without requiring factor models to aggregate the risks across different instruments and portfolios.

As suggested by its name, MPT optimizes its portfolios using mean-variance optimization techniques. MPT is well aware that the optimal portfolios produced by mean-variance optimizers are sensitive to estimation errors in both the expected returns and covariance matrices and that these problems can be especially severe in portfolios that mix long and short positions. For this reason, it uses proprietary Bayesian statistical approaches to estimate the parameters. These combine the historical data with prior information about the parameter values and thereby reduce the sampling variation from the historical sample that is the source of the estimation error. For this example, we do not worry about the source or quality of the estimates of the mean returns and covariance matrix but simply use them to illustrate the use of value-at-risk and risk decomposition.

MPT'S PORTFOLIO AND PARAMETER ESTIMATES

We consider a fund benchmarked to the S&P 500 that uses only stock index futures contracts in its active portfolio. Restricting attention to stock index futures contracts simplifies the example without sacrificing anything of importance, because bond futures and currency forwards would be treated in the same way as the stock index futures. This active futures position is shown in Table 11.1. The second column of the Table shows the weights in the several markets, where the weight in the ith market w_i is the value of the cash market position equivalent to the futures position divided by the fund net asset value, that is, the weight is

$$w_i = \frac{\text{value of cash market position equivalent to futures position}}{\text{fund net asset value}}.$$

Negative weights indicate short positions. Currently the active portfolio of futures contracts has a large (40%) long position in the Swiss market and somewhat smaller long positions in Canada, Italy, and the Netherlands. The largest short position is in the U.S. market (−25%), with other short positions in Australia, Spain, France, and Japan. The weights on the long positions sum to 100%, while those on the short positions sum to −95%.

The portfolio also has a weight of 100% in a benchmark portfolio that tracks the S&P 500. Due to the need to maintain futures margin accounts,

TABLE 11.1 Current "active" portfolio weights, expected returns, and standard deviations

	Portfolio Weight (%)	Expected Return (% per month)	Standard Deviation of Prediction Error (% per month)	Standard Deviation Based on Constant Expected Return (% per month)
Australia (SPI)	−15.0	0.90	4.84	5.23
Canada (TSE 300)	30.0	2.40	5.96	6.44
Switzerland (SMI)	40.0	2.30	6.46	7.00
Germany (DAX-30)	−20.0	1.50	7.40	8.06
Spain (IBEX 35)	−10.0	1.20	7.99	8.66
France (CAC-40)	−5.0	0.70	6.88	7.53
Great Britain (FT-SE 100)	0.0	0.40	5.03	5.48
Italy (MIB 30)	15.0	2.50	8.77	9.57
Japan (Nikkei 225)	−20.0	0.40	6.29	6.75
Netherlands (AEX)	15.0	1.80	6.28	6.70
New Zealand (NZSE)	0.0	1.60	6.09	6.56
United States (S&P 500)	−25.0	0.10	5.07	5.53

it is impossible to achieve this 100% weighting by investing the net asset value in the benchmark portfolio. Instead, approximately 90% of the net asset value is invested in a passively managed stock portfolio that tracks the S&P 500, and 10% of the net asset value is invested in money market instruments used for futures margin. The allocation of 100% to the benchmark is then obtained by establishing a long position in S&P 500 index futures contracts in an amount equivalent to approximately 10% of the net asset value.

The third and fourth columns of Table 11.1 show the estimates of the conditional expected returns (per month) on the various markets and standard deviations of the prediction errors (also per month) from MPT's forecasting model. These estimates (together with the correlations of the prediction errors) will be used in estimating the expected return and risk of the portfolio. The fifth column of Table 11.1 shows *naïve* estimates of the standard deviations of monthly returns, computed assuming that the expected returns on the various markets are constant. These naïve standard deviations ignore the fact that MPT's forecasting model explains some of the variability of monthly returns and thus are larger than the standard deviations of the prediction errors.

MPT manages this portfolio to have an annualized tracking error volatility less than or equal to 10% per year, equivalent to $10/\sqrt{12} = 2.887\%$ per month. Given the assumptions and parameter choices it makes, this is identical to its value-at-risk. Due to its desire to maximize the portfolio return, MPT tries to fully utilize this risk budget, that is, it manages the portfolio so that the tracking error volatility is close to (but less than) 2.887% per month.

VALUE-AT-RISK

The value-at-risk estimates are used by MPT for portfolio construction and managing the risk-taking process, rather than by an outside organization or risk manager for use in monitoring and controlling the portfolio managers. As discussed in the previous chapter and illustrated in Table 11.1, to the extent that a portfolio manager is able to predict expected returns, the predictive model will explain some of the variability of returns, and the variability of the unexplained component of returns (the prediction errors) will be less than the variability of returns computed assuming the expected return is constant. From the perspective of the portfolio manager, the risk stems from the variability of these prediction errors, and value-at-risk estimates should be based on the distribution of the prediction errors. This is the choice made by MPT.

In addition to this choice, MPT must also choose a method for computing value-at-risk, a holding period, and a confidence interval. Because the fund is benchmarked to the S&P 500 index, it focuses on the value-at-risk of the relative return $r_P - r_B$, where r_P is the return on the portfolio and r_B is the return on the benchmark, the portfolio underlying the S&P 500 index. Due to the linearity of the changes in value of the futures and the approximate normality of returns on the underlying stock markets, the delta-normal method is a reasonable choice. The liquidity of the futures contracts enables MPT to alter its portfolio frequently, and it sometimes does so, suggesting that it is reasonable to use a short time horizon; MPT uses one month. Finally, MPT computes a one-sigma (84% confidence) value-at-risk and defines value-at-risk relative to the expected value of the excess return $r_P - r_B$, rather than relative to zero. With these choices, the value-at-risk is identical to the standard deviation, or volatility of the tracking error.

The excess (relative to the benchmark) return on the portfolio can be written

$$r_P - r_B = \sum_{i=1}^{12} w_i r_i + r_B - r_B$$

$$= \sum_{i=1}^{12} w_i r_i,$$

where r_i is the return on the ith market, w_i is the corresponding weight, $\sum_{i=1}^{12} w_i r_i$ is the return on the active portfolio, and $\sum_{i=1}^{12} w_i r_i + r_B$ is the portfolio return, including the return on the passive benchmark portfolio. The one-sigma value-at-risk, or tracking error volatility σ, is the standard deviation of the return on the active portfolio

$$\sigma = \sqrt{\mathrm{var}\left(\sum_{i=1}^{12} w_i r_i \right)}$$

$$= \sqrt{\sum_{i=1}^{12} \sum_{j=1}^{12} w_i w_j \mathrm{cov}(r_i, r_j)},$$

where $\mathrm{cov}(r_i, r_j) = \rho_{ij} \sigma_i \sigma_j$, σ_i is the standard deviation of the prediction error for market i, and ρ_{ij} is the correlation between the prediction errors for markets i and j. The σ_is were shown above in Table 11.1, while these correlations are shown in Table 11.2. Using these parameters, the VaR/tracking error volatility is VaR $= \sigma = 3.215\%$ per month, or approximately 11.14% per year. This is greater than the target of 2.887% per month, implying that MPT needs to reduce the risk of the active portfolio.

In contrast to the VaR/tracking error volatility of 3.215%, the value-at-risk based on the naïve standard deviations (and for simplicity assuming that the correlations of returns are identical to the correlations of the prediction errors) is 3.477% per month, or approximately 12.05% per year. This illustrates that the value-at-risk computed using the standard deviations of returns exceeds that computed using the standard deviations of the prediction errors. Such an estimate of value-at-risk might be useful to a risk manager or portfolio-management client who wanted to measure the risk under the assumption that the portfolio manager's predictive model is flawed and actually does not predict expected returns.

TABLE 11.2 Estimates of the correlations of prediction errors

	AUD	CAD	CHF	DEM	ESP	FRF	GBP	ITL	JPY	NLG	NZD	USD
AUD	1.00	0.40	0.36	0.36	0.38	0.34	0.44	0.27	0.30	0.38	0.45	0.39
CAD	0.40	1.00	0.39	0.43	0.36	0.40	0.40	0.29	0.28	0.41	0.33	0.53
CHF	0.36	0.39	1.00	0.45	0.44	0.47	0.48	0.33	0.26	0.52	0.37	0.46
DEM	0.36	0.43	0.45	1.00	0.45	0.54	0.41	0.45	0.27	0.55	0.28	0.41
ESP	0.38	0.36	0.44	0.45	1.00	0.49	0.42	0.46	0.29	0.46	0.30	0.36
FRF	0.34	0.40	0.47	0.54	0.49	1.00	0.44	0.47	0.28	0.53	0.26	0.41
GBP	0.44	0.40	0.48	0.41	0.42	0.44	1.00	0.31	0.25	0.50	0.38	0.47
ITL	0.27	0.29	0.33	0.45	0.46	0.47	0.31	1.00	0.25	0.42	0.20	0.25
JPY	0.30	0.28	0.26	0.27	0.29	0.28	0.25	0.25	1.00	0.27	0.24	0.26
NLG	0.38	0.41	0.52	0.55	0.46	0.53	0.50	0.42	0.27	1.00	0.33	0.45
NZD	0.45	0.33	0.37	0.28	0.30	0.26	0.38	0.20	0.24	0.33	1.00	0.34
USD	0.39	0.53	0.46	0.41	0.36	0.41	0.47	0.25	0.26	0.45	0.34	1.00

IS COMPUTING THE VALUE-AT-RISK ENOUGH?

Unfortunately, simply computing the value-at-risk is not enough. Single summary measures of value-at-risk are useful for disclosure to investors and (when this is relevant) reporting to regulators and may sometimes be sufficient for the board of directors. But, they are not sufficient for managing the portfolio.

A portfolio or risk manager will almost certainly want to know the effect on risk of increasing or decreasing the position in each of the futures contracts. He or she will want to know the marginal contribution to risk and return of each of the futures contracts, that is, he or she will be interested in decomposing the risks of the portfolio, or *risk decomposition*. This identifies the portfolio's hot spots, or areas of particular concern to the risk or portfolio mangers, and will help him or her decide what positions to reduce (or increase) if the risk of the portfolio is above (or below) the desired level.

Combined with information about expected returns, the risk decomposition can also help optimize the risk-return tradeoff. For example, it will help the portfolio manager identify the expected return forecasts implicit in the choice of a particular portfolio, that is, the portfolio's *implied views*. It can also help the portfolio manager decide if the benefits of altering a position are large enough to justify the transaction costs of trading. The portfolio manager will want this information even if an optimizer is used in helping to select a portfolio, because a manager who relies blindly on a mean-variance optimizer will likely not be a portfolio manager for long.

RISK DECOMPOSITION OF THE CURRENT PORTFOLIO

Table 11.3 presents the risk decomposition of the current portfolio. The second column shows the portfolio weights w_i, the third and fourth columns show the risk contributions $(\partial \sigma(w)/\partial w_i)(w_i)$ and percentage risk contributions $(\partial \sigma(w)/\partial w_i)/\sigma(w)$, and the fifth column shows the partial derivatives $\partial \sigma(w)/\partial w_i$. Although these partial derivatives are typically not presented in most uses of risk decomposition, they are shown in the Table because they clarify the interpretation of the risk contributions of the short positions. In particular, for the short positions increasing the size means establishing a larger short position, which can be seen from the fact that for the short positions the sign of the risk contribution is opposite the sign of the partial derivative.

TABLE 11.3   Risk decomposition of the current portfolio

	Risk Contribution (% per month)	Risk Contribution (% of total risk)	Portfolio Weight (%)	Partial Derivative
Australia (SPI)	0.043	1.3	−15.0	−0.0029
Canada (TSE 300)	0.661	20.6	30.0	0.0220
Switzerland (SMI)	1.488	46.3	40.0	0.0372
Germany (DAX-30)	0.056	1.7	−20.0	−0.0028
Spain (IBEX 35)	−0.021	−0.7	−10.0	0.0021
France (CAC-40)	−0.041	−1.3	−5.0	0.0081
Great Britain (FT-SE 100)	0.000	0.0	0.0	0.0080
Italy (MIB 30)	0.428	13.3	15.0	0.0285
Japan (Nikkei 225)	0.303	9.4	−20.0	−0.0152
Netherlands (AEX)	0.293	9.1	15.0	0.0195
New Zealand (NZSE)	0.000	0.0	0.0	0.0066
United States (S&P 500)	0.006	0.2	−25.0	−0.0002
Total	3.215	100.0		

Examining the risk decomposition, we see that the risk contribution of the large (w_3 = 40%) long position in the Swiss market is 1.488%, or 46.3% of the portfolio risk. The long positions in the Canadian and Italian markets also make significant contributions to the risk of the portfolio, contributing 20.6% and 13.3%, respectively. The risk contributions of these positions are large because the weights of these positions in the portfolio (combined with the fact that these positions are not serving primarily to hedge other positions) imply that the portfolio return is highly correlated with the returns on these markets. Thus, increasing the positions in these markets contributes to the portfolio risk.

Of the short positions, the largest risk contribution is from the Japanese market, with a risk contribution equal to 9.4% of the total. Strikingly, the risk contribution of the Japanese market is considerably larger than those of the German and U.S. markets (1.7% and 0.2% of the total, respectively), even though the short positions in these markets are the same size or larger (–20% and –25% for the German and U.S. markets, respectively, versus –20% for the Japanese market). This illustrates that a large position does not necessarily imply a large risk contribution. Here, the risk contributions of the U.S. and German markets are low because these positions function as hedges of the rest of the portfolio, which has large long positions in the Canadian and Swiss markets. In contrast, the short position in the Japanese market does not play this role.

Two of the positions, those in the Spanish and French markets, make negative contributions to portfolio risk. This is because these short positions serve to hedge the remainder of the portfolio, so increasing the size of these positions actually reduces risk. In particular, the positive partial derivatives of 0.0021 and 0.0081 reveal that long positions in these markets are positively correlated with the portfolio return, of course implying that short positions in these markets are negatively correlated with the portfolio return. The negative risk contributions reflect the short positions through the negative weights w_i and therefore capture the negative correlations between the short positions and the portfolio return. The interpretation of these risk contributions is that larger short positions will reduce the portfolio risk.

This risk decomposition clearly highlights the positions that should be the focus of the portfolio or risk manager's attention. In the terminology of Litterman (1996), these positions are the portfolio's *hot spots*. As indicated above, the hot spots are not necessarily the largest positions. Thus, the risk decomposition also indicates the positions that need *not* be the focus of concern, even though they may be large. For example, the large short positions in the U.S. and German markets are responsible for little of the portfolio's risk.

RISK DECOMPOSITION AND HEDGING

Recalling that the current tracking error volatility of 3.215% per month (11.14% per year) exceeds the target of 2.887% per month (10% per year), MPT needs to reduce the risk of the portfolio. The risk decomposition above identifies obvious candidates for trades to reduce the risk. These may be either reductions in the positions that contribute to the risk or increases in the sizes of positions that function as hedges. The decomposition also allows MPT to compute the effect of changing the positions on the portfolio risk.

The position in the Swiss market has the largest risk contribution and is an obvious candidate for a trade to reduce the risk. The effect of reducing the position in the Swiss market from 40% to 35% can be obtained from the equation

$$
\begin{aligned}
\text{change in risk} &\approx \frac{\partial \sigma(w)}{\partial w_i} w_i \times \frac{(w_i^* - w_i)}{w_i} \\
&= (\text{risk contribution}) \times (\text{proportional change in volatility}) \\
&= 1.488\% \times \frac{35\% - 40\%}{40\%} \\
&= -0.186\%,
\end{aligned}
$$

yielding a new volatility of approximately 3.215% − 0.186% = 3.029%, or 10.49% per year. The actual change in risk resulting from this change in the position is −0.174, yielding a new volatility of 3.041% per month. The difference is due to the fact that the risk decomposition is a marginal analysis and is only exactly correct for infinitesimally small changes in the positions. In this example, the exact decrease in risk of 0.174 is smaller than the approximate decrease in risk of 0.186 because the covariance between the Swiss market and the portfolio declines as w_3 declines, so that reductions in w_3 have decreasing effect on the risk.

This analysis can be reversed to (approximately) determine the trade necessary to have a desired effect on the volatility. For example, to determine the (approximate) change in the Swiss market position necessary to reduce the volatility by 30 basis points, solve the equation

$$
\begin{aligned}
-0.3\% &= (\text{risk contribution}) \times (\text{proportional change in position}) \\
&= 1.488 \times \frac{\Delta w_3}{40\%}.
\end{aligned}
$$

The solution of $\Delta w_3 = 8.06\%$ implies that a reduction in the weight in the Swiss market from 40% to about 32% would reduce the monthly volatility by about 30 basis points.

The positions in the Spanish and French markets both serve as hedges. The approximate effect of increasing the short position in the French market from 5% to 6% is

$$\text{change in risk} \approx \frac{\partial \sigma(w)}{\partial w_i} w_i \times \frac{(w_i^* - w_i)}{w_i}$$

$$= (\text{risk contribution}) \times (\text{proportional change in volatility})$$

$$= -0.041\% \times \frac{-6\% - (-5)\%}{-5\%}$$

$$= -0.008\%,$$

yielding a new volatility of approximately $3.215\% - 0.008\% = 3.207\%$. The exact change in volatility is 0.007%, indicating that the estimate of 0.008% is a good approximation of the effect of increasing the hedge (the short position) from $w_6 = -5$ to -6%.

The risk decomposition can also be used to compute risk-minimizing trades, or *best hedges,* for each of the markets. We illustrate this using the position in the Swiss market. Letting Δw_3 denote the change in the position in the Swiss market, the risk-minimizing trade is the Δw_3 that minimizes the portfolio variance, or the solution of

$$\min_{\Delta w_3} \left[\sum_{i=1}^{12} \sum_{j=1}^{12} w_i w_j \, \text{cov}\,(r_i, r_j) + (\Delta w_3)^2 \text{var}(r_3) + \sum_{i=1}^{12} \Delta w_3 w_i \, \text{cov}\,(r_i, r_3) \right].$$

The first-order condition for the minimum is

$$2\Delta w_3 \, \text{var}(r_3) + 2\sum_{i=1}^{12} w_i \, \text{cov}\,(r_i, r_3) = 0,$$

which implies that the risk-minimizing trade is

$$\Delta w_3 = \frac{\sum_{i=1}^{12} w_i \, \text{cov}\,(r_i, r_3)}{\text{var}(r_3)}$$

The numerator of the term on the right-hand side, $\sum_{i=1}^{12} w_i \, \text{cov}\,(r_i, r_3)$, is the covariance between the return r_3 and the active portfolio return $\sum_{i=1}^{12} w_i r_i$, so the right-hand side is the negative of the ratio of the covariance between the portfolio return and r_3 to the variance of r_3. This implies that the right-hand side can be interpreted as the negative of the regression coefficient, or beta, obtained by regressing the portfolio return on r_3. This result is intuitive, for it says that the risk-minimizing trade in the Swiss market is the trade that offsets or hedges the sensitivity of the portfolio return to the Swiss market return. For MPT's portfolio, the risk-minimizing trade is $\Delta w_3 = -28.7\%$. If this trade is made, the new position in the Swiss market of $40 - 28.7 = 11.3\%$ will be uncorrelated with the returns of the resulting portfolio.

Table 11.4 shows the best hedges for each of the markets, along with the volatility of the resulting portfolio and the percentage reduction in volatility. Not surprisingly, the risk-minimizing trades are largest for the Swiss and Canadian markets and smallest for the U.S. market. These are consistent with the risk contributions of the portfolio; in particular, the position in the U.S. market was already very nearly a best-hedge position, so the risk-minimizing trade is nearly zero. Also as expected, the best hedges in

TABLE 11.4   Risk-minimizing trades or best hedges

	Volatility at the Best Hedge (% per month)	Reduction in Volatility (% of total risk)	Portfolio Weight (%)	Trade Required to Reach Best Hedge (Change in port. weight)
Australia (SPI)	3.210	0.17	−15.0	3.9
Canada (TSE 300)	2.987	7.09	30.0	−20.0
Switzerland (SMI)	2.628	18.26	40.0	−28.7
Germany (DAX-30)	3.213	0.07	−20.0	1.6
Spain (IBEX 35)	3.214	0.03	−10.0	−1.1
France (CAC-40)	3.193	0.70	−5.0	−5.5
Great Britain (FT-SE 100)	3.174	1.27	0.0	−10.1
Italy (MIB 30)	3.041	5.42	15.0	−11.9
Japan (Nikkei 225)	3.120	2.95	−20.0	12.3
Netherlands (AEX)	3.056	4.96	15.0	−15.9
New Zealand (NZSE)	3.196	0.59	0.0	−5.7
United States (S&P 500)	3.215	0.00	−25.0	0.3

the Spanish and French markets involve increasing the short positions. More surprisingly, the risk-minimizing trade in the Netherlands market is larger than that in the Italian market, even though the risk contribution of the Italian market is larger. This occurs because the return on the Netherlands market is more highly correlated with the large Canadian and Swiss market positions, so that its risk contribution decreases less rapidly as the position in the Netherlands market is decreased.

Although we do not show them, it is also possible to compute the risk-minimizing, or best hedge, trade involving two or more markets. If a particular set of H markets has been selected, the risk-minimizing trade in each market is the multiple regression coefficient of the portfolio return on the returns of each of the H markets, and the volatility at the best hedge is the standard deviation of the residual from that regression. By searching over all possible sets of H markets, it is straightforward to compute the risk-minimizing trade involving this number of markets. The H markets that are identified as the best hedges are those that explain the variation in the value of the portfolio, so this analysis also reveals the portfolio's principal exposures.

IMPLIED VIEWS ANALYSIS

Even though transaction costs in the futures markets are very low, it still doesn't make sense for MPT continuously to update its portfolios to match the optimal portfolios produced by the mean-variance optimizer. This raises the question: to what extent is the existing portfolio consistent with the expected returns from the forecasting model? Phrased differently, what are the market views implied by the existing portfolio? Do they even make any sense?

Determining these *implied views* involves the reverse engineering of the portfolio. Fortunately, this is easier than the phrase reverse engineering might suggest: the implied views can be determined immediately from the risk decomposition. As discussed in the next section of this chapter, portfolio optimization involves selecting positions, so that the return contribution of a position is proportional to the risk contribution. If this condition is not satisfied, the risk-return tradeoff can be improved by altering the positions until it is. To determine the implied views, we do not need actually to do this but only need to find the expected returns that make the return contributions proportional to the risk contributions. The easiest way to do this is to look at a mean-variance optimization problem.

The risk-return tradeoff (*mean-variance frontier*) can be obtained by maximizing the utility function

$$U = \text{portfolio expected return} - \lambda(\text{portfolio variance}),$$

where the coefficient λ determines the extent to which the utility function penalizes risk. Letting λ vary between 0 and ∞ maps out the usual efficient frontier. For example, as $\lambda \to \infty$, the utility function penalizes risk infinitely much, and the optimal portfolio obtained by maximizing the utility function approaches the minimum variance portfolio, while as $\lambda \to 0$, risk is not penalized and the optimal portfolio involves "plunging" into a levered position in the asset or market with the highest expected return, financed by a short position in the asset with the lowest expected return.

Using our notation, the maximization of the utility function becomes

$$\max_{\{w_i\}}\left[\sum_{i=1}^{12} w_i E[r_i] - \lambda \sum_{i=1}^{12}\sum_{j=1}^{12} w_i w_j \, \text{cov}(r_i,r_j)\right].$$

The first-order conditions are

$$E[r_i] = 2\lambda \sum_{j=1}^{12} w_j \, \text{cov}(r_i,r_j), \qquad \text{for } i = 1, 2, \ldots, 12.$$

The expected returns on the left-hand side are the expected returns, or implied views, that are consistent with the positions (and covariances) on the right-hand side. That is, they are implied by the choice of the w_i. Recalling that $\sum_{j=1}^{12} w_j \text{cov}(r_i, r_j)$ is the covariance between the return on the ith market and the active portfolio return $\sum_{j=1}^{12} w_j r_j$, this result says that the expected returns implicit in a choice of portfolio weights w_i are proportional to the covariances. Multiplying both sides of each equation by w_i and 1 in the form of σ/σ,

$$w_i E[r_i] = (2\lambda\sigma)\dfrac{\displaystyle\sum_{j=1}^{12} w_j \, \text{cov}(r_i,r_j)}{\sigma} \times w_i$$

$$= (2\lambda\sigma) \times (\text{risk contribution of } i\text{th position}).$$

This says that the expected return contribution $w_i E[r_i]$ is proportional to the risk contribution.

Table 11.5 shows these implied views for MPT's current portfolio and the expected returns from MPT's forecasting model, with λ chosen so that the equally weighted average of the implied views matches the equally weighted average of the expected returns. The most obvious feature of the implied views is that they are generally more extreme than the expected returns from the forecasting model. This follows directly from the risk decomposition in Table 11.3. The dramatic differences in the risk contributions are rationalized only by the conclusion that the portfolio manager has extreme views about expected returns; otherwise the differences in the risk contributions are too large.

A closer examination of Table 11.5 reveals a more interesting feature of the implied views: they do not necessarily correspond to whether the positions are long or short. More generally, the implied views of a portfolio do not necessarily correspond to the deviations from the benchmark.

To see this, consider the French market. The position of $w_5 = -5\%$ might be interpreted as indicating that the manager had a negative view on France, but the implied view for the French market is positive, at 1.16% per month. How can this be? The answer lies back in the risk contributions and best hedge analysis, which indicate that the portfolio volatility can be

TABLE 11.5 Implied views of the current portfolio

	Implied View (% per month)	Expected Return (% per month)	Portfolio Weight (%)
Australia (SPI)	−0.41	0.90	−15.0
Canada (TSE 300)	3.14	2.40	30.0
Switzerland (SMI)	5.31	2.30	40.0
Germany (DAX-30)	−0.40	1.50	−20.0
Spain (IBEX 35)	0.30	1.20	−10.0
France (CAC-40)	1.16	0.70	−5.0
Great Britain (FT-SE 100)	1.14	0.40	0.0
Italy (MIB 30)	4.07	2.50	15.0
Japan (Nikkei 225)	−2.17	0.40	−20.0
Netherlands (AEX)	2.79	1.80	15.0
New Zealand (NZSE)	0.94	1.60	0.0
United States (S&P 500)	−0.03	0.10	−25.0

reduced by increasing the short position in the French market. The failure of the manager to do this indicates a positive implied view. The same analysis applies to Great Britain: here the neutral position does not indicate a neutral view, because the best hedge trade in the British market is to establish a short position of −10.1%. Given this, the zero weight in the British market indicates a positive implied view.

In general, the implied views of a portfolio depend on all the other positions and the correlations among them. This is precisely because of the relationship between the implied views and the risk contributions: the implied views depend on all of the other positions in exactly the same way the risk contributions do.

RISK DECOMPOSITION AND PORTFOLIO OPTIMIZATION

We conclude this chapter by going to the final step of portfolio optimization. The risk decomposition in Table 11.3 makes clear that the existing portfolio is not optimal, for that Table shows that increasing the position in the Spanish and French markets results in a reduction in risk. Table 11.1 shows that these markets have positive expected returns, so increasing the positions in them increases the portfolio expected return. Therefore, the existing portfolio cannot be optimal.

If we expand Table 11.3 to include the marginal expected returns and the positions' contributions to portfolio expected returns, MPT can determine what other trades will improve the risk-return tradeoff and by how much they will do so. Determining marginal expected returns is straightforward, because the expected return of a portfolio is the weighted average of the expected returns of its components, and the marginal effect of increasing the position in the ith market is just the expected return of the ith market. In symbols, the marginal expected return is

$$\text{marginal expected return} = \frac{\partial E[r_P]}{\partial w_i}$$

$$= \frac{\partial \left(\sum_{i=1}^{12} w_i E[r_i] \right)}{\partial w_i}$$

$$= E[r_i].$$

The expected return contribution of the ith position is then just the product of the expected return of the ith market and the position size, or $E[r_i]w_i$.

Table 11.6 includes the position sizes, risk sensitivities, and risk contributions from Table 11.3, as well as the market expected returns and expected return contributions. In addition, the rightmost column shows the ratio of the expected return contribution to the risk contributions. When these ratios are not all equal, the risk-return tradeoff can by improved by reallocating assets among the markets. For example, the ratio of expected return to risk is 1.090 for the Canadian market and 0.618 for Switzerland. The difference indicates that there is an opportunity to improve the risk-return tradeoff by reallocating assets from the Swiss market to the Canadian market.

TABLE 11.6   Risk decomposition and contributions to expected return of the current portfolio

	Portfolio Weight (%)	Partial Derivative	Contribution to Risk (% per month)	Market Expected Return (% per month)	Contribution to Portfolio Expected Return (% per month)	Ratio of Return to Risk
Australia (SPI)	−15.0	−0.0029	0.043	0.90	−0.1	−3.148
Canada (TSE 300)	30.0	0.0220	0.661	2.40	0.7	1.090
Switzerland (SMI)	40.0	0.0372	1.488	2.30	0.9	0.618
Germany (DAX-30)	−20.0	−0.0028	0.056	1.50	−0.3	−5.368
Spain (IBEX 35)	−10.0	0.0021	−0.021	1.20	−0.1	5.734
France (CAC-40)	−5.0	0.0081	−0.041	0.70	0.0	0.859
Great Britain (FT-SE 100)	0.0	0.0080	0.000	0.40	0.0	0.501
Italy (MIB 30)	15.0	0.0285	0.428	2.50	0.4	0.877
Japan (Nikkei 225)	−20.0	−0.0152	0.303	0.40	−0.1	−0.264
Netherlands (AEX)	15.0	0.0195	0.293	1.80	0.3	0.921
New Zealand (NZSE)	0.0	0.0066	0.000	1.60	0.0	2.427
United States (S&P 500)	−25.0	−0.0002	0.006	0.10	0.0	−4.461
Total			3.215		1.59	

The negative ratios for some of the short positions reveal even greater opportunities for improving the risk-return tradeoff. To interpret them, one must know whether they are negative because increasing the position reduces risk and increases expected return or increases risk and reduces expected return. For the short positions with negative ratios, it turns out that increasing the magnitude of the short position increases risk and reduces expected return, so the risk-return tradeoff is improved by reducing the magnitudes of the short positions. For example, the ratio of -3.148 for the position in the Australian market reflects the fact that reducing the short position from 15% to 14% (changing w_1 from -15% to -14%) reduces risk by approximately 0.043% and increases the expected return by 1% of 0.90%, or 0.009%.

From this discussion, it should be clear that the optimal active portfolio of futures contracts is characterized by equal ratios. (An important exception is when constraints, perhaps self-imposed, on the position size in any market lead to smaller than optimal allocations for some markets.) The actual optimum can be computed using a mean-variance optimizer; in this example, with no constraints on the portfolio, the solution is easy to obtain. Table 11.7 shows the optimal portfolio (maximum expected return), subject to the constraint that the VaR/tracking error volatility be less than or equal to 2.887% per month (10% per year). This Table also shows the risk sensitivities (partial derivatives), risk contributions, expected returns, expected return contributions, and ratios of expected return to risk at the optimal allocations. As expected, the ratios are equal across markets.

Consistent with the preceding discussion of ratios of the expected return to the risk contributions in the Canadian and Swiss markets, the optimal allocation reflects a smaller position in the Swiss market and a larger position in the Canadian market; in fact, the largest position is now in the Canadian market. Also, the optimal short positions in the Spanish and French markets are larger than in the current portfolio, reflecting the fact that, given the current positions, they serve as hedges. The short position in Australia of -15% has been reduced, and in fact turns into a long position of 2.1%. All of these positions are unsurprising in light of the expected returns and risk decomposition of the existing portfolio in Table 11.6.

The change in the position in the British market can be understood in terms of the best hedge and implied views analyses. The best hedge trade in the British market is to establish a short position of -10.1%; the existing zero weight in the British market indicates an implied view greater than the expected return. In order to be consistent with the expected return forecast, the position in the British market must be decreased.

TABLE 11.7 Risk decomposition and contributions to expected return of the optimal portfolio

	Portfolio Weight (%)	Risk Sensitivity	Risk Contribution (% per month)	Market Expected Return (% per month)	Contribution to Portfolio Expected Return (% per month)	Ratio of Return to Risk
Australia (SPI)	2.1	0.01395	0.030	0.90	0.02	0.645
Canada (TSE 300)	35.4	0.03719	1.317	2.40	0.85	0.645
Switzerland (SMI)	24.2	0.03565	0.862	2.30	0.56	0.645
Germany (DAX-30)	−1.5	0.02325	−0.035	1.50	−0.02	0.645
Spain (IBEX 35)	−4.4	0.01860	−0.082	1.20	−0.05	0.645
France (CAC-40)	−13.0	0.01085	−0.141	0.70	−0.09	0.645
Great Britain (FT-SE 100)	−16.9	0.00620	−0.105	0.40	−0.07	0.645
Italy (MIB 30)	11.7	0.03874	0.454	2.50	0.29	0.645
Japan (Nikkei 225)	−6.0	0.00620	−0.037	0.40	−0.02	0.645
Netherlands (AEX)	14.2	0.02790	0.397	1.80	0.26	0.645
New Zealand (NZSE)	11.2	0.02480	0.277	1.60	0.18	0.645
United States (S&P 500)	−32.4	0.00155	−0.050	0.10	−0.03	0.645
Total			2.887		1.86	

The reasons for the changes in the weights in the U.S. and New Zealand markets are not obvious from the previous discussion. The best hedges analysis indicated little change in the U.S. market position and that the initial zero position in New Zealand should be changed to a short position. Why does the optimal portfolio reflect an increase in the short position in the United States and a significant long position in New Zealand? The explanation lies in the changes in the positions in the other markets. The changes in the portfolio, and in particular the increase in the size of the Canadian position, make the position in the U.S. market a better hedge of the portfolio, leading to the new optimal U.S. position of $w_{12} = -32.4\%$. This, combined with the optimal large short position in Great Britain, serves to hedge the

New Zealand market. Thus, it is possible to have a significant long position in New Zealand without contributing too greatly to the risk of the portfolio.

NOTES

The implied views analysis is described in Winkelman (2000a; 2000b). This analysis is closely related to mean-variance optimization, the literature on which is too large to attempt to survey here.

CHAPTER 12

Aggregating and Decomposing the Risks of Large Portfolios

A key feature of MPT's portfolio discussed in the preceding chapter is that it consists of positions in only 12 instruments, the stock index futures contracts. For this reason, we were able to work directly with the covariance matrix of changes in the values of the individual instruments. Unfortunately, the MPT portfolio contains too few instruments to be representative of most actual institutional portfolios, which contain hundreds, or even thousands, of instruments. In particular, this is true of the aggregate portfolios of plan sponsors, which are composed of the sums of the different portfolios controlled by the sponsors' managers. For such large portfolios, factor models of the sort discussed in Chapters 7 and 8 play a crucial role in simplifying and estimating the risk.

Factor models play a background role in simple value-at-risk computations, in that they are only a means to an end. Typically, the user of simple value-at-risk estimates has little interest in the factor models *per se*, provided that the resulting VaR estimate is reasonably accurate. In contrast, factor models play an important role in the foreground of risk decomposition. To understand why, imagine taking a portfolio with approximately equal weights in 1000 common stocks and decomposing the portfolio risk into the risk contributions of the 1000 stocks, along the lines of the previous chapter. With so many stocks, the risk contribution of each common stock will be somewhere between zero and a few tenths of one percent of the total portfolio risk. Such risk decompositions reveal little of the important risks in the portfolio. More meaningful risk decompositions are in terms of industry or other groupings, or in terms of the market factors to which the portfolio is exposed. In this latter case, the factor models play a highly visible role because the risk contributions of market risk factors that do not appear in the factor model cannot be measured. Thus, the choice of factors determines the possible risk decompositions of the total portfolio risk.

This chapter describes risk decomposition by both groups of securities and factors. The risk decomposition by groups of securities allows the identification of undesirable country, regional, or industry concentrations, for example, an unintended overweighting in technology stocks. The risk decomposition by groups of securities also allows the measurement of the risk contribution of particular portfolio managers, because the risk contribution of a manager's portfolio is just the risk contribution of the group of securities that constitute the portfolio.

The ability to decompose risk by market factors can be equally, or even more, valuable. An excessive exposure to a growth factor, or unintended interest rate risk in an equity portfolio, can be difficult to identify because such exposures stem from many stocks in different industries. The risk decomposition by factors is very flexible because a wide range of variables can be used in factor models. The returns on portfolios, changes in interest rates, unexpected changes in growth in gross domestic product (GDP), or the unexpected component of the change in almost any other variable of interest are all legitimate factors. Further, a stock's factor model residuals can be viewed as yet another factor that affects the return on only one stock, permitting residual risk to be considered in the same framework. Thus, a wide range of risk decomposition questions can be addressed using the framework provided by factor models.

This chapter illustrates the use of factor models to aggregate and decompose risk across portfolios with an example of a portfolio consisting of three subportfolios, perhaps managed by different portfolio managers. It begins with a brief description of the portfolios, securities, and parameter estimates and then turns to the risk decompositions. The risk decomposition by individual securities and groups of securities is illustrated first and is followed by the risk decomposition by factors.

THE PORTFOLIOS, SECURITIES, AND PARAMETER ESTIMATES

The three subportfolios that make up the aggregate portfolio consist of a common stock portfolio, a fixed-income portfolio, and a portfolio containing both long and short positions in both stocks and bonds. This last portfolio is interpreted as the portfolio of a market-neutral hedge fund manager. For simplicity, all of the portfolios are composed of positions in only four common stocks and three bonds and there are only two stock market factors and three bond market factors.

SECURITIES AND PARAMETER ESTIMATES

The two stock market factors are the growth and value indexes used in the factor model in Chapter 7, and the four hypothetical common stocks are identical to those used in Chapter 7, except that the stocks are now assumed to have some limited interest rate exposure. The three bond market factors are the first three principal components used in Chapter 8, and the three bonds are those used in Chapter 8. Table 12.1 shows the factor loadings of the seven securities on the five market factors, as well as the residual volatilities (standard deviations) of the common stock returns. (The bond residuals are identically zero because the three principal components are assumed to capture all of their risks.) Stocks 1 and 2 have large loadings on the growth factor and negative loadings on the value factor and thus are naturally labeled growth stocks; below it is assumed that they can also be labeled technology stocks. Stocks 3 and 4 have relatively large loadings on the value factor and small (−0.1 and 0.2, respectively) loadings on the growth factor and are labeled value stocks. Three of the four common stocks now have some limited interest rate exposure, but the bonds have no equity market exposure because the three principal components are assumed to capture completely their risks, reflected in the residual volatilities of zero. For convenience, the residuals of the four common stocks are assumed to be uncorrelated.

Table 12.2 shows the monthly volatilities and correlation matrix of the five market factors. The volatilities of the stock market factors (the growth and value indexes) are expressed as percentages (per month), while the volatilities of the principal components are expressed in basis points. Table 12.3 shows the covariance matrix corresponding to the correlations and volatilities in Table 12.2. Not surprisingly, the two stock market indexes are highly correlated, with a correlation coefficient of 0.80. While the principal components are of course uncorrelated with each other by construction, Tables 12.2 and 12.3 show that they are somewhat correlated with the stock market indexes. This reflects the fact that stock prices are affected by changes in interest rates.

TABLE 12.1 Factor loadings of the securities

	Growth Index	Value Index	Principal Comp. 1	Principal Comp. 2	Principal Comp. 3	Residual Volatility
Stock 1	2.5	−1.1	−0.08	0.08	0.00	8.0%
Stock 2	2.1	−0.8	−0.05	0.05	0.00	7.0%
Stock 3	−0.1	1.2	0.00	0.00	0.00	6.0%
Stock 4	0.2	0.8	−0.05	0.00	0.00	5.5%
Bond 1	0.0	0.0	−1.59	0.00	−0.11	0.0 bp
Bond 2	0.0	0.0	−2.55	−1.08	0.35	0.0 bp
Bond 3	0.0	0.0	−3.72	−2.91	2.47	0.0 bp

TABLE 12.2 Volatilities and correlations of market factors

	Factors				
	Growth Index	Value Index	Principal Comp. 1	Principal Comp. 2	Principal Comp. 3
Volatilities:	4.30%	4.10%	88.93 bp	25.22 bp	12.36 bp
Correlations:					
Factors	Growth Index	Value Index	Principal Comp. 1	Principal Comp. 2	Principal Comp. 3
Growth Index	1.00	0.80	−0.20	−0.10	0.00
Value Index	0.80	1.00	−0.15	−0.07	0.00
Prin. Comp. 1	−0.20	−0.15	1.00	0.00	0.00
Prin. Comp. 2	−0.10	−0.07	0.00	1.00	0.00
Prin. Comp. 3	0.00	0.00	0.00	0.00	1.00

TABLE 12.3 Market factor covariances

	Factors				
Factors	Growth Index	Value Index	Principal Comp. 1	Principal Comp. 2	Principal Comp. 3
Growth Index	18.49	14.10	−76.48	−10.85	0.00
Value Index	14.10	16.81	−54.69	−7.24	0.00
Prin. Comp. 1	−76.48	−54.69	7908.36	0.00	0.00
Prin. Comp. 2	−10.85	−7.24	0.00	636.29	0.00
Prin. Comp. 3	0.00	0.00	0.00	0.00	152.81

FACTOR MODELS FOR THE PORTFOLIO RETURNS

The portfolio return r_p is a weighted average of the returns on the three subportfolios

$$r_p = w_{p_1} r_{p_1} + w_{p_2} r_{p_2} + w_{p_3} r_{p_3}, \tag{12.1}$$

where w_{p_j} is the return of the jth subportfolio and $w_{p_1} = 0.4$, $w_{p_2} = 0.4$, and $w_{p_3} = 0.2$ are the weights of the three subportfolios in the aggregate portfolio. The returns on the subportfolios are given by weighted averages of the returns of the securities that compose them of the form

$r_{p_j} = \sum_{i=1}^{N} u_{ij} r_i$, where u_{ij} is the weight of the ith security in the jth sub-portfolio, r_i is the return on the ith security, and here $N = 7$. Alternatively, the portfolio return can be written in terms of the returns of the individual assets in the portfolios, that is,

$$r_p = \sum_{i=1}^{N} w_i r_i, \tag{12.2}$$

where w_i is the weight of the ith asset in the aggregate portfolio. Each of these aggregate portfolio weights w_i is simply the weighted sum $w_i = \sum_{j=1}^{3} w_{p_j} = u_{ij}$, of the weights in the subportfolios. Table 12.4 shows the weights u_{ij} of the three subportfolios, along with the weights w_i of the securities in the aggregate portfolio. The common stock portfolio is equally split between the growth, or technology, and value stocks, while the fixed-income portfolio has large positions in the 10- and 30-year bonds. The hedge fund manager is long the two technology stocks and short an equal dollar amount of the value stocks, long the 30-year bond, and short the five-year bond. Although it is not apparent from Table 12.4, the magnitude of the short position in the five-year bond is chosen so that it almost completely

TABLE 12.4 Portfolio weights

	Weights of Securities in Subportfolios			Weights of Securities in Aggregate Portfolio
	Subportfolio 1 (equity)	Subportfolio 2 (fixed income)	Subportfolio 3 (hedge fund)	
Stock 1	0.4	0.0	0.3	0.22
Stock 2	0.1	0.0	0.3	0.10
Stock 3	0.3	0.0	−0.2	0.08
Stock 4	0.2	0.0	−0.4	0.00
Bond 1	0.0	0.2	−0.9	−0.10
Bond 2	0.0	0.4	0.0	0.16
Bond 3	0.0	0.4	0.4	0.24
Cash	0.0	0.0	1.5	0.30
Sum	1.0	1.0	1.0	1.00
Weights of Subportfolios in Aggregate Portfolio	0.4	0.4	0.2	

offsets the exposure of the 30-year bond to the first principal component, the level of the yield curve. Through these positions, the hedge fund manager is expressing the views that technology stocks will outperform value stocks and that the yield curve will flatten.

As discussed in Chapter 7, when the number of assets is large, factor models are very useful in estimating the covariance matrix and calculating the value-at-risk. In a factor model, the return on each asset is written as

$$r_i = \beta_{i0} + \sum_{k=1}^{K} \beta_{ik} f_k + \varepsilon_i, \tag{12.3}$$

where K is the number of factors (here $K = 5$), f_k is the change in or return on the kth factor, β_{ik} is the beta of the ith asset with respect to the kth factor, and ε_i is the residual for the ith asset, assumed to be uncorrelated both with the factor returns and with the residuals for the other assets. Combining equations (12.2) and (12.3) and then rearranging,

$$
\begin{aligned}
r_p &= \sum_{i=1}^{N} w_i r_i \\
&= \sum_{i=1}^{N} w_i \left(\beta_{i0} + \sum_{k=1}^{K} \beta_{ik} f_k + \varepsilon_i \right) \\
&= \sum_{i=1}^{N} w_i \beta_{i0} + \sum_{k=1}^{K} \left(\sum_{i=1}^{N} w_i \beta_{ik} \right) f_k + \sum_{i=1}^{N} w_i \varepsilon_i \\
&= \beta_{p0} + \sum_{k=1}^{K} \beta_{pk} f_k + \sum_{i=1}^{N} w_i \varepsilon_i \\
&= \beta_{p0} + \sum_{k=1}^{K} \beta_{pk} f_k + \varepsilon_p,
\end{aligned} \tag{12.4}
$$

where $\beta_{p0} = \sum_{i=1}^{N} w_i \beta_{i0}$, $\beta_{pk} = \sum_{i=1}^{N} w_i \beta_{ik}$ is the portfolio factor loading on the kth factor, and $\varepsilon_p = \sum_{i=1}^{N} w_i \varepsilon_i$ is the portfolio residual. Similar expressions can be obtained for the factor loadings of each of the subportfolios.

The factor loadings of the subportfolios and the aggregate portfolio can be computed from the factor loadings from Table 12.1 and the portfolio

TABLE 12.5   Factor loadings of the portfolios

	Factors					Residuals			
	Growth Index	Value Index	Principal Comp. 1	Principal Comp. 2	Principal Comp. 3	Stock 1	Stock 2	Stock 3	Stock 4
Subportfolio 1	1.22	0.00	−0.05	0.04	0.00	0.40	0.10	0.30	0.20
Subportfolio 2	0.00	0.00	−2.83	−1.60	1.10	0.00	0.00	0.00	0.00
Subportfolio 3	1.32	−1.13	−0.07	−1.12	1.09	0.30	0.30	−0.20	−0.40
Aggregate Portfolio	0.75	−0.23	−1.16	−0.85	0.66	0.22	0.10	0.08	0.00

weights from Table 12.4 and are shown in Table 12.5. Not surprisingly, the aggregate portfolio has significant exposure to the growth factor because of the long positions in growth stocks in subportfolios 1 and 3 and has negative exposures to the first two principal components (level and slope) and a positive exposure to the third principal component (curvature) due to the long positions in the 10- and 30-year bonds in subportfolios 2 and 3. However, despite the long positions in value stocks in subportfolio 1, the aggregate portfolio has a negative exposure to the value factor due to the negative loadings of the growth stocks on the value factor and the short positions in value stocks in subportfolio 3.

VALUE-AT-RISK

The last two lines of (12.4) are factor models for the portfolio return r_p and provide a framework for computing the portfolio standard deviation and value-at-risk estimates. Using the fact that the variance of the portfolio residual is $\text{var}(\varepsilon_p) = \sum_{i=1}^{N} w_i^2 \text{var}(\varepsilon_i)$ the portfolio variance and standard deviation of the portfolio return are

$$\text{var}(r_p) = \sum_{k=1}^{K} \sum_{l=1}^{K} \beta_{pk}\beta_{pl} \, \text{cov}\,(f_k, f_l) + \sum_{i=1}^{N} w_i^2 \, \text{var}(\varepsilon_i) \qquad (12.5)$$

and

$$\sigma_p = \sqrt{\text{var}(r_p)} = \sqrt{\sum_{k=1}^{K} \sum_{l=1}^{K} \beta_{jk}\beta_{jl} \, \text{cov}\,(f_k, f_l) + \sum_{i=1}^{N} w_i^2 \, \text{var}(\varepsilon_i)}.$$

If we continue to measure the value-at-risk relative to the expected return rather than relative to zero, the 95% confidence value-at-risk is just VaR $= 1.645\sigma_p$. Using the parameters in Tables 12.1–12.5, the value-at-risk is VaR $= 1.645\sigma_p = 1.645(3.55\%) = 5.85\%$ of the value of the portfolio.

Alternatively, if we define a benchmark we can compute benchmark-relative value-at-risk. As discussed in previous chapters, this would just involve changes to the weights in Table 12.4 to reflect a short position in the benchmark. These changes in the weights would then flow through to the factor loadings in Table 12.5 and the value-at-risk calculation.

RISK CONTRIBUTIONS OF THE SECURITIES

In addition to simplifying the computation of the value-at-risk, the factor models (12.3) and (12.4) also allow for the risk decomposition of the portfolio. We start with relatively simple decompositions in which the factor models play a background role and then turn to the explicit use of the factor models.

Equation (12.2) says simply that the portfolio return is a weighted average of the returns on the securities in the portfolio and provides the basis for decomposing the portfolio risk into the risk contributions of the individual securities. This decomposition proceeds exactly along the lines of the risk decomposition carried out in the previous chapter: the risk contribution of a security is determined by the covariance of the returns on that security with the returns on the portfolio. The covariance of the returns on the ith security with the portfolio return is

$$\operatorname{cov}(r_i, r_p) = \sum_{k=1}^{K} \sum_{\ell=1}^{K} \beta_{ik}\beta_{p\ell} \operatorname{cov}(f_k, f_\ell) + w_i \operatorname{var}(\varepsilon_i), \qquad (12.6)$$

where the variance of only one residual appears because each ε_i is assumed to be uncorrelated with the others. As in the previous chapter, if we use a delta-normal approach and define value-at-risk relative to the expected return, the risk contribution of the ith security is

$$\text{risk contribution} = \frac{\operatorname{cov}(r_i, r_p)w_i}{\sqrt{\operatorname{var}(r_p)}}. \qquad (12.7)$$

The second column of Table 12.6 shows the risk contributions of the seven securities, expressed in monthly terms (percent per month), while the third shows the percentages of the total risk due to each of the seven securities. As they must, the risk contributions sum to the portfolio standard deviation of 3.55% per month, and the percentages sum to 100%. This table shows that the first security accounts for the bulk of the risk, that is, 2.18 percentage points out of 3.55, or 61.3% of the total risk. This occurs because the first subportfolio constitutes a large fraction of the aggregate portfolio ($w_1 = 0.22$) and has returns that covary highly with it. This high covariance results from the combination of the security's volatility, its large weight in the aggregate portfolio, and its positive correlation with the second stock, which also has a relatively high volatility and appears with a positive weight in the aggregate portfolio.

The second largest risk contribution is made by stock 2 (the second growth stock), and the third largest by bond 3 (the 30-year bond). These risk contributions are large due to the volatilities of these instruments, their large weights in the portfolio, and their positive correlations with stock 1. The risk decomposition tells us that, if we want to reduce the risk of the portfolio, stocks 1 and 2 and bond 3 are the instruments that merit attention. Conversely, increasing positions in stocks 1 or 2 or bond 3 would result in the largest increase in risk.

The decomposition into the risk contributions of the individual securities is useful if there are only a limited number of positions. This, for example, was the case with MPT's portfolio in the preceding chapter. (It is also the case in the example in this chapter, but only because the number of securities has been

TABLE 12.6 Risk decomposition by securities

Security	Risk Contribution (Percent)	Percentage Contribution
Stock 1	2.18	61.3
Stock 2	0.66	18.6
Stock 3	0.24	6.8
Stock 4	0.00	0.0
Bond 1	−0.06	−1.7
Bond 2	0.16	4.6
Bond 3	0.37	10.4
Total	3.55	100.0

limited for simplicity.) However, for portfolios involving thousands of securities, the decomposition into the risk contributions of individual securities is usually uninformative. Except when a single asset or position is large relative to the portfolio, the risk contribution of a single asset is almost always small.

RISK DECOMPOSITION IN TERMS OF GROUPS OF ASSETS

Equation (12.1) provides the basis for decomposing the portfolio risk into the risk contributions of the three subportfolios. In this case, the risk contribution of a subportfolio is determined by the covariance of the returns on that subportfolio with the returns on the total portfolio. This covariance is given by an expression similar, though slightly more complicated, than equation (12.6): because the same asset may appear in more than one subportfolio, the residual for the ith subportfolio is now correlated with the residuals for the other subportfolios. For example, the residuals from factor models describing the returns of the first and third subportfolios are correlated because these two subportfolios both include positions in the four common stocks and thus include the effects of the same four residuals. Combining (12.6) with the fact that $r_{p_j} = \sum_{i=1}^N u_{ij} r_i$, for the jth subportfolio we have

$$ \text{cov}(r_{p_j}, r_p) = \sum_{k=1}^K \sum_{\ell=1}^K \beta_{pjk} \beta_{p\ell} \, \text{cov}(f_k, f_\ell) + \sum_{i=1}^N u_{ij} w_i \, \text{var}(\varepsilon_i), \quad (12.8) $$

where u_{ij} is the weight of the ith asset in the jth subportfolio and, as before, w_i is the weight of the ith asset in the aggregate portfolio. In (12.8), the residuals ε_i and weights u_{ij} and w_i play the roles of factors and factor loadings, respectively. This can be understood by looking back at (12.3), where each ε_i can be interpreted as a factor for which the ith security has a factor loading of 1 and all other securities have a factor loading of 0. The weights u_{ij} and w_i are then just the weighted averages of these factors loadings of 1 or 0.

The second column of Table 12.7, headed "Risk Contribution," shows the risk contributions of the three subportfolios, expressed in monthly terms (percent per month). As expected, they sum to the portfolio standard deviation of 3.55% per month. The percentages of the total risk of 3.55% due to each of the three subportfolios are shown in the third column. This table shows that the first subportfolio accounts for the bulk of the risk, that is, 2.40 percentage points, or 67.6% of the total risk of 3.55% per month. This occurs because the first subportfolio constitutes a large fraction of the aggregate portfolio $w_{p_1} = 0.40$ and has returns that covary highly with it.

TABLE 12.7　Risk decomposition by subportfolios

Subportfolio	Risk Contribution (Percent)	Percentage Contribution
1	2.40	67.6
2	0.46	12.9
3	0.69	19.5
Total	3.55	100.0

This high covariance results from the combination of the volatilities of the stocks in the first subportfolio and their large weights in the aggregate portfolio. Although the third subportfolio includes short positions in stocks 3 and 4, the net position in stock 3 in the aggregate portfolio is still positive; moreover, the third subportfolio includes large long positions in stocks 1 and 2, which are the most volatile.

Perhaps surprisingly, Table 12.7 also shows that the market-neutral subportfolio 3 makes a significant risk contribution. These results that subportfolios 1 and 3 make the largest risk contributions are consistent with the early risk decomposition by securities, for both subportfolios 1 and 3 have significant long positions in stocks 1 and 2. This risk decomposition by managers allows the sponsor to set and monitor individual risk budgets for the managers of the subportfolios. In particular, the sponsor could set a target for the risk contributions and total portfolio risk and then monitor the managers by comparing the entries in the column headed "Risk Contribution" to the managers' risk budgets.

A bit of thought about the decompositions into the risk contributions of the individual securities and the subportfolios suggests that a wide range of risk decompositions is possible, because one need not restrict attention to the original subportfolios. There is no limit to the number of possible subportfolios into which the assets can be partitioned, each leading to a different decomposition. For example, if we group the securities into technology stocks and others (i.e., the other stocks and the bonds), the portfolio return can be written

$$r_p = \sum_{i=1}^{N} w_i r_i$$

$$= \underbrace{\sum w_i r_i}_{\substack{\text{technology} \\ \text{stocks}}} + \underbrace{\sum w_i r_i}_{\substack{\text{other} \\ \text{securities}}}.$$

Going further, we can look at technology stocks in each of the subportfolios, that is,

$$r_p = \sum_{i=1}^{N} w_i r_i$$

$$= \underbrace{\sum w_i r_i}_{\substack{\text{technology} \\ \text{stocks in} \\ \text{subport. 1}}} + \underbrace{\sum w_i r_i}_{\substack{\text{technology} \\ \text{stocks in} \\ \text{subport. 2}}} + \underbrace{\sum w_i r_i}_{\substack{\text{technology} \\ \text{stocks in} \\ \text{subport. 3}}} + \underbrace{\sum w_i r_i}_{\substack{\text{other} \\ \text{securities}}}.$$

The risk decompositions corresponding to these groupings of the assets are shown in Table 12.8. They indicate the risk contribution of both the aggregate technology bet in the entire portfolio and the technology bets made by each of the managers of the subportfolios. As must be the case, the risk contribution of the technology stocks of 2.84% per month, or 79.9% of the risk of the portfolio, equals the sum of the risks of stocks 1 and 2 (the two technology stocks) shown in Table 12.6.

Table 12.8 reveals that a significant contributor to the risk is the *hidden* technology bet in subportfolio 3, stemming from the long leg of the long-short equity position. The technology stocks in subportfolio 3 account for 27.9% of the total portfolio risk, despite the fact that their weight in the aggregate portfolio is only $w_{p_3}(u_{13} + u_{23}) = 0.2(0.3 + 0.3) = 0.12$, or 12%, and the position in them is offset by a short position in the value stocks with weight $w_{p_3}(u_{33} + u_{43}) = 0.2(-0.2 - 0.4) = -0.12$, or -12%. This technology bet is hidden in the sense that one might not ordinarily expect such a hedged position in a market-neutral fund to be so highly correlated with the

TABLE 12.8   Risk contributions of technology stocks

Subportfolio	Risk Contributions of Technology Stocks (Percent)	Percentage Contributions
1	1.85	52.0
2	0.00	0.0
3	0.99	27.9
Total Technology Stocks	2.84	79.9
Other Securities	0.71	20.1
Total Risk	3.55	100.0

diversified equity portfolio, subportfolio 1. Nonetheless, it is; this is partly because the technology stocks are the most volatile stocks in the aggregate portfolio, but also because the technology stocks' negative factor loadings on the value factor exacerbate the risk of the short position in the value stocks and their negative factor loadings on the first principal component exacerbate the risk of the bond position. One of the contributions of risk decomposition is that it allows the identification of such positions.

Of course, the approach can be applied to other industries or sectors. In fact, a similar decomposition could be carried out for any possible grouping of securities that the portfolio or risk manager considers interesting. Such risk decompositions allow plan sponsors to set and monitor risk budgets on industry and sectoral exposures, and, as in the example of the New York City Retirement Systems mentioned in the notes, they allow the portfolio or risk manager to identify particular industry or sectoral concentrations of risk, which may be hidden across multiple portfolios controlled by different managers.

RISK DECOMPOSITION IN TERMS OF THE FACTORS

Rather than group securities by characteristics (e.g., technology, growth, or value), an alternative approach is to think of each portfolio as consisting of a set of factor exposures and to measure the risk contributions of the market factors. As indicated in the discussion of factor models in Chapters 7 and 8, for equities these factors might include the market, value, growth, or other variables such as the exposure to unexpected growth in GDP; for interest rates they might include various key rates, forward rates, or factors corresponding to the level, slope, and curvature of the yield curve. An advantage of the risk decomposition in terms of factors is that the use of factors allows one to measure the risks of factors, such as unexpected growth in GDP or yield curve factors that do not correspond to any partition or grouping of securities. It also allows the risk decomposition to capture the fact that, even for factors such as growth and value that do correspond to groupings of securities, different stocks will have different loadings on the factors.

Using factor models for risk decomposition is a more direct use of the factor models than we have previously seen. Above, and in Chapters 7 and 8, we used the factor models to render manageable the computation of the variances and covariances, for example, through equations (12.5), (12.6), and (12.8). In Chapter 8 we also described how the principal components (a particular choice of factors) could be used to simplify Monte Carlo simulation. For these purposes, the identity and interpretation of the factors was unimportant: all that mattered was that they captured the possible changes in the portfolio value. In contrast, the factors come to the forefront when we use them for risk decomposition, for in doing this we interpret the portfolio as a set of factor exposures. For the risk decomposition in terms of the factors to be useful, the factors must correspond to the risks in which we are interested and should have intuitive interpretations.

To see the risk decomposition in terms of the factors, return to equations (12.6) and (12.8) and recall that the residuals ε_i and weights u_{ij} and w_i play the role of factors and factor loadings, respectively. In particular, rewrite (12.6) as

$$
\begin{aligned}
\text{cov}(r_i, r_p) = & \sum_{k=1}^{K}\left(\sum_{\ell=1}^{K} \text{cov}(\beta_{ik} f_k, \beta_{p\ell} f_\ell)\right) \\
& + \sum_{i=1}^{N}\sum_{h=1}^{N} \text{cov}(\varepsilon_i, w_h \varepsilon_h),
\end{aligned}
\tag{12.9}
$$

indicating that the covariance $\text{cov}(r_i, r_p)$ can be written as a sum of K terms each of the form $\sum_{\ell=1}^{K} \text{cov}(\beta_{ik} f_k, \beta_{p\ell} f_\ell)$ and N terms of the form $\sum_{h=1}^{N} \text{cov}(\varepsilon_i, w_h \varepsilon_h)$. From (12.7), the risk contribution of the ith security is

$$
\frac{\text{cov}(r_i, r_p)w_i}{\sqrt{\text{var}(r_p)}} = \sum_{k=1}^{K}\left(\frac{w_i \sum_{\ell=1}^{K} \text{cov}(\beta_{ik} f_k, \beta_{p\ell} f_\ell)}{\sqrt{\text{var}(r_p)}}\right)
$$

$$
+ \sum_{i=1}^{N}\left(\frac{w_i \sum_{h=1}^{N} \text{cov}(\varepsilon_i, w_h \varepsilon_h)}{\sqrt{\text{var}(r_p)}}\right).
\tag{12.10}
$$

Define

$$
C_{ik} \equiv \left(\frac{w_i \sum_{\ell=1}^{K} \text{cov}(\beta_{ik} f_k, \beta_{p\ell} f_\ell)}{\sqrt{\text{var}(r_p)}}\right)
$$

to be the risk contribution of the ith security's exposure to the kth factor, and

$$c_{ii} \equiv \frac{w_i \sum_{h=1}^{N} \text{cov}\,(\varepsilon_i,\, w_h \varepsilon_h)}{\sqrt{\text{var}(r_p)}} = \frac{w_i^2\, \text{var}(\varepsilon_i)}{\sqrt{\text{var}(r_p)}}$$

to be the risk contribution stemming from the ith security's exposure to its own residual. Then equation (12.10) implies that the risk contribution of the ith security can be written as the sum of the risk contributions of its exposures to the K factors and N residuals, that is,

$$\text{risk contribution} = \frac{\text{cov}\,(r_i,\, r_p)w_i}{\sqrt{\text{var}(r_p)}} = \sum_{k=1}^{K} C_{ik} + c_{ii}. \qquad (12.11)$$

A similar analysis for the jth subportfolio reveals that the risk contribution of the jth subportfolio is

$$\frac{\text{cov}\,(r_{p_j},\, r_p)w_{p_j}}{\sqrt{\text{var}(r_p)}} = \sum_{k=1}^{K} \left(\frac{w_{p_j} \sum_{l=1}^{K} \text{cov}\,(\beta_{p_j k} f_k,\, \beta_{pl} f_l)}{\sqrt{\text{var}(r_p)}} \right)$$

$$(12.12)$$

$$+ \sum_{l=1}^{N} \left(\frac{w_{p_j} \sum_{h=1}^{N} \text{cov}\,(u_{ij} \varepsilon_i,\, w_h \varepsilon_h)}{\sqrt{\text{var}(r_p)}} \right).$$

Similar to above, defining

$$C_{p_j k} \equiv \left(\frac{w_{p_j} \sum_{l=1}^{K} \text{cov}\,(\beta_{p_j k} f_k,\, \beta_{pl} f_l)}{\sqrt{\text{var}(r_p)}} \right)$$

to be the risk contribution stemming from the jth subportfolio's exposure to the kth factor and

$$c_{p_j i} \equiv \frac{w_{p_j} \sum_{h=1}^{N} \text{cov}\,(u_{ij}\varepsilon_i,\, w_h\varepsilon_h)}{\sqrt{\text{var}(r_p)}}$$

to be the jth subportfolio's exposure to the ith residual, we have

$$\text{risk contribution} = \frac{\text{cov}\,(r_{p_j},\, r_p)w_{pj}}{\sqrt{\text{var}(r_p)}} = \sum_{k=1}^{K} C_{p_j k} + \sum_{i=1}^{N} c_{p_j i}. \qquad (12.13)$$

These further decompositions (12.11) and (12.13) of the risk contributions of the ith security and jth subportfolio into the risk contributions of the factors and residuals follow from the somewhat mechanical fact that covariances of the form (12.6) can be rewritten in the form of (12.9). In the common case when the factors f_k can be interpreted as the returns on portfolios, the right-hand sides of equations (12.11) and (12.13) can also be interpreted in terms of the risk contributions of portfolios, as follows.

Equation (12.4) above says that the portfolio return r_i can be written as

$$r_i = \beta_{i0} + \sum_{k=1}^{K} \beta_{ik}f_k + \varepsilon_i, \qquad (12.14)$$

which is repeated as (12.14) for convenience. If the factors f_k are the returns on securities or portfolios, then (12.14) says that the portfolio return is a weighted average of the K returns f_k, the constant β_{i0}, and the residual ε_i. The constant β_{i0} can be interpreted as a portfolio return, because it can be written in the form $\beta_{i0} = w_{i0}r_0$, where r_0 is the risk-free rate or return on cash and $w_{i0} = \beta_{i0}/r_0$ is the portfolio weight in cash. Then, because the residual $\varepsilon_i = r_i - (\beta_{i0} + \sum_{k=1}^{K} \beta_{ik}f_k)$ can be interpreted as the return on the security minus the return $\beta_{i0} + \sum_{k=1}^{K} \beta_{ik}f_k$ on a combination of cash and the factor portfolios, the residual ε_i is also the return on a portfolio. Thus, the second line of (12.14) says that r_i can be interpreted as the return on a portfolio consisting of a risk-free component $\beta_{i0} = w_{i0}r_0$, K factor portfolios with weights β_{ik}, and a residual return with weight 1. To emphasize this, we write the return as

$$r_i = w_{i0}r_0 + \sum_{k=1}^{K} w_{ik}f_k + w_\varepsilon\varepsilon_i, \qquad (12.15)$$

where $w_{i0} = \beta_{i0}/r_0$, $w_{ik} = \beta_{ik}$, and $w_\varepsilon = 1$ are the portfolio weights. This is just a rearrangement of the portfolio return into the returns on other portfolios, analogous to our rearrangement of the assets into technology stocks and other securities. It allows the decomposition on the right-hand side of equation (12.11) to be interpreted as the sum of the risk contributions of factor and residual portfolios. A similar analysis would allow the right-hand side of equation (12.13) to be interpreted similarly.

Table 12.9 shows the risk decomposition by securities and factors or residuals; each entry in the Table shows the risk contribution of the exposure of a particular security to a particular factor or residual, expressed as a percentage of the total risk of the portfolio. For example, the entry of 51.0 in the row labeled "Growth Index" and column headed "Stock 1" indicates that the exposure of the first stock to the growth index accounts for 51.0% of the total portfolio risk. The next four rows show the contributions of the securities' other factor exposures, and the next four after that show the risk

TABLE 12.9   Risk decomposition by factors and securities

Factor or Residual	Stock 1	Stock 2	Stock 3	Stock 4	Bond 1	Bond 2	Bond 3	Aggregate Portfolio
Growth Index	51.0	19.5	−0.7	0.0	0.0	0.0	0.0	69.7
Value Index	−14.4	−4.8	5.7	0.0	0.0	0.0	0.0	−13.4
Prin. Comp. 1	0.2	0.1	0.0	0.0	−1.7	4.4	9.7	12.6
Prin. Comp. 2	0.0	0.0	0.0	0.0	0.0	0.2	0.7	0.8
Prin. Comp 3	0.0	0.0	0.0	0.0	0.0	0.0	0.0	0.1
Residual 1	24.5	0.0	0.0	0.0	0.0	0.0	0.0	24.5
Residual 2	0.0	3.9	0.0	0.0	0.0	0.0	0.0	3.9
Residual 3	0.0	0.0	1.8	0.0	0.0	0.0	0.0	1.8
Residual 4	0.0	0.0	0.0	0.0	0.0	0.0	0.0	0.0
Residuals	24.5	3.9	1.8	0.0	0.0	0.0	0.0	30.2
Total	61.3	18.6	6.8	0.0	−1.7	4.6	10.4	100.0

The heading "Risk Contributions (Percentage of total risk)" spans the stock/bond/aggregate columns.

contributions of the four stocks' residuals; the row labeled "Residuals" shows the sum of the risk contribution of the residuals of the individual securities. Of course, because this risk decomposition is by individual securities, only the aggregate portfolio shows a positive risk contribution for more than one residual.

In Table 12.6 we saw that stock 1 has the largest risk contribution and stock 2 the second largest. Table 12.9 reveals that these large risk contributions are due to the growth factor and the residuals and that the risk contributions of these stocks' exposures to the value factor are negative. The rightmost column of the Table reveals that, while the exposure to the growth factor is most important, the exposure to stock 1's residual is the second most important source of risk in the portfolio. The third-largest risk contribution is due to the first principal component (level of the yield curve), mostly stemming from the position in the 30-year bond (bond 3). The risk contribution of the exposure to the value factor is negative, due to both the net short position in stock 3 and the negative exposures of stocks 1 and 2 to the value factor.

Table 12.10 shows the risk decomposition by subportfolios and factors or residuals; similar to Table 12.9, each entry in the Table shows the

TABLE 12.10   Risk decomposition by factors and subportfolios

Factor or Residual	Risk Contributions (Percentage of Total Risk)			
	Subportfolio1	Subportfolio2	Subportfolio3	Aggregate Portfolio
Growth Index	45.2	0.0	24.5	69.7
Value Index	0.0	0.0	−13.4	−13.4
Prin. Comp. 1	0.2	12.3	0.2	12.6
Prin. Comp. 2	0.0	0.6	0.2	0.8
Prin. Comp 3	0.0	0.0	0.0	0.1
Residual 1	12.8	0.0	6.7	24.5
Residual 2	1.6	0.0	2.3	3.9
Residual 3	2.7	0.0	−0.9	1.8
Residual 4	0.0	0.0	0.0	0.0
Residuals	22.1	0.0	8.1	30.2
Total	67.6	12.9	19.5	100.0

risk contribution of the exposure of a particular subportfolio to a particular factor or residual, expressed as a percentage of the total risk of the portfolio. As suggested by the decomposition by subportfolio in Table 12.6 and the decomposition by securities in Table 12.9, it shows that the growth stocks in subportfolio 1 make the largest contributions to the portfolio risk, both through their exposures to the growth factor and their residual risk. However, subportfolio 3 is not as far behind as its characterization as a market-neutral portfolio might lead one to guess: the exposure of subportfolio 3 to the growth factor contributes 24.5% of the total portfolio risk, and the exposure to the residuals contributes 8.1%. As one might expect, the first principal component makes the largest contribution of the interest rate factors.

Although we do not do so, it is possible to drill down even further; for example, the risk contribution of stock 1 in portfolio 1 is 26.3% of the total risk and the residual is 14% of the total risk. This process can be carried out for every possible subset of the securities and for every factor or residual. This makes it possible to examine the risks in as fine a detail as one might desire.

Such risk decompositions allow plan sponsors to identify unintended factor and residual exposures, to identify uncompensated risks, and to decide how and to what extent to hedge each factor. The ability to decompose risk by factors and subportfolios also allows sponsors to assign risk budgets for exposures to portfolio managers and to monitor them. As discussed in the notes to this chapter, software firms are developing such tools, and plan sponsors are increasingly using them. The risk decomposition analysis also allows for implied views analysis and portfolio optimization, but now with factors and residuals substituted for securities. This is discussed further in the next chapter.

NOTES

As indicated in the notes to Chapter 10, the approach to risk decomposition here is that exposited by Litterman (1996); closely related work includes Litterman and Winkelman (1996), Litterman, Longerstaey, Rosengarten, and Winkelman (2000), and Winkelman (2000a, 2000b). Dowd (1999) uses marginal value-at-risk to examine the risk-return tradeoff.

A clear example of the use of risk decomposition to identify an unintended sector bet is provided by Cass (2000), who reports that the

New York City Retirement Systems used the risk-decomposition capabilities of Barra's Total Risk for Asset Management (TRAM) to identify a series of technology stock bets one manager was taking that were outside the manager's risk profile. In particular, the risk decomposition allowed the plan to identify "which specific securities have a much greater contribution to the marginal risk of the portfolio," allowing the plan to "have a much more structured conversation with the managers, [and] engage in a qualitatively different conversation with them." While it is easy to identify undesirable industry concentrations of risk after a loss has occurred, the ability to do this on a "forward-looking" basis is crucial. This is particularly valuable when market volatilities or correlations are changing, because in this situation the historical performance of the managers sheds less light on the risks they are taking.

Risk (2000) reports that Putnam Investments uses risk-decomposition analytics that enable it to decompose portfolio risk "into common factors and specific factors." This allows Putnam to identify uncompensated risks and to "decide how and to what extent to hedge each factor."

An alternative approach to risk decomposition is an *incremental* approach based on regression analysis and described in Golub and Tilman (2000). In this approach, one begins by expressing the portfolio return in terms of the changes in (or returns to) K factors, as in the last line of (12.4). For any such factor model, it is possible to compute the proportion of the variance of the return r_p explained by the K factors, which we denote R_K^2 because it is analogous to the R-squared of a multiple regression. To compute the risk contribution of the Kth factor, one considers a $(K-1)$-factor model of the form

$$r_p = \beta_{p0} + \sum_{k=1}^{K-1} \beta_{pk} f_k + \varepsilon_p$$

and computes the proportion of the variance of r_p explained by the $K-1$ factors, R_{K-1}^2. The risk contribution of the kth factor is then the difference in the proportions of the explained variances, $R_K^2 - R_{K-1}^2$.

A limitation of incremental decomposition is that it depends on the order in which the factors are considered. While some situations might have a natural ordering of factors, in most cases the order is less apparent. In such cases, Golub and Tilman (2000) suggested that at each step one should search over all of the remaining factors (or groups of factors) to find the factor (or group of factors) with the largest risk contribution.

As of the writing of this book, risk decomposition is increasingly being used. Cass (2000), Falloon (1999), and *Risk* (2000) report on some users of risk decomposition and indicate a number of software firms that include at least some risk decomposition functionality in their recent releases. Further applications of risk decomposition are discussed in Gurnani (2000), Layard-Liesching (2000), Putnam, Quintana, and Wilford (2000), Rawls (2000), and Winkelman (2000a, 2000b).

CHAPTER 13

Risk Budgeting and the Choice of Active Managers

The previous two chapters illustrated how risk decomposition can be used to understand and manage the risks in both bond and equity portfolios. There we saw how to compute the risk contributions of various assets and how these can be used to manage the risk of a portfolio. The analysis in these chapters is broadly applicable. At the level of a portfolio manager, it can be used to identify, structure, and manage the risks in the portfolio. At the level of a risk manager, it can be used to monitor the portfolio managers. Finally, at the level of an organization that hires portfolio managers, it can be used to control risks, including aiding in the identification of unintended risks. Thus, this analysis is useful for a wide range of organizations.

In this chapter, we look at a more specific application of risk decomposition and risk budgeting. In particular, we take the perspective of a pension plan sponsor or other organization that hires active portfolio managers and show how the ideas of this book can be applied to the problem of managing active risk at the total fund or plan level. The problem of managing active risk at the plan level can be decomposed into two pieces: the analysis of the existing manager roster and the determination of the optimal manager roster. In determining this optimal manager roster, we use the idea that risk should be taken up to the point where the ratio of the marginal impact of performance to the marginal impact on the risk of the total portfolio is the same for each manager and asset class.

Decomposing the problem in this way is sensible because most large pension plans have an existing manager roster, and it is not practical to start *de novo* with a wholly new roster. Rather, the question in practice is to consider what incremental changes should be made to the existing roster. Comparing an existing manager roster to the optimal one can provide insight into those changes that are likely to have the greatest impact on the risk-adjusted performance of the total fund or plan.

This chapter is built around the example described below. The example is deliberately kept simple, with unrealistically small numbers of asset classes and managers, in order to avoid cluttering the chapter with unnecessary detail. For convenience, the example assumes that the distributions of asset returns are normally distributed and defines value-at-risk relative to the expected value of the excess (over a benchmark) return on the portfolio, using an annual holding period. In particular, letting $r - r_B$ denote the excess return over the benchmark return r_B, the 95% confidence value-at-risk is 1.645 σ rather than $-1.645(E[r - r_B])$. This simplifies the example because it allows value-at-risk to be equated with the standard deviation of the tracking error, which corresponds to a view of risk common in portfolio management. The last section of the chapter briefly discusses what parts of the analysis depend on this assumption.

THE EXISTING ASSET ALLOCATION AND MANAGER ROSTER

To keep things simple, we restrict attention to the seven asset classes listed in Table 13.1. The table also lists the index used as a benchmark for each asset class, the expected excess returns (over cash), the expected returns, and the standard deviations of returns. The fund may also invest in money market instruments (i.e., cash), which offer a return of 6% per year.

The plan has the existing manager roster and asset allocations shown in Table 13.2. Included in this table are a number of managers who currently do not have any allocations but who are under consideration. For each manager, the plan sponsor (or its consultant) has estimated the manager's beta, alpha, and tracking error volatility (standard deviation) relative

TABLE 13.1   Asset classes and benchmarks used in the example

Asset Class	Benchmark	Expected Excess Return (% per year)	Expected Return (% per year)	Standard Deviation (% per year)
U.S. Large Cap	S&P 500	5.5	11.5	20.0
U.S. Small Cap	Russel 2000	6.5	12.5	25.0
International	MSCI EAFE	6.0	12.0	25.0
Emerging Markets	MSCI EMF	6.5	12.5	40.0
U.S. Bonds	Lehman Aggregate	1.0	7.0	5.0
High Yield	ML High Yield	2.0	8.0	10.0
Non–U.S. Bonds	WGBIxUS	1.0	7.0	10.0

TABLE 13.2 Existing managers and asset allocations

Asset Class	Manager	Benchmark	Beta	Alpha (% per year)	Tracking Error Volatility (% per year)	Allocation (Percent)	Asset Class Allocation (Percent)	Expected Return (% per year)
U.S. Large Cap	1	S&P 500	1.20	0.3	6.0	10.0	30.0	12.90
	2	S&P 500	1.10	0.2	4.0	10.0		12.25
	3	S&P 500	0.95	0.8	6.0	10.0		12.03
U.S. Small Cap	4	Russel 2000	1.10	1.0	8.0	5.0	10.0	14.15
	5	Russel 2000	0.90	2.0	6.0	5.0		13.85
International	6	MSCI EAFE	1.00	0.5	7.0	5.0	10.0	12.50
	7	MSCI EAFE	1.10	1.0	8.0	5.0		13.60
Emerging Markets	8	MSCI EMF	1.00	3.0	8.0	0.0	0.0	15.50
U.S. Bonds	9	Lehman Aggregate	1.00	0.1	2.0	10.0	20.0	7.10
	10	Lehman Aggregate	1.05	0.1	2.4	10.0		7.10
	11	Lehman Aggregate	1.00	0.1	1.2	0.0		7.05
High Yield	12	ML High Yield	1.00	1.5	6.0	0.0	0.0	9.50
	13	ML High Yield	1.00	1.5	4.0	0.0		9.50
Hedge Funds	14	Cash		6.0	20.0	0.0	0.0	12.00
	15	Cash		10.0	25.0	0.0		16.00
Strategic Benchmark	16		0.0	0.0	0.0	30.0	30.0	9.30

to the appropriate benchmark. The table lists these estimates, estimates of the expected returns based on them, and the existing asset allocations to the managers. The two largest allocations are to large capitalization U.S. equities and U.S. bonds, constituting 30% and 20% of the portfolio, respectively. Currently 70% of the plan assets have been allocated to the active managers, with the remaining 30% allocated to a passive portfolio of index funds corresponding to the strategic benchmark described below.

Table 13.3 shows the estimates of correlations among the various asset classes (i.e., the various benchmarks). The analysis below also requires the correlations of returns among the active managers. These are determined by the correlations and standard deviations of the benchmarks, the managers' betas with respect to the benchmarks, and the correlations and standard deviations of the managers' tracking errors. The standard deviations of the tracking errors are in the column of Table 13.2 labeled "Tracking Error Volatility." For simplicity, we assume that the correlations of the tracking errors across different managers are zero. This assumption will not be satisfied to the extent that managers deviate from their benchmarks in similar ways. It is straightforward to introduce correlations among the managers' tracking errors, but this would clutter the analysis below.

The expected return on the portfolio can be computed from the asset allocations and expected returns in Table 13.2 and is 10.63% per year. Subtracting the cash yield of 6%, the expected excess return on this portfolio is 4.63% per year. The standard deviation of portfolio returns is 13% per year. Of this, 1% can be ascribed to the tracking error of the active managers, because a calculation of standard error that does not include the tracking

TABLE 13.3   Correlations among the benchmark returns

	S&P 500	Russell 2000	MSCI EAFE	MSCI EMF	Lehman Aggregate	ML High Yield	WGBIxUS
S&P 500	1.00	0.67	0.52	0.5	0.43	0.46	0.35
Russel 2000	0.67	1.00	0.41	0.55	0.19	0.54	0.21
MSCI EAFE	0.52	0.41	1.00	0.48	0.18	0.27	0.28
MSCI EMF	0.50	0.55	0.48	1.00	0.00	0.33	0.12
Lehman Aggregate	0.43	0.2	0.18	0.00	1.00	0.37	0.58
ML High Yield	0.46	0.54	0.27	0.33	0.37	1.00	0.36
WGBIxUS	0.35	0.21	0.28	0.12	0.58	0.36	1.00

errors is 12% per year. Following the procedure in the previous chapters, we could decompose the risk of the portfolio, that is, determine the risk contributions of each of the managers and asset classes. However, in the context of portfolio management it is common to measure the risk relative to a benchmark, so we first introduce the benchmark.

THE STRATEGIC BENCHMARK

Many plan sponsors begin the asset-allocation process by setting a strategic benchmark, reflecting its allocations across asset classes. In the simplest case, this strategic benchmark is the portfolio of assets that best hedges the liability stream. For example, if the liability stream can be interpreted as a short position in a fixed-income portfolio, the strategic benchmark might consist of the return on that fixed-income portfolio. If no perfect hedge is possible, the strategic benchmark might be the return on the portfolio that minimizes the volatility of the surplus, that is, the difference between the return on the assets and the return on a short position in the liabilities.

Alternatively, one might choose the benchmark using mean-variance optimization. In this case, one would proceed by first determining the risk and return characteristics of the liability stream and of each of the asset classes that will be used. These may be estimated from long-run historical average returns, from the returns predicted by a model of market equilibrium, from fundamental views, or from some mix of these sources. Given the expected returns, volatilities, and correlations, one then uses an optimizer to find the efficient frontier, that is, the maximum expected return for each risk level. Selecting a point on this risk-return tradeoff amounts to selecting a particular portfolio, that which achieves this expected return and risk. The portfolio weights for this portfolio are then used to define the strategic benchmark. For example, if the selected portfolio has weights of 50% on both large-cap U.S. equities and U.S. corporate bonds, then the strategic benchmark would consist of $r_B = 0.5r_{S\&P500} + 0.5r_{LA}$, where r_B, $r_{S\&P500}$, and r_{LA} are the total returns on the strategic benchmark and the portfolios underlying S&P 500 index and the Lehman Aggregate.

Regardless of how it is chosen, if we use the asset classes and benchmarks above, then in general the strategic benchmark will consist of a portfolio return of the form

$$r_B = w_{S\&P500}r_{S\&P500} + w_{R2000}r_{R2000} + w_{EAFE}r_{EAFE} + w_{EMF}r_{EMF}$$
$$+ w_{LA}r_{LA} + w_{HY}r_{HY} + w_{xUS}r_{xUS} + w_{cash}r_{cash} + \varepsilon,$$

where the rs represent the returns on the various indexes or benchmarks listed in Table 13.1 and the ws are portfolio weights. The extra term, or residual ε, will be zero if the strategic benchmark is chosen by applying an optimizer to portfolios that track the various asset indexes, because in this case the strategic benchmark is a linear combination of the returns on various benchmarks. The residual ε might be nonzero if the return on the liability stream is used as the strategic benchmark. For example, if the strategic benchmark is chosen to be the return on the liability stream and that return is highly but not perfectly correlated with the Lehman Aggregate, then the strategic benchmark might be $r_B = w_{LA}r_{LA} + (1 - w_{LA})r_{cash} + \varepsilon$, where the coefficient w_{LA} and the volatility of ε are determined by the exact relation between the liability stream and the Lehman Aggregate.

Here we assume that the process of choosing a strategic benchmark has already been completed, that it has the weights shown in Table 13.4, and that $\varepsilon = 0$. With these choices, the return on the strategic benchmark is

$$r_B = 0.3r_{S\&P500} + 0.1r_{R2000} + 0.1r_{EAFE} + 0.2r_{LA} + 0.1r_{HY} + 0.2r_{cash}.$$

Given this strategic benchmark, the focus is on the excess return $r - r_B$, where the portfolio return r is $r = \sum_{i=1}^{15} w_i r_i + (1 - \sum_{i=1}^{15} w_i) r_B$, r_i is the return on the portfolio managed by manager i, and w_i is the fraction of the portfolio allocated to manager i. In particular, the problem is to choose the allocations w_i to obtain the best possible risk-return tradeoff. In this process we assume that the plan sponsor has access to index funds corresponding to all of the indexes in the strategic benchmark, so that one option is simply to invest in the strategic benchmark through the index funds. The coefficient $1 - \sum_{i=1}^{15} w_i$ that appears in the definition of r_B allows for this and is interpreted as the passive investment in a portfolio of index funds that corresponds to the strategic benchmark. An extremely risk-averse plan sponsor who could not accept any risk of underperformance might choose to allocate close to 100% of the portfolio in this way.

Table 13.4 also shows the existing active, passive, and total allocations to each of the asset classes. Comparing the existing allocations to the strategic benchmark, one can see that relative to the benchmark the current portfolio is overweight in U.S. and international equities and U.S. bonds and underweight in cash.

Table 13.5 decomposes the risks of the strategic benchmark into the marginal risk contributions using the procedure of Chapter 10. Because it decomposes the risk of the strategic benchmark rather than the risk of the excess return over the present value of the liability stream, it is equivalent to assuming that the liability stream acts like cash. As in Chapter 10, these risk contributions

TABLE 13.4 Weights used in forming the strategic benchmark and existing allocation

Asset Class	Asset Class Benchmark	Weight in Strategic Benchmark (Percent)	Existing Allocations		
			Allocation to Active Managers (Percent)	Passive Allocation to Index Funds (Percent)	Total Allocation to Asset Class (Percent)
U.S. Large Cap	S&P 500	30	30	9	39
U.S. Small Cap	Russel 2000	10	10	3	13
International	MSCI EAFE	10	10	3	13
Emerging Markets	MSCI EMF	0	0	0	0
U.S. Bonds	Lehman Aggregate	20	20	6	26
High Yield	ML High Yield	10	0	3	3
Non–U.S. Bonds	WGBIxUS	0	0	0	0
Cash	Cash	20	0	6	6
Total		100	70	30	100

TABLE 13.5 Risk decomposition of the strategic benchmark

Asset Class	Asset Class Benchmark	Marginal Risk $\partial\sigma/\partial w_i$	Risk Contribution (% per year)
U.S. Large Cap	S&P 500	0.0197	5.68
U.S. Small Cap	Russel 2000	0.0207	1.98
International	MSCI EAFE	0.0177	1.70
Emerging Markets	MSCI EMF	0.0236	0.00
U.S. Bonds	Lehman Aggregate	0.0025	0.47
High Yield	ML High Yield	0.0062	0.59
Non–U.S. Bonds	WGBIxUS	0.0043	0.00
Cash	Cash	0.0000	0.00

show the marginal effect on the portfolio standard deviation of increasing the allocation to each asset class, starting from the existing portfolio. Not surprisingly, the marginal risks of the equity asset classes are considerably greater than those of the fixed-income asset classes, ranging from 0.177 to 0.236. These equity risks are high due to the interaction of three factors: (i) the high standard deviations of the returns on the equity asset classes; (ii) the correlations among the equity returns; and (iii) the relative weights of the equity asset classes in the strategic benchmark. Due to the second and third reasons, the equity asset classes are highly correlated with the existing portfolio, leading to the high measures of their marginal risk. In fact, the effect of the correlations among the equity asset classes is strong enough (and the volatility of the emerging markets asset class high enough) that the marginal risk of the emerging markets asset class is the highest, despite its current weight of zero.

In many cases, the risks of the strategic benchmark are the largest and most relevant from the perspective of the plan sponsor. This occurs when returns on the strategic benchmark deviate from changes in the present value of the liability stream, as in this example. In other cases, to the extent that the plan sponsor chooses the strategic benchmark to hedge the liability stream, the risks of the net position consisting of the benchmark and the liability stream will be much smaller than those of the strategic benchmark itself. In fact, in the extreme case in which the strategic benchmark is a perfect hedge of the liability stream, the risk of the net position is zero.

Regardless, another set of risks arises by deviating from the strategic benchmark. Most commonly, these arise through the active managers.

RISK DECOMPOSITION OF THE EXISTING MANAGER ROSTER

As discussed above, many institutional investors have manager rosters that blend a number of portfolio-management styles. We assume that the plan has the existing roster of managers shown in Table 13.2, which also shows various characteristics of the asset classes. The number of asset classes and managers shown in Table 13.2 is fewer than the numbers used by many plans, but we use a small set of asset classes and managers in order to illustrate the main points without cluttering the example.

A quick examination of Table 13.2 suggests that the existing allocations might not be the best choice. For example, manager 11 has the same alpha, lower beta, and smaller tracking error than the other two U.S. bond managers but has no allocation, while each of the other two U.S. bond managers currently manages 10% of the portfolio. Farther down the table, there is no allocation to the emerging markets and hedge fund managers (managers 8, 14, and 15), even though managers 14 and 15 have the highest alphas and manager 8 is tied for the third-highest alpha. These observations suggest that the plan might benefit by increasing the allocations to some of the managers and either decreasing the allocations to the other managers or decreasing the passive allocation of 30%.

However, this analysis was only suggestive. To reach correct conclusions about whether the risk-return tradeoff would be improved by increasing or decreasing each of the allocations, for each manager we must determine how changes in the allocation affect both the expected return and the risk. Determining the effect of the managerial allocations on the expected return is straightforward, because the expected return of a portfolio is the weighted average of the expected returns of its components, and the return contribution of an asset is just the product of the expected return and the portfolio weight. Thus, our focus is on the risk.

Once the effect of altering the allocations has been determined, one can increase allocations to those managers for which this increases expected return more than risk and decreases others. Implicitly, this is what underlies the earlier comparison of alphas, betas, and tracking errors. Alpha and beta translate directly into higher expected return, and higher beta and tracking error are positively related to risk. However, our quick examination of alphas, betas, and tracking error was incomplete, and thus only suggestive, because it failed to reflect the effect of the correlations among the various asset classes and managers.

Given that we are now measuring risk relative to the strategic benchmark, risk decomposition asks, "what is the effect of changing the allocations on the value-at-risk of the excess return

$$r - r_B = \sum_{i=1}^{15} w_i r_i + \left(1 - \sum_{i=1}^{15} w_i\right) r_B - r_B$$

$$= \sum_{i=1}^{15} w_i (r_i - r_B)?\text{"}$$

The terms $\sum_{i=1}^{15} w_i r_i$ and $(1 - \sum_{i=1}^{15} w_i) r_B$ on the right-hand side of the first equality are the returns on the actively managed part of the portfolio and the passive allocation to the benchmark portfolio, and the second equality follows immediately from the first.

Given the assumption of normally distributed returns, the focus is on the variance and standard deviation of the portfolio excess return $r - r_B$. Using the definitions above, the excess return variance σ^2 can be written as

$$\sigma^2 = \sum_{i=1}^{15} \sum_{j=1}^{15} w_i w_j \, \text{cov} \, (r_i - r_B, r_j - r_B)$$

$$= \sum_{i=1}^{15} \sum_{j=1}^{15} w_i w_j [\text{cov} \, (r_i, r_j) - \text{cov} \, (r_i, r_B) - \text{cov} \, (r_j, r_B) + \text{var} \, (r_B)],$$

where cov $(r_i, r_j) = \rho_{ij}\sigma_i\sigma_j$, ρ_{ij} is the correlation between the returns on the portfolio managed by managers i and j, and σ_i is the volatility of the portfolio of manager i. The covariances among the 15 active managers, and those between the active managers and the benchmark, can be computed from the standard deviations in Table 13.1, the correlations in Table 13.3, and the assumption that the tracking errors across managers are uncorrelated.

Asking "what is the effect of changing the allocations w_i on the excess return standard deviation σ?" amounts to asking "what are the partial derivatives, or marginal risks $\partial\sigma/\partial w_i$, for each of the 15 active managers?" taking account the fact that $w_B = -\sum_{i=1}^{15} w_i$. Defining v_i to be the standard deviation of the excess return $r_i - r_B$ and γ_{ij} to be the correlation between the excess returns $r_i - r_B$ and $r_j - r_B$, the excess return variance σ^2 becomes

$$\sigma^2 = \sum_{i=1}^{15}\sum_{j=1}^{15} w_i w_j \, \text{cov}(r_i - r_B, r_j - r_B)$$

$$= \sum_{i=1}^{15}\sum_{j=1}^{15} w_i w_j \gamma_{ij} v_i v_j,$$

and the marginal risks are

$$\frac{\partial\sigma}{\partial w_1} = \left[\sum_{j=1}^{15} w_j \gamma_{ij} v_i v_j\right] / \sigma,$$

for $i = 1, \ldots, 15$. These marginal risks are shown in Table 13.6.

It should be emphasized that these are *marginal* risks. Starting from the current allocation, the ith marginal risk measures the effect of increasing the allocation to the ith manager. As discussed in Chapter 10, the risk contributions are obtained by multiplying these by the portfolio weights. Also, the calculation of these marginal risks takes account of the restriction $w_B \equiv -\sum_{i=1}^{15} w_i$. Thus, the marginal risk for the ith manager measures the change in risk that would result from increasing the allocation to the ith manager, while simultaneously reducing the allocation to the passive benchmark.

Examination of Table 13.6 reveals that the marginal risks are greatest for the equity managers. Similar to the risk decomposition of the strategic benchmark, these equity risks are high due to the interaction of three factors: (i) the high standard deviations of the returns of the equity portfolios; (ii) the correlations among the equity returns; and (iii) the relatively large allocations to the equity asset classes. Due to the second and third reasons, the equity portfolios are highly correlated with the existing total portfolio, leading to the high measures of their risk contribution. In striking contrast,

TABLE 13.6 Risk decomposition of the existing manager roster

Asset Class	Manager	Marginal Risk $\partial\sigma/\partial w_i$
U.S. Large Cap	1	9.24
	2	8.56
	3	9.24
U.S. Small Cap	4	8.65
	5	8.17
International	6	7.65
	7	7.91
Emerging Markets	8	10.63
U.S. Bonds	9	−6.97
	10	−6.91
	11	−7.10
High Yield	12	−6.12
	13	−6.12
Hedge Funds	14	−9.01
	15	−9.01

the marginal risks of the U.S. bond portfolios, high-yield portfolios, and hedge funds are negative. To understand this, recall that the risk measures shown in Table 13.6 represent the net effect of reallocating assets from the passive benchmark portfolio to the active managers. The U.S. bond and high-yield asset classes have both relatively low volatility and relatively low correlations with the equity asset classes, while the hedge fund returns are uncorrelated with the other asset classes. Due to these factors, reallocating assets from the passive benchmark portfolio to these portfolios results in a reduction in risk. These negative marginal risks are particularly striking because the expected returns of the high-yield and hedge fund portfolios are greater than the expected return of the passive benchmark portfolio. Thus, by reallocating assets from the passive benchmark portfolio to these asset classes, it is possible simultaneously to decrease risk and increase expected return.

RISK DECOMPOSITION OF THE EXISTING ASSET CLASS ALLOCATIONS

Another question of interest is the risk of the existing asset allocations. Since we are measuring risk using risk contributions, or marginal risks, this amounts to asking what happens to the risk if we increase the allocation to a particular asset

TABLE 13.7 Risk decomposition of the existing asset classes

Asset Class	Asset Class Benchmark	Marginal Risk $\partial\sigma/\partial w_i$
U.S. Large Cap	S&P 500	9.02
U.S. Small Cap	Russel 2000	8.41
International	MSCI EAFE	7.78
Emerging Markets	MSCI EMF	10.63
U.S. Bonds	Lehman Aggregate	−6.99
High Yield	ML High Yield	−6.12
Non–U.S. Bonds	WGBIxUS	−9.01

class, starting from the current allocations. For example, what happens if we increase the allocation to the actively managed equity portfolios from 30%?

Table 13.7 shows the marginal risks by asset classes, using the assumption that an increase in the allocation to an asset class is spread equally among the managers in that class. Not surprisingly, the pattern of marginal risks is similar to that in Table 13.6.

OPTIMAL MANAGER ROSTER AND ASSET ALLOCATION

Tables 13.6 and 13.7 make clear that the existing manager roster and asset allocations are not optimal. Most notably, risk can be decreased by increasing the allocation to U.S. bonds, high-yield bonds, or hedge funds. As can be seen in Table 13.2, the managers in the latter two of these asset classes have expected returns greater than the expected excess return on the strategic benchmark of 9.30%. Thus, by increasing the allocations to these managers, it is possible simultaneously to decrease risk and increase expected return. Of course, this is not surprising: only by chance (or carefully rigged example) would the existing manager roster be exactly optimal.

Table 13.8 compares the risk measures (marginal risks) and expected excess returns for each of the managers. In this table, the expected excess return is the difference between the expected return on the portfolio and that on the benchmark and represents the (expected) return benefit that can be obtained by reallocating assets away from the passive benchmark and into that portfolio. The rightmost column shows the ratio of the expected excess return to the marginal risks. When these ratios are not all equal, there is gain from reallocating assets among the managers. For example, the ratio of excess return to risk is 0.39 for the first U.S. large-capitalization managers, 0.34 for the second, and 0.29 for the third. The difference indicates that there

TABLE 13.8 Risk decomposition and marginal expected return of the existing manager roster

Asset Class	Manager	Marginal Risk $\partial\sigma/\partial w_i$	Expected Excess Return (Percent)	Ratio of Expected Excess Return to Marginal Risk
U.S. Large Cap	1	9.24	3.60	0.39
	2	8.56	2.95	0.34
	3	9.24	2.73	0.29
U.S. Small Cap	4	8.65	4.85	0.56
	5	8.17	4.55	0.56
International	6	7.65	3.20	0.42
	7	7.91	4.30	0.54
Emerging Markets	8	10.63	6.20	0.58
U.S. Bonds	9	−6.97	−2.20	0.32
	10	−6.91	−2.20	0.32
	11	−7.10	−2.25	0.32
High Yield	12	−6.12	0.20	−0.03
	13	−6.12	0.20	−0.03
Hedge Funds	14	−9.01	2.70	−0.30
	15	−9.01	6.70	−0.74

is an opportunity to (slightly) improve the risk-return tradeoff by reallocating assets from the third U.S. manager to the first or second and from the second to the first.

The negative ratios toward the bottom of the table indicate the opportunity for even greater gains. To interpret these, remember their definition: they are the ratios of the expected excess return to the (marginal) risk measures. Here the ratios are negative because the numerator (the expected return) is positive and denominator (the risk measure) is negative, indicating that reallocating assets simultaneously increases expected return and decreases risk.

From this discussion, it should be clear that optimal allocations to the active managers are characterized by equal ratios. (An important exception is when constraints, perhaps self-imposed, on the fraction of the portfolio that may be allocated to a manager lead to a smaller than optimal allocation.) The actual optimum can be computed using a mean-variance optimizer and is shown in Table 13.9. This table also shows the expected excess returns, the marginal risks at the optimal allocations, and their ratios. As expected, the ratios are equal across managers.

The largest asset allocations are for managers 2 and 11, in the U.S. large-capitalization equity and U.S. bond asset classes, respectively. The

TABLE 13.9 Optimal allocations to active managers

Asset Class	Manager	Benchmark	Existing Allocation (Percent)	Optimal Allocation (Percent)	Marginal Risk $\partial\sigma/\partial w_i$	Expected Excess Return (Percent)	Ratio of Expected Excess Return to Marginal Risk
U.S. Large Cap	1	S&P 500	10.0	8.81	4.29	3.60	0.84
	2	S&P 500	10.0	11.69	3.51	2.95	0.84
	3	S&P 500	10.0	3.95	3.24	2.73	0.84
U.S. Small Cap	4	Russel 2000	5.0	3.80	5.77	4.85	0.84
	5	Russel 2000	5.0	5.09	5.42	4.55	0.84
International	6	MSCI EAFE	5.0	3.10	3.81	3.20	0.84
	7	MSCI EAFE	5.0	5.81	5.12	4.30	0.84
Emerging Markets	8	MSCI EMF	0.0	0.49	7.38	6.20	0.84
U.S. Bonds	9	Lehman Aggregate	10.0	6.35	-2.62	-2.20	0.84
	10	Lehman Aggregate	10.0	4.41	-2.62	-2.20	0.84
	11	Lehman Aggregate	0.0	10.68	-2.68	-2.25	0.84
High Yield	12	ML High Yield	0.0	3.47	0.24	0.20	0.84
	13	ML High Yield	0.0	7.80	0.24	0.20	0.84
Hedge Funds	14	Cash	0.0	3.08	3.21	2.70	0.84
	15	Cash	0.0	3.25	7.98	6.70	0.84

distinguishing feature of these managers is their small tracking errors: they have the smallest tracking error in their asset classes. Manager 13, the second high yield manager, also has a small tracking error and a relatively large allocation. The combination of these small tracking errors and the relatively large weights on these asset classes in the strategic benchmark accounts for the large allocations, because these factors make it possible for these managers to receive large allocations without creating excessive risk. Manager 2 actually has the lowest alpha of any of the equity managers, illustrating the importance of the risk contribution.

The same point is illustrated by the smaller optimal allocations. In spite of a large alpha, the allocation to manager 8, the sole emerging markets manager, is only 0.49% both because this asset class does appear in the strategic benchmark and because this manager has a large tracking error (which is assumed to be independent of the index returns). Thus, the marginal risk of manager 8's portfolio is considerable and leads to a small allocation in spite of the large expected return. The same factors lead to the relatively small allocations (3.08% and 3.25%) to the hedge fund managers 14 and 15, respectively. Even though these managers have very high alphas, even with these small allocations their marginal risks are relatively large.

NOTES

This chapter draws upon Winkelman (2000a, 2000b). The computation of the optimal manager roster is the outcome of a mean-variance optimization. It is well known that the results of mean-variance optimization are very sensitive to the estimates of expected returns and that it is difficult, at best, to come up with good estimates of expected returns (see, e.g., Michaud 1989). Moreover, the expected returns, volatilities, and correlations are likely to change over time, especially during periods of market stress. Even setting aside the issue of the stability of the volatilities and correlations, the estimation of the covariance matrix can also be problematic (see Chapter 17), although this is not so widely recognized. These considerations suggest that the approach be used with caution.

Refinements
of the Basic Methods

Delta-Gamma Approaches

As discussed in earlier chapters, a limitation of the delta-normal method is that it amounts to replacing the portfolio with a linear approximation and then computing the value-at-risk of the linear approximation. Thus, use of the delta-normal method leads to significant errors in the value-at-risk estimate when the portfolio value is a highly nonlinear function of the underlying market factors, because in such cases a linear approximation will not adequately capture the risks of the portfolio. The *delta-gamma-theta-normal* method represents a natural next step, in that it uses a second-order or quadratic approximation of the portfolio. The approach involves computing the first four moments (mean, variance, skewness, and kurtosis) of the second-order approximation to the value of the portfolio and then finding a flexible distribution that matches these four moments. Once this has been done, the value-at-risk is then computed from that flexible distribution.

To illustrate the main idea, we use a portfolio that depends on only one underlying market factor. In particular, the position consists of a portfolio of common stocks, along with some index options. To keep things simple, we assume that returns on the stock portfolio are perfectly correlated with the returns on the S&P 500 index, so the level of the S&P 500 is the only market factor. The current level of the S&P 500 index is 1087 and the value of the stock portfolio is $10,000,400. The options position consists of 90 S&P 500 (SPX) put options with a strike level of 1075 and two months until expiration. The multiplier for the SPX options is 100, so the payoff of each of the options is $100 \times \max[1075 - S, 0]$, where S denotes the level of the index on the expiration date of the options. The options position has a current value of $260,985, so the initial value of the portfolio is $1,000,400 + $260,985 = $1,261,385. Figure 14.1 shows the value of the portfolio of stock and index options as a function of the level of the S&P 500 index.

To find the second-order approximation upon which the delta-gamma-normal method is based, we need the delta, gamma, and theta of the portfolio, which in turn depend upon the same derivatives of the put options. Letting V^{put} denote the value (per share) of the SPX puts, the delta, gamma, and theta are

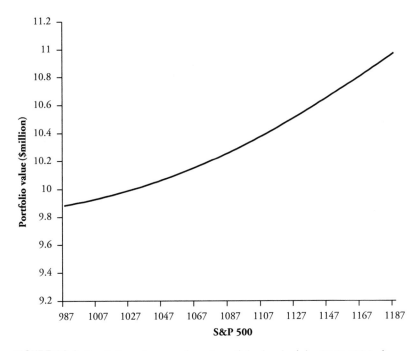

FIGURE 14.1 Portfolio value as a function of the level of the S&P 500 index

$$\text{option delta} = \frac{\partial V^{\text{put}}}{\partial S} = 100 \times (-0.3969) = -39.69,$$

$$\text{option gamma} = \frac{\partial^2 V^{\text{put}}}{\partial S^2} = 100 \times 0.003949 = 0.3949,$$

$$\text{option theta} = \frac{\partial V^{\text{put}}}{\partial t} = 100 \times 89.90 = 8990.$$

These were computed by taking the appropriate derivatives of the dividend-adjusted Black-Scholes formula, using a volatility of 22% per year, a continuous dividend yield of 1.6% per year, and a continuously compounded interest rate of 5% per year.

Since the current level of the S&P 500 is 1087 and the value of the stock portfolio is $10,000,400, the value of the stock portfolio is $10,000,400/1087 = 9200 times the level of the S&P 500 index, which implies that the stock portfolio has a delta of 9200 with respect to the S&P 500 index. Using this, and the fact that the portfolio contains 90 put options, the portfolio delta, gamma, and theta are

$$\frac{\partial V}{\partial S} = 9200 + 90(-39.69) = 5627.6,$$

$$\frac{\partial^2 V}{\partial S^2} = 90(0.3949) = 35.5,$$

$$\frac{\partial V}{\partial t} = 90(-8990.0) = -809,098.$$

To compute the moments of the delta-gamma-theta approximation, let $V = V(S, t)$ denote the value of the portfolio, and let Δt and ΔS denote the horizon of the value-at-risk estimate and change in the market factor (the S&P 500) over that horizon, respectively. (Note that the meaning of the symbol Δ has changed.) The approximation of the change in value of the portfolio is

$$\Delta V \approx \frac{\partial V}{\partial S}(\Delta S) + \left(\frac{1}{2}\right)\frac{\partial^2 V}{\partial S^2}(\Delta S)^2 + \frac{\partial V}{\partial t}\Delta t$$

$$= \frac{\partial V}{\partial S}S\left(\frac{\Delta S}{S}\right) + \left(\frac{1}{2}\right)\frac{\partial^2 V}{\partial S^2}S^2\left(\frac{\Delta S}{S}\right)^2 + \frac{\partial V}{\partial t}\Delta t. \tag{14.1}$$

The delta-gamma-theta-normal approach proceeds by computing the first four moments of the distribution of the approximation of the change in the portfolio value and then matching them to the moments of another distribution. To simplify these computations, we assume that $E[\Delta S] = 0$. Using this assumption, the first four moments of the second-order approximation are

$$E[\Delta V] = E\left[\frac{\partial V}{\partial S}(\Delta S) + \left(\frac{1}{2}\right)\left(\frac{\partial^2 V}{\partial S^2}(\Delta S)^2\right) + \frac{\partial V}{\partial t}\right]$$

$$= \left(\frac{1}{2}\right)\frac{\partial^2 V}{\partial S^2}S^2\sigma^2 + \frac{\partial V}{\partial t}\Delta t, \tag{14.2}$$

$$\text{var}[\Delta V] = E\left[\left(\frac{\partial V}{\partial V}(\Delta S) + \left(\frac{1}{2}\right)\frac{\partial^2 V}{\partial S^2}(\Delta S)^2 + \frac{\partial V}{\partial t}\Delta t\right.\right.$$

$$\left.\left. - E\left[\frac{\partial V}{\partial S}(\Delta S) + \left(\frac{1}{2}\right)\frac{\partial^2 V}{\partial S^2}(\Delta S)^2 + \frac{\partial V}{\partial t}\Delta t\right]\right)^2\right] \tag{14.3}$$

$$= \left(\frac{\partial V}{\partial S}\right)^2 S^2\sigma^2 + \frac{1}{2}\left(\frac{\partial^2 V}{\partial S^2}\right)^2 S^4\sigma^4,$$

$$
\text{skewness}[\Delta V] = E\left[\left(\frac{\partial V}{\partial V}(\Delta S) + \left(\frac{1}{2}\right)\frac{\partial^2 V}{\partial S^2}(\Delta S)^2 + \frac{\partial V}{\partial t}\Delta t\right.\right.
$$
$$
\left.\left. - E\left[\frac{\partial V}{\partial S}(\Delta S) + \left(\frac{1}{2}\right)\frac{\partial^2 V}{\partial S^2}(\Delta S)^2 + \frac{\partial V}{\partial t}\Delta t\right]\right)^3\right] \quad (14.4)
$$
$$
= 3\left(\frac{\partial V}{\partial S}\right)^2 \frac{\partial^2 V}{\partial S^2} S^4\sigma^4 + \left(\frac{\partial^2 V}{\partial S^2}\right)^3 S^6\sigma^6,
$$

$$
\text{kurtosis}[\Delta V] = E\left[\left(\frac{\partial V}{\partial V}(\Delta S) + \left(\frac{1}{2}\right)\frac{\partial^2 V}{\partial S^2}(\Delta S)^2 + \frac{\partial V}{\partial t}\Delta t\right.\right.
$$
$$
\left.\left. - E\left[\frac{\partial V}{\partial S}(\Delta S) + \left(\frac{1}{2}\right)\frac{\partial^2 V}{\partial S^2}(\Delta S)^2 + \frac{\partial V}{\partial t}\Delta t\right]\right)^4\right] \quad (14.5)
$$
$$
= 3\left(\frac{\partial V}{\partial S}\right)^4 S^4\sigma^4 + 15\left(\frac{\partial V}{\partial S}\right)^2\left(\frac{\partial^2 V}{\partial S^2}\right)^2 S^6\sigma^6 + \frac{15}{4}\left(\frac{\partial^2 V}{\partial S^2}\right)^4 S^8\sigma^8,
$$

where $\sigma^2 = E[(\Delta S/S)^2]$ is the variance of the percentage change in the market factor over the horizon used in computing value-at-risk, and we have used the facts that $E[(\Delta S/S)^4] = 3\sigma^4$, $E[(\Delta S/S)^6] = 15\sigma^6$, $E[(\Delta S/S)^8] = 105\sigma^8$, and that all of the odd moments are zero. Notice that in the special case when $\partial^2 V/\partial S^2 = 0$ these results are exactly what one expects in that the variance is proportional to the square of $\partial V/\partial S$, the skewness is zero, and the kurtosis is proportional to the fourth power of $\partial V/\partial S$.

To complete the computation of the moments we need Δt, the horizon over which the value-at-risk is being measured, and σ. In this example, we set $\Delta t = 1/12$ (i.e., one month) and $\sigma = 0.06357$, respectively, which is consistent with a volatility of 22% per year. Combining these assumptions with the partial derivatives computed above, the moments of the distribution of the delta-gamma approximation of ΔV are

$$
E[\Delta V] = 1.7439 \times 10^4,
$$
$$
\text{var}[\Delta V] = 1.6564 \times 10^{11},
$$
$$
\text{skewness}[\Delta V] = 7.7142 \times 10^{16},
$$
$$
\text{kurtosis}[\Delta V] = 1.3396 \times 10^{23}.
$$

Given these moments, the next steps are to find a flexible distribution that matches them and then read the value-at-risk off that flexible distribution. A convenient choice for matching a distribution with positive skewness is the three-parameter lognormal distribution. One drawback of the three-parameter lognormal is that it can match only three of the four moments above, but we use it for this example because of its simplicity. If ΔV follows a three-parameter lognormal distribution, then $\ln(\Delta V - c)$ has a normal distribution with a mean of a and standard deviation of b. In the two-parameter lognormal distribution widely used in finance, $c = 0$, so the three-parameter lognormal is obtained by shifting ΔV by an amount c that is the lower bound of the distribution. The first three moments of the three-parameter lognormal are

$$E[\Delta V] = \exp\left(a + b^2/2\right) + c, \tag{14.6}$$

$$\mathrm{var}[\Delta V] = e^{2a}e^{b^2}\left(e^{b^2} - 1\right), \tag{14.7}$$

$$\mathrm{skewness}[\Delta V] = e^{3a}\exp\left(\tfrac{3}{2}b^2\right)\left(e^{b^2} - 1\right)\left(e^{b^2} + 2\right). \tag{14.8}$$

Setting the right-hand sides of equations (14.6), (14.7), and (14.8) equal to the first three moments calculated above and solving for the parameters, we obtain $a = 13.86$, $b = 0.353843$, and $c = -1,096,934$.

Figure 14.2 shows the density function of the three-parameter lognormal distribution with these parameters, along with the value-at-risk estimate of $-513,934$ dollars obtained from this distribution using a critical probability of 5%. The Figure also shows the density function of the normal distribution with mean zero and variance 1.5123×10^{11} used in the delta-normal approximation and the true density function of profits and losses on the portfolio, which incorporates the exact relation between the S&P 500 index and the portfolio value. The value-at-risk estimate based on the delta-normal approximation (and a probability of 5%) is 643,217 dollars, while the value-at-risk using the true distribution (and a probability of 5%) is 411,800 dollars.

Comparing the three density functions shown in Figure 14.2, it is clear that the delta-gamma-theta-normal approach represents an improvement over the delta-normal approach, but the delta-gamma-theta-normal value-at-risk is still considerably different from the value-at-risk computed using the true distribution of possible profits and/or losses. The improvement

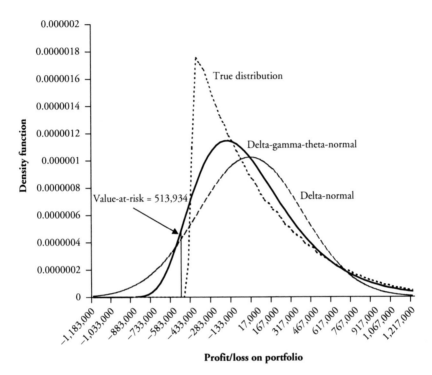

FIGURE 14.2 Density function of the true distribution of changes in portfolio value, along with the density functions used in the delta-gamma-theta-normal and delta-normal approximations

over the delta-normal approach occurs because the delta-gamma-theta approximation captures some of the curvature that is apparent in Figure 14.1. However, the approximation does not capture all of the curvature in Figure 14.1. In particular, the approximation replaces the function shown in Figure 14.1 with a second-order approximation, in which the second derivative (the gamma) is constant. Although it is not readily apparent from Figure 14.1, for index values between 1021 and 1087, the gamma is greater than it is at 1087. One implication of this is that for index values less than 1087 the delta-gamma-theta approximation lies slightly below the portfolio value graphed in Figure 14.1, so that the actual losses on the portfolio are slightly greater than the losses implied by the delta-gamma-theta approximation. More importantly, the gamma also changes as time passes, and for a range of index values around the strike price it increases considerably. For example, if one month passes without any change in the index value, the gamma will be 0.5569 instead of 0.3949. These increases in gamma have the effect of mitigating the losses due to large decreases in the level of the S&P 500 index and are not reflected in the approximation in which the second derivative is constant. Thus, in this example the approximation overstates the probability of large losses.

In general, whether the delta-gamma approximation over- or understates the probability of large losses depends on the properties of the options in the portfolio and whether they are bought or written. In this example, if the options had been written, the delta-gamma approximation would have understated the probability of large losses.

It is straightforward to extend the delta-gamma-normal approach to cases when there are two or more underlying market factors. For example, if there are two market factors with values denoted by x_1 and x_2, the approximation is

$$
\Delta V \approx \frac{\partial V}{\partial x_1}(\Delta x_1) + \frac{\partial V}{\partial x_2}(\Delta x_2) + \left(\frac{1}{2}\right)\frac{\partial^2 V}{\partial x_1^2}(\Delta x_1)^2 + \left(\frac{1}{2}\right)\frac{\partial^2 V}{\partial x_2^2}(\Delta x_2)^2
$$

$$
+ \frac{\partial^2 V}{\partial x_1 \partial x_2}(\Delta x_1)(\Delta x_2) + \frac{\partial V}{\partial t}\Delta t
$$

$$
= \frac{\partial V}{\partial x_1}x_1\left(\frac{\Delta x_1}{x_1}\right) + \frac{\partial V}{\partial x_2}x_2\left(\frac{\Delta x_2}{x_2}\right) + \left(\frac{1}{2}\right)\frac{\partial^2 V}{\partial x_1^2}x_1^2\left(\frac{\Delta x_1}{x_1}\right)^2
$$

$$
+ \left(\frac{1}{2}\right)\frac{\partial^2 V}{\partial x_2^2}x_2^2\left(\frac{\Delta x_2}{x_2}\right)^2 + \frac{\partial^2 V}{\partial x_1 \partial x_2}x_1 x_2\left(\frac{\Delta x_1}{x_1}\right)\left(\frac{\Delta x_2}{x_2}\right) + \frac{\partial V}{\partial t}\Delta t.
$$

Similar expressions can be obtained when there are more than two factors. From these, it is straightforward to compute the first four moments of ΔV along the lines of equations (14.2) through (14.5), though the computations are lengthy and tedious and the resulting expressions are much more complicated than (14.2) through (14.5). In particular, they involve various moments of the form $E[(\Delta x_i)(\Delta x_j)\ldots(\Delta x_K)]$, where K is the number of market factors.

One way to simplify the computation is to replace the market factors with an equivalent set of market factors whose changes have a diagonal covariance matrix and to express the change in the portfolio value in terms of the equivalent set of market factors. To consider a two-dimensional example, let

$$
\Delta x = \begin{bmatrix} \Delta x_1 \\ \Delta x_2 \end{bmatrix}
$$

denote the vector of changes in the market factors, and

$$\Sigma = \begin{bmatrix} \sigma_1^2 x_1^2 & \sigma_1 \sigma_2 \rho_{12} x_1 x_2 \\ \sigma_1 \sigma_2 \rho_{12} x_1 x_2 & \sigma_2^2 x_2^2 \end{bmatrix}$$

denote the covariance matrix, and again assume for convenience that $E[\Delta x] = 0$. Define $y = \Sigma^{-1/2} x$, so that

$$\begin{bmatrix} \Delta y_1 \\ \Delta y_2 \end{bmatrix} = \Sigma^{-1/2} \begin{bmatrix} \Delta x_1 \\ \Delta x_2 \end{bmatrix},$$

where $\Sigma^{-1/2}$ is the inverse of a square root of Σ. With y defined this way, Δy_1 and Δy_2 are uncorrelated, that is, they have a diagonal covariance matrix. If we write the portfolio value V in terms of y, we have $V(x, t) = V(\Sigma^{1/2} y, t) \equiv W(y, t)$, and

$$\Delta V \approx \frac{\partial W}{\partial y_1}(\Delta y_1) + \frac{\partial W}{\partial y_2}(\Delta y_2) + \left(\frac{1}{2}\right)\frac{\partial^2 W}{\partial y_1^2}(\Delta y_1)^2 + \left(\frac{1}{2}\right)\frac{\partial^2 W}{\partial y_2^2}(\Delta y_2)^2$$

$$+ \frac{\partial^2 W}{\partial y_1 \partial y_2}(\Delta y_1)(\Delta y_2) + \frac{\partial W}{\partial t}\Delta t$$

$$= \frac{\partial W}{\partial y_1} y_1 \left(\frac{\Delta y_1}{y_1}\right) + \frac{\partial W}{\partial y_2} y_2 \left(\frac{\Delta y_2}{y_2}\right) + \left(\frac{1}{2}\right)\frac{\partial^2 W}{\partial y_1^2} y_1^2 \left(\frac{\Delta y_1}{y_1}\right)^2$$

$$+ \left(\frac{1}{2}\right)\frac{\partial^2 W}{\partial y_2^2} y_2^2 \left(\frac{\Delta y_2}{y_2}\right)^2$$

$$+ \frac{\partial^2 W}{\partial y_1 \partial y_2} y_1 y_2 \left(\frac{\Delta y_1}{y_1}\right)\left(\frac{\Delta y_2}{y_2}\right) + \frac{\partial W}{\partial t}\Delta t,$$

where

$$\frac{\partial W}{\partial y_i} = \frac{\partial W}{\partial x_1}\frac{\partial x_1}{\partial y_i} + \frac{\partial W}{\partial x_2}\frac{\partial x_2}{\partial y_i} \tag{14.9}$$

and

$$\frac{\partial^2 W}{\partial y_i \partial y_j} = \frac{\partial^2 V}{\partial x_1^2}\left(\frac{\partial x_1}{\partial y_i}\right)^2 + 2\frac{\partial^2 V}{\partial x_1 \partial x_2}\left(\frac{\partial x_1}{\partial y_i}\right)\left(\frac{\partial x_2}{\partial y_i}\right) + \frac{\partial^2 V}{\partial x_2^2}\left(\frac{\partial x_2}{\partial y_i}\right)^2. \tag{14.10}$$

The moments of ΔV may now be computed, and a flexible distribution may be fitted to match them.

In the general (K-dimensional) case, we have

$$\Delta V = \left(\frac{\partial W}{\partial y}\right)'(\Delta y) + \frac{1}{2}(\Delta y)'\frac{\partial^2 W}{\partial y \partial y'}(\Delta y) + \left(\frac{\partial W}{\partial t}\right)\Delta t,$$

where

$$\frac{\partial W}{\partial y} = \begin{bmatrix} \dfrac{\partial W}{\partial y_1} \\ \vdots \\ \dfrac{\partial W}{\partial y_K} \end{bmatrix} = \left(\frac{dx}{dy}\right)'\frac{\partial V}{\partial x} = (\Sigma^{1/2})\frac{\partial V}{\partial x}, \tag{14.11}$$

and

$$\frac{\partial^2 W}{\partial y \partial y'} = \begin{bmatrix} \dfrac{\partial^2 W}{\partial y_1^2} & \cdots & \dfrac{\partial^2 W}{\partial y_1 \partial y_K} \\ \vdots & \ddots & \vdots \\ \dfrac{\partial^2 W}{\partial y_K \partial y_1} & \cdots & \dfrac{\partial^2 W}{\partial y_K^2} \end{bmatrix} = \left(\frac{dx}{dy}\right)'\frac{\partial^2 W}{\partial x \partial x'}\left(\frac{dx}{dy}\right)$$

$$= (\Sigma^{1/2})\frac{\partial^2 W}{\partial x \partial x'}(\Sigma^{1/2}). \tag{14.12}$$

The advantage of this transformation to uncorrelated random variables $\Delta y_1, \Delta y_2, \ldots,$ is that it permits the computation of the moments of ΔV without having to compute all of the (even) moments of the multivariate normal distribution through eighth order. Instead, one need only compute the moments of each of the marginal distributions. The cost, however, is that it complicates calculation of the derivatives, as in (14.9) and (14.10) or (14.11) and (14.12).

NOTES

The approach described here is essentially that of Zangari (1996c) and is perhaps the simplest delta-gamma approach. Zangari (1996c) suggests using a distribution from the *Johnson family*, of which the three-parameter lognormal is one member. Other members of the Johnson family allow all four moments to be matched. See Johnson, Kotz, and Balakrishnan (1994, Chapter 12) for further discussion of the Johnson family, and Johnson, Kotz, and Balakrishnan (1994, Chapter 14) for discussion of the three-parameter lognormal. Zangari (1996a) suggests an alternative delta-gamma approach using the *Cornish-Fisher approximation*, while Fong and Vasicek (1997) suggest the use of the gamma distribution. Limitations of delta-gamma approaches are discussed in Mina and Ulmer (1999) and Pichler and Selitsch (2000).

El-Jahel, Perraudin, and Sellin (1999) describe a more sophisticated delta-gamma approach that allows for stochastic volatility, so that changes in the market factors are no longer multivariate normal. They derive the characteristic function of the process for the market factors to calculate their moments, and from these calculate the moments of a delta-gamma approximation of the portfolio value. Then, similar to the approach in this chapter, they select a member of the Pearson or Johnson families of distributions that matches the moments of the delta-gamma approximation and use the fitted distribution to compute the value-at-risk.

Cardenás, Fruchard, Koehler, Michel, and Thomazeau (1997) and Rouvinez (1997) also describe approaches based on the characteristic function of the delta-gamma approximation of the change in portfolio value. However, rather than match moments, they invert the characteristic function to obtain either the density or distribution of the change in portfolio value and then read off the VaR estimate. Duffie and Pan (1999) use a similar approach in a more general framework that allows for jumps and credit risk. Feuerverger and Wong (2000) describe an alternative approach based on the moment-generating function and *saddlepoint approximations*, while Britten-Jones and Schaeffer (1998) express the distribution of a delta-gamma approximation of portfolio value in terms of a sum on noncentral chi-square random variables.

CHAPTER 15

Variants of the Monte Carlo Approach

In order to avoid the computational burden of the full Monte Carlo method, various strategies are used to reduce N, K, and M without foregoing too much accuracy. Strategies to reduce the number of instrument valuations M have the greatest payoff, because valuing the instruments is typically the most burdensome part of the process. The mapping approach discussed in earlier chapters is the simplest strategy for reducing the burden of computing the values of the financial instruments. For example, a portfolio of hundreds, thousands, or tens of thousands of fixed-income instruments such as bonds or interest-rate swaps denominated in a particular currency can be mapped to a set of approximately 15 zero-coupon bonds. Once this has been done for each simulated realization of the market factors, one need only compute the value of this portfolio of bonds. This is much less burdensome than separately computing the values of each of the bonds or swaps.

Unfortunately, mapping is less effective for options and other instruments with option-like payoffs. One of the principal motivations for employing the Monte Carlo approach is precisely that using options' deltas to map them onto a set of standardized positions fails to capture the nonlinearity of the option values. This can lead to large errors in the value-at-risk estimate because the option values may be highly nonlinear functions of the underlying market factors.

The approach of mapping using instruments' deltas is equivalent to computing the value-at-risk of a linear approximation of the portfolio value. This observation, combined with the inability of the option deltas fully to capture the risks of options, suggests trying other, more complicated approximations. Several different approximations have been suggested and used. All share the feature that the portfolio is replaced by an approximating function that is easy to evaluate (more precisely, its evaluation is less costly in terms of computer resources). While the approximating functions do not have easy interpretations in terms of portfolios of standard instruments, they nonetheless offer considerable savings in terms of computation.

A DELTA-GAMMA APPROXIMATION

Perhaps the simplest approach is to replace the portfolio value function with a second-order or so-called delta-gamma-theta (or delta-gamma) approximation, leading to the *delta-gamma Monte Carlo method*. To illustrate the idea, return to the example discussed in Chapters 3 and 6. The portfolio has a current value of $101,485,220 and consists of an investment in a well-diversified portfolio of large-capitalization U.S. equities, together with positions in S&P 500 index futures, FT-SE 100 index futures, (written) S&P 500 index call options, and (written) FT-SE 100 index call options. It is assumed that the returns of the portfolio of U.S. equities can be treated as perfectly correlated with the returns on the S&P 500 index, implying that the value of the portfolio is a function of the levels of the S&P 500 and FT-SE 100 indexes, the exchange rate, time (because the option prices depend on time), and the other determinants of the option prices, such as interest rates and volatilities.

The first step in the approximation is to think of the portfolio value as a function of the two index values, the exchange rate, and time, holding constant all of the other determinants of the option prices. Letting V denote the value of the portfolio, we have

$$\text{portfolio value} = V(S_1, S_2, e, t),$$

where S_1 and S_2 denote the levels of the two indexes, e denotes the exchange rate, and t denotes time. However, rather than work with the function V, one replaces it by the approximation

$$\hat{V}(S_1, S_2, t) = 101,485,220 + \frac{\partial V}{\partial S_1}(S_1 - 1097.6) + \frac{\partial V}{\partial S_2}(S_2 - 5862.3)$$

$$+ \frac{\partial V}{\partial e}(e - 1.6271) + \frac{\partial V}{\partial t}(t - t_0) + \left(\frac{1}{2}\right)\frac{\partial^2 V}{\partial S_1^2}(S_1 - 1097.6)^2$$

$$+ \left(\frac{1}{2}\right)\frac{\partial^2 V}{\partial S_2^2}(S_2 - 5862.3)^2 + \left(\frac{1}{2}\right)\frac{\partial^2 V}{\partial e^2}(e - 1.6271)^2$$

$$+ \frac{\partial^2 V}{\partial S_1 \partial S_2}(S_1 - 1097.6)(S_2 - 5862.3)$$

$$+ \frac{\partial^2 V}{\partial S_1 \partial e}(S_1 - 1097.6)(e - 1.6271)$$

$$+ \frac{\partial^2 V}{\partial S_2 \partial S_2}(S_2 - 5862.3)(e - 1.6271),$$

where $101485,220 = V(1097.65862.3, 1.6271, t_0)$ is the current value of the portfolio, t_0 is the date at which the approximation is done (the current date), and the derivatives are evaluated at t_0 and the current values of the market factors, $S_1 = 1097.6$, $S_2 = 5862.3$, and $e = 1.6271$. This approximation is second-order in the underlying assets and first-order in time. It is referred to as a *delta-gamma* or *delta-gamma-theta approximation* because the first and second derivatives with respect to the underlying asset are called delta and gamma, and the time derivative is called theta. When value-at-risk is computed over a short time horizon, such as one day, the time derivative $\partial V / \partial t$ is sometimes omitted, leading to the approximation

$$\hat{V}(S_1, S_2, e, t) = 101,485,220 + \frac{\partial V}{\partial S_1}(S_1 - 1097.6) + \frac{\partial V}{\partial S_2}(S_2 - 5862.3)$$

$$+ \frac{\partial V}{\partial e}(e - 1.6271) + \left(\frac{1}{2}\right)\frac{\partial^2 V}{\partial S_1^2}(S_1 - 1097.6)^2$$

$$+ \left(\frac{1}{2}\right)\frac{\partial^2 V}{\partial S_2^2}(S_2 - 5862.3)^2 + \left(\frac{1}{2}\right)\frac{\partial^2 V}{\partial e^2}(e - 1.6271)^2$$

$$+ \frac{\partial^2 V}{\partial S_1 \partial S_2}(S_1 - 1097.6)(S_2 - 5862.3)$$

$$+ \frac{\partial^2 V}{\partial S_1 \partial e}(S_1 - 1097.6)(e - 1.6271)$$

$$+ \frac{\partial^2 V}{\partial S_2 \partial S_2}(S_2 - 5862.3)(e - 1.6271).$$

For this portfolio the deltas with respect to the S&P 500 index, FT-SE 100 index, and the exchange rate are

$$\frac{\partial V}{\partial S_1} = 4863.7, \quad \frac{\partial V}{\partial S_2} = 2821.5, \quad \text{and} \quad \frac{\partial V}{\partial e} = -2,127,725,$$

respectively. The time derivative theta (with time measured in years) is $\partial V / \partial t = 12,761,464.5$, and the gammas with respect to the S&P 500 and FT-SE 100 indexes are

$$\frac{\partial^2 V}{\partial S_1^2} = -218.5 \quad \text{and} \quad \frac{\partial^2 V}{\partial S_2^2} = -4.68,$$

respectively, and the partial derivative $\frac{\partial^2 V}{\partial S_2 \partial e} = -3331.6$. The other second derivatives are all zero.

The delta-gamma-theta (or delta-gamma) Monte Carlo approach involves using the approximation in place of $V(S_1, S_2, e, t)$. That is, for each of the N samples of the changes in the market factors, instead of computing the exact change in value $V(S_1, S_2, e, t) - 101,485,220$, one computes the approximate change in value

$$
\begin{aligned}
\hat{V}(S_1, S_2, e, t) - 101,485,220 \; = \; & 4863.7(S_1 - 1097.6) \\
& + 2821.5(S_2 - 5862.3) \\
& - 2,127,725(e - 1.6271) \\
& + 12,761,464.5(t - t_o) \\
& - (1/2)(218.5)(S_1 - 1097.6)^2 \\
& - (1/2)4.68(S_2 - 5862.3)^2 \\
& - 3331.5(S_2 - 5862.3)(e - 1.6271)
\end{aligned}
$$

The advantage of this is that it is easy to compute the approximation, because the derivatives are evaluated at the current values of the indexes and therefore are the same for each of the N samples. Given the derivatives, the approximation is a simple quadratic function in S_1, S_2, e, and $t - t_o$, and is therefore easy to evaluate. Even though computing the derivatives may be of equal or greater difficulty than computing the portfolio value $V(S_1, S_2, e, t)$, the approach saves greatly on computation because the derivatives need be computed only once. In contrast, in the full Monte Carlo method the function V must be evaluated N times. If it is costly to compute the portfolio value, either because the instruments in the portfolio are difficult to value or because the portfolio involves a large number of different instruments, then it is useful to avoid the need to compute the portfolio value repeatedly.

Figure 15.1 shows the results of the simulation, using a simulation sample size of $N = 10,000$ drawn from the multivariate normal distribution used in Chapter 6. The distribution is asymmetric and is similar in shape to that shown in Figure 6.2. This is not surprising, because the goal of the method is precisely to capture the nonlinearity of the portfolio value as a function of the underlying market factors and the resulting asymmetry of the distribution of possible profits and losses. However, close examination of the figures reveals that the details differ. First, Figure 15.1 is somewhat less peaked; the bars at 1,500,000 and 2,000,000 represent 2237 and 1287 realizations, while the corresponding bars in Figure 6.2 represent 2264 and 1574 observations, respectively. Second, Figure 6.2 covers a different range and has a longer and fatter left tail. The maximum value in Figure 6.2 is

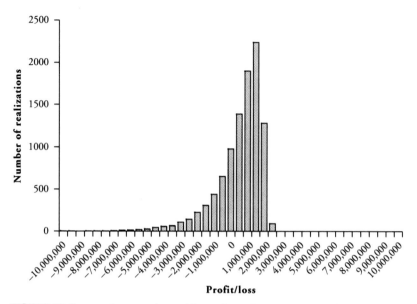

FIGURE 15.1 Distribution of possible profit and loss on the portfolio estimated using the delta-gamma-theta Monte Carlo method

2,300,405, and no bar is visible at 2,500,000, while in Figure 15.1 the maximum value is 2,675,209, and the bar labeled 2,500,000 represents 90 realizations. (The bin labeled 2,500,000 includes all observations between 2,250,000 and 2,750,000. There was one realization in this range (2,300,405), but the resulting bar is too small to be seen on the figure.) In the left tail of Figure 6.2, the bar labeled −10,000,000 represents eight observations, of which the smallest is −11,504,265. The corresponding bar of Figure 15.1 represents only 2 observations, of which the smallest is −10,638,541. Also, in Figure 6.2 the left tail is fatter. For example, there are 154 observations less than or equal to −4,750,000, while in Figure 15.1 there are only 91 observations less than or equal to −4,750,000. Due to these differences in the estimated distributions, the value-at-risk estimate from the delta-gamma-theta approximation (Figure 15.1) is only 2,270,032, while the value-at-risk estimate obtained using the full Monte Carlo method (Figure 6.2) is 2,582,663.

Figures 6.2 and 15.1 illustrate both the advantages and disadvantages of the delta-gamma-theta Monte Carlo approach. It is able to capture important features of the distribution of possible profits and losses, and in particular is able to capture the asymmetry of that distribution. In both Figures 6.2 and 15.1, the truncations of the right-hand tails and the long left-hand tail are due to the fact that the gammas $\partial^2 V/\partial S_1^2$ and $\partial^2 V/\partial S_2^2$ are negative. The delta-gamma-theta approach captures this, and as a result it is much more accurate than the delta-normal approach. This may be seen by comparing Figures 15.1 and 6.2 to Figure 6.3, which shows the estimate of the density obtained using the delta-normal approach.

However, there are errors in the delta-gamma-theta approximation that stem from its inability to capture completely the nonlinearity in the value of the portfolio. The key feature of the approximation is that it is quadratic in S_1 and S_2, which of course implies that it has constant gammas (second derivatives). But, for index values near the exercise prices of the options, the gammas become smaller (i.e., negative and larger in absolute value) as time passes. This change in the gammas is not captured by the delta-gamma-theta approximation, and as a result the left-hand tail of the exact distribution (Figure 6.2) is longer and the truncation of the right-hand tail is more pronounced.

In general, the delta-gamma-theta Monte Carlo method will perform poorly for portfolios for which the gammas change greatly as time passes and/or the prices of the underlying assets change. In this example, the errors in the delta-gamma-theta approximation are exacerbated by the relatively long holding period of one month. In this example, the option gammas change as time passes, and the long holding period allows this time dependence of the gammas to manifest itself. It also makes large changes in the indexes more likely, which exacerbates the dependence of the gammas on the index levels. Typically, the delta-gamma-theta Monte Carlo method will perform much better with a short holding period (e.g., one day), because the assumption of constant gammas is then more reasonable. However, even for a short holding period, the delta-gamma-theta approximation can perform poorly for some portfolios of exotic options for which the gammas vary greatly even for small changes in time or the underlying market factors.

A GRID MONTE CARLO APPROACH

The *grid Monte Carlo approach* replaces the portfolio value function with a different approximation, based on a grid of values of the underlying assets. For portfolios with varying gammas, the grid approximation can be better than the delta-gamma-theta approximation. Due to the inability to display graphically both three underlying market factors and the portfolio value, we illustrate the grid approach by fixing the value of the exchange rate at $e = 1.6271$ dollar/pound and therefore work with a grid of values for the S&P 500 and FT-SE 100 indexes. Specifically, we pick five levels for each of the market factors to construct a 5-by-5 grid. For each of the combinations of index values shown in the grid, one computes the corresponding portfolio value, using the appropriate futures price formulas and option pricing models. Using the equally spaced values (997.6; 1047.6; 1097.6; 1147.6; 1197.6) for the S&P 500 index and (5262.3; 5562.3; 5862.3; 6162.3; 6462.3) for the FT-SE 100, the 25 portfolio values are shown in Table 15.1. The grid approximation used to replace the portfolio value function V is then obtained by interpolating between the values in the table. Figure 15.2 shows the approximating function obtained by interpolation.

The advantage of grid Monte Carlo is that the 25 portfolio values need be computed only once, at the outset. Then, for each of the N Monte Carlo samples or draws, one computes an approximate portfolio value by interpolating between the portfolio values in Table 15.1, which requires little in the way of computer resources. Thus, the N portfolio valuations required by full Monte Carlo are replaced by only 25 portfolio valuations.

This example overstates the advantage of the grid Monte Carlo method, because a 5-by-5 grid may not give an adequate approximate of the portfolio value function, and a denser grid may be needed. More important, however, is the "curse of dimensionality," that is, the fact that the number of points on the grid grows exponentially with the number of factors. Specifically, if there are K market factors and one constructs a grid using five values of each market factor, then the grid approximation requires 5^K portfolio valuations. For example, if there are 10 market factors and one builds a grid using nine possible values of each market factor, then there are $9^{10} = 3.487 \times 10^9$ nodes at which the portfolio must be revalued. Using such a high-dimensional grid is not just more burdensome than full Monte Carlo, but can often simply be infeasible. If K is not small, then the construction of the grid can require more portfolio valuations than would be required by full Monte Carlo. Thus, this approach is useful only when the number of market factors is small, that is, less than or equal to three or perhaps four.

TABLE 15.1 Grid of possible values of the S&P 500 and FT-SE 100 indexes and the associated portfolio values. The grid is centered at the current index values of 1097.6 and 5862.3.

	FT-SE 100				
S&P 500	5262.3	5562.3	5862.3	6162.3	6462.3
997.6	97,322,917	98,817,267	99,879,499	100,524,319	100,814,190
1047.6	98,406,251	99,900,600	100,962,832	101,607,653	101,897,524
1097.6	98,928,638	100,422,988	101,485,220	102,130,040	102,409,911
1147.6	98,406,251	100,404,232	101,466,463	102,111,284	102,401,155
1197.6	98,909,882	99,920,201	100,982,433	101,627,253	101,917,424

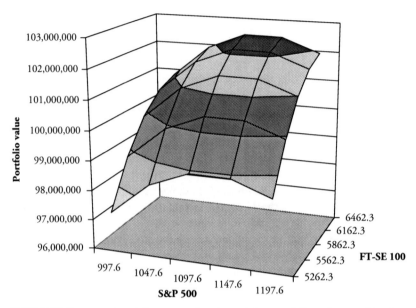

FIGURE 15.2 Example of the approximation of the portfolio value used in the grid Monte Carlo method

PRINCIPAL COMPONENTS GRID MONTE CARLO

Recognition of this limitation suggests attacking the problem by reducing the number of factors. For fixed-income portfolios, the *principal components grid Monte Carlo approach* uses the method of principal components to reduce the dimension of possible yield-curve changes to a manageable one. For example, in the case of term structure models, the first three principal components, often interpreted as level, slope, and curvature, explain most of the risk of changes in interest rates. The approach is to use the first few (e.g., three) principal components as factors, express the portfolio values in terms of these factors, and then proceed as in naïve grid Monte Carlo: specify a grid of possible values of the factors, reprice the portfolio exactly on the nodes of the grid, and then use linear interpolation to reprice the portfolio for factor realizations that fall between the nodes.

If one builds a grid using nine possible values of each market factor, then there are $9^3 = 729$ nodes at which the portfolio must be repriced. Also, it can make sense to use fewer grid points for the second and third factors because the principal components analysis has identified them as making a smaller contribution to the risk than the first factor, so the error from using a crude approximation is smaller. For example, if one used nine possible changes in the term structure level, five possible changes in slope, and three possible changes in curvature, there would be only $9 \times 5 \times 3 = 135$ nodes on the grid for which the portfolio would need to be revalued. This is certainly feasible. However, the argument to use a cruder grid for the second and third factors is undermined to the extent that the risk of the first and/or second factor has been hedged. In this case, the risk of the portfolio is driven by the factor or factors for which a crude approximation is used.

This approach can be useful if: (i) the first few principal components or other factors account for almost all of the risk, as is often the case in term structure modeling; and (ii) the approximate portfolio values computed by linear interpolation from the grid are adequate. However, it is less useful for portfolios of instruments, such as options on individual common stocks, for which the residual risk not explained by factor models is important.

SCENARIO SIMULATION

Scenario simulation is another method that breaks the link between the number of Monte Carlo draws and number of portfolio repricings. It does this by approximating the distributions of changes in the factors rather than by approximating the portfolio value. As in principal components grid Monte Carlo, principal components analysis is used to reduce the number of factors. Each risk factor is then assumed to take only a small number of distinct values, leading to a small (or, at least, manageable) number of possible scenarios, each corresponding to a portfolio value that needs to be computed only once. Monte Carlo simulation is then done by sampling among these scenarios, leading to a great reduction in the number of portfolio revaluations required.

OTHER MONTE CARLO APPROACHES

From the examples discussed above, it should be clear that the number of potential variations of the Monte Carlo method is limited only by the number of possible methods for approximating the portfolio value function and/or the distribution of changes in the market factors. For example, one could conceivably add higher-order terms to the delta-gamma-theta approximation or omit the second-order terms for factors that are deemed less important. In the context of grid approaches, Pritsker (1997) discusses the *modified grid Monte Carlo approach*. This approach combines a grid approximation for a handful of factors for which nonlinearity is important and then uses a linear approximation to capture the effect of the other factors. For any choice of approximating function, the key issue is the trade off between the accuracy of the approximation and the computer resources required to evaluate the approximating function. All of the variants of the Monte Carlo method retain the features of full Monte Carlo, except that they explicitly trade off accuracy for saving in computational time to varying degrees.

NOTES

Delta-gamma Monte Carlo is described in Duffie and Pan (1997). Using a portfolio of European-style foreign currency options, Pritsker (1997) examined the trade off between accuracy and computational time for the standard delta-normal method, full Monte Carlo, delta-gamma Monte Carlo, and modified grid Monte Carlo. Principal components grid Monte Carlo is described by Frye (1998). Scenario simulation was proposed by Jamshidian and Zhu (1997) and evaluated by Abken (2000) and Gibson and Pritsker (2000/2001).

Gibson and Pritsker (2000/2001) suggest the use of partial least squares rather than principal components to select the factors in grid Monte Carlo approaches. The motivation for this choice is that the partial-least-squares method chooses as factors the random variables that best explain the changes in portfolio value, in contrast to the principal components approach, which chooses as factors the random variables that best explain changes in the yield curve. If the portfolio has limited exposure to the most important factors driving the yield curve, choosing the principal components as factors will not fully capture its risks. A limitation of the partial-least-squares approach is that the factors it selects may be unintuitive and difficult to interpret.

Strategies to reduce the sample size N without sacrificing accuracy include use of standard variance reduction techniques such as antithetic variates, control variates, and stratified sampling, and the use of quasi-random sequences. These are beyond the scope of this book but are discussed in standard references on Monte Carlo methods. Cardenás, Fruchard, Picron, Reyes, Walters, and Yang (1999) describe the use of control variates and stratified sampling in computing value-at-risk. Boyle, Broadie, and Glasserman (1997) discuss the use of variance-reduction techniques and quasi-random sequences in option pricing.

This method is sometimes called the delta-gamma or delta-gamma-theta method instead of the delta-gamma-theta Monte Carlo method. In this book, the names *delta-gamma* and *delta-gamma-theta* are reserved for the approach described in Chapter 14.

CHAPTER 16

Extreme Value Theory and VaR

It is well known that the actual distributions of changes in market rates and prices have fat tails relative to the normal distribution, implying that an appropriately fat-tailed distribution would provide better value-at-risk estimates for high confidence levels. However, since by definition the data contain relatively few extreme observations, we have little information about the tails. As a result, selecting a reasonable fat-tailed parametric distribution and estimating the parameters that determine the thickness of the tails are inherently difficult tasks. Similarly, the historical simulation method provides imprecise estimates of the tails.

Extreme value theory (EVT) has recently attracted a great deal of attention because it offers a potential solution to the problem of estimating the tails. Loosely, EVT tells us that the behavior of certain extreme values is the same (i.e., described by a particular parametric family of distributions) regardless of the distribution that generates the data.

Two broad classes of models appear in EVT. The models in the more modern group are known as *peaks over threshold* (POT) models. These are based on a mathematical result that, for a large class of distributions that includes all of the commonly used continuous distributions, extreme realizations above a high (or below a low) threshold are described by a particular distribution, the *generalized Pareto distribution* (GPD). Thus, EVT solves the problem of how to model the tails: they are described by the generalized Pareto distribution, regardless of the distribution that generates the data. Since knowing the tail of the distribution is exactly what is required for value-at-risk estimates at high confidence levels, the applicability of this result to value-at-risk calculations is clear.

Classical extreme value theory gives us *block maxima* models, which are models for the maxima out of large samples of (identically distributed) observations. These are based on a long-standing result that, for large blocks, the maxima satisfy the generalized extreme value (GEV) distribution. For example, if the observations are daily interest-rate changes and the

245

blocks are years, a block maxima model using the GEV distribution might be used to estimate the distribution of the maximum one-day interest-rate change within the year. Such models can offer guidance regarding the scenarios that should be considered in stress testing.

EVT has a long history of applications in hydrology, climatology, engineering, and, somewhat more recently, insurance. Its use in financial risk measurement is only nascent, partly because its applicability to financial risk management has only recently been recognized by nonspecialists in EVT, and partly because there are important limitations to EVT, particularly in the area of multivariate EVT. Thus, to some extent EVT is a field of future promise rather than current application. Nonetheless, EVT speaks so directly to key issues in financial risk measurement that it is clear that it is here to stay and that financial risk managers should be aware of its main ideas.

With this goal in mind, this chapter provides a brief introduction to the main ideas of EVT and its use in risk measurement. After describing the data used to illustrate EVT, it explains the GPD and its potential role in value-at-risk calculations, presents one approach for fitting the GPD to the data, and then illustrates the differences in the estimates of the tails. It then briefly describes the classical result on the distribution of maxima and its potential role in stress testing. The last section of the chapter then indicates some open issues in EVT that limit its use in value-at-risk calculations.

DISTRIBUTION OF YIELD CHANGES

Figure 16.1 illustrates the distribution of changes in the 10-year constant maturity treasury (CMT) yield over the period 1990–1999, a total of 2503 business days. These data are used below to illustrate the application of extreme value theory to value-at-risk calculations. Each point on the line labeled "Empirical frequency" represents the number of yield changes observed in an interval 2 basis points wide, centered around the value indicated on the horizontal axis. For example, the point (0, 523) indicates that 523 of the yield changes satisfy the condition −1 basis point ≤ yield change < 1 basis point. The Figure also shows the frequencies predicted by a normal distribution with mean and variance equal to the mean and variance of the changes in the 10-year CMT yields. Figure 16.2 provides a more detailed look at the right-hand tail of the distribution.

Comparison of the empirical frequencies in Figure 16.1 to those predicted from the normal distribution reveal that the distribution of changes in the 10-year CMT yield has a higher peak than the normal distribution with the same mean and variance, while comparison of the frequencies in

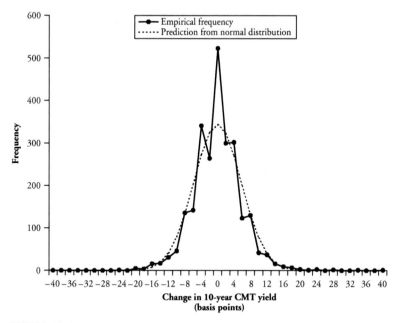

FIGURE 16.1 Distribution of changes in the 10-year CMT yield

Figure 16.2 reveals that the empirical distribution has more probability in the right-hand tail than the normal, that is, that the empirical distribution has fat or heavy tails relative to the normal. For example, Figure 16.2 shows that the empirical and normal frequencies are approximately the same for yield changes of 12, 14, and 16 basis points, but that larger changes occur more frequently than predicted by the normal distribution. Though not shown, a similar pattern is found in the left-hand tail. Then, for intermediate changes of between 6 and 10 basis points, the empirical frequencies are less than those predicted by the normal distribution.

These characteristics are commonly found in financial data and can have significant effects on value-at-risk estimates, especially for high confidence levels. For example, for the empirical and normal distributions quantiles of 16 and 14 basis points, respectively, leave approximately 1% of the probability in the right-hand tail. To leave approximately 0.3% in the right-hand tail, the quantiles are 22 basis points and slightly more than 16 basis points, respectively. These differences in the quantiles map into differences in value-at-risk estimates and indicate that the use of the normal distribution may lead to underestimates of value-at-risk. (However, for a lower confidence level, for example, 90% or 95%, the situation can

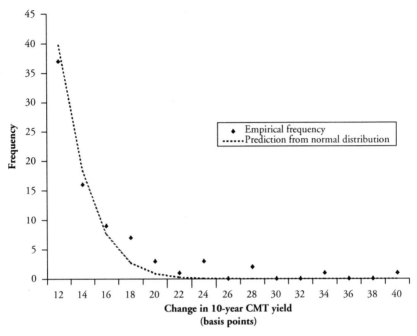

FIGURE 16.2 Right-hand tail of the distribution of changes in the 10-year CMT yield

be reversed due to the fact that the empirical frequencies are less than those predicted by the normal distribution for intermediate changes of between 6 and 10 basis points.) As indicated above, EVT offers some hope of overcoming this problem.

THE GENERALIZED PARETO DISTRIBUTION AND VALUE-AT-RISK

Peaks over threshold models are based on a mathematical result that, for a large class of distributions, extreme realizations above a high (or below a low) threshold follow the generalized Pareto distribution. We focus on the upper (right-hand) tail of the distribution, though this choice is of no importance; the left-hand tail can be transformed into the right-hand tail by switching the sign of the random variable X we introduce next. To explain the result, we first need to introduce a bit of notation.

Let X be the random variable under consideration (e.g., a mark-to-market loss), and use F to denote its distribution function. Consider a threshold u, and define $X - u$ to be the excess loss over the threshold, often called the *exceedance*.

The conditional distribution function $F(x \mid X > u)$ gives the conditional probability that the excess loss $X - u$ is less than x, given that the loss exceeds u. It follows that $1 - F(x \mid X > u)$ is the conditional probability that the excess $X - u$ exceeds x.

The key result underlying POT models is that, in the limit as the threshold $u \to \infty$, the conditional distribution function $F(x \mid X > u)$ approaches the generalized Pareto distribution (GPD) given by

$$
G(x) = \begin{cases} 1 - \left(1 + \xi\dfrac{x}{\beta}\right)^{-1/\xi} & \text{if } \xi \neq 0, \\[2mm] 1 - \exp\left(-\dfrac{x}{\beta}\right) & \text{if } \xi = 0, \end{cases} \tag{16.1}
$$

where $x \geq 0$ if $\xi \geq 0$ and $0 \leq x < -\beta/\xi$ if $\xi < 0$. The parameter ξ is a shape parameter that determines the fatness of the tail, while β is an additional scaling parameter. The GPD is generalized in that it subsumes three distributions as special cases: if the shape parameter $\xi > 0$, it is equivalent to the ordinary Pareto distribution, used in insurance as a model for large losses; if $\xi = 0$, it is the exponential distribution; and if $\xi < 0$, it is the Pareto type II distribution.

The case $\xi > 0$ is the one most relevant for financial data, as it corresponds to heavy tails. Considering this case, the preceding equation implies that the conditional probability that the excess loss $X - u$ is greater than x is approximated by

$$
P(X - u > x \mid X > u) \approx 1 - G(x) = \left(1 + \xi\frac{x}{\beta}\right)^{-1/\xi}, \tag{16.2}
$$

where $P(A)$ is the probability of the event A. In applications, one cannot actually let the threshold $u \to \infty$. Instead, one picks a threshold high enough to approximate infinity and above that threshold treats equation (16.2) as though it holds exactly. Doing this, the unconditional probability that the excess loss is greater than a number x depends on the probability that the random variable X exceeds u, and is given by

$$
\begin{aligned} P(X - u > x) &= P(X > u)P(X - u > x \mid X > u) \\ &\approx P(X > u)\left(1 + \xi\frac{x}{\beta}\right)^{-1/\xi}. \end{aligned} \tag{16.3}
$$

Thus, provided u is chosen to be large enough that the approximation in (16.2) and (16.3) is sufficiently accurate, it is possible to compute value-at-risk without knowledge of the distribution that describes the data.

As will be seen below, it is reasonably straightforward to estimate the threshold u above which the GPD provides a good approximation and also straightforward to estimate the parameters β and ξ. Then using the obvious fact that $P(X - u > x) = P(X > u + x)$, the $1 - \alpha$ percent confidence value-at-risk is the number $\mathrm{VaR} = u + x$ such that

$$
\begin{aligned}
\alpha &= P(X > \mathrm{VaR}) \\
&= P(X > u + x) \\
&= P(X > u)\left(1 + \xi\frac{x}{\beta}\right)^{-1/\xi} \\
&= P(X > u)\left(1 + \xi\frac{\mathrm{VaR} - u}{\beta}\right)^{-1/\xi},
\end{aligned}
$$

implying that

$$
\mathrm{VaR} = u + \frac{\beta}{\xi}\left[\left(\frac{\alpha}{P(X > u)}\right)^{-\xi} - 1\right]. \tag{16.4}
$$

Typically it is also straightforward to estimate the probability of exceeding the threshold $P(X > u)$, allowing the value-at-risk to be computed from this formula.

THE MEAN EXCESS FUNCTION AND THE THRESHOLD *u*

The *mean excess function* is

$$
e(u) = E[X - u | X > u],
$$

that is, it is the expected value of the excess $X - u$, conditional on an excess. For a given data set and threshold u, the mean excess can be estimated from the data as

$$
\frac{1}{n_u}\sum_{i=1}^{n_u}(X_i - u), \tag{16.5}
$$

where n_u is the number of observations X_i that exceed the threshold u. Repeated use of (16.5) for a range of values of u then produces an estimate of the mean excess as a function of the threshold u, that is, it produces an empirical estimate $\hat{e}(u)$ of the mean excess function. Figure 16.3 illustrates the mean excess function for the CMT yield data summarized in Figure 16.1 and thresholds between 0 and 30 basis points. The numbers of excesses used to compute the means range from 1344 for the threshold of 0 basis points to 2 for the threshold of 30 basis points.

The threshold u above which it is reasonable to use the approximations (16.2) and (16.3) can be estimated from the empirical mean excess function because the mean excess function for a GPD is linear in the threshold; in particular, it is of the form

$$e(u) = \frac{\beta + \xi u}{1 - \xi}. \tag{16.6}$$

The threshold u at which the empirical mean excess function constructed from (16.5) becomes approximately linear, then provides an estimate of the threshold above which the GPD (16.5) provides a reasonable approximation of the tail.

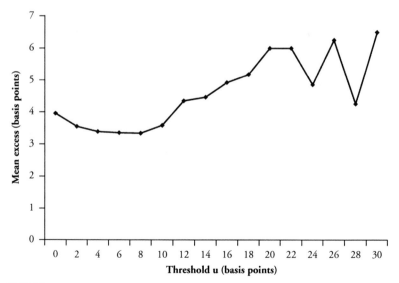

FIGURE 16.3 Mean excess function for the CMT yield data

The mean excess is closely related to the popular *expected shortfall* measure, which is discussed in Chapter 19 in the context of coherent risk measures. In particular, the expected shortfall is the expected loss given that the loss is greater than or equal to the value-at-risk, or equivalently the sum of the value-at-risk and the mean excess using the value-at-risk as the threshold:

$$\text{expected shortfall} = \text{VaR}_{1-\alpha} + \text{mean excess over VaR}$$
$$= \text{VaR}_{1-\alpha} + E[X - \text{VaR}_{1-\alpha} | X > \text{VaR}_{1-\alpha}]. \qquad (16.7)$$

The distribution (16.1) implies that, if excesses over a threshold u have the distribution (16.1), then excesses over $\text{VaR}_{1-\alpha} > u$ have the same distribution function with the scaling parameter β replaced by $\beta + \xi(\text{VaR}_{1-\alpha} - u)$, and the mean excess is given by (16.6), with u replaced by $\text{VaR}_{1-\alpha} - u$. Combining this fact with (16.7), the expected shortfall is

$$\text{expected shortfall} = \text{VaR}_{1-\alpha} + \frac{\beta + \xi(\text{VaR}_{1-\alpha} - u)}{1 - \xi}$$
$$= \frac{\text{VaR}_{1-\alpha}}{1 - \xi} + \frac{\beta - \xi u}{1 - \xi}.$$

ESTIMATING THE PARAMETERS OF THE GPD AND COMPUTING VALUE-AT-RISK

The first step in estimation is to pick the threshold u above which it is reasonable to use the approximations (16.2) and (16.3). Figure 16.3 indicates that the empirical mean excess function is approximately linear above the threshold of $u = 10$ basis points. A total of 86 data points, or approximately 4.075% of the sample, exceed this threshold, while 118 data points, or 4.751% of the yield changes, equal or exceed it. While the empirical mean excess function appears again to become nonlinear at a threshold of about 22 basis points, the means for thresholds of 22 to 30 basis points are estimated using only between eight observations (at 22 basis points) and two observations (at 30 basis points). Thus, it seems reasonable to discount the apparent nonlinearity in this region.

Next, we need estimates of the parameters β and ξ and the probability $P(X > u)$. The parameters β and ξ were estimated using the method of maximum likelihood, discussed in the notes to this chapter. The maximum likelihood estimates are $\hat{\xi} = 0.264$ and $\hat{\beta} = 0.031$.

Letting n_u denote the number of observations that exceed the threshold $u = 10$ basis points, a straightforward estimate of the probability $P(X > u)$ is given by the ratio of n_u to the total number of observations, n_u/n. As indicated above, a total of 86 of the yield changes are greater than 10 basis points. However, a small complication stems from the fact that the precision of the data is one basis point, so that 32 of the reported yield changes are exactly 10 basis points. We handle this detail by treating one-half of these as if they were less than 10 basis points and one-half as if they were greater. Doing this, we treat a total of $86 + (1/2)32 = 102$ observations as exceeding the threshold of 10 basis points, yielding an estimate of the probability of $P(X > u) = 102/2503 = 0.0475$, or 4.75%.

Using these estimates, Figure 16.4 shows the estimated distribution function of the GPD,

$$G(x) = 1 - \left(1 + \hat{\xi}\frac{x}{\hat{\beta}}\right)^{-1/\hat{\xi}}.$$

This gives an estimate of the conditional probability $P(X - u < x \mid (X > u))$ as a function of x, that is, it gives the estimated probability that the excess is less than a level x, conditional on an excess. Figure 16.4 also shows the corresponding probabilities computed from the conditional empirical distribution, as well as the conditional probabilities of excesses computed from the normal distribution with mean and variance equal to the sample mean and variance of the yield changes. These conditional normal probabilities are given by

$$
\begin{aligned}
P(X - u < x \mid X > u) &= 1 - P(X - u > x \mid X > u) \\
&= 1 - \frac{P(X > x + u)}{P(X > u)} \\
&= 1 - \frac{1 - N(x + u; \hat{\mu}, \hat{\sigma}^2)}{1 - N(u; \hat{\mu}, \hat{\sigma}^2)},
\end{aligned}
$$

where $N(x; \hat{\mu}, \hat{\sigma}^2)$ is the cumulative normal distribution function with mean $\hat{\mu}$ and variance $\hat{\sigma}^2$.

The probability that a yield change exceeds a level y can be computed directly from the distribution function of excesses using the fact that the yield change is the sum of the threshold and the excess, giving the relations $y = u + x$ and $P(X > y) = P(X - u > x)$. Combining these relations with

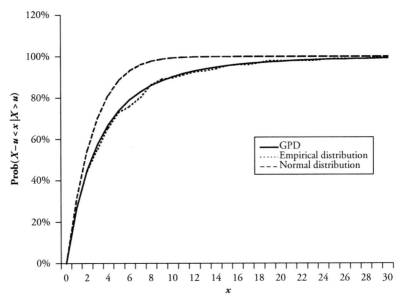

FIGURE 16.4 Estimated distribution functions, conditional on an excess

equation (16.3) and using the estimates $\hat{\beta}$, $\hat{\xi}$, and n_u/n, for the GPD the probability of exceeding a level y is estimated by

$$P(X > y) = \frac{n_u}{n}\left(1 + \hat{\xi}\frac{y - u}{\hat{\beta}}\right)^{-1/\hat{\xi}}.$$

For the normal distribution, the probability of exceeding a level y is simply $1 - N(y; \hat{\mu}, \hat{\sigma}^2)$. Figure 16.5 shows the estimates of the probabilities $P(X > y)$ for the generalized Pareto, normal, and empirical distributions for y in the range from 10 to 40 basis points.

Figures 16.4 and 16.5 reveal that the GPD matches the empirical distribution in the right-hand tail quite closely, but that the normal distribution does not. For example, the normal distribution indicates a 1% probability of a yield change larger than about 13.5 basis points, while the GPD assigns the same probability to a yield change greater than 15 basis points. The differences become larger farther out in the tail; the normal distribution indicates a 0.28% probability of a yield change greater than 16 basis points, while the GPD assigns the same probability to a yield change of 22 basis points. The differences translate directly into differences in the

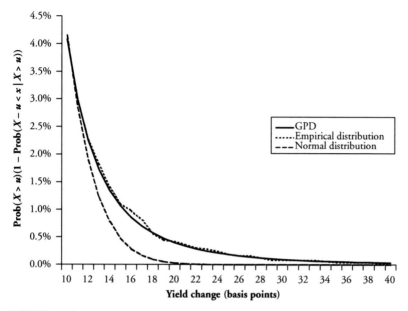

FIGURE 16.5 Probabilities $P(X > y)$ for the generalized Pareto, normal, and empirical distributions

value-at-risk estimates implied by the different distributions. For a portfolio with a linear exposure to changes in the 10-year CMT yield (and no other significant exposures), the $100\% - 0.28\% = 99.72\%$ confidence value-at-risk estimate implied by the GPD would be $22/16 = 1.375$ times as large as that implied by the normal distribution.

The GPD approach to computing value-at-risk can be adapted to incorporate changing volatilities by first scaling the changes in the market factors by estimates of their volatilities and then fitting the GPD to the tails of the scaled changes. This is similar to the approach Hull and White (1998) suggest for incorporating changing volatilities in the historical simulation method.

THE GENERALIZED EXTREME VALUE DISTRIBUTION AND STRESS TESTING

Classical extreme value theory focuses on the limiting distribution of appropriately centered and normalized maxima of sequences of random variables. Specifically, let $X_1, X_2, \ldots, X_n$ denote a sequence of n independent and identically distributed random variables, for example, n returns on an asset or changes in interest or exchange rates. Then if $M_n = \max[X_1, X_2, \ldots, X_n]$ is the maximum of the sequence $X_1, X_2, \ldots, X_n$ and b_n are appropriately chosen normalizing constants, as the number of observations $n \to \infty$, the distribution of the centered and normalized maximum $m_n = (M_n - a_n)/b_n$ approaches the *generalized extreme value (GEV) distribution*. In its most general form, the distribution function is

$$
H(x) = \begin{cases} \exp\left[-\left(1 + \xi\left(\dfrac{x-u}{\psi}\right)\right)^{-1/\xi}\right] & \text{if } \xi \neq 0, \\[4mm] \exp\left[-e^{-\left(\frac{x-u}{\psi}\right)}\right] & \text{if } \xi = 0. \end{cases}
\tag{16.8}
$$

Up to the asymptotic approximation, this distribution function is the probability that $m_n < x$, so $1 - H(x)$ gives the probability that the level x will be exceeded. Similar to the GPD, the GEV distribution subsumes three special cases: if $\xi > 0$, it reduces to the *Frechet distribution*; if $\xi = 0$, it reduces to the *Gumbel*; and if $\xi < 0$, it reduces to the *Weibull*.

One should not be bothered by the fact that the result is a statement about a centered and normalized variable, for this is actually a familiar situation. Suppose, for example, that each of the random variables X_i above has a mean of μ and a standard deviation of σ. Then a version of the central limit theorem says that the mean $\frac{1}{n}\sum_{i=1}^{n} X_i$ converges in distribution to a normal random variable with mean μ and standard deviation $\mu/\sqrt{n}$, or that $\frac{1}{n}\sum_{i=1}^{n} X_i - \mu$ has a limiting distribution with mean zero and standard deviation $\sigma/\sqrt{n}$. Doing a bit of rewriting, we obtain

$$
\frac{1}{n}\sum_{i=1}^{n} X_i - \mu = \frac{1}{n}\left(\sum_{i=1}^{n} X_i - n\mu\right),
$$

and thus see that the familiar central limit theorem is a statement about a centered and normalized variable, the sum $\sum_{i=1}^{n} X_i$. Here the centering and normalizing constants are $n\mu$ and n, respectively.

Because value-at-risk is not concerned with the distribution of the maximum, the GEV distribution is not directly relevant to value-at-risk calculations. However, the distribution of the maximum is directly relevant for stress testing, because it can provide guidance about what scenarios are reasonable to consider. A key feature of EVT is that it can provide such guidance even though few extreme events have ever been observed.

To develop stress-testing scenarios using a block maxima model and the GEV distribution, one would partition the data into blocks of approximately equal size and then fit the GEV to the block maxima. For example, 30 years of daily returns data might be formed into 60 semiannual blocks, each consisting of approximately 125 returns. Then, the parameters would be estimated from the 60 block maxima, perhaps using the method of maximum likelihood based on the density implied by (16.8). Doing this involves the assumption that the 125 observations in each block are sufficiently many for the limiting distribution (16.8) to apply. Once the estimates are obtained, the GEV distribution function can be used to make statements about the (estimated) probabilities of semiannual maxima, for example, with a high probability q the largest daily stock market decline observed in the next six months will be less than 30%. Such estimates can be used to make judgments about whether a stock market decline of this magnitude should be included in the scenarios used for stress testing.

LIMITATIONS OF EVT IN COMPUTING VALUE-AT-RISK

At first glance, EVT seems like a magic bullet. Through the GPD, it provides a way of estimating the tail behavior of random variables without knowledge of the true distribution. Thus, it seems ideally suited for value-at-risk computations. Through the GEV distribution, it provides a way of assessing the magnitudes of scenarios for use in stress testing. Moreover, the theory underlying EVT is well established, with certain of the basic results dating back to 1928. Why then isn't everyone using it?

Crucially, note that the discussion above has been of using EVT to model the tails of the distribution of a single random variable. For value-at-risk calculations, we are typically interested in the joint distribution of changes in multiple market factors. A multivariate extreme value theory characterizing the joint distribution of the tails does exist, but it is less well developed than its univariate counterpart and more difficult to implement. Multivariate extreme value theory is developed using the concept of *copulas*, which describe the dependence structure of random variables. In principle, one can estimate the (parameters of the) copulas for the tails of the joint distribution. However, recognizing that each random variable has both an upper and a lower tail and both are relevant for risk measurement due to short positions and portfolio effects, a collection of K random variable has 2^K tails. Thus, implementation of this approach is infeasible when there are more than a handful of market factors. Nonetheless, multivariate extreme value theory does appear to be useful for developing scenarios for stress testing, because in this case one is often interested in the joint dependence of a handful of key market factors.

To apply EVT to calculate the value-at-risk of portfolios that depend on multiple sources of risk, the best approach seems to be to turn the problem into a univariate one by first estimating the distribution of profits and losses by historical simulation, that is, by using the technique of *portfolio aggregation*. Then, one fits the GPD to the tail of this univariate distribution of profits and losses. This is straightforward but requires that one accept most of the limitations of the historical simulation method. Also, the available empirical evidence does not bear directly on the question of whether EVT is useful for measuring the VaR of portfolios that depend (perhaps nonlinearly) on multiple sources of risk.

NOTES

For further discussion of extreme value theory and its applications in insurance and finance, see Embrechts, Klüppelberg, and Mikosch (1997, hereafter EKM). Other recent books include Beirlant, Teugels, and Vynckier (1996), Leadbetter, Lindgren, and Rootzen (1983), Reiss and Thomas (1997), and Resnick (1987). Embrechts, Resnick and Samorodnitsky (1998) and McNeil (1999) are overviews of the use of extreme value theory in risk measurement, with McNeil's overview being somewhat longer (and thus more complete). Diebold, Schuermann, and Stroughair (1998) provide a critical review of the use of extreme value theory in risk measurement, focusing on issues of estimation. Embrechts (2000) is a collection of recent articles on applications of EVT to financial risk measurement. Smith (2000) outlines areas of current theoretical development.

The data used in the example are the 10-year constant maturity U.S. Treasury yields, obtained from the Board of Governors of the Federal Reserve System at *http://www.federalreserve.gov/releases/H15/data.htm* and described there. The result that the limiting distribution of excesses over high thresholds is the generalized Pareto distribution dates to Balkema and de Haan (1974) and Pickands (1975) and is further developed by Smith (1987) and Leadbetter (1991). Properties of the GPD are summarized in EKM (1997, Theorem 3.4.13). Important papers illustrating the use of the GPD in modeling extreme values (of nonfinancial data) include Smith (1989), Davison (1984), and Davison and Smith (1990).

The use of the mean excess function in selecting the threshold u is discussed by EKM (1997, section 6.5) and the references therein. The empirical mean excess function in Figure 16.3, in which there is no obvious unique choice of the threshold u and the function is estimated imprecisely for high thresholds, is common.

The maximum likelihood estimation of the parameters of the generalized Pareto distribution is studied by Smith (1987) and described by EKM (1997, section 6.5). The density function of the GPD for the case $\xi > 0$ and a given threshold u is

$$g(x) = \frac{1}{\beta}\left(1 + \xi\frac{x}{\beta}\right)^{-\frac{1}{\xi}-1}, \quad x \in [0, \infty),$$

and the log-likelihood is

$$\ell(\xi, \beta) = (-n_u)\ln\beta - \left(\frac{1}{\xi} + 1\right)\sum_{i=1}^{n_u}\ln\left(1 + \frac{\xi}{\beta}X_i\right),$$

where n_u is the number of excesses over the threshold u and $X_i \in [0, \infty)$ is the ith excess. With only two parameters β and ξ, computation of the maximum likelihood estimates is straightforward.

There are alternative semiparametric approaches to estimating the tail, of which the best known approach is the Hill (1975) estimator. Recent work in this area includes Danielsson and de Vries (1997a; 1997b) and Danielsson, de Haan, Peng, and de Vries (1999), who cite additional references. Danielsson, Hartmann, and de Vries (1998) discuss the use of this approach in computing value-at-risk.

Neftci (2000) uses the maximum likelihood approach to fit the GPD to extreme changes for a number of foreign exchange rates and U.S. dollar interest rates and uses the resulting estimates to compute the 1% tail probabilities for the distributions. The out-of-sample performance of the estimated tail probabilities is good in the sense that approximately 1% of the out-of-sample observations fall into the predicted 1% tails. These results are encouraging, in that they indicate that the GPD would provide accurate 99% confidence value-at-risk forecasts for a portfolio with a (single) linear exposure to any of the exchange or interest rates studied. McNeil and Frey (2000) do this for several stock return series and other market factors and then compute and back test value-at-risk estimates at the 95, 99, and 99.5%

quantiles. The conditional GPD-based value-at-risk estimates perform well at all quantiles, and significantly better than the other approaches to which they compare it at the 99 and 99.5% quantiles. They also obtain promising results for conditional GPD-based estimates of the expected shortfall.

Other applications of the GPD in insurance and finance include Danielsson and de Vries (1997c; 2000), Danielsson and Morimoto (2000), Gavin (2000), Këllezi and Gilli (2000), McNeil (1997a), McNeil and Frey (2000), McNeil and Saladin (1997; 1998), and the papers in Embrechts (2000).

The result regarding the limiting distribution of maxima dates to Fisher and Tippet (1928) and is discussed in the previously cited books on EVT. Estimation of the centering and scaling constants is discussed in EKM, section 6.4 and the references cited there; section 3.3 provides explicit calculations for several distributions. McNeil (1997b; 1998) describes such an analysis (using annual blocks) and argues it could have predicted the 1987 stock market break in the sense that it estimated that a decline of that magnitude had a nontrivial probability. Other applications of the GEV in financial risk measurement include Këllezi and Gilli (2000) and Parisi (2000). The *worst-case scenario* measure proposed by Boudoukh, Richardson, and Whitelaw (1995) is similar to block maxima models in that it also measures the distribution of the largest loss, though without use of EVT.

Embrechts, de Haan, and Huang (1999) discuss some of the issues in multivariate extreme value theory. Embrechts, McNeil, and Straumann (1999, 2001) criticize reliance on correlation to measure the dependence between random variables. Longin (2000) proposes an approximate approach to use multivariate EVT model for value-at-risk calculations and applies it to stock returns. Starica (1999) estimates the dependence between the extreme movement of various exchange rates. All of these authors provide references to the statistics literature on multivariate EVT.

five

Limitations of Value-at-Risk

CHAPTER 17

VaR Is Only an Estimate

Value-at-risk estimates are just that: estimates. Errors occur because the distributional assumptions may not correspond to the actual distribution of changes in the market factors (and will never correspond *exactly* to the actual distribution of changes in the market factors), because the delta-normal, delta-gamma-normal, and grid Monte Carlo methods are based on approximations to the value of the portfolio, and because the estimates are based on past data that need not reflect current market conditions. Further, even users who choose the same framework and avoid implementation errors will make different implementation choices, leading to different value-at-risk estimates. For example, there can be differences in the choice of basic market factors, the mappings of various instruments, the methods for interpolating term structures, the formulas or algorithms used to value various instruments (e.g., options), and the number of past data used to estimate the distributions of changes in the market factors. In addition, some value-at-risk systems will embody logical or computer coding errors of varying degrees of severity, and it is conceivable that in some situations users will have incentives to introduce biases or errors into value-at-risk estimates.

As a result, back testing is crucial to verify model accuracy and identify areas in which improvement is needed. While some of the impetus for back testing has come from banking regulators, who need to ensure VaR models used to determine capital requirements are not systematically biased, verifying VaR models is important for anyone who uses them for decision making. This chapter explains several approaches for back testing VaR models and then briefly summarizes some of the evidence on the performance of the various methods for computing value-at-risk.

SIMPLE APPROACHES FOR BACK TESTING

Underlying the simplest back testing framework is the idea that, for a $1 - \alpha$ confidence VaR model, one expects to observe exceptions on $\alpha\%$ of the days.

For example, if $\alpha = 0.05$ and the model is back tested using the last 250 daily returns, the expected number of exceptions is $0.05 \times 250 = 12.5$. Of course, the actual number of exceptions depends on the random outcomes of the underlying market factors in addition to the quality of the VaR model; even if the VaR model is correct, the actual number typically will differ from the expected number. This leads to a rule based on a range, determined by the willingness to reject a correct VaR model. For example, Figure 17.1 shows the distribution of the number of exceptions out of 250 daily returns for a correct model with $\alpha = 0.05$. Even though the expected number of exceptions is 12.5, the probability that the number of exceptions e is outside the range $7 \leq e \leq 19$ is 5.85%. If 250 daily returns are used and a probability of rejecting a correct VaR model of 5.85% is tolerable, then the model should be rejected if the number of exceptions is outside this range and not rejected otherwise.

This simple approach is widely used and is enshrined in Basle framework, allowing banks to use internal risk models to determine capital requirements. However, a crucial limitation should be clear—many incorrect VaR models will generate between 7 and 19 exceptions out of 250 returns.

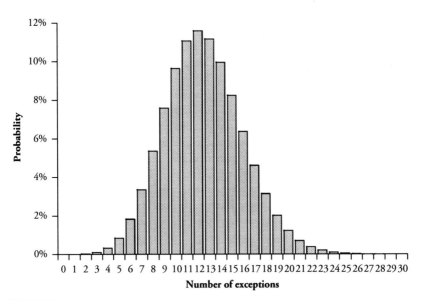

FIGURE 17.1 Distribution of number of exceptions for a VaR model with exception probability $\alpha = 0.05$

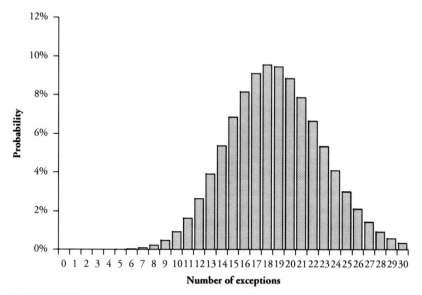

FIGURE 17.2 Distribution of number of exceptions for a VaR model with exception probability $\alpha = 0.075$

For example, Figure 17.2 shows the distribution of exceptions of a biased VaR model for which the probability of an exception is actually 7.5%. For such an incorrect model, the probability that the number of exceptions is between 7 and 19 is 58.4%; even the expected number of exceptions, 18.75, is within the range $7 \leq e \leq 19$. If each day the probability of an exception is 10%, the probability that the total number of exceptions out of 250 returns is between 7 and 19 is 12.1%.

In short, this approach is just not very powerful: a range wide enough that a correct model is rejected with only low probability is so wide that many incorrect models are also rejected with only low probability, while a range narrow enough that most incorrect models are rejected with high probability results in a high probability of rejecting correct models. The problem stems from the fact that a large sample of daily returns is required to have a reasonable number of exceptions of 95% confidence VaR estimates. The situation is even worse if one wants to back test 99% confidence VaR models. Because large samples of weekly or monthly data are either not available or include past periods no longer relevant, this leads to back testing VaR models using daily data even if VaR is intended to be used with a longer horizon. Unfortunately, even using daily data it takes a long time to generate a large sample, because only one observation is generated during each holding period (e.g., day); thus it can take a long time to identify a biased model. This is problematic, because the biased model may be in use.

The problem can be ameliorated by using a lower confidence level, because there will be more exceptions to provide information about the performance of the model. While use of a lower confidence level is useful if the purpose of the VaR model is to serve as a broad gauge of risk, it does not help when the user is concerned primarily with the tail of the distribution of portfolio returns.

Further, to pass back tests of this sort a VaR model need only be correct on average. In statistical terminology, the approach considers only the marginal distribution of the exceptions. As a result, even grossly deficient VaR models can pass these simple tests. For example, consider a silly model that estimates VaR to be $100 billion on 99 out of every 100 days and then on the 100th day estimates VaR to be $0. Since this model would generate an exception on every 100th day and on only two or three days out of every 250, it would pass simple tests based on exceptions, even though it provides no useful risk information.

A more realistic example is a VaR model that does not respond fully to changes in market volatility, thereby producing downward-biased estimates during high-volatility periods and upward-biased estimates during low-volatility periods. So long as it is right on average, tests based on the marginal distribution of exceptions will not be able to distinguish it from a model that correctly reflects changes in volatility. Since the exceptions from a model that does not respond fully to volatility changes will tend to follow one another, given a sufficiently large sample of portfolio returns and VaR estimates the problem can be uncovered by looking at the conditional probabilities of exceptions. For the $1 - \alpha$ confidence VaR, it should be the case that the probability of an exception at time $t + 1$ is α, independent of whether there was an exception at time t. That is, it should be that

$$P(-r_{t+1} > \mathrm{VaR}_{t+1} \mid -r_t > \mathrm{VaR}_t) = P(-r_{t+1} > \mathrm{VaR}_{t+1} \mid -r_t \le \mathrm{VaR}_t) = \alpha,$$

where VaR_t denotes the $1 - \alpha$ percent confidence VaR computed at time t and $P(A)$ is the probability of the event A. However, the effectiveness of this approach is still limited by the relative paucity of exceptions.

BACK TESTS BASED ON THE ENTIRE DISTRIBUTION

A different way of stating the problem with back tests based on exceptions is that by considering only the exceptions they ignore much of the information in the sample of returns.

Most value-at-risk models produce an estimate (perhaps implicit) of the entire probability distribution as an intermediate step in computing the value-at-risk. The trick is how to exploit this information. The estimated distributions are conditional distributions, which change each day as both the portfolio and volatility estimates change. From each distribution one observes only one realization, the portfolio return for that day. At first glance this might not seem like sufficient information to evaluate the VaR model.

Knowing a distribution function F amounts to knowing all of its quantiles x, for example, to knowing the quantile x such that $0.01 = P(r \leq x)$, the quantile y such that $0.02 = P(r \leq y)$, and so on. Of course, when using a VaR model the estimates of these quantiles change every day as the estimate of the distribution function changes. Imagine collecting a sample of say 500 portfolio returns, computing the (estimates of the) quantiles for each of the 500 days, and then comparing the returns to the estimated quantiles. One expects five of the returns to be less than or equal to the 1% quantiles, another five to be between the 1% and 2% quantiles, another five to be between the 2% and 3% quantiles, and so on. It is not necessary that these intervals all contain the same probability; in general, a fraction $F(x) - F(y)$ of the returns r should satisfy $y < r \leq x$. After picking a set of intervals, one can evaluate the VaR model by comparing the observed proportion of the sample falling into each interval to the proportion that would be expected if the VaR model were correct. This is the same idea that underlies the simple back tests, except that one looks at many intervals instead of simply the losses that exceed the value-at-risk.

The statement that a fraction $F(x) - F(y)$ of the returns r should satisfy $y < r \leq x$ is equivalent to the statement that a fraction $F(x)$ should satisfy $r \leq x$; this in turn implies that a fraction $F(x)$ should satisfy $F(r) \leq F(x)$. But if a fraction $F(x)$ satisfies $F(r) \leq F(x)$, then the transformed variable $u = F(r)$ is uniformly distributed on the interval $[0,1]$. (If this seems confusing, just substitute y for $F(x)$; if $P(u \leq y) = y$ for $y \in [0,1]$, then the random variable u is uniformly distributed on the interval $[0,1]$.) This leads immediately to a statistical test: if the estimate of the distribution function F actually is the distribution function of the return r, then the transformed random variable $u = F(r)$ should be distributed uniformly on the interval $[0,1]$. This can be examined using standard tests of goodness of fit such as the Kolmogorov-Smirnov test. Some authors have advocated a variant known as Kuiper's statistic, described in sources cited in the notes.

These tests appear to require a minimum of between 500 and 1000 observations for the results to be meaningful. This is practical when the purpose of back testing is to select among approaches for computing VaR but may be a problem if the purpose is to monitor the performance of a model currently in use.

Similar to the simple tests based on exceptions described above, this is a test of the marginal distribution. If the VaR model correctly estimates the conditional distributions, the *u*s from different dates should be independent, that is, u_{t+j} should be independent of u_t for $j > 0$. This can be evaluated using time-series tests for dependence. An additional caveat is that tests based on the entire distribution are not necessarily the best approach, precisely because they are based on the entire distribution. Errors in modeling the center of the distribution can lead to rejection of the VaR model, even though such errors are unimportant for risk management. This criticism can be addressed by introducing a weighting function that weights deviations in one part of the distribution more heavily than those in others.

The approach of transforming the returns to construct uniformly distributed random variables can be extended by introducing another transformation to create normal random variables. If F is the distribution function of a random variable z and the transformed random variable $u = F(z)$ is uniformly distributed on [0,1], then the random variable $z = F^{-1}(u)$ has the distribution F, where F^{-1} is the inverse of F. Applying this idea to the standard normal distribution function N, the random variable $z = N^{-1}(u)$ has a standard normal distribution. This observation, together with the earlier one that $u = F(r)$ is uniformly distributed if F is the distribution function of r, implies that, if F is the distribution function of r, then the transformed random variable

$$z = N^{-1}(u) = N^{-1}(F(r)) \qquad (17.1)$$

has a standard normal distribution. Also, the zs from different dates should be independent, that is, z_{t+j} should be independent of z_t for $j > 0$.

The transformation in equation (17.1) is convenient, because it sets the problem in the standard Gaussian likelihood-based testing framework. Whether F correctly describes the location and dispersion of the return r can be evaluated by testing whether the mean and variance of z are 0 and 1, respectively, while whether it captures the fatness of the tails of the distribution of returns can be tested by nesting the normal within a fat-tailed family, such as the t-distribution that includes the normal as a special case. Time-series dependence among the zs for different dates can be evaluated by testing that the autocorrelation coefficient is 0. If one is interested exclusively in a certain part of the distribution, it is possible to base tests on the truncated normal distribution. Results in a source cited in the notes indicate that these tests have reasonable power to detect biased VaR models with as few as 100 observations.

WHAT DO WE KNOW ABOUT THE PERFORMANCE OF THE VARIOUS APPROACHES?

Little information is publicly available about the performance of VaR models applied to actual portfolios. However, there have been several studies of artificial test portfolios, using simple tests based on exceptions. In this setting the limitations of the simple tests based on exceptions can be overcome by simulating results for many different portfolios with many different samples.

PORTFOLIOS WITH LINEAR VALUE FUNCTIONS

When the value of the portfolio is a linear function of the underlying market factors, the linear and quadratic approximations used in the delta-normal and delta-gamma-normal methods are exact and do not introduce any errors. Thus, differences among the methods are due to the fact that the distributions used may not correspond to the distribution of the actual changes used in the historical simulation method.

Hendricks (1996) examines the performance of the different methodologies with a range of foreign exchange portfolios using the U.S. dollar prices of the foreign currencies as the market factors. Specifically, he considered: (i) the historical simulation approach using four samples of past data (the past 125, 250, 500, and 1250 days); (ii) the delta-normal method using an equally weighted covariance matrix estimator with five samples of data (the past 50, 125, 250, 500, and 1250 days); and (iii) the delta-normal method using an exponentially weighted covariance matrix estimator with three choices of λ (0.94, 0.97, and 0.99). For each of the 12 value-at-risk methodologies, he calculated one-day value-at-risk measures for 1000 randomly selected foreign currency portfolios for each of 3005 days.

Hendricks found no systematic difference between 95% confidence level value-at-risk measures obtained using the historical simulation method and those obtained using the delta-normal method, in that the averages (over time and portfolios) of the value-at-risk measures were very similar. However, at the 99% confidence level, the historical simulation value-at-risk measures were significantly larger than those obtained using the delta-normal method. This occurs because the distributions of changes in exchange rate and other financial variables have fat tails relative to the normal distribution, that is, extreme price changes are more frequent than the normal distribution would predict. Because it directly uses the actual price changes, the historical simulation method captures the actual frequency of extreme price changes and computes a larger value-at-risk.

The lack of systematic differences between the historical simulation and delta-normal methods in computing the 5% value-at-risk measures is perfectly consistent with this explanation, because the fat tails of the actual data are observed farther out in the tails of the distribution. Specifically, for many financial time series the 5% quantile of the actual distribution (that is, the loss that is exceeded with a probability of only 5%) appears to be not much different from the 5% quantile of a normal distribution with the same mean and variance. Since the 5% value-at-risk is the negative of the 5% quantile of the distribution, this is just another way of saying that the heaviness happens too far out in the tails to have an important impact on the 5% value-at-risk.

The statement that Hendricks found no important systematic differences between the methods in computing 5% value-at-risk is a statement that the *averages* across time and portfolios were similar. The averages, however, mask the variability in the estimates. For a particular portfolio on a particular date, the value-at-risk estimates computed using the different methods often differed considerably. Thus, for any particular portfolio and date some of the methods must have provided poor estimates, and it may be that all methods provided poor estimates. This is true for both 5% and 1% value-at-risk measures. In fact, Hendricks (1996, p. 48) writes, "differences in the range of 30 to 50 percent between the risk measures produced by specific approaches on a given day are not uncommon." The 99% confidence VaR measures computed using the historical simulation method display the greatest differences with the other methods. This is not surprising, because the historical simulation estimate of value-at-risk is based on the observations in the tail of the distribution. Inherently there are few observations in the tail and very few observations in the extreme tail. Thus, the historical simulation 1% value-at-risk estimates are in effect based on a small number of observations, and it is inevitable that they display considerable sampling variation. This is consistent with Jorion's (1996) analysis of the estimation error in value-at-risk estimates.

Overall Hendricks's results suggest that the delta-normal method does a good job of computing 5% value-at-risk measures for linear portfolios but appears to result in downward-biased 1% value-at-risk measures due to the failure of the normal distribution to reflect the fat tails in the data. Unfortunately, it is difficult to generalize about the magnitude of the bias in computing 1% value-at-risk measures because the fatness of the tails differs across equity, foreign exchange, and interest-rate series, and even across interest rates of different maturities. The historical simulation method, which does not suffer from this bias, tends to be inaccurate in computing 1% value-at-risk measures because the estimate of the value-at-risk is based on only a very few observations. When only small samples of past data are used, the historical simulation method is inaccurate in computing the 95% confidence value-at-risk measures for the same reason. Other sources cited in the notes also find that the delta-normal approach provides downward-biased estimates of the 99% confidence value-at-risk for linear portfolios.

PORTFOLIOS WITH NONLINEAR VALUE FUNCTIONS

For portfolios that include options and other portfolios in which the value is a nonlinear function of the underlying market factors, there is a compelling theoretical reason to be concerned about the performance of the delta-normal method, for this method is based on a linear approximation to the value of the portfolio. To the extent that the nonlinearity in the portfolio value is important and large changes in the market factors are possible, the delta-normal method will result in incorrect estimates of the value-at-risk because the linear approximation will not capture the impact of large changes in the market factors on the value of the portfolio. This concern is ameliorated when the value-at-risk is computed over short horizons, such as one day, because large changes in the market factors are less likely and the linear approximation is therefore more likely to be adequate.

Similar concerns exist for the delta-gamma-theta-normal method, which is based on a quadratic approximation of the portfolio value. To the extent that a quadratic approximation does not capture the effect of changes in the market factors on the value of the portfolio, the delta-gamma-theta-normal method will not fully reflect the risk of the portfolio.

In a paper devoted to studying the tradeoff between accuracy and computational time, Pritsker (1997) compares the accuracy of the delta-normal, full Monte Carlo, delta-gamma Monte Carlo, and modified grid Monte Carlo methods using portfolios of European-style foreign exchange options. The modified grid Monte Carlo method uses a low-order grid for the market factors for which the value is nonlinear and a first-order Taylor series (i.e., delta) approximation for the other factors. With the options portfolios, he finds that full Monte Carlo, which captures the nonlinearity in the values of the options, can produce value-at-risk estimates considerably different from the analytic methods. As expected, the delta-normal method overstates the value-at-risk of portfolios that include long options positions and understates the value-at-risk of portfolios that include short options positions. This is also the case for the method Pritsker calls *delta-gamma-delta*, though the over- and understatements are smaller. The delta-gamma Monte Carlo and modified grid Monte Carlo methods perform much better than the analytic methods, though these methods still over- or understated value-at-risk for about 25% of the portfolios.

Abken (2000) examined the performance of scenario simulation on a portfolio involving interest-rate derivatives. Gibson and Pritsker (2000) compared the performance of scenario simulation and principal components grid Monte Carlo, also using portfolios of interest-rate derivatives. Not surprisingly, delta-normal is fastest but least accurate, and the approximate Monte Carlo methods are slower but more accurate than the delta-normal approach but faster and less accurate than the full Monte Carlo. Modified grid Monte Carlo turns out to be more accurate than scenario simulation, because the errors due to the approximation of the value function in modified grid Monte Carlo are smaller than those stemming from the discrete approximation of the distribution in scenario simulation. While neither Abken nor Gibson and Pritsker compared principal components and modified grid Monte Carlo, one should expect that the accuracies of the two methods are similar, a reasonable assumption because the grid in modified grid Monte Carlo could be chosen to have the same structure as that used in principal components grid Monte Carlo. More surprising is the fact that scenario simulation, modified grid Monte Carlo, and principal components Monte Carlo are dominated by the delta-gamma-theta Monte Carlo method. This is presumably because the delta-gamma-theta approximation provided a good description of the changes in the values of the portfolios used in the comparisons. There are likely to be many portfolios for which this is not the case.

Smithson (1998, Chapter 19) considers weakly and strongly nonlinear portfolios, including swaps, FX-forward contract, and interest-rate and FX options. For the weakly nonlinear portfolio, the historical simulation, Monte Carlo simulation, delta-gamma, and delta-gamma-normal methods produce similar value-at-risk estimates. However, for the strongly nonlinear portfolio, the historical and Monte Carlo simulation methods produce value-at-risk estimates that are markedly different from those produced by the two analytic methods.

It is difficult to generalize from these results, because how to identify *ex ante* which portfolios are strongly nonlinear is not clear. In this context, a strongly nonlinear portfolio is one in which the delta-normal approximation does not perform well. Regardless, these results confirm that there is reason to be concerned about the delta-normal and delta-gamma-normal methods for portfolios that include options or other instruments with values that are nonlinear functions of the underlying market factors.

IMPLEMENTATION RISK

In an intriguing study, Marshall and Siegel (1997) provided identical portfolios of financial instruments of varying complexity to different vendors of risk-management systems and asked them to compute value-at-risk estimates using a common model (RiskMetrics™) and a common data set (the RiskMetrics™ data set from a particular day).

Strikingly, the value-at-risk estimates for the same portfolios provided by different software vendors differed, sometimes considerably. The differences were small for the portfolios of simple instruments (FX forwards and money market instruments) but were significant for the government bond, swap, FX-option, and interest-rate option portfolios. Specifically, for these portfolios the standard deviations (across different vendors) of the estimates were 17%, 21%, 25%, and 23% of the medians (across vendors) of the value-at-risk estimates. Value-at-risk estimates for the FX-option portfolio computed using a variety of simulation methods displayed even more striking variation, as the standard deviation of the estimates was 63% of the median estimate. These differences in results due to differing implementations of the same formal model are what Marshall and Siegel call *implementation risk*.

The variation in estimates appears to be at least partly due to a combination of differences in vendors' valuations of the instruments, differences in the way instruments are mapped, and other factors, such as differences in interpolating term structures. Given that Marshall and Siegel did not have access to the details of the implementations but had only the model outputs, it is impossible to determine the exact importance of these differences relative to other factors, such as logical and coding errors. However, the results suggest that one vendor did not understand completely the valuation and risk of interest-rate swaps. Even setting aside this issue, the differences in value-at-risk estimates across different vendors using the same basic methodology and data are not comforting.

NOTES

The discussion of the simple approach to back testing based on exceptions draws upon Kupiec (1995), who provides a likelihood ratio test for evaluating

VaR models and analyzes its power. Kupiec (1995) also analyzes statistical tests based upon the length of time elapsed before the first exception, which he terms a *failure*. The idea behind the test based on the time until first failure is that a model that systematically underestimates value-at-risk will tend to have a short time until the first failure, while a model that overestimates value-at-risk will likely have a long time until the first failure. Lopez (1999) analyzes other back testing methods.

Conditional exceptions from a VaR model are one form of conditional interval forecast, which is analyzed by Chatfield (1993) and Christoffersen (1998), who provides a likelihood ratio test of conditional coverage. Christoffersen, Hahn, and Inoue (1999) present a moment-based framework for evaluating VaR models.

The transformation $u = F(r)$ is due to Rosenblatt (1952); its use in evaluating value-at-risk models is due to Crnkovic and Drachman (1996), as is the suggestion to use Kuiper's statistic. Diebold, Gunther, and Tay (1998) also suggest the use of the transformation $u = F(r)$. Kuiper's statistic is described in Crnkovic and Drachman (1996) and Press *et al.* (1992) and the references therein. The Kolmogorov-Smirnov test is described in many mathematical statistics texts.

Morgan Guaranty Trust Company (1994; 1996) presents evidence that the delta-normal method works reasonably well for 5% value-at-risk for portfolios with linear value functions, which implies that the 5% quantiles of the actual distribution of the changes in the market factors and the normal distribution with the same variance are reasonably close. Smithson (1998, Chapter 19) also reports results consistent with this.

Gizycki and Hereford (1998) find considerable dispersion in Australian banks' estimates of the market risk in a number of pre-specified portfolios. Crouhy, Galai, and Mark (1998) provide an overview of model risk.

CHAPTER 18

Gaming the VaR

As emphasized in the previous chapter, value-at-risk measures are estimates of market risk based on past data, for example, the squared returns used to estimate the covariance matrix. While pure statistical error in value-at-risk estimates clearly exists, at first glance there seems to be no reason to think VaR estimates are systematically biased. Standard estimators of the covariance matrix are (at least approximately) unbiased, suggesting that value-at-risk estimates are just as likely to overestimate as underestimate risk. But this reasoning does not hold when portfolio managers seek to evade risk or position limits based on value-at-risk. To the extent that the portfolio manager or trader understands the errors in and limitations of the value-at-risk estimate, he will be able to game the value-at-risk and enter into positions for which the value-at-risk estimate understates the portfolio risk.

To illustrate this, this chapter describes a simple example involving the use of delta-normal value-at-risk. It shows the extent to which estimation errors in value-at-risk due to sampling variation in the estimated covariance matrix permit a portfolio manager or trader to exceed the risk limits. Although the example allows for only linear positions, it is clear that VaR can be gamed if the portfolio manager is allowed to sell options. In this case, the portfolio manager can sell options with probabilities of exercise less than the probability α used to compute the VaR estimate.

GAMING ESTIMATION ERRORS IN THE COVARIANCE MATRIX

Given some knowledge of market implied volatilities, on many days the portfolio manager will know for which markets and instruments historical estimates of market volatility underestimate current market volatility and for which markets and instruments historical estimates overestimate current market volatility. He is also likely to have information about the relationship between current market correlations and historical estimates of them. For example, shortly prior to the departure of the U.K. pound and Italian lira from the European

Exchange Rate Mechanism in September 1992, one could have predicted that the relatively high historical correlations among dollar/pound, dollar/lira, and dollar/Deutsche mark exchange rates were unlikely to persist. Due to such market knowledge, on many days a portfolio manager will have a good understanding of the errors in the value-at-risk estimate. If he wants, he will be able to evade risk limits based on value-at-risk by choosing portfolios for which he knows that the value-at-risk estimate is less than the true value-at-risk. To the extent that he does this, the estimated value-at-risk will be downward-biased, i.e., the true value-at-risk will exceed the estimated value-at-risk.

To illustrate the problem, we consider an extreme case in which the portfolio manager knows the true covariance matrix and deliberately exploits his knowledge of the sampling errors in the estimated covariance matrix in order to take on as much risk as possible. Assuming knowledge of the true covariance matrix is an extreme case of assuming that the portfolio manager has information about the errors in the estimated covariance matrix and provides an upper bound on the bias in estimated value-at-risk. The portfolio manager may be evading risk limits due to hubris, in a desperate gamble to recover previous losses, or because convexities in the manager's compensation package make this the strategy that maximizes expected compensation.

The setup involves K assets, which may be interpreted as either individual assets or the standard positions often used in value-at-risk systems. The asset returns have a multivariate normal distribution with a mean vector μ and a (nonsingular) covariance matrix Σ. The value-at-risk measure is not based on the covariance matrix Σ, but rather on an estimate

$$\Psi = \sum_{n=1}^{N} \lambda_n (r_n - \mu)(r_n - \mu)', \tag{18.1}$$

where r_n is a $K \times 1$ vector consisting of the returns n periods in the past and the weights $\{\lambda_1, \lambda_2, \lambda_3, \ldots, \lambda_N\}$ satisfy $\sum_{n=1}^{N} \lambda_n = 1$. Equation (18.1) includes as special cases both the equally weighted covariance matrix estimator defined by $\lambda_n = 1/N$ and the exponentially weighted covariance matrix estimator defined by $\lambda_n = ((1-\lambda)/(1-\lambda^N))\lambda^{n-1}$, for $n = 1, \ldots, N$. In estimating the covariance matrix it is commonly assumed that $\mu = 0$, because for the data commonly used in financial applications the mean has only trivial impact on the estimate of the covariance matrix.

Using Ψ, the estimated portfolio variance and value-at-risk are $w'\Psi w$ and $k\sqrt{w'\Psi w}$, respectively, where k is a constant determined by the probability level of the value-at-risk estimate (often $k = 1.645$ or 2.326), w is a $K \times 1$ vector of portfolio weights, and for simplicity we make the common assumption $\mu = 0$. In contrast, the true value-at-risk is $k\sqrt{w'\Sigma w}$, where, as above, Σ is the actual covariance matrix of changes in the market values of the positions. We are interested in the relationship between the estimated and true value-at-risk measures $k\sqrt{w'\Psi w}$ and $k\sqrt{w'\Sigma w}$, under the assumption that the portfolio manager maximizes the true value-at-risk $k\sqrt{w'\Sigma w}$ subject to a constraint that the estimated value-at-risk $k\sqrt{w'\Psi w}$ equals a constant.

The difference between the estimated and true value-at-risk measures stems from the fact that the number of observations N used to estimate the covariance matrix may be small relative to its dimension K. In extreme cases, the dimension of the covariance matrix may equal or exceed the number of observations, and as a result the estimated covariance matrix Ψ is singular. This implies that there are many risky portfolios for which the estimated portfolio variance $w'\Psi w$, and therefore the estimated value-at-risk $k\sqrt{w'\Psi w}$, are zero. Were a portfolio manager permitted to execute trades in all markets, it would be possible to enter into an arbitrarily risky position for which the estimated value-at-risk is zero. If value-at-risk is used in setting position limits or in performance evaluation, the manager may have an incentive to do so.

Most portfolio managers have access to a limited range of markets, so the case of a portfolio manager who is able to enter into a risky position with an estimated value-at-risk of zero because the estimated covariance matrix is singular is not realistic. However, a fixed-income portfolio manager will often be able to execute transactions in all segments of the U.S. dollar yield curve, and some hedge fund managers do have access to large numbers of markets. In the context of some risk-measurement systems, these situations correspond to K equal to approximately 20 or greater. In such situations, it turns out that the estimated covariance matrix, while not singular, can be nearly so. To the extent that the trader enters into positions that systematically exploit errors in the estimated covariance matrix, the true value-at-risk can be much larger than the value-at-risk measure based on the estimated covariance matrix.

GAMING ESTIMATION ERRORS IN THE COVARIANCE MATRIX: A SIMPLE EXAMPLE

We begin with a simple example to provide a geometric interpretation of the bias. In the example there are two assets, the returns of which are multivariate normal with $\sigma_1 = 0.06$, $\sigma_2 = 0.04$, and $\rho = 0.6$, so that the true covariance matrix is

$$\Sigma = \begin{bmatrix} 0.0036 & 0.00144 \\ 0.00144 & 0.0016 \end{bmatrix}.$$

The estimated covariance matrix is not equal to Σ, but instead is

$$\Psi = \begin{bmatrix} 0.00378 & -0.00087 \\ -0.00087 & 0.00158 \end{bmatrix}.$$

Letting $w = (w_1, w_2)'$ denote the portfolio weights, the restriction that the estimated value-at-risk be equal to a constant defines an ellipse in the (w_1, w_2) space of the form $k\sqrt{w'\Psi w} = c$, equivalent to $w'\Psi w = (c^2/k^2)$. The solid curve in Figure 18.1 shows this ellipse for $c/k = 1$. That is, it shows the portfolio weights $w = (w_1, w_2)$ for which the estimated portfolio variance is one.

For each choice of the true value-at-risk, the true covariance matrix Σ defines an ellipse of the form $k\sqrt{w'\Sigma w} = \mathrm{VaR}$ or $w'\Sigma w = (\mathrm{VaR})^2/k^2$. The two dotted curves in Figure 18.1 show two such true ellipses. The inner ellipse, labeled $w'\Sigma w = 1$, corresponds to a portfolio variance of one. It differs from the solid curve, which displays the ellipse corresponding to an estimated portfolio variance of one, because $\Psi \neq \Sigma$. The outer ellipse, labeled $w'\Sigma w = 2.45$, corresponds to a portfolio variance of 2.45.

Recognizing that each true ellipse describes the set of portfolios with a given true value-at-risk, choosing the portfolio to maximize the true value-at-risk subject to a constraint on the estimated value-at-risk amounts to picking a portfolio that is on the largest possible true ellipse (i.e., the largest possible ellipse of the form $w'\Sigma w = (\mathrm{VaR})^2/k^2$), while still intersecting the constraint ellipse $w'\Psi w = 1$. This occurs at the two points labeled w^* and $-w^*$, where the true ellipse $w'\Sigma w = 2.45$ is tangent to the constraint ellipse $w'\Psi w = 1$. These portfolios have variance 2.45.

Figure 18.1 shows the optimal portfolio for only one realization of the estimated covariance matrix Ψ. While for this realization w^* and $-w^*$ lie outside the ellipse $w'\Sigma w = 1$, they will not always lie outside it. When the sample results in an estimated correlation close to the true correlation, the ellipse $w'\Psi w = 1$ will have the same orientation as the true ellipse $w'\Sigma w = 1$; when the estimated variances are large relative to the true variances, the constraint on estimated value-at-risk will force w to be small and the ellipse $w'\Psi w = 1$ will lie inside $w'\Sigma w = 1$. With $K = 2$ and reasonable values of N the bias is not large, because when $K = 2$ the covariance matrix can be estimated reasonably precisely with relatively few observations. However, the next section shows that the bias can be large for realistic choices of K and N.

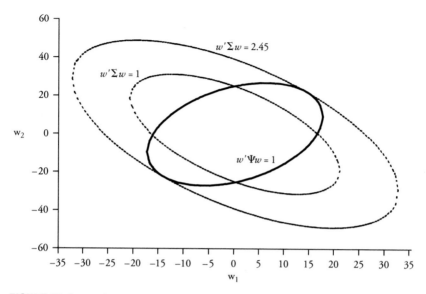

FIGURE 18.1 Portfolio choices when the trader seeks to maximize the true value-at-risk subject to a constraint on the estimated value-at-risk

GAMING ESTIMATION ERRORS IN THE COVARIANCE MATRIX: GENERAL CASE

To analyze the general case, we consider the problem of maximizing the value-at-risk

$$\max_{w} k\sqrt{w'\Sigma w} \tag{18.2}$$

subject to the constraint

$$k\sqrt{w'\Psi w} = c, \tag{18.3}$$

where we allow short positions, that is, negative elements of w. Letting w^* denote the solution, the true value-at-risk is $k\sqrt{w^{*'}\Sigma w^*}$. The relationship between the estimated and true value-at-risk is summarized by the ratio

$$R(\Psi) = \frac{k\sqrt{w^{*'}\Psi w^*}}{k\sqrt{w^{*'}\Sigma w^*}} = \frac{c}{k\sqrt{w^{*'}\Sigma w^*}}.$$

We focus on the distribution of the ratio of estimated to true value-at-risk rather than the ratio of true to estimated value-at-risk because the estimated value-at-risk is often close to zero, distorting some of the statistics we examine.

A nice feature of the ratio is that it depends on neither k, c, the choice of units, nor the overall level of volatility. Although less obvious, the ratio above also does not depend on the correlations among the asset returns. In particular, a source cited in the notes shows that $R(\Psi)$ is the square root of the minimal eigenvalue of $\hat{I}$, where $\hat{I}$ is the estimated covariance matrix constructed using a sample of N vectors z_n drawn from a multivariate normal distribution with a mean of zero and covariance matrix I. That is, letting $\Sigma^{1/2}$ be the symmetric square root of Σ, the vector z_n defined $z_n \equiv \Sigma^{-1/2}x_n$ is distributed multivariate normal with a covariance matrix I, and

$$\hat{I} = \sum_{n=1}^{N} \lambda_n z_n z_n',$$

and $R(\Psi)$ is the square root of the minimal eigenvalue of $\hat{I}$.

One way to understand why the covariance matrix Σ does not affect the distribution of the ratio is to notice that the vector $z = \Sigma^{-1/2}r$ can be interpreted as the returns of K new assets formed from linear combinations of the original K assets. For the new assets, the portfolio equivalent to w is $y = \Sigma^{1/2}w$, for $y'z = w'\Sigma^{1/2}\Sigma^{-1/2}r = w'r$. The choice to work with y and z instead of w and r is of no importance, because the portfolio returns and value-at-risk measures that may be achieved are identical. Then, in terms of y, the optimization problem corresponding to (18.2) and (18.3) is

$$\max_{y} k\sqrt{y'y} \text{ subject to } k\sqrt{y'\hat{I}y} = c.$$

Since the covariance matrix Σ does not appear in this problem, the solution cannot depend on it. On a figure analogous to Figure 18.1 but in the (y_1, y_2) space, the dotted ellipses would be circles, and the solid ellipse would not be a circle only because of sampling variation, that is, only because $\hat{I} \neq I$.

Table 18.1 shows the expected values of $R(\Psi)$, the ratio of estimated to true value-at-risk, for $K = 10, 20, 50$, and 100 when $\hat{I}$ is estimated using the equally weighted covariance matrix estimator

$$\hat{I} = \frac{1}{N} \sum_{n=1}^{N} z_n z_n'$$

with various values of N. In addition, the first row of the table shows the expected value of the ratio when the covariance matrix is estimated using the exponentially weighted covariance matrix estimator

$$\hat{I} = (1 - \lambda) \sum_{n=1}^{N} \lambda^{n-1} z_n z_n',$$

where $\lambda = 0.94$. The results in the table show that the bias is large except when the number of available instruments is small and the number of observations used in estimating the covariance matrix is large. For example, when $K = 50$ and $N = 200$, the average ratio of estimated to true value-at-risk is 0.518. Even when $N = 1000$, which corresponds to using about four years of daily data to estimate the covariance matrix, when $K = 50$ the average ratio of estimated to true value-at-risk is 0.786. Moreover, the bias is very large for the exponentially weighted covariance matrix estimator. Even when K is only 10 the mean ratio of estimated to true value-at-risk is 0.551, and when $K = 100$ it is only

TABLE 18.1   Expected values of $R(\Psi)$, the ratio of estimated to true value-at-risk, for various combinations of K and N. The expected values are calculated under the assumption that the portfolio manager maximizes value-at-risk subject to a constraint on estimated value-at-risk.

Number of Observations Used to Estimate Covariance Matrix (N)	Dimension of Covariance Matrix (K)			
	10	20	50	100
Exponential Weighting with $\lambda = 0.94$	0.551	0.372	0.131	0.029
50	0.606	0.405	0.000[1]	0.000
100	0.725	0.586	0.312	0.000
200	0.809	0.710	0.518	0.306
500	0.879	0.817	0.697	0.563
1000	0.915	0.871	0.786	0.692

[1]Entries of zero indicate that the estimated covariance matrix is singular for those combinations of K and N.

0.029, that is, estimated value-at-risk is typically only 2.9% of true value-at-risk.

To interpret these values of K, note that, in value-at-risk systems, it is common to summarize the yield curve in each currency in terms of approximately 20 market factors or standard positions, and an actual instrument (e.g., a bond or interest-rate swap) is interpreted as a portfolio of the 20 standardized positions. From the perspective of the risk-measurement system, a fixed-income portfolio manager is just working with portfolios of these 20 standardized positions. Thus, $K = 20$ corresponds to a portfolio manager who trades the entire yield curve in one currency, while $K = 50$ and $K = 100$ correspond to trading the yield curves in two to three and five to six currencies, respectively. For some hedge funds, $K = 100$ may actually understate the available trading opportunities.

Table 18.2 reports various percentiles of the distributions of $R(\Psi)$. The medians in this table are close to the means in Table 18.1, indicating that the means provide a reasonable measure of the center of the distributions of the ratios of estimated to true value-at-risk. Strikingly, even many of the 90th percentile values are relatively small, and none of them exceeds 1. For example, when $K = 50$ and $N = 200$, the 90th percentile of the ratio of estimated to true value-at-risk is 0.569, only slightly higher than the mean of 0.518. Even when $N = 1000$, when $K = 50$ the 90th percentile of the ratio of estimated to true value-at-risk is 0.798. Also, as one might expect after examining the means, all of the percentiles are strikingly small for the exponentially weighted covariance matrix estimator. Even when K is only 10, the 90th percentile of the ratio of estimated to true value-at-risk is 0.612, and when $K = 100$ it is only 0.032.

OTHER ASSUMPTIONS ABOUT THE PORTFOLIO MANAGER'S BEHAVIOR

In the analysis above, it was assumed that the portfolio manager knows the true covariance matrix Σ and seeks to evade risk limits and take on as much risk as possible. As a result, the measures of bias above represent upper bounds on the bias in estimated value-at-risk in the delta-normal setting. If the trader had a better estimate than Ψ, but did not know Σ, these upper bounds would not be reached.

Sources cited in the notes show that the value-at-risk estimate can be biased even if the portfolio manager relies on the estimated market variances and covariances and does not have knowledge of the true covariance matrix. For example, the manager would underestimate the risk by determining a

TABLE 18.2 Percentiles of the distributions of $R(\Psi)$, the ratio of estimated to true value-at-risk, for various combinations of K and N. The expected values are calculated under the assumption that the portfolio manager maximizes value-at-risk subject to a constraint on estimated value-at-risk.

Number of Observations Used to Estimate Covariance Matrix (N)	Percentile	Dimension of Covariance Matrix (K)			
		10	20	50	100
Exponential Weighting with $\lambda = 0.94$	10th	0.490	0.333	0.117	0.026
	25th	0.520	0.351	0.124	0.027
	50th	0.554	0.374	0.132	0.029
	75th	0.581	0.394	0.139	0.030
	90th	0.612	0.409	0.145	0.032
50	10th	0.539	0.352	0.000^2	0.000
	25th	0.571	0.378	0.000	0.000
	50th	0.607	0.405	0.000	0.000
	75th	0.643	0.433	0.000	0.000
	90th	0.674	0.456	0.000	0.000
100	10th	0.675	0.543	0.282	0.000
	25th	0.700	0.563	0.298	0.000
	50th	0.728	0.588	0.312	0.000
	75th	0.754	0.609	0.328	0.000
	90th	0.774	0.627	0.342	0.000
200	10th	0.772	0.680	0.494	0.288
	25th	0.791	0.693	0.506	0.297
	50th	0.810	0.712	0.519	0.306
	75th	0.829	0.727	0.531	0.315
	90th	0.846	0.740	0.543	0.323
500	10th	0.855	0.795	0.681	0.548
	25th	0.866	0.805	0.688	0.556
	50th	0.880	0.818	0.697	0.563
	75th	0.892	0.828	0.706	0.571
	90th	0.903	0.836	0.713	0.577
1000	10th	0.899	0.856	0.774	0.682
	25th	0.907	0.863	0.781	0.687
	50th	0.915	0.871	0.787	0.693
	75th	0.924	0.879	0.793	0.698
	90th	0.932	0.886	0.798	0.702

[2]Entries of zero indicate that the estimated covariance matrix is singular for those combinations of K and N.

hedge based on the estimated covariance matrix of two assets, and then, after establishing the hedge, estimating the risk of the hedged portfolio using the same estimated covariance matrix. Similarly, the risk will be underestimated if the portfolio manger uses the sampling error to select a portfolio to achieve a small estimated portfolio standard deviation or mean-variance efficient portfolio.

In the case of a trader who seeks to evade risk limits and take on as much risk as possible, the bias is large, except when the number of available assets is small (i.e., less than or equal to 20) and the number of observations used in estimating the covariance matrix is large (greater than or equal to 500). In the other two cases, the bias in estimated value-at-risk is smaller but still large for some reasonable combinations of parameters. In particular, the bias is very large when the covariance matrices are estimated by weighting the data using exponentially declining weights. This raises concerns about the use of this approach.

HOW REASONABLE IS THIS?

First, it is explicitly assumed that the trader is deliberately behaving badly. Also, our analysis does not consider other mechanisms to control risk-taking, such as position limits on individual instruments. Nonetheless, in considering the use of value-at-risk in the control function, it is reasonable to consider the worst case. Thus, these results raise questions about the use of value-at-risk in the control and performance evaluation of individual decision-making units such as portfolio managers, traders, or trading desks. For firms or companies with multiple portfolios or trading desks, whether and how the biases at the level of the individual decision-making unit aggregate to biases at the firm level will depend upon the interactions among the portfolios chosen by the individual units.

Setting this issue aside, if value-at-risk is to be used to control individual traders or trading desks, the results in Tables 18.1 and 18.2 push one in the direction of estimating the covariance matrix using a large sample of past price changes. However, this comes at the cost of capturing changes in volatility, which may be a more important consideration.

One additional issue is that the analysis is restricted to the delta-normal setting, in which the changes in the value of the portfolio are linear in the changes in the underlying market factors. A trader who writes options could do additional damage by entering into portfolios for which the loss, while no more likely than indicated by the value-at-risk estimate, is very large when it does occur.

NOTES

The analysis of the case of a trader who seeks to maximize true value-at-risk subject to a constraint on estimated value-at-risk is due to Ju and Pearson (2000), who also analyze two other cases: (i) a trader who seeks to maximize expected return subject to a constraint on estimated value-at-risk; and (ii) a trader who has identified a preferred portfolio but is unable to hold it because the estimated value-at-risk of the portfolio exceeds some specified limit. In this case, they assume that the trader seeks to hold a portfolio as close as possible to the preferred portfolio, subject to the constraint on estimated value-at-risk. For each of these situations, they determine the bias for different assumptions about the number of different instruments to which the trader has access and the number of observations used in estimating the covariance matrix.

CHAPTER 19

Coherent Risk Measures

Value-at-risk was criticized from the outset because it says nothing about the magnitude of losses greater than the value-at-risk estimate. Artzner, Delbaen, Eber, and Heath (hereafter, ADEH) (1997; 1999a) offer a subtler, and much deeper, criticism: value-at-risk does not correctly aggregate risk across portfolios. Combined with another property that ADEH argue any reasonable risk measure must possess, this implies that value-at-risk does not correctly capture the effect of diversification. Ironically, aggregating risk across portfolios and capturing the benefits of diversification are two of the commonly cited advantages of value-at-risk.

As a substitute for value-at-risk, ADEH propose a new class of *coherent risk measures*. They argue that one should restrict attention to coherent risk measures because only such measures are consistent with certain basic properties that any reasonable risk measure must have. Value-at-risk is a coherent risk measure if the possible change in portfolio value is described by the normal distribution, but not generally. However, it turns out that both scenario-based measures and the *expected shortfall,* defined as the expected loss conditional on a loss greater than or equal to the value-at-risk, are coherent measures of risk.

LIMITATIONS OF VALUE-AT-RISK

To see the problems with value-at-risk, consider two portfolios of digital puts and calls on the same underlying asset, price, or rate. Portfolio A consists of $400,000 in cash and a short digital put with a notional amount of $10 million, a 4% probability of being exercised, and time to expiration equal to the time horizon of the value-at-risk estimate. Portfolio B consists of $400,000 in cash together with a short digital call with a notional amount of $10 million, a 4% probability of being exercised, and a time to expiration equal to the time horizon of the value-at-risk estimate. Assume for simplicity that the interest rate is zero and that the risk-neutral probabilities of exercise of both options are also 4%. These assumptions imply

that the current mark-to-market values of the two portfolios are both
$400,000 − 0.04($10,000,000) = $0.

For both portfolios, the probability distribution of possible profits and
losses over the time horizon of the value-at-risk estimate is

$$\text{profit} = \begin{pmatrix} \$400,000 & \text{with probability } 0.96, \\ -\$10,000,000 & \text{with probability } 0.04. \end{pmatrix}$$

Clearly these portfolios have some risk. But because the probability of a loss
is only 4%, 95% value-at-risk measures would indicate that the two portfolios have none. Even worse, a 95% value-at-risk measure would also indicate
no risk for a third portfolio consisting of $40 million in cash, a short digital
call with a notional amount of $1 billion, and a profit and loss distribution of

$$\text{profit} = \begin{pmatrix} \$40 \text{ million} & \text{with probability } 0.96, \\ -\$1 \text{ billion} & \text{with probability } 0.04. \end{pmatrix}$$

This simple example illustrates that value-at-risk does not reflect the risk of
low probability outcomes, even though these may entail large or even crip-
pling losses. Such positions can be created by selling out-of-the-money options
or through other transactions that are equivalent to selling such options. While
99%-confidence value-at-risk measures would identify the portfolios above as
risky, similar positions with loss probabilities of less than 1% would continue
to be identified as risk-free.

To see a less obvious problem, consider the aggregate portfolio consisting of the sum of portfolios A and B, and the diversified portfolio consisting
of one-half of portfolio A and one-half of portfolio B. Because the digital put
and call will not both be exercised, the distribution of profit and loss for the
aggregate portfolio is

$$\text{profit of aggregate portfolio} = \begin{pmatrix} \$800,000 & \text{with probability } 0.92, \\ -\$10,000,000 & \text{with probability } 0.08, \end{pmatrix}$$

and the distribution of profit and loss for the diversified portfolio is

$$\text{profit of diversified portfolio} = \begin{pmatrix} \$400,000 & \text{with probability } 0.92, \\ -\$5,000,000 & \text{with probability } 0.08. \end{pmatrix}$$

Thus, the 95%-confidence value-at-risk measures of the aggregate and
diversified portfolios are $10 million and $5 million, respectively. The

problem is that the value-at-risk of the aggregate portfolio exceeds the sum of the value-at-risk measures of portfolios A and B (which are both zero), and the value-at-risk estimate of the diversified portfolio exceeds the average of the value-at-risk estimates of portfolios A and B. ADEH argue that no reasonable risk measure can have these properties, implying that value-at-risk cannot be a reasonable risk measure.

COHERENT RISK MEASURES

The setup in ADEH (1997; 1999a) is a capital market with a finite number K of outcomes or *states of the world*. Let x and y be K-dimensional vectors representing the possible state-contingent payoffs of two different portfolios, $\rho(x)$ and $\rho(y)$ the portfolios' risk measures, a and b arbitrary constants (with $a > 0$), and r the risk-free interest rate. ADEH argue that any reasonable risk measure should satisfy the following four properties:

(i) $\rho(x + y) \leq \rho(x) + \rho(y)$ (subadditivity)
(ii) $\rho(ax) = a\rho(x)$ (homogeneity)
(iii) $\rho(x) \geq \rho(y)$, if $x \leq y$ (monotonicity)
(iv) $\rho(x + b(1 + r)) = \rho(x) - b$ (risk-free condition)

In property (iii), $x \leq y$ means that each element of y is at least as large as the corresponding element of x.

The first property says that the risk measure of an aggregate portfolio must be less than or equal to the sum of the risk measures of the smaller portfolios that constitute it and ensures that the risk measure should reflect the impact of hedges or offsets. If this condition is not satisfied, then one can reduce the risk of a portfolio by splitting it into two or more parts. In a banking context, this would imply that it is possible to reduce the capital requirement by splitting a bank into parts. This condition also permits decentralized calculation of risk, since the sum of the risk measures of subportfolios provides a conservative estimate of the risk of the aggregate portfolio.

The second property says that the risk measure is proportional to the scale of the portfolio; for example, halving the portfolio halves the risk measure. The first two properties together imply that the risk of a diversified portfolio must be less than or equal to the appropriate weighted average of the risks of the instruments or subportfolios that make up the diversified portfolio. For example, if the payoff of a diversified portfolio is $z = wx + (1 - w)y$, where w and $1 - w$ are the weights on two subportfolios with payoffs x and y, then properties (i) and (ii) require that $\rho(z) \leq w\rho(x) + (1 - w)\rho(y)$. Risk measures that do not satisfy these conditions fail to capture the benefits of diversification.

Value-at-risk satisfies (ii), (iii), and (iv), but is not a coherent risk measure because it fails to satisfy (i). For example, the aggregate portfolio of the digital put and call discussed above fails to satisfy (i), while the diversified portfolio fails to satisfy the combination of (i) and (ii) with $a = 1/2$. However, value-at-risk satisfies property (i) if the price changes of all instruments are described by a multivariate normal distribution. Under this assumption it correctly aggregates risk and reflects the benefit of diversification.

Property (iii) says it is good to receive cash. Specifically, if the portfolio with payoffs y dominates that with payoffs x in the sense that each element of y is at least as large as the corresponding element of x (i.e., $x \leq y$), then the portfolio with payoffs y must be of lesser or equal risk. One implication of this is that delta-normal value-at-risk measures of the form

$$\begin{aligned} \text{VaR} &= -(\text{expected value} - k \times \text{standard deviation}) \\ &= (k \times \text{standard deviation} - \text{expected value}) \end{aligned}$$

are not coherent for portfolios with non-normal distributions. To see this, compare the null portfolio (payoff of zero) to a free lottery ticket paying m with probability $1/m$. Clearly the lottery ticket is more desirable. However, it has expected value $m(1/m) + 0(m - 1)/m = 1$, standard deviation

$$\sqrt{(m-1)^2(1/m) + (0-1)^2(m-1)/m} = \sqrt{m-1},$$

and value-at-risk $k\sqrt{m-1} - 1$, which is greater than zero whenever $m > 1.37$ and $k \geq 1.645$. Thus, the delta-normal approximation implies that the lottery ticket is riskier than the null portfolio, inconsistent with (iii).

Property (iv) says that adding a risk-free instrument to a portfolio decreases the risk by the size of the investment in the risk-free instrument. This property ensures that coherent risk measures can be interpreted as the amount of capital needed to support a position or portfolio.

A key result in ADEH (1999a) is that all coherent risk measures can be represented in terms of *generalized scenarios*. To construct a generalized scenario risk measure, first construct a list of N scenarios of future market factors and portfolio values, as might be done in Monte Carlo simulation or deterministic scenario analysis. Second, assign probabilities to the N scenarios. These probabilities determine how the different scenarios are weighted in the risk measure and need not reflect the likelihood of the scenarios; they are probabilities in the sense that they are numbers between 0 and 1 whose sum (over the N scenarios) is 1.

Third, repeat the assignment of probabilities M times to construct a set of M probability measures on the N scenarios; these are the M generalized scenarios. For example, one measure might say that the N scenarios are equally likely, while another might say that the nth scenario occurs with probability 1 while the other scenarios have probability 0. At most one of the probability measures will correspond to the likelihoods of events, so unless $M = 1$ (and sometimes even in that case) the probability measures will not be based on the risk manager's assessment of the likelihood of the scenarios. Fourth, for each of the M probability measures, calculate the expected loss. Finally, the risk measure is the largest of the M expected losses.

This seemingly abstract procedure corresponds to two widely used risk measures, the expected shortfall measure defined by $E[\text{loss} \mid \text{loss} < \text{cutoff}]$ and the measure produced by the Standard Portfolio Analysis of Risk$^{\circledR}$ (SPAN$^{\circledR}$) system developed by the Chicago Mercantile Exchange and used by many others.

SPAN$^{\circledR}$

The SPAN$^{\circledR}$ system uses 16 scenarios of changes in the price of the underlying instrument and the option implied volatility, the last two of which are extreme scenarios. The performance bond (capital) requirement is computed as the maximum of the loss on each of the first 14 of the scenarios and 30% of the loss on each of the two extreme scenarios. This system can be characterized in terms of 16 generalized scenarios if we introduce an implicit 17th scenario of no change. The first 14 generalized scenarios each assign probability 1 to one of the first 14 scenarios and probability 0 to all other scenarios. The expected values for each of these generalized scenarios are then just the losses on the first 14 scenarios. The 15th and 16th generalized scenarios assign probability 0.3 to each of the two extreme scenarios and probability 0.7 to the no-change scenario. The expected values for these two generalized scenarios are just 30% of the losses on the two extreme scenarios. Taking the maximum expected loss over the 16 generalized scenarios then produces the SPAN$^{\circledR}$ performance bond.

EXPECTED SHORTFALL

Although it is less obvious, another coherent risk measure is the expected shortfall measure defined by $E[\text{loss} \mid \text{loss} \geq \text{cutoff}]$, or $E[\text{loss} \mid \text{loss} \geq \text{VaR}_{1-\alpha}]$ if the cutoff is set equal to the $1-\alpha$ confidence value-at-risk. Given an estimate of the physical probability distribution reflecting the likelihoods of the various outcomes, consider all events with a probability of at least α. Supposing that there are M such events A_i, $i = 1, \ldots, M$, assign to the outcomes that constitute the event A_i their conditional probabilities $P(x_k \mid A_i) = P(x_k)/P(A_i)$, yielding M probability measures. The M events A_i together with these probability measures make up M generalized scenarios, with expected losses $E[\text{loss} \mid A_i]$. Because the losses that except the $1 - \alpha$ percent value-at-risk are the worst α percent, the maximum expected loss $\max_i E[\text{loss} \mid A_i]$ from among the M generalized scenarios is precisely the expected shortfall $E[\text{loss} \mid \text{loss} \geq \text{VaR}_{1-\alpha}]$.

WHAT SHOULD ONE TAKE AWAY FROM THIS?

Are conditions (i) through (iv) reasonable requirements for a risk measure? This is up to the reader. ADEH offer them as axioms, and one either finds them compelling or not. At a minimum, the analysis of ADEH serves to highlight and clarify some of the limitations of value-at-risk. VaR is subadditive if price changes are multivariate normal, and this approximation is widely used. This avoids the issues raised by ADEH, at the cost of the approximation.

In addition, ADEH (1997; 1999a) provide a strong impetus for the use of expected shortfall measures, which at first glance seem to dominate VaR. A convenient feature of expected shortfall is that it is only a small step beyond value-at-risk, and virtually any approach for computing value-at-risk can readily be adapted to compute expected shortfall.

Regardless, and despite their appeal, the ideas of ADEH seem so far to have had limited impact on risk-management practice. The explicitly scenario-based SPAN® system predates the analysis of ADEH, and value-at-risk appears to be even more firmly established in risk-management practice than it was when ADEH first presented their ideas in 1996. A drawback of expected shortfall is that, while only a small one, it is a step beyond value-at-risk. A convenient feature of value-at-risk is that it is accessible to unsophisticated constituencies. This may not be true of expected shortfall.

A drawback of explicitly scenario-based approaches is that it is unclear how reasonably to select scenarios and probability measures on scenarios in situations in which portfolio values depend on dozens or even hundreds of risk factors. This requires significant thought and probably knowledge of the portfolio. (ADEH (1997) argue that an approach that "requires thinking before calculating . . . can only improve risk management.") In situations with many market factors, scenario-based approaches lose intuitive appeal and can be difficult to explain to senior managers, boards of directors, regulators, and other constituencies.

NOTES

Applied work within the framework of coherent risk measures has mostly centered on expected shortfall. Measures equivalent to expected shortfall are widely used in the actuarial and insurance literature and elsewhere. Rockafellar and Uryasev (2001) argue that expected shortfall (which they call *conditional value-at-risk*) is useful for portfolio optimization and cite some of the recent literature. Clarke (1998) provides a traditional view of expected shortfall and other risk measures from a portfolio-management perspective.

Other than this, there has been only limited work on and analysis of coherent risk measures. Studer (1999) suggests a method for finding the worst loss in a given set of scenarios, which turns out to be a coherent risk measure. Delbaen (2000) extends the theory of coherent risk measures to general probability spaces and relates them to value-at-risk and game theory. ADEH (1999b) and Delbaen and Denault (2000) analyze the internal allocation of capital and risk limits among the several divisions or trading desks of a financial firm.

The SPAN® system dates to 1988 and is described more completely at http://www.cme.com/span/span-ov1.htm.

six

Conclusion

CHAPTER 20

A Few Issues in Risk Budgeting

Most of this book has focused on techniques for accomplishing risk budgeting, namely, value-at-risk and risk decomposition. Suppose that you decide to implement a set of either soft or hard risk targets, budgets, or limits using these techniques. What issues will arise?

RISK BUDGETING CHOICES

One needs first to determine what risk measures and risk contributions will be monitored and to establish a hierarchy of risk limits. Chapter 13, discussing the choice of active managers, illustrated a simple two-level hierarchy involving the risk contributions of the strategic benchmark and the active managers, using the simplifying assumption that the active returns of the different managers were uncorrelated. Additional levels of monitoring could be obtained by looking at factor and industry risk contributions of the individual portfolios, along the lines of Chapter 12. Even if no hard (or even soft) limits are placed on such risk contributions, knowledge of them allows the plan sponsor to initiate conversations with managers who deviate from the anticipated factor and industry exposures.

As illustrated in Chapters 11 through 13, risk contributions can be computed for any factor, portfolio, industry group, or other subset of securities. In principle, risk budgets can be assigned to any factor or group of securities whose risk contribution can be computed, though hard risk budgets with a very fine granularity make little sense because they come close to specifying all of the portfolio positions. If the plan sponsor is going to specify all of the positions, why is it paying the portfolio managers? However, monitoring the factor and industry exposures can be a useful way of identifying unintended risks and deviations from historical styles.

Once one determines what will be monitored, one needs to determine the risk targets or budgets. This is often inevitably a combination of an ad hoc evaluation of the sponsor's or customers' risk tolerance and return expectations, combined with (perhaps implicit) analysis of the risk-return tradeoff to determine the allocations to asset classes, managers, and factors. One insight that came out of Chapters 11 and 13 is that risk contributions should be proportional to return expectations. Even if one does not engage in explicit optimization, this insight should guide the determination of the relative sizes of risk budgets for different asset classes and managers. Their overall level is then determined by the fact that the risk contributions sum to the portfolio VaR.

A related issue is the hardness of the risk budgets. Risk budgets will be violated, perhaps frequently. In fact, risk budgets should be violated at least occasionally. If a portfolio manager is close to his risk budget and volatility increases, he will likely exceed it unless he quickly alters the portfolio. Given the transactions costs associated with quickly altering large portfolios, this is unlikely to be considered a desirable outcome. Thus, the sponsor needs to determine what risk budget excessions are acceptable and what the reaction to them should be. If it is acceptable to exceed the risk budget due to a change in volatility, is it also acceptable to enter into a transaction that causes an excession? How quickly should the portfolio manager come back into compliance following a change in volatility? Never? That is, is the risk budget excession just the starting point of a conversation, which need not necessarily lead to a change in the portfolio? If the risk budgets indicate a change in asset allocation is needed, should this be carried by the staff or should the board be involved?

In this regard, it is crucial to recall that value-at-risk is an *estimate* of market risk. Sometimes the risk budgets will be violated because the value-at-risk numbers overstate the risk. This argues strongly against hard risk limits and in favor of treating the risk budget excession as the beginning of an investigation into the reasons for the excession. Does it in fact mean that the portfolio manager is taking undesirable risks? On the other hand, budgets that are never enforced lose their value. This is a delicate issue.

CHOICES IN VALUE-AT-RISK

Choices must also be made about the value-at-risk estimate. Most obviously, which method should be used? For that method, what parameters (e.g., time horizon and critical probability) should be selected? In considering these issues, it is useful to think in terms of a trade off between precision, bias, and computational time.

The delta-normal method relies on the strong assumption that the changes in the underlying market factors are described by a multivariate normal distribution and bases the value-at-risk calculation on a linear, or delta, approximation of the portfolio value. If these assumptions are correct, errors in the estimate will stem primarily from errors in the estimates of the variances and covariances of changes in the market factors. Because variances and covariances can be estimated relatively precisely, the delta-normal method will yield relatively precise value-at-risk estimates if its assumptions are satisfied. Of course, if the assumptions are not satisfied, it will yield biased estimates. The delta-gamma-normal relies on a somewhat more general quadratic, or delta-gamma, approximation of the portfolio value and a similar statement can be made about it. If these strong assumptions are satisfied, they increase the precision of the estimate; if they are not satisfied, they result in biased estimates.

The historical simulation method makes no assumptions about the distribution of changes in the market factors, except that the distribution is constant over time. Thus, biases are not introduced by reliance on assumptions that are not satisfied. But this is achieved at a cost in terms of the precision of the estimate. Specifically, the historical simulation estimate of value-at-risk is based on the realizations in the tail of the distribution of changes in the value of the portfolio. Inherently, there are relatively few realizations in the tail of the distribution. Thus, the historical simulation value-at-risk estimate is based on a relatively small number of observations. As a result, this method is inherently less precise than the others.

In principle, the limitations of the delta-normal, delta-gamma, and historical simulation methods can be overcome by full Monte Carlo. By relying on full revaluation of the portfolio, the biases introduced through the linear and quadratic approximations used in the delta-normal and delta-gamma-normal methods are avoided. However, these benefits in terms of bias and precision come at the cost of considerably increasing the computational burden of the procedure. When the portfolio includes large numbers of instruments, and in particular when it includes large numbers of American or exotic options with prices that must be computed by numerical methods, the computations can be very time consuming. The tradeoff between bias and computational time can be seen very clearly in the delta-gamma and grid Monte Carlo methods. In these methods, one explicitly accepts some error (i.e., potential bias) through the delta-gamma (or delta-gamma-theta) and grid approximations in order to save on computational time.

The choice of method is also intimately connected to the choices of the critical probability and holding period, which in turn depend upon the purposes to which the value-at-risk estimate is to be put. Other things equal, a short time horizon inclines one toward the use of delta or delta-gamma (or delta-gamma-theta) approximations. These approximations tend to work well for small changes in the values of the market factors, and shorter time horizons are characterized by smaller changes in the values of the underlying market factors. Longer time horizons, or portfolios with options, incline one toward use of Monte Carlo methods. Longer time horizons argue against the use of the historical simulation method, because large samples of non-overlapping past monthly or quarterly changes in the market factors are usually not available.

The choice of confidence level amounts to a decision about how far out in the tail of the distribution of possible losses one should look. Organizations using value-at-risk to assess worst case scenarios will, of course, tend to use higher confidence levels or smaller critical probabilities. If their portfolios contain options, this inclines them toward the use of Monte Carlo methods, because the other methods do less well in capturing the effect of large price changes on option values. Alternatively, organizations that use value-at-risk to assess the extent of day-to-day, month-to-month, or quarter-to-quarter changes in the level of risk being taken will be less interested in extreme events. This permits the use of a lower confidence level, and the Monte Carlo approach will confer fewer benefits.

The complicated nature of these trade-offs makes difficult the choice among the various approaches. The user must also decide what assets to include in the value-at-risk calculation. For a pension fund, should the value-at-risk calculation include only the assets in the investment portfolio or should it also include the present value of the pension liabilities? The answer depends on the purpose for which the risk estimates are being used. For example, if a pension fund uses value-at-risk to monitor the risks being taken by the portfolio managers it uses, it might include only the asset portfolio in the calculation. However, if it is concerned about the risk of underfunding, it would likely include the present value of the pension liabilities in the calculation. Then, since underfunding is a risk that is typically realized over the course of years rather than days or months, the value-at-risk calculation might use a holding period of a year or more. This then has implications for the choice of method.

RISK AGGREGATION

While risk decomposition and risk budgeting may be of interest to individual portfolio managers in measuring the risk of and managing their own portfolios (see the example in Chapter 11), the leading application is at the level of the plan sponsor. It is the plan sponsor who wants to know which asset classes, and which portfolio managers, contribute the most to the plan's risk. But the plan may be very large, spread across many portfolios and portfolio managers.

From a purely technical point of view, the problem of aggregating risk across large and complex portfolios clearly is capable of solution and, in fact, has been solved. The large bank derivative dealers who are the traditional users of value-at-risk also have large portfolios with a full range of instruments, including many complex ones. Descriptions of value-at-risk methodologies focus on issues such as mapping and the choice of market factors precisely because these are the tools used to solve the problems involved in measuring and aggregating the risks of large portfolios. But in investment-management organizations, risk decomposition and aggregation raise a new issue.

Throughout this book, an implicit assumption has been that the risks of different portfolios and portfolio managers are measured using the same risk model. One implication of this is that the work is done at the level of the plan (perhaps by its consultants) or its custodian. Furthermore, for a pension plan or other large investment organization, it may be that not all instruments (e.g., derivatives) are held by the plan's custodian. Thus, a prerequisite is that the plan obtain timely position data on all of the instruments in all of its portfolios as frequently as the risk analysis is to be performed. This may be one of the largest challenges to implementing a risk-budgeting framework.

IS IT WORTH THE TROUBLE?

We close by returning to an issue discussed in the introduction: is risk budgeting worth the trouble? Clearly risk budgeting involves significant costs. These are not just the costs of the risk-measurement system and necessary data, but also the time and energy needed to establish and monitor a set of risk budgets. Staff with the skills to do this are costly and could be spending their time on other valuable activities. Not least, risk budgeting imposes significant costs on the portfolio managers and, to the extent that trades are done in order to maintain compliance with risk budgets, on the portfolios themselves. The benefits—careful risk monitoring and management, and as a result perhaps better sleep—are limited by the imprecision in value-at-risk estimates.

No one can deny these costs and limitations. One response, made in the introduction, is that increases in the extent of risk-management education and knowledge and the evolution of risk-measurement systems will both increase the benefits and reduce the costs of the risk-budgeting process. Although overstated, an alternative response to critics of VaR would be: "Emphasizing its faults is like discovering iron in the Stone Age and getting complaints about rust" (Bever, Kozun, and Zvan 2000). VaR and related risk measures are imperfect and difficult to work with. But they are better than the currently available alternatives.

references

Abken, P.A. 2000. An empirical evaluation of value-at-risk by scenario simulation. *Journal of Derivatives* 7, 4 (summer): 12–30.

Anderson, T.W. 1984. *An introduction to multivariate statistical analysis.* 2nd ed. New York: John Wiley & Sons.

Aragonés, J.R., C. Blanco, and K. Dowd. 2001. Incorporating stress tests into market risk modeling. *Derivatives Quarterly* 7, 3 (spring): 44–49.

Artzner, P., F. Delbaen, J.-M. Eber, and D. Heath. 1997. Thinking coherently. *Risk* 10, 11 (November): 68–71.

———1999a. Coherent measures of risk. *Mathematical Finance* 9, 3 (July): 203–228.

———1999b. Risk management and capital allocation with coherent measures of risk. Working paper, University of Strasbourg.

Balkema, A.A., and L. de Haan. 1974. Residual lifetime at great age. *Annals of Probability* 2: 792–804.

Barone-Adesi, G., K. Giannopoulos, and L. Vosper. 1999. VaR without correlations for nonlinear portfolios. *Journal of Futures Markets* 19 (April): 583–602.

———2000a. Filtering historical simulation backtest analysis. Working paper, University of Westminster.

———2000b. Nonparametric VaR techniques: myths and realities. Working paper, University of Westminster.

Basel Committee on Banking Supervision. 2001. *Public disclosures by banks: results of the 1999 survey.* Basel, Switzerland: Bank for International Settlements.

Basel Committee on Banking Supervision, and the Technical Committee of the International Organization of Securities Commissions (IOSCO). 1999. *Trading and derivatives disclosures of banks and securities firms: results of the survey of public disclosures in 1998 annual reports.* Basel, Switzerland: Bank for International Settlements.

Beirlant, J., J.L. Teugels, and P. Vynckier. 1996. *Practical analysis of extreme values.* Leuven: Leuven University Press.

Berkowitz, J. 1999. Evaluating the forecasts of risk models. Working paper, Federal Reserve Board.

———1999/2000. A coherent framework for stress testing. *Journal of Risk* 2, 2 (winter): 5–15.

303

————2000. Breaking the silence. *Risk* 13, 10 (October): 105–108.

Bodie, Z., A. Kane, and A.J. Marcus. 1993. *Investments.* Homewood, Ill.: Richard D. Irwin.

Bookstaber, R. 1997. Global risk management: are we missing the point? *Journal of Portfolio Management* 23, 3 (spring): 102–107.

Boudoukh, J., M. Richardson, and R.F. Whitelaw. 1995. Expect the worst. *Risk* 9, 9 (September): 100–101.

————1997. Investigation of a class of volatility estimators. *Journal of Derivatives* 4, 3: 62–89.

————1998. The best of both worlds. *Risk* 11, 5 (May): 64–66.

Boyer, B.H., M.S. Gibson, and M. Loretan. 1997. Pitfalls in tests for changes in correlation. International Finance Discussion Paper 597, Board of Governors of the Federal Reserve System.

Boyle, P., M. Broadie, and P. Glasserman. 1997. Monte Carlo methods for security pricing. *Journal of Economic Dynamics and Control* 21: 1267–1321.

Britten-Jones, M., and S.M. Schaeffer. 1998. Non-linear value-at-risk. *European Finance Review* 2, 2: 161–187.

Brooks, C., and G. Persand. 2000. Value-at-risk and market crashes. *Journal of Risk* 2, 4: 5–26.

Brooks, C., B. Scott-Quinn, and J. Whalmsey. 1998. Adjusting VaR models for the impact of the Euro. Working paper, ISMA Center.

Burmeister, E., R. Roll, and S. Ross. 1994. *A practitioner's guide to factor models.* Charlottesville, Va.: Research Foundation of the Institute of Chartered Financial Analysts.

Butler, J.S., and B. Schachter. 1996. Improving value-at-risk estimates by combining kernel estimation with historical simulation. In *Proceedings of the 32nd Annual Conference on Bank Structure and Competition.* Chicago: Federal Reserve Bank of Chicago.

————1998. Estimating value-at-risk by combining kernel estimation with historical simulation. *Review of Derivatives Research* 1: 371–390.

Cardenás, J., E. Fruchard, J.-F. Picron, C. Reyes, K. Walters, and W. Yang. 1999. Monte Carlo within a day. *Risk* 12, 2 (February): 55–59.

Cardenás, J., E. Fruchard, E. Koehler, C. Michel, and I. Thomazeau. 1997. VaR: one step beyond. *Risk* 10, 10 (October): 72–75.

Carverhill, A., and C. Strickland. 1992. Money market term structure dynamics and volatility expectations. Working paper, Financial Options Research Center, University of Warwick.

Cass, D. 2000. VaR and risk budgeting: who wants them? *Risk* 13, 7: 6–7.

Chatfield, C. 1993. Calculating interval forecasts. *Journal of Business and Economic Statistics* 11: 121–135.

Cherubini, U., and G. Della Lunga. 1999. Stress testing techniques and value-at-risk measures: a unified approach. Working paper, Polyhedron Computational Finance.

Christoffersen, P. 1998. Evaluating interval forecasts. *International Economic Review* 39, 4: 841–862.

Christoffersen, P., J. Hahn, and A. Inoue. 1999. Testing, comparing, and combining value-at-risk measures. Working paper, McGill University.

Cizeau, P., M. Potters, and J.-P. Bouchaud. 2001. Correlation structure of extreme market returns. Working paper, Capital Fund Mgt.

Clarke, R.C. 1998. Alternative measures of risk. In *Investment management*, ed. P. L. Bernstein and A. Damodoran. New York: John Wiley & Sons.

Crnkovic, C., and J.Drachman. 1996. Quality control. *Risk* 9, 9 (September): 138–143.

Crouhy, M., D. Galai, and R. Mark. 1998. Model risk. *Journal of Financial Engineering* 7, 3/4: 267–288.

Danielsson, J., and C.G. de Vries. 1997a. Tail index and quantile estimation with very high frequency data. *Journal of Empirical Finance* 4: 241–257.

———1997b. Beyond the sample: extreme quantile and probability estimation. Technical report, Tinbergen Institute, Rotterdam.

———1997c. Extreme returns, tail estimation, and value-at-risk. Working paper, London School of Economics and Tinbergen Institute, Rotterdam.

———2000. Value-at-risk and extreme returns. Working paper, London School of Economics and Tinbergen Institute, Rotterdam.

Danielsson, J., L. de Haan, L. Peng, and C. G. de Vries. 1999. Using a bootstrap method to choose the sample fraction in tail index estimation. Working paper, Tinbergen Institute, Rotterdam.

Danielsson, J., P. Hartmann, and C. G. de Vries. 1998. The cost of conservatism. *Risk* 11, 1 (January): 101–103.

Danielsson, J., and Y. Morimoto. 2000. Forecasting extreme financial risk: a critical analysis of practical methods for the Japanese market. Bank of Japan Institute for Monetary and Economic Studies discussion paper series 2000-E-8.

Davison, A.C. 1984. Modelling excesses over high thresholds, with an application. In *Statistical Extremes and Applications.*, ed. J. Tiego de Olivera. Dordrecht: Reidel.

Davison, A.C., and R.L. Smith. 1990. Models for exceedances over high thresholds (with discussion). *Journal of the Royal Statistical Society Series B* 52, no. 3: 393–442.

De Bever, L., W. Kozun, and B. Zvan. 2000. Risk budgeting in a pension fund. In: *Risk budgeting: A new approach to investing.*, ed. Leslie Rahl. London: Risk Books.

Delbaen, F. 2000. Coherent risk measures on general probability spaces. Working paper, ETH Zürich.

Delbaen, F., and M. Denault. 2000. Coherent allocation of risk capital. Working paper, ETH Zürich.

Dembo, R.S., A.R. Aziz, D. Rosen, and M. Zerbs. 2000. *Mark to future: a framework for measuring risk and reward.* Toronto: Algorithmics Publications.

Diebold, F.X., T.A. Gunther, and A.S. Tay. 1998. Evaluating density forecasts. *International Economic Review* 39, 4: 863–906.

Diebold, F.X., T. Schuermann, and J.D. Stroughair. 1998. Pitfalls and opportunities in the use of extreme value theory in risk management. In *Decision technologies for computational finance,* ed. A.-P.N. Refenes, A.N. Burgess, and J.E. Moody. Boston: Kluwer Academic Publishers.

Dowd, K. 1999. A value-at-risk approach to risk-return analysis. *The Journal of Portfolio Management* 20, 4 (summer): 60–67.

Duffie, D., and J. Pan. 1997. An overview of value-at-risk. *Journal of Derivatives* 4, 3: 7–49.

———1999. Analytical value-at-risk with jumps and credit risk. Working paper, Graduate School of Business, Stanford University.

Dybvig, P. 1989. Bond and bond option pricing based on the current term structure. Working paper, Washington University.

El-Jahel, L., W. Perraudin, and P. Sellin. 1999. Value-at-risk for derivatives. *Journal of Derivatives* 6, 3 (spring): 7–26.

Elton, E., and M. Gruber. 1994. *A practitioner's guide to factor models.* Charlottesville, Va.: Research Foundation of the Institute of Chartered Financial Analysts.

Embrechts, P., editor. 2000. *Extremes and integrated risk management.* London: Risk Books.

Embrechts, P., L. de Haan, and X. Huang. 1999. Modeling multivariate extremes. Working paper, ETH Zürich.

Embrechts, P., C. Klüppelberg, and T. Mikosch. 1997. *Modeling extremal events for insurance and finance.* Vol. 33, Applications of Mathematics. New York: Springer-Verlag.

Embrechts, P., A.J. McNeil., and D. Straumann. 1999. Correlation: pitfalls and alternatives. A short non-technical article. *Risk* 12, 5 (May): 69–71.

Embrechts, P., A.J. McNeil, and D. Straumann. 2000. Correlation and dependence in risk management: properties and pitfalls. In *Risk management beyond value-at-risk,* ed. M.A.H. Dempster and H.K. Moffat, Cambridge: Cambridge University Press.

Embrechts, P., S. Resnick, and G. Samorodnitsky. 1998. Living on the edge. *Risk* 11, 1 (January): 96–100.

Engle, R.F., and S. Manganelli. 1999. CaViaR: conditional value-at-risk by regression quantiles. Working paper 7341, National Bureau of Economic Research.

Falloon, William. 1999. Growin' up. *Risk* 12, 2 (February): 26–31.

Feuerverger, A., and A.C.M. Wong. 2000. Computation of value-at-risk for nonlinear portfolios. *Journal of Risk* 3, 1 (Fall): 37–56.

Figlewski, S. 1997. Forecasting volatility. *Financial markets, institutions, and instruments* 6: 1–88.

Finger, C. 1996. Testing RiskMetrics volatility forecasts on emerging markets data. *RiskMetrics Monitor* (fourth quarter): 3–19.

———1997. A methodology for stress correlation. *RiskMetrics Monitor* (fourth quarter): 3–11.

Fong, G., and O.A. Vasicek. 1997. A multidimensional framework for risk analysis. *Financial Analysts Journal* (July/August): 51–57.

Frye, J. 1997. Principles of risk: finding value-at-risk through factor-based interest rate scenarios. In *VAR: understanding and applying value-at-risk.* London: Risk Publications.

———1998. Monte Carlo by day. *Risk* 11, 11 (November): 66–71.

Gavin, J. 2000. Extreme value theory—an empirical analysis of equity price risk. Working paper, UBS Warburg.

Gibson, M.S. 2001. Incorporating event risk into value-at-risk. Working paper, Trading Risk Analysis Section, Federal Reserve Board.

Gibson, M.S., and M. Pritsker. 2000/2001. Improving grid-based methods for estimating value-at-risk of fixed-income portfolios. *Journal of Risk* 3, 2 (winter): 65–89.

Gizycki, M., and N. Hereford. 1998. Assessing the dispersion in bank's estimates of market risk: the results of a value-at-risk survey. Working paper, Reserve Bank of Australia.

Glasserman, P., P. Heidelberger, and P. Shahabuddin. 2000. Variance reduction techniques for estimating value-at-risk. *Management Science* 46: 139–164.

Golub, B.W., and L.M. Tilman. 1997. Measuring yield curve risk using principal components analysis, value-at-risk, and key rate durations. *Journal of Portfolio Management* (summer): 72–84.

———2000. *Risk management: approaches for fixed income markets.* John Wiley & Sons: New York.

Greenspan, A. 2000. Speech at the 36th Annual Conference on Bank Structure and Competition of the Federal Reserve Bank of Chicago, Chicago, Illinois.

Grinold, R., and R. Kahn. 1994. *A practitioner's guide to factor models.* Charlottesville, Va.: Research Foundation of the Institute of Chartered Financial Analysts.

Group of Thirty. 1993. *Derivatives: practices and principles.* New York: Group of Thirty.

Guldimann, T. 2000. The story of RiskMetrics. *Risk* 13, 1 (January): 56–58.

Gurnani, D. 2000. Managing risks in a multimanager hedge fund portfolio: the use of value-at-risk methodology. In *Risk budgeting: a cutting edge guide to enhancing fund management*, ed. R. Layard-Liesching. New York: Institutional Investor, Inc.

Hayt, G.S., and R.M. Levich. 1999. Class notes: who uses derivatives. *Risk* 12, 8 (August): 96–97.

Hendricks, D. 1996. Evaluation of value-at-risk models using historical data. *Federal Reserve Bank of New York Economic Policy Review* 2, 1 (April): 39–69.

Henrard, M. 2000. Comparison of cashflow maps for value-at-risk. *Journal of Risk* 3, 1 (fall): 57–72.

Hill, B.M. 1975. A simple general approach to inference about the tail of a distribution. *Annals of Statistics* 3: 1163–1174.

Ho, T.S.Y. 1992. Key rate durations: measures of interest rate risks. *Journal of Fixed Income* 2, 1: 29–44.

Hosking, J., G. Bonti, and D. Siegel. 2000. Beyond the lognormal. *Risk* 13, 5 (May): 59–62.

Hull, J. 2000. *Options, futures, and other derivatives.* Upper Saddle River, N.J.: Prentice Hall.

Hull, J., and A. White. 1998a. Incorporating volatility up-dating into the historical simulation method for value-at-risk. *Journal of Risk* 1, 1 (fall): 5–19.

———1998b. Value-at-risk when daily changes in market variables are not normally distributed. *Journal of Derivatives* 5, 3 (spring): 9–19.

James, J., and N. Webber. 2000. *Interest rate modelling.* New York: John Wiley & Sons.

Jamshidian, F., and Y. Zhu. 1997. "Scenario simulation: theory and methodology. *Finance and Stochastics* 1, 1 (January): 43–67.

Jarrow, R.A. 1996. *Modelling fixed income securities and interest rate options.* New York: McGraw-Hill.

Joe, H. 1997. *Multivariate models and dependence concepts.* London: Chapman & Hall.

Johnson, N.L., S. Kotz, and N. Balakrishnan. 1994. *Continuous univariate distributions.* vol. 1, 2d ed. New York: John Wiley & Sons.

Joliffe, I.T. 1986. *Principal components analysis.* New York: Springer-Verlag.

Jorion, P. 1996. Risk^2: measuring the risk in value-at-risk. *Financial Analysts Journal* (November/December): 47–56.

Ju, X., and N.D. Pearson. 1999. Using value-at-risk to control risk taking: how wrong can you be? *Journal of Risk* 1, 2: 5–36.

Këllezi, E., and M. Gilli. 2000. Extreme value theory for tail-related risk measures." Working paper, University of Geneva (April).

Kim, J., and C.C. Finger. 2000. A stress test to incorporate correlation breakdown. *Journal of Risk* 2, 3 (spring): 5–19.

Koedjik, K., R. Huisman, and R. Pownall. 1998. VaR-x: fat tails in financial risk management. *Journal of Risk* 1, 1 (fall): 47–62.

Kupiec, P. 1995. Techniques for verifying the accuracy of risk measurement models. *Journal of Derivatives* 3, 2 (winter): 73–84.

————1998. Stress testing in a value-at-risk framework. *Journal of Derivatives* 6, 1 (fall): 7–24.

Layard-Liesching, R. 2000. Risk budgeting. In *Risk budgeting: a cutting edge guide to enhancing fund management*, ed. R. Layard-Liesching. New York: Institutional Investor, Inc.

Leadbetter, M.R. 1991. On the basis for "peaks over threshold" modeling. *Statistics and Probability Letters* 12: 357–362.

Leadbetter, M.R., G. Lindgren, and H. Rootzen. 1983. *Extremes and related properties of stationary sequences and processes.* New York: Springer-Verlag.

Levich, R.M., G.S. Hayt, and B. A. Ripston. 1999. 1998 survey of derivatives and risk management practices by U.S. institutional investors. Working paper FIN-99-074, New York University Stern Graduate School of Business.

Linsmeier, T. J., and N.D. Pearson. 1996. Risk measurement: an introduction to value-at-risk. Working paper, University of Illinois.

Litterman, R. 1996. Hot Spots™ and hedges. *The Journal of Portfolio Management* 23 (December special issue): 52–75.

Litterman, R., J. Longerstaey, J. Rosengarten, and K. Winkelman. 2000. *The green zone: assessing the quality of returns.* New York: Goldman Sachs Investment Management Division.

Litterman, R., and J. Scheinkman. 1991. Common factors affecting bond returns. *Journal of Fixed Income* (June): 54-61.

Litterman, R., and K. Winkelman. 1996. Managing market exposure. *Journal of Portfolio Management* 22, 4 (summer): 32–49.

Longin, F.M. 2000. From value-at-risk to stress testing: the extreme value approach. *Journal of Banking and Finance* 24, 7: 1097–1130.

Lopez, J.A. 1999. Regulatory evaluation of value-at-risk models. *Journal of Risk* 1, 1: 37–64.

Mardia, K.V., J.T. Kent, and J.M. Bibby. 1979. *Multivariate analysis*. London: Academic Press.

Marshall, C., and M. Siegel. 1997. Value-at-risk: implementing a risk measurement standard. *Journal of Derivatives* 4, 3: 91–111.

McNeil, A.J. 1997a. Estimating the tails of loss severity distributions using extreme value theory. *ASTIN Bulletin* 27: 117–137.

———1997b. On extremes and crashes. Working paper, Departement Mathematik, ETH Zentrum.

———1998. History repeating. *Risk* 11, 1: 99.

———1998. Calculating quantile risk measures for financial time series using extreme value theory. Working paper, Departement Mathematik, ETH Zentrum.

———1999. Extreme value theory for risk managers. *Internal Modelling and CAD II*. London: Risk Books.

McNeil, A.J., and R. Frey. 2000. Estimation of tail-related risk measures for heteroscedastic financial time series: an extreme value approach. *Journal of Empirical Finance* 7, 3–4: 271–300.

McNeil, A.J., and T. Saladin. 1997. The peaks over thresholds method for estimating high quantiles of loss distributions. *Proceedings of the 28th International ASTIN Colloquium*.

McNeil, A.J., and T. Saladin. 1998. Developing scenarios for future extreme losses using the POT method. Working paper, Departement Mathematik, ETH Zentrum.

Michaud, R.O. 1989. The Markowitz optimization enigma: is "optimized" optimal? *Financial Analysts Journal* (January/February): 31–42.

Mina, J. 1999. Improved cash-flow map. Working Paper, RiskMetrics Group.

Mina, J., and A. Ulmer. 1999. Delta-gamma four ways. Working paper, RiskMetrics.

Mina, J., and J.Y. Xiao. 2001. *Return to RiskMetrics: the evolution of a standard*. New York: RiskMetrics Group.

Morgan Guaranty Trust Company. 1994. *RiskMetrics™ technical document*. New York: Global Research, Morgan Guaranty Trust Company.

———1996. *RiskMetrics™ technical document*. 4th ed. New York: Global Research, Morgan Guaranty Trust Company.

Neftci, S.N. 2000. Value-at-risk calculations, extreme events, and tail estimation. *Journal of Derivatives* 7, 3 (spring): 23–37.

Nelson, R.B. 1999. *An introduction to copulas*. New York: Springer-Verlag.

Niffikeer, C.I., R.D. Hewins, and R.B. Flavell. 2000. A synthetic factor approach to the estimation of value-at-risk of a portfolio of interest rate swaps. *Journal of Banking and Finance* 24: 1903–1932.

Parisi, Francis. 2000. Extreme value theory and Standard & Poors ratings. ABS Research Special Report. New York: Standard & Poors.

Pickands, J. 1975. Statistical inference using extreme order statistics. *Annals of Statistics* 3: 119–131.

Pichler, S., and K. Selitsch. 2000. A comparison of analytical and VaR methodologies for portfolios that include options. In *Model risk, concepts, calibration, and pricing*, ed. R. Gibson. London: Risk Books.

Press, W.H., S.A. Teukolsky, W.T. Vetterling, and B.P. Flannery. 1992. *Numerical recipes in C: the art of scientific computing*. Cambridge: Cambridge University Press.

Pritsker, M. 1997. Evaluating Value-at-Risk methodologies: accuracy versus computational time. *Journal of Financial Services Research* 12, 2/3 (October): 201–242.

———2001. The hidden dangers of historical simulation. Working paper, University of California at Berkley.

Putnam, B.H., J.M. Quintana, and D.S. Wilford. 2000. Understanding risk is key to long-term return management. In *Risk budgeting: a cutting edge guide to enhancing fund management*, ed. R. Layard-Liesching. New York: Institutional Investor, Inc.

Rawls, S.W. 2000. Why is everyone talking about risk allocation? In *Risk budgeting: a cutting edge guide to enhancing fund management*, ed. R. Layard-Liesching. New York: Institutional Investor, Inc.

Rebonato, R., and P. Jackel. 1999/2000. The most general methodology for creating a valid correlation matrix for risk management and option pricing purposes. *Journal of Risk* 2, 2 (winter): 17–27.

Reiss, R., and M. Thomas. 1997. *Statistical analysis of extreme values*. Basel, Switzerland: Birkhauser.

Resnik, S.I. 1987. *Extreme values, regular variation, and point processes*. New York: Springer-Verlag.

Risk. 2000. Asset management risk manager of the year: Putnam Investments. *Risk* 13, 1 (January): 36.

Rockafellar, R.T., and S. Uryasev. 2001. Optimization of conditional value-at-risk. *Journal of Risk* 2, 3 (spring): 21–40.

Ronn, E., A. Sayrak, and S. Tompaidis. 2000. The impact of large changes in asset prices on intra-market correlations in the domestic and international markets. Working paper, University of Texas at Austin.

Rosenblatt, M. 1952. Remarks on a multivariate transformation. *Annals of Mathematical Statistics* 23: 470–472.

Roth, B., and A. Layng. 1998. Tools for trading. *Risk* 11, 6 (June): 51–55.

Rouvinez, C. 1997. Going Greek with VAR. *Risk* 10, 2 (February): 57–65.

Shimko, D., B. Humphreys, and V. Pant. 1998. Hysterical simulation. *Risk* 11, 6 (June): 47.

Simons, K. 1996. Value-at-Risk: new approaches to risk management. *New England Economic Review* (September/October): 3–13.

Singh, M.K. 1997. Value-at-risk using principal components analysis. *Journal of Portfolio Management* (fall): 101–112.

Smith, R.L. 1987. Estimating tails of probability distributions. *Annals of Statistics* 15, 3: 1174–1207.

———1989. Extreme value analysis of environmental time series: an application to trend detection in ground-level ozone. *Statistical Science* 4: 367–393.

———1994. Multivariate threshold methods. In *Extreme value theory and its applications,* ed. J. Galambos. Boston: Kluwer Academic Publishers.

———2000. Measuring risk with extreme value theory. Working paper, Department of Statistics, University of North Carolina.

Smithson, C.W. 1998. *Managing financial risk: a guide to derivative products, financial engineering, and value maximization.* New York: McGraw-Hill.

Stambaugh, R. 1995. Discussion of "Why do markets move together? An investigation of U.S.–Japan stock return comovements using ADR's" (by A. Karolyi, and R. Stulz) presented at the NBER Conference on Financial Risk Management.

Starica, C. 1999. Multivariate extremes for models with constant conditional correlations. *Journal of Empirical Finance* 6, 5: 515–553.

Steeley, J.M. 1990. Modelling the dynamics of the term structure of interest rates. *The Economic and Social Review* 24, 4 (July), 337–361.

Studer, G. 1999. Market risk computation for nonlinear portfolios. *Journal of Risk* 1, 4: 33–53.

Venkataraman, S. 1997. Value-at-Risk for a mixture of normal distributions: the use of quasi-Bayesian estimation techniques. *Economic Perspectives* (March–April): 2–13.

Wilson, T. 1994. Debunking the myths. *Risk* 7, 4 (April): 67–73.

Winkelman, K. 2000a. *Risk budgeting: managing active risk at the total fund level.* New York: Goldman Sachs Investment Management Division.

———2000b. Risk budgeting: managing active risk at the total fund level. In *Risk budgeting: a cutting edge guide to enhancing fund management,* ed. R. Layard-Liesching. New York: Institutional Investor, Inc.

Zangari, P. 1996a. A VaR methodology for portfolios that include options. *RiskMetrics Monitor* (first quarter): 4–12.

———1996b. An improved methodology for measuring VaR. *RiskMetrics Monitor* (second quarter): 7–25.

———1996c. How accurate is the delta-gamma methodology? *RiskMetrics Monitor* (third quarter): 12–29.

———1996d. When is non-normality a problem? The case of 15 time series from emerging markets. *RiskMetrics Monitor* (fourth quarter): 20–34.

———1997a. Finding gamma: a path of less resistance. *Derivatives Strategy* (February): 43–44.

———2000. Applying scenario analysis and stress testing to measure extreme events. Presentation notes, Goldman Sachs Asset Management.

index

Abken, P. A., 242, 272, 303
Absolute return funds, 163
Aggregation and decomposition of
    risks of large portfolios,
    183–203
    factor models for portfolio returns,
    186–189
    portfolios, securities, and parameter
    estimates, 184
    risk contributions of securities,
    190–192
    risk contributions in terms of asset
    groups, 192–195
    risk contributions in terms of factors,
    195–201
    securities and parameters estimates,
    184–186
    and VaR, 189–190
Anderson, T. W., 133, 303
Aragonés, J. R., 303
Artzner, P., 287, 292, 293, 303
Autoregressive Conditional
    Heteroscedasticity
    (ARCH) model, 49, 51, 73
Aziz, A. R., 102, 306

Balakrishnan, N., 103, 232, 309
Balkema, A. A., 258, 303
Barone-Adesi, G., 73, 303
Basel Committee on Banking
    Supervision, 11, 303

Beirlant, J., 258, 303
Berkowitz, J., 149, 303
Best hedges, 172
Bibby, J. M., 133, 310
Black-Scholes formula, 224
Blanco, C., 303
Block maxima models, 245
Board of Governors of the Federal
    Reserve System, 258
Bodie, Z., 114, 304
Bonti, G., 102, 308
Bookstaber, R., 148, 304
Bouchaud, J.-P., 149, 305
Boudoukh, J., 52, 73, 260, 304
Boyer, B. H., 149, 304
Boyle, P., 243, 304
Britten-Jones, M., 232, 304
Broadie, M., 243, 304
Broken arrow stress test, 144–145, 148
Brooks, C., 149, 304
Burmeister, E., 114, 304
Butler, J. S., 72, 304

Cardenás, J., 232, 242, 304
Carverhill, C., 304
Cass, D., 11, 201, 203, 304
Chatfield, C., 274, 304
Cherubini, U., 305
Choice of active managers, 205–219
    existing allocation and manager
    roster, 206–209

decomposition of existing asset class allocations, 215–216
optimal manager roster and asset allocation, 216–219
risk decomposition of existing manager roster, 212–215
strategic benchmark, 209–212
Cholesky decomposition, 103
Christoffersen, P., 274, 305
CIBI World Markets, 11
Cizeau, P., 149, 305
Clarke, R. C., 293, 305
Coherent risk measures, 287–293
Conditional VaR, 293
Copulas, 257
Cornish-Fisher approximation, 232
Crnkovic, C., 274, 305
Crouhy, M., 274, 305

Danielson, J., 259, 260, 305
Davison, A. C., 258, 305
De Bever, L., 72, 302, 305
De Haan, L., 258, 259, 260, 303, 306
De Vries, C. G., 259, 260, 305
Delbaen, F., 287, 292, 293, 303
Della Lunga, G., 305
Delta equivalent positions, 37
Delta-gamma approaches, 223–232
Delta-gamma-delta method, 272
Delta-gamma Monte Carlo approximation, 234
Delta-gamma-theta-normal method, 223
Delta-mixture-of-normals method, 49
Delta-normal method, 29, 33–53
covariance estimates and exponential weighting, 45–48
and explicit consideration of FX risk, 39–45
limitations of the, 48–50
mapping options, 37–39
sample portfolio, 34–36
Delta-normal method for a fixed-income portfolio, 75–89

computing portfolio variance, standard deviation, and VaR, 82–83
determining the distribution of changes in market factor shares, 79–81
differing payment dates, 83–85
identifying basic market factors and standard positions, 77
mapping interest-rate swaps, 85
mapping options, 85–86
mapping the portfolio into positions in the standard instruments, 78–79

Delta-t model. *See* Delta-mixture-of-normals method
Dembo, R. S., 102, 306
Denault, M., 293, 306
Diebold, F. X., 258, 274, 306
Dowd, K., 201, 303, 306
Drachman, J., 274, 305
Duffie, D., 52, 53, 73, 232, 242, 306
Dybvig, P., 306

Eber, J.-M., 287, 292, 293, 303
El-Jahel, L., 232, 306
Elton, E., 114, 306
Embrechts, P., 258, 260, 306, 307
Engel, R. F., 73, 307
Euler's law, 154, 161
Exceedance, 248–249
Expected shortfall, 287, 291–292, 303
Extreme value theory, 149–150, 245–260
distribution of yield changes, 246–248
estimating parameters of the GPD and computing VaR, 252–255
generalized Pareto distribution and VaR, 248–250
limitations of EVT in computing VaR, 257–258
mean excess function and the threshold u, 250–252

Factor models in computation of the VaR
  of equity portfolios, 105–114
delta-normal VaR, 106–109
factor models, 105–106
full Monte Carlo VaR, 111–113
inclusion of options in computing
  delta-normal VaR, 109–111
methods other than full Monte
  Carlo, 113
Feuerverger, A., 232, 307
Figlewski, S., 51, 307
Falloon, W., 203, 307
Filtered historical simulation, 73
Finger, C. C., 53, 148, 149, 307
Flannery, B. P., 103, 311
Flavell, R. B., 134, 311
Fong, G., 232, 307
Frechet distribution, 256
Fruchard, E., 232, 242, 304
Frye, J., 134, 242, 260, 307, 310

Galai, D., 274, 305
Gaming the VaR, 275–285
  assumptions about portfolio
    manager's behavior, 282–284
  gaming estimation errors in covari-
    ance matrix, 275–277
  general case of gaming estimation
    errors, 279–282
  simple example of gaming estimation
    errors, 277–279
Gavin, J., 260, 307
Generalized Autoregressive
  Conditional Heteroscedasticity
  (GARCH) model, 49, 51–52
  GARCH (1,1) model, 49, 52, 71, 73
Generalized extreme value distribution,
  245, 248–250, 256
Generalized Pareto distribution, 245
Generalized scenarios, 290
Giannopoulos, K., 73, 303
Gibson, M. S., 53, 149, 242, 272, 304,
  307
Gilli, M., 260, 309
Gizycki, M., 274, 307

Glasserman, P., 102, 243, 304, 307
Golub, B. W., 134, 202, 307
Greenspan, Alan, 148, 307
Grinold, R., 114, 308
Group of Thirty, 10, 308
Gruber, M., 114, 306
Guldimann, T., 10, 308
Gumbel distribution, 256
Gunther, T. A., 274, 306
Gurnani, D., 203

Hahn, J., 274, 305
Hartmann, P., 259, 305
Hayt, G. S., 11, 308, 309
Heath, D., 287, 292, 293, 303
Heidelberger, P., 102, 307
Hendricks, D., 47, 269–270, 308
Henrard, M., 86–87
Hereford, N., 274, 307
Hewins, R. D., 134, 311
Hidden technology bets, 194
Hill, B. M., 259, 308
Historical method, 28–29
Historical simulation method, 24, 29,
  55–74
  advantages and limitations of the,
    67–70
  and analysis of a simple fixed-
    income portfolio, 57–63
  features, 56–57
  and options and other more
    complicated instruments, 63–67
  refinements to the, 70–72
Ho, T. S. Y., 308
Homogeneity, 289
Hosking, J., 102, 308
Huang, X., 260, 306
Hull, J., 73, 102, 134, 308
Humphreys, B., 73, 312
Huisman, R., 53, 309
Hull, J. 255–257, 308

Implementation risk, 273
Implied views analysis, 168–169,
  174–177

Incremental approach, 202
Inoue, A., 274, 305
International Organization of
    Securities Commissions, 11

Jäckel, P., 148, 311
James, J., 134, 308
Jamshidian, F. 242, 308
Jarrow, R. A., 134, 308
Joe, H., 308
Johnson, N. L., 103, 232, 308
Johnson family distributions, 232
Joliffe, I. T., 133, 309
Jorion, P., 270, 309
Ju, X., 285, 309

Kahn, R., 114, 308
Kane, A., 114, 304
Këllezi, E., 260, 309
Kent, J. T., 133, 310
Key rates, 124–129
Kim, J., 148, 149, 309
Klüppelberg, C., 258, 306
Koedjik, K., 53, 309
Koehler, E., 232, 304
Kolmogorov-Smirnov test, 267,
    274
Kotz, S., 103, 232, 309
Kozun, W., 72, 302, 305
KPMG, 11
Kuiper's statistic, 267, 274
Kupiec, P., 148, 273, 309
Kurtosis, 223

Layard-Liesching, R., 203
Layng, A., 72, 312
Leadbetter, M. R., 258, 309
Lehman aggregate, 209, 210
Levich, R. M., 11, 308, 309
Lindgren, G., 258, 309
Linear homogeneity, 154
Linsmeier, T. J., 309
Lirtzman, Harris, 11
Litterman, R., 30, 134, 161, 170,
    201, 309

Long-short hedge fund manager,
    163–181
    computation of VaR not enough,
        168–169
    MPT portfolio and parameter
        estimates, 164–166
    MPT and VaR, 166–168
    risk decomposition of current
        portfolio, 169–170
    risk decomposition and hedging,
        171–174
    risk decomposition and portfolio
        optimization, 177–181
Longerstaey, J., 201, 309
Longin, F. M., 149, 260, 303
Lopez, J. A., 274, 309
Loretan, 149, 304

Manganelli, S., 73, 307
Marcus, A. J., 114, 304
Mardia, K. V., 133, 310
"Marginal," nonstandard usage of,
    161
Marginal risk decomposition, 21
Mark, R., 274, 305
Mark to future, 102
Marshall, C., 273, 310
McNeil, A. J., 258, 259, 260, 306,
    310
Mean, 223
Mean-variance frontier, 175
Michaud, R. O., 219, 310
Michel, C., 232, 304
Mikosch, T., 258, 306
Mina, J., 50, 87, 161, 232, 310
Monotonicity, 289
Monte Carlo simulation, 28, 29, 73
    advantages and limitations of,
        99–101
    application of hypothetical pseudo-
        random market share changes,
        95–96
    identification of market factors,
        92–94
    identification of Var, 96–98

liquidity-adjusted VaR and, 98–99
selection of a statistical distribution,
    94–95
similarities and differences with
    historical simulation, 91–92
simulation of multivariate normal
    random variables, 102–103
Morgan Guaranty Trust Company
    (J. P. Morgan), 10, 47, 50, 53,
    60, 274, 310
Morimoto, Y., 260, 305
MPT Asset Manager, 163

Naïve historical method, 29
Neftci, S. N., 259, 310
Nelson, R. B., 310
New York Retirement System, 202
New York University, 11
Niffikeer, C. I., 134, 311

1 – α percent confidence VaR, 10
Ontario Teachers Pension Plan, 72
Option delta, 37
Option elasticity, 109

Pan, J., 52, 53, 73, 232, 242, 306
Pant, V., 73, 312
Parametric method, 28
Parisi, Francis, 260, 311
Parraudin, W., 232, 306
Peaks over threshold models, 245
Pearson, N. D., 285, 309
Peng, L., 259, 305
Persand, G., 149, 304
Pichler, S., 232, 311
Pickands, J., 258, 311
Picron, J.-F., 242, 304
Portfolio aggregation, 73, 258
Portfolio standard deviation, 6
Potters, M., 149, 305
Pownall, R., 53, 309
Press, W. H., 103, 311
Principal components in computation
    of VaR of fixed-income
    portfolios, 115–134

computing principal components,
    120–121
decomposition of a random vector,
    116–118
example of a term structure of,
    124–129
general case, the, 123–124
limitations of the use of principal
    components, 132–133
numerical example of, an, 121–123
principal components, 118–120
principal components decomposi-
    tion, 115
using principal components to com-
    pute VaR, 129–132
using principal components with
    Monte Carlo simulation, 132
Pritsker, M., 73, 74, 242, 271, 272,
    311
Putnam, B. H., 203, 311
Putnam Investments, 202

Quintana, J. M., 203, 311

Rawls, S. W., 203, 311
Rebonato, R., 134, 148, 311
Reiss, R., 258, 311
Resnick, S. I., 258, 307, 311
Reyes, C., 242, 304
Richardson, M., 52, 73, 260, 304
Ripston, B. A., 11, 309
Risk, 202, 203
Risk,
    contribution, 21, 154
    difficulty of measuring, 3
    mapping, 33–34
    measures of, 3
Risk budgeting,
    and choice of active managers,
        205–219
    choices in, 297–298
    connection of, to VaR, 9
    controversy whether it makes sense,
        9–10
    definition of, 4, 7–8

issues in, 297–302
process, 8
risk aggregation, 300–301
Risk decomposition, 6–7, 153–162, 168
  for historical and Monte Carlo
    simulation, 157–158
  and expected returns, 158–161
  and large portfolios, 183–203
Risk-free condition, 289
RiskMetrics methodology, 47, 50, 60,
  161, 273
Rockafellar, R. T., 293, 311
Roll, R., 114, 304
Ronn, E., 149, 311
Rootzen, H., 258, 309
Rosen, D., 102, 306
Rosenblatt, M., 274, 312
Rosengarten, J., 201, 309
Ross, S., 114, 304
Roth, B., 72, 312
Rouvinez, C., 312

Saddlepoint approximations, 232
Saladin, T., 260, 310
Samarodnitsky, G., 258, 307
Sayrak, A., 149, 311
Schachter, B., 73, 304
Schaeffer, S. M., 232, 304
Scheinkman, J., 134, 309
Schuermann, T., 258, 306
Scott-Quinn, B., 304
Selitsch, K., 232, 311
Sellin, P., 232, 306
Shahabuddin, P., 102, 307
Shimko, D., 73, 312
Siegel, D., 102, 273, 308, 310
Simons, K., 28, 312
Simulation, 29
Singh, M. K., 134, 312
Skewness, 223
Smith, R. L., 258, 259, 312
Smithson, C. W., 272, 274, 312
SPAN®, 291, 292, 293
Stambaugh, R., 149, 312
Starica, C., 260, 312

Steeley, J. M., 312
Stochastic volatility models, 49
Straumann, D., 260, 306
Stress testing, 135–150
  anticipatory stress scenarios, 139–140
  anticipatory stress scenarios with
    "stress" correlations, 144–145
  construction of stress scenarios, 137
  issues in designing good stress tests,
    147–148
  portfolio-specific stress tests, 147
  predictive anticipatory stress
    scenarios, 140–144
  purpose of, 135
  and shortcomings of VaR, 135–136
  solutions to shortcomings, 136
  stressing factors left out of model, 146
  stressing VaR estimates, 145–146
  using actual past market events,
    137–138
  zero-stress scenarios, 138–139
Strickland, C., 304
Stroughair, J. D., 258, 306
Studer, G., 293, 312
Subadditivity, 289
Survey of Derivative and Risk
    Management Practices by U. S.
    Institutional Investors (1998), 11

Tay, A. S., 274, 306
Teugels, J. L., 258, 303
Teukolsky, S. A., 103, 311
Thomas, M., 258, 311
Thomazeau, I., 232, 304
Tilman, L. M., 134, 202, 307
Tompaidis, S., 149, 311
Total Risk for Asset Management
    (TRAM), 202

Ulmer, A., 232, 310
Urasev, S., 293, 311

Value-at-Risk,
  other approaches to computing,
    24–28

benchmark-relative, 18–19
choices in, 298–300
definition of, 4
as estimate only, 263–274
features, 3–4
limits of, 5
origins of, 5, 10–11
purposes of, in portfolio
    management, 6–7
of a simple equity portfolio, 13–30
and risk decomposition, 19–23
standard, 14–18
using risk contributions, 23–24
Value-at-Risk estimates,
    back tests based on entire
        distribution, 266–269
    portfolios with linear value func-
        tions, 269–271
    simple approaches for back testing,
        263–266
Variance, 223
Variance-covariance method, 29
Variants of the Monte Carlo Approach,
    233–243
    Delta-gamma (theta)
        approximation, 234–238
    Grid Monte Carlo approach,
        238–239
    other Monte Carlo approaches,
        241–242

Principal components grid Monte
    Carlo, 240–241
Scenario simulation, 241

Vasicek, O. A., 232, 307
Venkataraman, S., 53, 312
Vetterling, W. T., 103, 311
Vosper, L., 73, 303
Vynckier, P., 258, 303

Walters, K., 242, 304
Webber, N., 134, 308
Weibull distribution, 256
Whalmsey, J., 304
White, A., 73, 102, 308
Whitelaw, R. F., 52, 73, 260, 304
Wilford, D. S., 203, 311
Wilson, T., 134, 312
Winkelman, K., 181, 201, 203, 219,
    309
Wong, A. C. M., 232, 307
Worst-case scenario measure, 260

Xiao, J. Y., 50, 161, 310

Yang, W., 242, 304
Zangari, P., 53, 73, 231, 232, 313
Zerbs, M., 102, 306
Zhu, Y., 242, 308
Zvan, B., 72, 302, 305

Lightning Source UK Ltd.
Milton Keynes UK
08 April 2011

170607UK00001B/31/A